Biblical Theology

Biblical Theology

Issues, Methods, and Themes

JAMES K. MEAD

Westminster John Knox Press
LOUISVILLE • LONDON

Book design by Sharon Adams
Cover design by Mark Abrams / Jennifer K. Cox
Cover art courtesy of Sisse Brimberg/Cotton Coulson/Keenpress National Geographic/Getty Images

First edition
Published by Westminster John Knox Press
Louisville, Kentucky

This book is printed on acid-free paper that meets the American National Standards Institute Z39.48 standard. ∞

PRINTED IN THE UNITED STATES OF AMERICA

Library of Congress Cataloging-in-Publication Data

Mead, James K.
 Biblical theology : issues, methods, and themes / James K. Mead.—1st ed.
  p. cm.
 Includes bibliographical references.
 ISBN-13: 978-0-664-22972-6 (alk. paper)
 ISBN-10: 0-664-22972-7 (alk. paper)
 1. Bible—Theology. I. Title.

BS543.M45 2007
230'.041—dc22   2006047098

Contents

Preface

The field of biblical theology has entered a new century with a tremendous surge of interest and vitality. Scholars and students from many and diverse communities are reading the Bible theologically, seeking to understand its message and shape the methods whereby we approach the Bible. The goal of this textbook, therefore, is to make biblical theology—in its historical and methodological complexity—accessible for students. The present work is thus meant to guide students as they encounter these complexities and situate themselves within the ever-growing number of concepts and proposals. Although I hope that this book will be helpful in a variety of contexts, I especially envision it as a resource for college and seminary professors who want to introduce their students to this field. As much as possible, I have tried to make my discussion both descriptive and representative. That is, while I surely point out criticisms and arguments between and among scholars, I have sought to do so with fairness to as many of the viewpoints as possible.

It is thus my hope to advance the current discussion by increasing the number of participants in biblical theology, widening the circle of interest and inviting a new generation to share in the journey. Indeed, the decision to speak about *biblical* theology in the first place grows out of the increasing interest in relating discussions of testamental theologies to larger canonical issues. The book should prove helpful to those working in either testament, but by providing an overview of biblical theology it becomes a resource for those academic departments that can perhaps only offer one course in this subject area.

The subtitle promises to introduce readers to three concept areas: issues, methods, and themes. In order to prepare for these areas, chapter 1 discusses the challenges of defining biblical theology in the first place, and chapter 2 surveys the discipline's historical development. The next three chapters reveal that there is considerable overlap between the issues, methods, and themes of biblical theology. While it is impossible to separate these areas from each other or from the history of the discipline, we can distinguish these concepts enough to discern what issues are at stake in theological interpretation of the Bible (chap. 3), what methods scholars use to address these issues and articulate the Bible's theological message (chap. 4), and what major themes describe that message in view of both the issues and the methods that are brought to bear upon biblical theology (chap. 5). Chapter 6 offers a brief engagement with the prospects for biblical theology in light of the questions and proposals encountered in the preceding chapters.

The reader should be aware that this book assumes some familiarity with basic biblical knowledge, such as one might receive in a college introductory course. Furthermore, by using the terms "Old Testament" and "New Testament" I am inevitably situating myself in a particular community of interpretation, namely, a Christian one. Significant portions of the book discuss the complexities of such terminology for the biblical canon, but as far as possible with this and other issues I have tried to prescind my own theological commitments in describing the discipline in a helpful and accessible way.

As with every publishing endeavor, there are a host of individuals who in one way or another walk alongside an author, providing insight and encouragement. I have been blessed with wonderful departmental colleagues at Northwestern College in Orange City, Iowa, with an administration that provided financial support for this project through two successive summer grants, and with the staff of Ramaker Library who went the extra mile in obtaining a number of resources for my work. In this connection, I would also like to thank the library of the North American Baptist Theological Seminary in Sioux Falls for their generous assistance during the research process. Many other people have played significant roles in bringing this book to completion. Two students, Amy Vander Holt and Elizabeth Pedersen, participated in research and editing at various stages of the project. Professors Patrick Miller, Brent Strawn, and Kavin Rowe graciously read the entire manuscript and made valuable suggestions. I am indebted to my editor, Jon Berquist, and the staff at Westminster John Knox Press for sharing in the vision of this textbook and providing all of the technical expertise at the publishing level. Finally, I would like to dedicate this book to my loving family—my wife, Anne, and my children, Andrew and Molly—for their unfailing support and numerous sacrifices during the book's long journey to completion.

1

The Challenge of Defining "Biblical Theology"

BIBLICAL STUDIES AND BIBLICAL THEOLOGY

The study of the Bible is a rich and rewarding experience that invites students and scholars into a conversation with this ancient work of religious literature. As with any intellectual inquiry, this conversation may begin with a number of legitimate questions, probe more deeply into some topics than others, move freely among a variety of interests, and draw on a vast array of skills, information, and methods of study. In biblical studies, this means exploring the many contexts of the Bible, such as its history and culture, its languages and literary forms, the perspectives of its authors, the arrangement of its writings, and the interpretation of individual passages and books. Each of these topics may be studied for its own sake, yielding insights that may illuminate our understanding of the Bible and its world, but it is also true that these contexts relate in some way to questions about the theological meaning or message of the Bible.

This search for theological meaning grows out of the actual experience of people who have used the Bible as a source for authoritative guidance and nurture in matters of faith and religious practice.[1] As readers of the Bible have studied its laws, stories, poetry, wisdom, prophecies, and letters of instruction, they have naturally asked theological questions about them. The theological dimensions of biblical texts have been explored in a variety of ways and settings for thousands of years, but biblical theology eventually developed as a particular discipline within biblical studies.[2] As a working definition, biblical theology seeks to identify and understand the Bible's theological message and themes, that is, what the Bible says about God and God's relation to all creation, especially to humankind.[3] To state the matter informally, biblical

1

theology is a discipline that attempts to answer the question "What is the Bible all about?"

> Biblical theology seeks to identify and understand the Bible's theological message, that is, what the Bible says about God and God's relation to all creation, especially to humankind.

Biblical theology shares with all aspects of biblical studies a common interest in biblical texts while also pressing on to discern what those texts communicate about God. Thus, biblical theology can be distinguished, for example, from the study of the Bible's historical, sociological, or literary backgrounds, but it must always be sensitive to and knowledgeable about those backgrounds. Almost any biblical passage could be chosen to demonstrate biblical theology's connections with other aspects of biblical studies. In Genesis 22, for example, one might study the near sacrifice of Isaac in order to explore the rhetoric of family and social relationships behind the story. The issue of child sacrifice might lead one to investigate such practices in ancient Near Eastern religions. The intricate use of literary devices within the passage could be a means for learning about the way this Hebrew narrative functioned as literature. These aspects of research do not have to be explicitly theological insofar as their goal may simply be to learn more about the society and literature of Israel in its own historical settings. At the same time, however, the results of such study provide information that can have implications for theological interpretation. Building on all of these features, a biblical-theological approach to Genesis 22 would explore how the passage communicated something about Israel's understanding *of God*. The same exercise could be applied to passages in the New Testament, such as in Paul's letter to the Galatians. Along with questions about that book's historical background, literary forms, and religious issues, the work of biblical theology would be to explore how this book offers us insights into Paul's understanding of God's work among the believers in Galatia.

These examples point to the fact that *theological* interpretation interacts with and builds on other questions one can ask of the Bible or the methods one might use to answer them. The above definition of biblical theology, however, entails a great deal more than a single interpretive step in the study of distinct passages. The definition speaks of the Bible as a whole and what it says about God. When we widen the scope from one passage to many, from one biblical book to the entire Bible, how is the goal of grasping its theological message to be accomplished? Is it even possible to ascertain what the whole Bible says about God?

CHALLENGES IN THE TASK OF DEFINING BIBLICAL THEOLOGY

It might seem that the definition of an academic discipline should be more straightforward than I have made it. After all, is there really much debate over the nature and scope of economics, history, or biology? But even with subjects like these, a little reflection reveals that distinctions can and should be made. For example, the term "history" can be applied both to events as well as to the recording of those events, and a careful historian does not assume that a work of recorded history offers a flawless portrait of the actual events it relates. Even in the physical sciences, explanations of data may depend, say, on distinctions between Newtonian or quantum mechanics. In every discipline where over-arching theories seek to explain greater and increasingly diverse amounts of information, there remains significant debate over the most appropriate models for describing the evidence gained from exploration, experimentation, or interpretation. Such is the case with biblical theology.

The challenge of defining biblical theology arises in at least three broad areas of concern: the concepts used in any and all definitions, the human dimensions of theological interpretation, and ambiguity about the nature of the task. In other words, defining biblical theology is problematic because the language of definitions lacks clarity, because we ourselves approach the task with a wide range of experiences and understandings, and because biblical scholars disagree over the precise nature, scope, and purpose of theological interpretation.

The Challenge of the Concepts Themselves

Identifying and understanding the Bible's theological message can suffice as a working definition of the discipline, but such language is not completely clear and unambiguous. One way to illustrate this problem is to consider the informal description mentioned earlier: "What is the Bible all about?" While this question seems plain enough in everyday speech, it needs considerable explanation and qualification. Consider these three issues that arise in the individual components of that question.

Unity and Diversity: *What Is* the Bible All About?

The singular form of the verb in this question implies a sense of unity to the Bible's theology that may not account for diverse concepts and interpretations. One of the issues now confronting the discipline is the thematic diversity in the Bible and within each testament and book. Indeed, the very word "Bible" derives from the Greek plural *biblia*, meaning "the books." It is thus fair to ask if the diversity of theological themes in the Bible is too great to use the singular "theology" for them. Erhard Gerstenberger has recently suggested as much in his work *Theologies in the Old Testament*. He explains that this title was deliberately chosen because "the Old Testament, a collection of many testimonies of faith from around a thousand years of the history of ancient Israel, has no unitary theology, nor can it."[4] If this assessment is accurate for one testament, then surely the quest for a singular "theology" of the whole Bible would be impossible. Many scholars agree with Gerstenberger on this matter, while others might still search for thematic unity in the midst of diversity. With respect to the Old Testament, Claus Westermann writes, "A theology of the Old Testament has the task of summarizing and viewing together what the Old Testament as a whole, in all of its sections, says about God."[5] This description distinguishes between the "whole" and the "sections" while also suggesting the possibility of summarizing theological concepts. Thus, the unity-diversity question is one that continues to challenge the field of biblical theology.

The Biblical Canon: What Is *the Bible* All About?

The mention of "the Bible" raises the question of which form and version of the Bible is in view. While even beginning students are aware of the plethora of English translations of the Bible, the issue here actually runs much deeper than the differences in modern versions. Jewish and Christian faith communities have selected and arranged their sacred scriptures in different ways, a fact that can influence the quest for theological meaning. Which Bible is meant by the term "biblical"? Are we referring to the Hebrew Bible, and if so, which particular version of it: the Masoretic Text or some ancient translation/version behind it or portions of it? Do we mean the Christian Bible, with its two testaments, or should the Old and New Testaments be studied separately? Should we include the so-called deuterocanonical literature from the intertestamental or postapostolic periods? One of these questions, the difference in terminology between "Hebrew Bible" and "Old Testament," has been of particular importance in scholarly circles. While it may be the prerogative of the Christian tradition to speak of its Old and New Testaments, this language—and the interpretations that proceed from such a perspective—can sound as if the "New" Testament has supplanted the "Old" one, a view scholars call supersessionism.[6] Other designations, like "First" and "Second Testament," have been proposed, but these too have their limitations and ambiguities. Do we privilege the First Testament by virtue of its antiquity relative to the Second? Do we regard the Second Testament as a later, authoritative interpretation of the First? Some recent works of "Old Testament theology" acknowledge the deficiencies of such designations while opting to keep the traditional language.[7]

Comprehensiveness: What Is the Bible *All About*?

The concluding phrase, "all about," seems to suggest that the discipline of biblical theology can actually grasp the entirety of the Bible's theological message. But how comprehensive can any expression of the Bible's theological meaning be, and do we need other theological disciplines to explore a fuller meaning? The unity-diversity question certainly implies the issue of comprehensiveness; if there are a number of diverse "theologies" in the Bible, then it will be difficult to articulate what the Bible is *all about*. But the matter of comprehensiveness also touches on other issues as well. The use of the word "theology" in the title of the discipline implicitly raises the question of whether the Bible actually contains theology, or whether its testimonies of faith provide the source for readers to do theological reflection. To ask the question bluntly, is the Bible even "about" theology? Gerhard Ebeling clearly stated the issue in a presentation in the 1950s: "The fact that the Bible itself does not use the word 'theology' is obviously not in itself a reason for not applying it to the Bible. But it is also a doubtful proceeding to use the concept 'theology' in such a wide sense that any talk of God and any religious statement whatever may be designated as theology."[8] While we may be comfortable speaking of the theology in the creation accounts of Genesis, the parables of Jesus in the Gospels, or Paul's discussion of the resurrection in 1 Corinthians 15, we may find it more difficult to identify the theology of Old Testament dietary laws or lengthy lists of names and places. And these examples do not even broach the theology of passages that raise ethical concerns, like the imprecatory psalms and their cursings, as in Psalm 137. Ebeling thus warns that not everything in the Bible is to be treated as an equally valid source of or for theological reflection.

The issue of comprehensiveness also raises the question of whether biblical theology is capable of being an arbiter of the full theological message of the Bible. In other words, is it fair to say that biblical theology is *the* discipline that answers the question of what the Bible is all about? How does biblical theology relate to other forms of theology, especially to disciplines like systematic theology and pastoral theology? These other theological disciplines obviously use the Bible to explain doctrinal beliefs and ministerial practice, but their methods and goals differ from those of biblical theology. Some biblical scholars and systematic theologians are now paying significant attention to the connection between their two disciplines.[9] It remains to be seen what might be the precise role of biblical theology in the current discussions. Will it inevitably be so closely associated with biblical studies that it is unable to converse with systematic theology? To widen the scope to still other theological concerns, the way biblical theology is defined can have important implications and applications for how ethicists, religious educators, and pastors undertake their vocations.

The Challenge of How We Approach the Task

Throughout the twentieth century, fields such as philosophy, sociology, the fine arts, literature, and many others drew attention to the role that human beings themselves play as interpreters and creators of meaning. The quest of the "modern" age for scientific and historical fact has been challenged by a "postmodern" awareness that who we are as persons and what we have experienced have a tremendous effect on the conclusions we draw about matters of truth.[10] And while the value and implications of these postmodern insights remain hotly debated, it is certainly fair to say that personal interests, social location, and religious beliefs can make the search for a common definition of biblical theology a challenging one. Consider just a few of the positions from which different groups might be reading this book.

Scholars may already be asking philosophical and linguistic questions about the use of terms such as "meaning" or "message" in this chapter's working definition of biblical theology. After all, how do texts communicate meaning, and is it either possible or desirable to discover meaning in the Bible? If we grant the worthiness of the pursuit of theological meaning, we still need to ask whether this meaning is something biblical authors intended for their works, or whether there are several layers of meaning, some of which might never have been intended by the authors themselves.[11] Moreover, are our own presuppositions so influencing our study of the Bible that we unavoidably find the meaning we were looking for?

College students may be trying to integrate this discussion about biblical theology with required religion courses or with the broader liberal arts. And because the academic study of the Bible is usually a new experience for students, they may be asking how all of this relates to the instruction they received in their respective communities of faith. Perhaps they are astonished to find so wide a range of methods and interpretations in academic biblical studies, and they now wonder whether there are any solid answers that might assuage their rising doubts about the Bible.

Theological students may have already confronted the challenges of critical biblical scholarship and have chosen a stance somewhere along the spectrum of complete embrace to complete rejection. But however they use critical methods of biblical study, they may now be asking how the Bible's message interprets and is interpreted by their own doctrinal traditions. If they are pursuing a call to ministry, how will they be able to communicate to parishioners the "message of the Bible"?

Beyond these rather conventional categories, there may be still other readers who simply desire a compendium of what the Bible teaches. They may want to cut through all the academic debates to arrive at a list of the Bible's primary themes.

Regardless of the perspective of its readers, the Bible has always invited people's questions about the nature of God and living in relationship to God. Thus, the challenges inherent in defining biblical theology—whether in the terms or in ourselves—do not mean that attempts to define the discipline are useless. In fact, such challenges are helpful insofar as they make us aware of the complexity of the task. Nevertheless, in spite of its multifaceted nature, biblical theology still suggests its own set of methods, issues, and themes, not all of which would be equally pertinent to linguistic or historical study, for example. While we may discover that the search for an adequate definition is finally more important than the precise definition itself, that very search will point to particular topics and concepts that, in turn, yield insights into the meaning and message of the Bible.

The Challenge of Disagreement over the Nature of the Discipline

This chapter has occasionally used the word "description" to explain the work of biblical theology. However, scholars have often disagreed over the precise nature of the biblical-theological task. Indeed, a distinction between "descriptive" and "normative" aspects has existed in some form in the discipline of biblical theology throughout its history. The way that these two aspects have been combined, separated, or distinguished by scholars remains a significant challenge to developing a definition of biblical theology. We could put the issue in terms of a choice between the two aspects: Is biblical theology concerned only with describing the theological concepts within the Bible, or is it also concerned with articulating theological views that become authoritative standards (i.e., norms) for today? Setting aside for the moment whether it is completely fair to separate these aspects, this choice arises partly from the fact that the term "biblical theology" can be understood in at least two ways. The adjective "biblical" can be interpreted to imply either a descriptive or a normative identity. On the one hand, the word "biblical" can be read as a possessive, as in "the Bible's theology." Thus, according to this emphasis, the nature of biblical theology is to describe the theology (or theologies) found in the biblical writings. Here the focus is more on the Bible itself and the challenges of its unity and diversity, relating its different authors to each other, and asking if there are any overarching trajectories. On the other hand, "biblical" can refer not to the Bible's theology but to our own. Does *our* theology have biblical characteristics or stand in accord with the theological concepts that are in the Bible? The nature of the discipline therefore moves beyond mere description and becomes more normative. The resulting task might, for example, be to develop theologies that match the Bible's teaching, culminating in a norm or standard to follow.

For several decades, this descriptive-normative distinction has been discussed in relation to an influential entry on contemporary biblical theology by New Testament scholar Krister Stendahl, which was published in the early 1960s in the *Interpreter's Dictionary of the Bible*.[12] Stendahl suggests that biblical theology begins with the "descriptive task" and only then considers "its implications for other aspects of theology," something he calls "the hermeneutical question."[13] The descriptive task helps to determine—as far as possible given the limits of our knowledge—the original theological meaning of biblical texts. In the hermeneutical task, theologians try to state the contemporary meaning of the biblical theology arrived at under the descriptive task. Stendahl restates the matter by comparing description with the past tense of "What *did* it mean?" and the hermeneutical step with the present tense of "What *does* it mean?"[14] Since it is appropriate to ask about connections between the Bible and our contemporary world, it can be tempting for readers to jump quickly to questions about what a passage "means to me." Thus, professors rightly caution their students to think critically about the "distance" between their own situation and the original context of a biblical passage.

Stendahl's Distinction	
Biblical Theology	*Hermeneutics*
Descriptive	Normative
What it meant	What it means

This "meant/means" distinction predates Stendahl. Indeed, it has its origins, as we will see, in the very issues that led to the development of a distinct discipline of biblical theology in the late 1700s. For now, it is important to explain that the descriptive-normative distinction allows for more interaction between these two aspects than the above discussion implies. Stendahl himself argued that the hermeneutical step was to be founded on careful descriptive study. People would probably not suggest that they had grasped the contemporary meaning of the Bible—in other words, that their theology was "biblical"—unless they had carefully researched the biblical writings in order to determine the elements of a normative biblical theology. Having done so, they might argue that they had rightly described the Bible's theology and thus adopted it as their own.

If a normative approach seems dependent upon the task of description, the reverse does not, at first glance, seem to be the case for those who emphasize an exclusively descriptive approach to biblical theology. Those whose sole purpose is simply to describe the theological themes of the biblical writings probably have little interest in translating these themes into normative theological claims for themselves or others. Nevertheless, the task of description, or deciding "what it meant," is not without its own set of difficulties. Equally competent scholars disagree over the best methods to use in gaining an accurate description of the Bible's theological meaning, or if gaining an accurate description is even possible. Then too, they might employ different models to articulate this description. Since every scholar approaches the descriptive task with presuppositions about what is, for example, historically reasonable, then even the seemingly neutral task of description is just that—only *apparently neutral*. It is often charged with debate over evidence, methodology, and conclusions.[15]

Many scholars make a case for the legitimacy of a normative aspect within biblical theology based on a variety of reasons, including the point just acknowledged, that descriptive methods are never completely neutral. Of course, great caution must be taken to avoid making biblical theology an exclusively normative enterprise, since the search merely for norms (theological, ethical, etc.) will tend to avoid serious issues related to the biblical text itself as well as its literary, historical, and cultural contexts.[16] Nevertheless, the normative aspect of biblical theology ought not to be dismissed altogether, insofar as the biblical books contain implicit theological claims that readers who regard the Bible as authoritative would naturally seek. Indeed, one of the reasons the Bible has been transmitted through the ages is because people of faith have believed it to be "God's word to us."[17] Finally, it could be argued that the ambiguity in the word "biblical"—which suggested the descriptive-normative distinction in the first place—might even be a good thing, encouraging greater conversation and interaction between biblical and systematic theology.[18]

Although not everyone will find such arguments persuasive, they help to demonstrate the impact this distinction has on the way scholars think about and practice biblical theology. My working definition of biblical theology clearly requires the work of description, but it also implies the validity of the search for normative applications. To be sure, students of the Bible will negotiate the relationship of these two aspects in different ways, but even if one refuses to relate them, simply choosing a descriptive approach, then it is clear that some decision on the matter has still been made. A great deal depends on the expectations, ideals, and habits of one's academic and/or faith communities, but regardless of the emphasis given to each aspect or the way they are held in tension, the task of biblical theology will naturally be suggestive of further reflection based on the theological thoughts of the biblical writers.

THE DEFINITION OF BIBLICAL THEOLOGY
AND THE CURRENT STATE OF THE DISCIPLINE

The primary goal of this chapter has been to offer a tentative definition of the discipline of biblical theology while at the same time acknowledging the serious questions that one can raise about all of the terms used in any potential definition. Beginning the study of biblical theology by grappling with the problem of definition grows out of the history of the discipline itself and, in some respects, presents a microcosm of the current state of the discipline. That is, the issues and arguments above are representative of many others we will encounter in the course of this book. Beginning students do not need to be confronted immediately with dozens of names, technical terms, and nuances of biblical scholarship, but they still need some awareness of the present situation in order to make connections between this chapter and those that follow.

The Issues, Methods, and Themes of Biblical Theology

The subtitle of this book alludes to three critical areas of concern that form the basic outline of the book: issues, methods, and themes. This threefold rubric is obviously not exhaustive of the categories in biblical theology, and other scholars may offer different approaches to the discipline from the one used here. Moreover, dividing this book among these areas should not imply a separation between and among issues, methods, and themes. On the contrary, I have chosen them precisely because of their interrelationships. The challenges to defining biblical theology have already suggested certain *theological issues*, such as the relationship between the two testaments of the Christian Bible or the connection between the descriptive and normative understandings of the discipline. In response to these kinds of issues, scholars have employed a variety of *theological methods* to guide the interpretive task. Then, growing out of the application of these methods to the Bible, biblical theologians have identified and emphasized different *theological themes* by which to organize or summarize the Bible's message.

This threefold approach to biblical theology is by no means a universally accepted standard for the discipline. For one thing, scholars often integrate their own theological method with, for example, the themes they have identified in the biblical text. Moreover, they are not always interested in all aspects of biblical theology when they are writing about the Bible's message. A methodological study does not have to rehearse all of the critical issues in the discipline, nor does it have to describe all of the themes that could arise from using certain methods. Thus, the vast number and variety of studies reflects the difficulty of embracing the whole field in just a few simple categories. In spite of these facts, however, studying biblical theology in light of its issues, methods, and themes offers a logical and helpful path into this vast and complex field, while bringing students into contact with most of the scholarship in biblical theology.

Biblical Theology and Theological Interpretation of the Bible

I have described biblical theology in a few places using the term "theological interpretation," and it will be my practice in this book to use these terms somewhat interchangeably, though they are not precisely identical in their scope and purpose. I will spend more time discussing these matters in chapter 3, but for now it suffices to offer some preliminary explanation of the terms. Theological interpretation, or theological exegesis as it is sometimes called, may be understood as the reading of biblical texts with a view toward their theological content and how they function as scripture for people of faith. This understanding is very close to the concerns of biblical theology, but theological interpretation/ exegesis, as it is used in contemporary scholarship, carries some distinct connotations. First, as the term "exegesis" implies, the focus of theological interpretation is generally on individual passages rather than the Bible's larger divisions. Second, as theological interpreters build on historical, linguistic, and cultural insights to discern a text's message or teaching about God, they go on to relate that message in some way to a faith community's theological traditions. This latter purpose explains why people often think of systematic theologians when they hear the phrase "theological interpretation of the Bible."

Therefore, both biblical theologians and systematic theologians want to interpret the Bible theologically, but they do so from different vantage points and with different goals in mind.[19] For example, both will wrestle with the meanings of "justification" for Paul and James, but where the biblical theologian focuses on the biblical roots and historical developments of the concept of justification, the systematic theologian may try to explicate, for example, how the doctrine of justification has been employed in confessional documents from the Reformation or the Council of Trent.

Theological interpretation is certainly not a recent phenomenon, and even the current interest among both biblical and systematic theologians has its roots in earlier scholarly discussion and debate. Still, for the past two decades there has been growing interest from both directions—biblical and systematic—as evidenced in a number of publishing endeavors.[20] But regardless of the approach, methods, and purposes, any and all attention to the Bible's theological message is a welcome occurrence for those who practice the discipline of biblical theology.

The Literature of Biblical Theology

The amount of scholarly literature that explicitly or implicitly deals with biblical theology is enormous and growing all the time. Even the most extensive treatments cannot list, much less analyze, everything that has been published or presented in the field. Scholarly literature in biblical theology follows similar distinctions in the literature of other fields. This book will cite (1) *major monographs* with titles like "Theology of the Old Testament" or "New Testament Theology," (2) *surveys of the discipline* that summarize the history and methodology of biblical theology, (3) *collections of essays* by different scholars who focus on particular aspects of biblical theology, (4) *scholarly journals* devoted to biblical-theological research, (5) *reference works* such as dictionaries containing brief but valuable entries related to biblical theology, and (6) *other works* such as introductions to the Bible, biblical commentaries, and theological treatments of sections of the canon or of key figures in the biblical story.

CONCLUSION

We have only begun our journey into this important discipline, but the challenge of defining biblical theology already suggests connections to other aspects we will study. Still, the complexity of the issues, the variety of methods, and the diversity of themes—not to mention the history and current state of biblical theology—can be overwhelming. I recall an illustration one of my professors used for topics and texts like those addressed in biblical theology. He said that there are two kinds of water that are difficult to see through: muddy water and deep water. Biblical theology is deep water. Although there may be times when the subjects in the following chapters seem to muddy the waters of scholarship, the persistent student of the discipline will see that the water is deep and will gradually begin to plumb its depths and discover its treasures.

2

The History of Biblical Theology

We cannot pinpoint the origins of biblical theology to a particular place and time, since people have been engaged in theological interpretation of the Bible for as long as there has been a Bible or portions of it. In spite of the vagueness about its roots, biblical theology, like every academic discipline, has a certain history—an account of the key figures, their writings, the intellectual movements, and significant moments when the nature, purpose, and scope of the discipline were advanced by critical reflection if not by unanimity of opinion. Several scholars have written comprehensive and detailed treatments that provide a wealth of information far surpassing the brief survey offered here. Their books await the reader who, in this chapter, will only begin to learn the names of some important biblical theologians, the titles of their works, and the intellectual currents in the discipline.

The primary approach here is to clarify the relative significance of the information and the possible trajectories and interconnections between people and eras, while also creating a structure by which to understand and recall the basic historical data. The following discussion does not survey the vast history of biblical interpretation in general, of which biblical theology is one expression. A number of fine scholarly works provide both background and selected readings from a variety of interpreters.[1]

The previous chapter introduced the current state of the discipline, acknowledging the diversity of viewpoints and interests, the magnitude of publications, and the numerous issues raised simply by defining biblical theology. But how did biblical theology arrive at this juncture? For instance, why is biblical theology usually practiced with a sharp distinction between Old Testament theology and New Testament theology? Why does it struggle with the relationship between the historical study of the Bible and its theological interpretation? What accounts for the emphasis placed upon the variety of contexts and perspectives from which we read the Bible? To help us understand how we got here, I will arrange the history of biblical theology around seven questions associated with critical concepts or moments, preparing us to understand the issues, methods, and themes of biblical theology today.

1. What kind of biblical theology existed before the discipline of that name arose?
2. Under what circumstances did the discipline of biblical theology develop?
3. Why did the division in the treatment of the testaments occur?
4. What intellectual movements influenced the methods of nineteenth-century biblical theology?
5. What is the difference between the history of religions and biblical theology?
6. Why is the middle of the twentieth century thought of as a great age of biblical theology?
7. What new developments arose in the closing decades of the twentieth century?

WHAT KIND OF BIBLICAL THEOLOGY EXISTED BEFORE THE DISCIPLINE OF THAT NAME AROSE?

This question prompts us to explore the nature and scope of theological interpretation prior to the 1700s, an era often used as a starting point for many scholarly surveys of the discipline. We may encounter statements such as the one in the introduction to G. B. Caird and L. D. Hurst's *New Testament Theology*: "Until J. P. Gabler published his essay on the distinction between biblical and dogmatic theology [1787], *nobody* thought of writing 'biblical' theology. They wrote theology: and the shape of theology was dictated by the traditional doctrines of the creeds."[2] Consider this similar observation by Donald Guthrie that pushes the date back to the 1500s: "Prior to the Reformation there was *little or no interest* in biblical theology."[3] There is certainly some truth in these statements. Just as the Reformation witnessed a renewal of interest in the role of the Bible for Christian faith and life, so also the Enlightenment marked the use of scientific and historical methods to study the Bible apart from long-standing social, political, and religious influences. Given these factors, it is appropriate to look to that era for the immediate roots of a critical and disciplined approach to biblical theology that became published in scholarly works.

Nevertheless, having recognized this distinctive advance in scholarship, it would be a vast overstatement to say that *nobody* thought of interpreting the Bible theologically. The practice of biblical interpretation may not have self-consciously employed terms such as "biblical theology" or "theological interpretation," but there were numerous methods that had their own rationale and plausibility consistent with their presuppositions, often outside the context of the Christian creeds to which Caird refers. Renewed interest in the history of biblical interpretation warrants the recognition not only of the validity of pre-Enlightenment biblical research but also of its usefulness for the contemporary interpreter.[4] Although the following treatment is necessarily selective, it aims to set the context for understanding the later history of the discipline by identifying expressions of theological interpretation that would eventually coalesce in the discipline of biblical theology. Against the background of intrabiblical interpretation, Jewish and Christian communities wrestled with decisions about what constituted the biblical canon even as they developed basic methods for interpreting the meaning and message of the Bible. Questions of canonicity and interpretive method came together in a dynamic way in the Reformation and post-Reformation eras.

Intrabiblical Theological Reflection

Scholars have long recognized that the Bible itself contains numerous instances of the theological interpretation of one text by later authors.[5] One notable example of such intrabiblical reflection begins with Exodus 34:6–7.[6]

The LORD passed before him, and proclaimed,

"The LORD, the LORD,
a God merciful and gracious,
slow to anger,
and abounding in steadfast love and faithfulness,
keeping steadfast love for the thousandth generation,
forgiving iniquity and transgression and sin,
yet by no means clearing the guilty,
but visiting the iniquity of the parents
upon the children
and the children's children,
to the third and fourth generation."

The revelation of the Lord's (=Yahweh's) character to Moses during the golden calf incident is picked up and applied by several biblical texts in different settings. In Numbers 14:18, Moses uses Yahweh's very words to appeal for forgiveness rather than destruction of the people in the wilderness. Ezra's prayer recalls this language as he recounts the history of Israel on a day of national confession and dedication (Neh. 9:17). Psalm 86:15 is part of a lament that employs the language of God's gracious character to appeal for help, whereas Psalm 103:8 offers praise for these and other attributes of Yahweh. Joel's prophecy employs this text as a call to repentance under threat of divine judgment (Joel 2:13). Jonah confesses that it was his very knowledge of these qualities that moved him to flee from the call to prophesy against Nineveh (Jonah 4:2). All of the later sources tend to focus on the positive side of things, or as one scholar has put it, "The canonical trajectory reveals God to be essentially a Lover rather than a Punisher." The Prologue to the Gospel of John also draws on this language, where the "grace and truth" revealed in Christ (John 1:14) "are the Greek equivalents of the Hebrew words translated 'steadfast love and faithfulness' in Ex 34:6."[7] This example demonstrates how a passage in one setting can be interpreted theologically in other contexts as a source for petition, praise, repentance, and wrestling with the will of God.

Beyond this direct use of specific language, there are also important themes that are picked up by other biblical authors both within and between the testaments. Later chapters will address the question of the New Testament's use of the Old Testament and also survey the major thematic emphases of biblical theologians, but the following list provides a sample of theological development within Scripture itself.

- The Pentateuch develops the promises to the ancestors not only by reaffirming them for each generation of patriarchs and matriarchs but also by connecting Yahweh's redemption of Israel from Egypt to the covenant with the ancestors.
- The book of Deuteronomy provides the theological backdrop for interpreting the successes and failures of Israel and its leaders in the books of Joshua through Kings, leading to the designation of these works as the Deuteronomistic History.
- The prophetic books indict the nations of Israel and Judah in light of the demands of the Mosaic law and covenant, explaining why judgment must come upon Yahweh's people.
- The Gospels and the book of Acts draw on specific Old Testament quotations and themes in order to demonstrate the fulfillment of God's kingdom in Jesus of Nazareth and his followers.
- The letters of Paul draw support from almost every book of the Old Testament in order to explore the theological implications of Jesus' death and resurrection.

These examples only scratch the surface of the biblical-theological connections in the Bible, but they demonstrate that the biblical writers consciously interpreted and applied texts that they found in other portions of the Bible.[8]

Theological Interpretation and the Growth
of the Canon (200 BCE–200 CE)

The postexilic period saw a new impetus in biblical interpretation as Jewish religious leaders in Palestine and other parts of the Persian Empire commented on the meaning of the sacred stories, laws, poetry, prophecy, and wisdom, leading to entire traditions of oral and written interpretation that were passed down with the Bible.[9] James Kugel speaks of this linking of interpretations with the texts they sought to explain as the "*interpreted* Bible," indeed, as what both Jews and Christians came to mean by "the Bible."[10] By the middle of the fifth century BCE a "Torah of Moses" was known, "which seems to have had an honored place as *the* text of Judea."[11] At least by the third century BCE we begin to see religious documents that interpret Scripture but were not included in the canon.[12] Both the Dead Sea Scrolls and the writings of Jewish scholars such as Philo of Alexandria (20 BCE–50 CE) often employ figurative readings of the Bible in order to apply its meaning and message to the particular contexts of their respective readers.[13]

Perhaps the definitive factor in establishing the significance of a biblical canon and its interpretation was the tragic fall of Jerusalem to the Romans in 70 CE, which brought an end to religious rituals associated with the temple. Without an active sacrificial and priestly system, rabbis emerged as the primary leaders at the close of the first century CE. This phenomenon also coincides with the culmination of a long and complex process of canonization of the Hebrew Scriptures, associated with rabbinic communities after the destruction of Jerusalem.[14]

The period from 70 to 200 CE witnessed the consolidation of numerous teachings into the Mishnah, a compendium of interpretations dealing with a variety of legal matters in the Torah. Since much of the Mishnah concerns itself with priestly matters that assume the existence of the defunct temple and sacrificial system, the purpose of the work seems to have been to help the Jewish community focus on "what really matters" and to express hope for the future.[15] Over the next several centuries, rabbis continued to interpret both Torah and Mishnah, resulting in two other collections, the Palestinian and Babylonian Talmuds, during the fifth and sixth centuries.[16]

For the Christian community, the beginning of the second century was also one of transition, bringing an end to the apostolic era and the completion of the last writings that would eventually constitute the New Testament. Ever since the ministry of Jesus and the apostles, the theological differences between Jews who followed Jesus and those who were committed to the Pharisees' understanding of the faith became increasingly serious. In the second century, polemical writings of Christians illustrate how wide this gulf was becoming, as in Justin Martyr's (ca. 114–165) *Dialogue with Trypho* and other works that upheld the fulfillment of Old Testament prophecies of Jesus Christ and affirmed the witness of both testaments to him as the Logos.[17] But in the midst of this growing division between Judaism and Christianity, voices such as that of Marcion completely repudiated the Hebrew Scriptures and any Christian writings that acknowledged their value. Over against Marcionism, apologists such as Irenaeus and Tertullian defended the writings of the Old Testament as authoritative for the Christian church.[18] Thus, the early church recognized both the Hebrew Scriptures and the twenty-seven writings that formed the New Testament.[19]

Interpretive Methods in Christian and Jewish Communities (200–1500 CE)

The patristic era is known for wide-ranging theological interests, perhaps best expressed through the christological debates and ecumenical councils of the fourth and fifth centuries. But before, during, and after these events, vibrant theological interpretation of Scripture continued in every sector of the Christian church. Pastors and theologians searched the biblical text for meaning on a number of levels, but as William Yarchin astutely observes, "Much of the history of biblical interpretation concerns the question of referentiality in the Bible: to what extent are the texts of Scripture to be read for what they *plainly* state, and to what extent *as figures* of something other than their plain reference?"[20] The New Testament clearly employs examples of both, such as Luke's setting his narrative of the early church within the first-century context (e.g., Acts 24:27) or Paul's designation of Adam as a "type" in Romans 5:14.[21] On the whole, while it is true that the church fathers did not approach the Bible as a historical document that could be studied scientifically and objectively, they surely expounded the Scriptures in an effort to achieve some kind of theological consistency.[22]

These methodological options for ascertaining the message of the Bible were represented by the so-called Alexandrian and Antiochene schools, which came to be associated with predominantly allegorical and literal interpretation, respectively. Allegorical exegesis was championed by Origen (185–254), who sought for figurative meanings in a manner reminiscent of Philo. Beginning with the presupposition that God is the divine author of Scripture, Origen argued that the biblical books needed to be understood in "[their] spiritual sense" rather than "according to the sound of the letter."[23] Although the more literal and historical exegesis of the Antiochene school should not be seen as a complete opposite of figurative exegesis, there can be no doubt that its representatives placed a premium on the literal meaning of the Old Testament in determining its meaning and application to New Testament events, especially

Christ's ministry.[24] St. Augustine (354–430) used both literal and allegorical exegesis in his interpretation, to the end that the ultimate meaning of all Scripture pointed to the great commandments to love God and neighbor.[25]

The use of both literal and figurative interpretations of Scripture characterized the greatest Jewish and Christian scholars throughout the medieval period. The terms "medieval" or "Middle Ages" can, of course, lead to inaccurate perceptions of the expanse of time from about the sixth century to the fifteenth century, as if that one-thousand-year period served solely as a bridge between the Roman Empire and the Renaissance. Nevertheless, sweeping changes in socioeconomic, political, and religious conditions in Europe did contribute to new expressions of scholarship. Jewish academies and Christian monasteries carried on the tradition of biblical learning and interpretation. One scholar, Rashi (1040–1105), balanced the plain sense (*peshat*) with other, derived meanings (*derash*).[26] As Yarchin puts it, for Rashi these were "two types of interpretation that synergistically face one another, with a resulting interplay that helped maintain the ancient Eastern midrashic way of exegetical thinking amid the growing Western rationality of Rashi's world."[27] Within Christendom, scholastic theologians such as St. Thomas Aquinas (1225–1274) drew on Greek philosophical categories that had been reintroduced to Western culture through the work of Arab scholars. Aquinas's systematic mind wrestled with the multiple senses employed by earlier medieval thinkers, since one might object that "many different senses in one text produce confusion and deception and destroy all force of argument." In answer to this dilemma, Aquinas suggested that meaning is found not only in the literal significance of the biblical words but also in the spiritual significance of the things of which the Bible speaks: "Thus in Holy Writ no confusion results, for all of the senses are founded on one—the literal—from which alone can any argument be drawn."[28]

Reformation and Post-Reformation Periods (1500–1700 CE)

The Reformation and the Subtle Turn toward Biblical Theology

A brief survey cannot even begin to explain all of the developments leading to the Protestant Reformation.[29] There were many contributing factors, such as the recovery of classical learning that defined the European Renaissance, the invention of the printing press for quick production and multiplication of the written word, and the rising power of the papacy. Although individuals such as the German monk Martin Luther (1483–1546) and the French scholar John Calvin (1509–1564) did not set out to foment rebellion against the Catholic Church, they were at the forefront of the two primary movements of religious protest, which eventually became institutionalized in the Lutheran and Reformed traditions. Luther and Calvin may be distinguished from each other in numerous theological and ecclesiastical emphases, but they also shared a commitment to the authority of the Bible in relation to the traditional teachings of the church. Church tradition—as defined by the classic creeds— remained a vital part of Christian faith, but Luther and Calvin asserted the primacy of Scripture in determining the content of that faith, a concept called *sola scriptura* (Latin, "Scripture alone"). Thus, it is no surprise that most of the Reformation leaders shifted attention away from the dogmatic pronouncements of the medieval church to a renewed study of the Bible by all believers, with particular attention to its plain or literal sense. Hans Frei describes this outlook as a "realistic" reading of the Bible—one that emphasized the historicity of its narratives, the unity of its larger story, and the way in which its story "embraced the experience" of each generation.[30]

Luther and Calvin's primary search for the literal and historical meaning of Scripture went hand in hand with their belief that this meaning would be consistent with the Christian gospel. For example, in Psalm 2, Luther understands David to be writing from his own situation "in order that he might console and teach the church about the spreading of Christ's kingdom in spite of the powers of the world and of the air."[31] Calvin makes a similar move from historical setting to theological meaning in his comments on the same passage: "As David's temporal kingdom was a kind of earnest to God's ancient people of the eternal kingdom, which at length was truly established in the person of Christ, those things which David declares concerning himself are not violently, or even allegorically, applied to Christ, but were truly predicted concerning him."[32] They did not call their work biblical theology, but all of the interpretation in their biblical commentaries involved this kind of theological exegesis.

In hindsight, we are able to see how key emphases of the Reformation led to interesting and perhaps unintended results for the interpreter, the focus of study, and the practice of theological interpretation. For one thing, the Reformers claimed that the Bible was a book for all Christians to study and interpret under the guidance of the Holy Spirit rather than being constrained solely by church dogma. With reasonable effort and skill, anyone could learn to interpret the Bible and therefore begin to speak accurately about its meaning. Although the Reformers imagined that individuals would be reading the Bible within a community of believers and be guided by the creedal traditions, they had taken the first step toward a less centralized and more personal interpretive enterprise, whether the primary emphasis was on one's rational or spiritual capacities. Second, once the Bible was wrested from the authoritative hands of the church, it now became a book—still revered above all books, of course—that could be studied with the mind as well as the heart. Thus, over the next two centuries there was a gradual reversal of the realistic perspective that Frei mentions. What began as a confident interpretive movement from the literal biblical story to its historical truth eventually became an obsession with the historical events that were attested to by the biblical story. Frei speaks of this effect as "a logical distinction and reflective distance between the stories and the 'reality' they depict."[33] Conceivably, scholars could use any number of methods to get at the real events of the past, making the Bible merely one ancient source among others, indeed, a source that could be questioned and critiqued like any other. Third, and the result of both of these observations, the notion of a *biblical* theology could come into its own. There were now people who could freely study the Bible and arrive at conclusions about its message apart from the interpretive traditions or doctrinal constraints of the church, even those churches stemming from the Reformation. It would therefore only be a matter of time before people began to use historical and critical methods to uncover the theological nature of the Bible's witness to the real and actual events of which it spoke.

The Post-Reformation Era and the Impetus for Biblical Theology

It was not all that long in historical terms that the vibrancy and freshness of the sixteenth-century Reformation began to give way to the institutional structures and organized systems of thought that grew out of the work of Luther, Calvin, and others. Historians of religion have called this the era of Protestant scholasticism or Protestant orthodoxy for at least two reasons. Not only were its theological methods reminiscent of the work of medieval scholastics such as Thomas Aquinas; its approach to faith and doctrine became more "scholastic," that is, more intellectual and perhaps more detached from piety or spirituality. The roots of this outlook were laid almost immediately as the first Reformation leaders realized they needed to organize or systematize their beliefs. Only four years after Martin Luther nailed his Ninety-five Theses to the door of the castle church in Wittenberg, Germany, his close associate Philip Melanchthon organized Christian beliefs and supported them with quotations of Scripture in a book called *Loci Communes Theologici* (1521). Melanchthon wove biblical citations into a discussion of doctrines, telling his readers that he was "sketching a common outline of the topics that you can pursue in your study of Holy Scripture."[34] In time, however, other works arose which listed doctrines and their supporting scriptures, and these came to be called *dicta probantia*, or "proof sayings." An early example of this method was Sebastian Schmidt's (1617–1696) collection of biblical texts from both testaments, organized in relation to theological topics.[35] The goal of this proof-text method was surely to base doctrines on the Bible, but the presentation of the material privileged doctrine as the governing factor. Once the biblical texts were arranged under the doctrines, it eventually was easier simply to remember the doctrines and not the texts related to them. The effect of this method was the gradual independence of doctrine from the Bible and a return to emphasizing doctrine over the Bible.[36]

The work of systematization should not be remembered merely for its proof-text methods or as a time completely antithetical to the Bible's theological message. The 1600s reveal some of the earliest examples of written works called "biblical theologies" that presented overarching systems of Scripture, often around the theme of covenant.[37] The best known of these was Johannes Cocceius's (1603–1669) *Doctrinal Summary of the Covenant and Testament of God* (1648). He believed that the various covenants that God made with people during the biblical history constituted the best organizing theme of the Bible's message. He traced these from the covenant of works with Adam (based on his obedience) to the covenant of grace in Christ, the new Adam. His system of theology is sometimes called "federal theology," from the Latin word for covenant (*foedus*).[38] Building on Cocceius's work, Francis Turretin (1632–1687) wrote a systematic work called *Theological Institutes* (1679). This work continued to be enormously influential in the Western Protestant world and was still being referred to as a basic theological text two hundred years later.[39]

The seventeenth century also saw the rise of rational and scientific methods for Bible study. Jewish scholar Baruch de Spinoza (1632–1677) presented far-reaching insights in his magnum opus, *Tractatus Religico-Politicus* (1670). Drawing on the influence of a variety of philosophical and religious currents, Spinoza believed that there was nothing inherently contradictory between the Bible and the insights of human reason.[40] Nevertheless, his use of historical criticism on the biblical books did call into question "the traditional views of the biblical canon and the authorship of biblical books."[41] Lurking behind these early expressions of a more scientific study of the Bible was the Reformation's emphasis on literal and historical interpretation. Disciplined study of the Bible carried with it the possibility of conclusions that ran counter to those assumed by the Reformers. According to Hans Frei, "The antitraditionalism in scriptural interpretation of [Protestant orthodoxy] bolstered the antiauthoritarian stance in matters of religious meaning and truth of [rationalist religious thought]."[42] There are, therefore, no easy dividing lines between one era and another or between acceptance and rejection of the Bible.

Other responses to Protestant scholasticism are found in major philosophical and intellectual schools of thought that had their own methods for discovering and describing truth. There were, of course, several forms of rationalism beyond the type espoused by Spinoza, not all of which related directly to religion, much less to theological interpretation of the Bible. English deists challenged a personal view of God revealed in the Bible and opted for a more detached deity believed to exist based on observation of an orderly cosmos.[43]

German rationalists assumed the complete adequacy of reason to guide in all matters religious and moral, the effect being that the Bible was placed in one category vis-à-vis philosophy and reason in another.[44]

Still other movements affirmed the great worth of Christian faith while redirecting the focus away from exclusively doctrinal concerns to the spiritual life of believers. Pietism held that what people experience in their faith relationship with Christ through Scripture is more important than knowing the dogmatic theological statements of the church.[45] The individual most associated with Pietism was Philip Jacob Spener (1635–1705), whose work *Pia Desideria* (1675) identified a number of "defects" among civil authorities, church leaders, and the common people. The Bible was to be the central means of reforming such abuses: "The Word of God remains the seed from which all that is good in us must grow. If we succeed in getting the people to seek eagerly and diligently in the book of life for their joy, their spiritual life will be wonderfully strengthened and they will become altogether different people."[46] From within the established church, Pietists drew their spiritual sustenance more from experience than from doctrine, for "it is by no means enough to have knowledge of the Christian faith, for Christianity consists rather of practice."[47]

Another current was romanticism, part of the eighteenth century's "growing inclination to trade the dryness and coldness of the Rationalist approach for the warmth and tenderness of feeling."[48] Johann Gottfried von Herder's (1744–1803) work *The Spirit of Hebrew Poetry* (1782–1783) revealed a deep appreciation for the poetic way ancient Israelite culture expressed its faith and not merely for the theological concepts that could be gleaned from the Old Testament. Although he shared Pietism's concern for basic content of the Bible's history of salvation, Herder's interest in that history was characterized by an embrace of the aesthetic context in which that history is told.[49]

Summary

This sweeping survey of the centuries prior to the Enlightenment does not reveal a discipline of biblical theology in any modern sense. Even so, what has been called precritical biblical interpretation does share something with the critical enterprise, insofar as many of the same basic problems or issues that occupied the Enlightenment era had been broached throughout the preceding centuries. We shall see again and again that the questions earlier scholars raised pertaining to the sources of theology (e.g., the development of the biblical canon), the nature of the interpretive task (e.g., literal or figurative exegesis), and the influence of one's historical context (e.g., living in an era of reform) have continued to surface in ways that demonstrate the enduring challenges of identifying and understanding the meaning and message of Scripture.

UNDER WHAT CIRCUMSTANCES DID THE DISCIPLINE OF BIBLICAL THEOLOGY DEVELOP?

The many intellectual and spiritual currents of the post-Reformation era set the stage for the development of biblical theology as a distinct academic discipline within biblical studies. The variety of these currents created a complex interaction of philosophical, scientific, theological, and political issues.[50] Even though we cannot engage in an in-depth study of these matters here, we should keep in mind the danger of oversimplifying the distinctions among these various developments in different parts of Europe. In the midst of this complexity, however, there does seem to be a center of gravity—namely, the dynamic between ecclesiastical use of the Bible on the one hand and the historical, scientific study of the Bible on the other. Depending on one's perspective, of course, this dynamic might rather be seen as "a life-and-death struggle between Christian theology and 'mere historicism,' a theory of interpretation which secularized and humanized Old Testament religion."[51]

At the dawn of the Enlightenment, there were different responses to this dynamic, but the respondents did not necessarily disagree with each other on every point. Much of post-Reformation scholasticism was discarded in the tenets of rationalism or the practices of Pietism, but neither of these alternatives rejected the Bible or church doctrine out of hand. Rather, they sought a different use of the Bible than the proof-text methods of Protestant scholasticism. As Brevard Childs points out, both Pietists and rationalists called for a "biblical theology," the first group meaning a return from scholasticism "to a theology based solely on the Bible" and the second meaning "a return to the 'simple' and 'historical' religion of the Bible apart from complex ecclesiastical formulations."[52] In spite of these different emphases, many scholars were appreciative both of rational-scientific methods for studying the Bible and their pastoral and educational use in the church. Thus, a key circumstance behind the rise of biblical theology was the effort by such scholars to resolve tensions that existed within the matrix of the church's ministerial use of the Bible and the scholar's academic study of the Bible.[53] Two figures stand out as particularly significant for this pivotal moment in the discipline's inception.

G. T. Zachariae and the Role of Biblical Theology

In an insightful study of Gotthelf Traugott Zachariae (1729–1777), John Sandys-Wunsch states that "Zachariae has generally been recognized as the father of biblical theology in the modern sense of the term."[54] This acclamation is supported by more than Zachariae's authorship of a four-volume work, the main title of which was *Biblical Theology*.[55] Although his original plan was to examine and challenge the use of biblical proof texts, he came to realize that a larger purpose and method was called for in studying the church's use of the Bible, namely, the presentation of biblical teaching in a way that would be distinct from both the practice of exegesis and the discipline of systematic theology.[56] This middle way between exegesis and dogmatics was what Zachariae understood as biblical theology, a discipline that distinguished the "incidental and historically conditioned" ideas in Scripture from principles that were "abiding and universal."[57] He categorized these universal principles in three areas: those related to God, to human sin and divine response to it, and to changes to the human condition and Christian conduct.[58]

Zachariae's larger purpose in doing biblical theology was to educate pastors and teachers by giving them resources to teach sound biblical truth in churches and schools. He believed his embrace of historical methods could work in concert with his commitment to the Bible as a divinely inspired revelation. While not directly dealing with all of the philosophical implications of the doctrine of inspiration, he nevertheless could assume it as he set forth to follow his biblical-theological method. In this way, his work offered some resolution to the intellectual tensions of his time, if not completely developing either the methodology or the results of his study.

J. P. Gabler and the Distinctiveness of Biblical Theology

Although there is some warrant in Sandys-Wunsch's claim that Zachariae is the father of biblical theology, many scholars today regard Johann Philip Gabler (1753–1826) as the person who commenced the modern discipline of biblical theology. Ben Ollenburger claims that "Old Testament theology is a series of very expansive footnotes to Gabler," while Jon Levenson identifies "the birthday" of biblical theology as March 30, 1787, the date of Gabler's inaugural lecture at the University of Altdorf.[59] Even though Gabler never actually published a major text of biblical theology, what he did contribute to the discipline was a proposal for relating the historical methods and insights gained since the Enlightenment to the theological beliefs expounded by church doctrine. His lecture was entitled "An Oration on the Proper Distinction between Biblical and Dogmatic Theology and the Specific Objectives of Each"[60] and "has come to be honored as the first systematic formulation of the basic issues involved in the pursuit of biblical theology."[61] To be sure, Gabler built on the work of Zachariae, whom he favorably mentions in the address. Gabler sensed the need to offer clearer methodological reflection than Zachariae had given a decade earlier. Thus, Sandys-Wunsch still avers that in spite of Gabler's distinctive contribution to the discipline, "the hands were J. Ph. Gabler's, the voice was G. T. Zachariae's."[62]

What, then, was Gabler's contribution? In the most basic sense, he proposed the terminology with which to define biblical theology over against the more systematic or dogmatic expressions of theology. As the subtitle of his address states, he wanted to clarify "the specific objectives of each" of these disciplines. For Gabler, "biblical theology" was "of historical origin, conveying what the holy [i.e., biblical] writers felt about divine matters," whereas "dogmatic theology" was "of didactic origin, teaching what each theologian philosophises rationally about divine things."[63] He believed that as long as one conducted the work of biblical theology in a consistent, historical fashion, all of the conclusions would be in harmony with each other. Dogmatic theology, however, was subject to many winds of change, such as time period, location, ecclesiastical affiliation, and so on. This fundamental distinction, therefore, set in motion the distancing of doctrinal or systematic theology from biblical studies, even though Gabler himself would never have wanted their study to be overly separated.

Gabler set forth a method for doing biblical theology that relied on yet another distinction between two basic steps in the process of studying the Bible.[64] The first stage sought what he called "the true sacred ideas typical of each author," and this task could only be undertaken by "carefully collecting and classifying" the ideas of each biblical author through a process that used every available linguistic or historical skill. Then, once these biblical ideas had been accurately interpreted for each passage or book, the second stage called for "a careful and sober comparison" of the distinct ideas from each writer (never forgetting the unique setting of each) in order to derive whatever universal ideas may arise when the biblical authors are in agreement. The result is a "biblical theology, pure and unmixed with foreign things."[65]

Some scholars suggest that this "pure" biblical theology involves a normative move, insofar as decisions have to be made about what is universal and thus what is always true and applicable. Or, to draw on Stendahl's terminology, a pure biblical theology would tell every new generation what the text means for them, but unlike Stendahl, Gabler wanted a determination of "what it means" to remain part of the biblical-theological task. He believed the biblical scholar could and should do both aspects of biblical theology, identifying the "true" ideas as well as the comparison of texts that resulted in pure, universal principles. His hope was that theologians of the church would take the universal ideas of pure biblical theology and be able to build a dogmatic theology with stronger foundations.

Many students of the discipline have lamented that Gabler never carried out his far-reaching plan for a comprehensive work of biblical theology; his oration provided only the faintest of outlines. From one perspective, of course, the two-hundred-year history of the discipline is the project Gabler envisioned, an ongoing task of description and a wrestling with the connection between what is described and what it might prescribe. From another perspective, however, biblical theology since Gabler has tended to produce the same multiplicity of views he decried in dogmatics. He could not have imagined the specialization of biblical studies in our own time, where scholars are comfortable addressing matters only in their area of expertise, perhaps a portion of the canon or even one book. The thought of sharply dividing the testaments was not in his plan, but his historical method so emphasized the careful exegesis of passages in their distinct contexts that it was only natural to let the testaments drift apart. It was a development that would not be long in the making.

WHY DID THE DIVISION IN THE TREATMENT OF THE TESTAMENTS OCCUR?

Beginning students are often surprised by the relative lack of recent books devoted to the theology of the whole Bible compared with treatments of the individual testaments. In fact, the percentage of *biblical* theologies in relation to *Old* or *New Testament* theologies seems small indeed. Since Brevard Childs's *Biblical Theology of the Old and New Testaments* was published in 1993, there have been few attempts to produce a major work of biblical theology covering both testaments.[66] It is therefore fair to ask what happened to bring about this state of affairs, having just gained the impression that Gabler intended the entire Christian Bible to be a source for coherent theological interpretation.

G. L. Bauer and the Initial Steps toward Division of the Testaments

Perhaps it is ironic that the first expression of distinct treatments of the testaments happened geographically and chronologically near to Gabler himself. In the year following his famous address, he was joined at Altdorf by Georg Lorenz Bauer (1755–1806), a rationalist biblical scholar who came to appreciate much of Gabler's thought. Less than a decade later, Bauer published a volume of Old Testament theology (1796), which he followed with a four-volume New Testament theology, completed in 1802.[67] His Old Testament theology focused on the concepts of God and humankind as reflected in the historical development of ideas.[68] His volumes on the New Testament focused on what he believed "Jesus and the apostles taught as essential truths of religion valid for all people and times."[69]

Most important for our purposes here, of course, are the reasons Bauer produced these *separate* works. After all, his bibliography reveals the breadth of

his interests across both testaments. Nevertheless, Bauer was convinced that
the theology of the testaments must be treated separately for several reasons.[70]
First, their vastly different historical contexts called for this separation. Since
the Old Testament contained within it the development of religious ideas and
institutions, one could not simply compare theological ideas across the gulf
created by different languages, cultures, and concepts. Second, as a rationalist
thinker, Bauer always looked for the pure, universal truths taught by the Bible,
and he thus considered the New Testament teachings of Jesus and the apostles to be superior to Old Testament religion.[71] Third, though perhaps less
explicit, a unified treatment of the testaments was associated with the proof-
text methods of Protestant scholasticism, while overlooking the unique historical setting of the Bible's different parts.

Increasing Division of the Testaments
in Nineteenth-Century Works

In the decades following the publication of G. L. Bauer's volumes, some scholars, such as Gottlieb Kaiser (1781–1848) and Daniel Von Cölln (1788–1833),
continued to employ the term "biblical theology" in the titles of their works,
but even here the division was evident in their treatment of the biblical materials. Kaiser's rationalistic view of history downplayed the contributions of
Israelite religion, furthering the distinction between Judaism and Christianity, and Von Cölln placed discussion of the testaments in separate volumes of
his work with little integration.[72] Wilhelm DeWette's (1780–1849) *Biblical
Dogmatics of the Old and New Testaments* (1813) also treated the testaments in
separate sections.[73] Still other works appeared with titles like *Biblical Theology
of the New Testament*.[74]

Throughout the nineteenth century there were, of course, moderate and
conservative scholars whose resistance to rationalism was motivated in part by
a commitment to the unity of Old and New Testaments. Ludwig Baumgarten-
Crusius's (1788–1843) *Basic Features of Biblical Theology* (1828) argued that the
concept of the "kingdom of God" held the testaments together.[75] In similar
fashion, the so-called salvation history school, perhaps best represented by
Johann von Hofmann (1810–1877), described the unity of the testaments in
terms of the developing story of God's salvation in history.[76] As von Hofmann
put the matter in *Interpreting the Bible* (1860), "In the New Testament the witnesses of salvation are expressed in terms that are derived from the Old Testament. The Old Testament manifestations must be understood spiritually,
however, as witnesses of the same salvation that has been given to us as Christians, if the terminology of the New Testament witness is to be interpreted
correctly."[77] Representing a less critical approach to the theological unity of

the testaments was E. W. Hengstenberg (1802–1869). His *Christology of the Old Testament* was a massive, four-volume work that interpreted the Old Testament as a source of prophecies and types of Jesus Christ. The bulk of the book discussed what he called "Messianic Predictions in the Prophets," with the largest portion devoted to Isaiah.

These efforts to articulate and advance a more holistic approach to the Bible were not to win the day, even though the occasional biblical theology continued to appear well into the twentieth century. Geerhardus Vos's *Biblical Theology: Old and New Testaments* (1948) was extremely influential in the middle of the last century and is still a good example of a covenantal theology. Nevertheless, the rise of the historical-critical method in the nineteenth century, particularly the advent of the "history of religions" approach, was to solidify what now seems to be a permanent mark on the separate study of the testaments. Thus, Childs's summary of Ebeling's work is to the point: "The theological unity of the Old and New Testaments has become extremely fragile and it seems now impossible to combine the testaments on the same level in order to produce a unified theology."[78] It remains to be seen what, if anything, might happen to change this fact of biblical studies. The rigorous treatment of and sensitivity to the historical contexts of each testament has resulted in Old and New Testament theology remaining distinct from each other. Perhaps the pendulum of scholarship has swung too far away from the treatment of the whole Bible, or perhaps the burden of proof still lies with those who would bring the two testaments together in one theological analysis.

WHAT INTELLECTUAL MOVEMENTS INFLUENCED THE METHODS OF NINETEENTH-CENTURY BIBLICAL THEOLOGY?

The nineteenth century was a time of significant debate over the nature of biblical history and theology, of experimentation in the use of philosophical systems for biblical interpretation, and ultimately of great change in the nature and task of biblical theology. It is true, of course, that every time period is marked by philosophical and religious movements that express themselves on questions of divine authority and human reason. But the nineteenth century stands out as a battleground "between the times," that is, between the growing acceptance of higher criticism in the eighteenth century and its ultimate victory in the twentieth-century. This conflict in the discipline of biblical theology involved many currents and occurred on more than one front. Some scholars found ways to transform emphases in their pietistic backgrounds with interpretive methods that sought the fundamental themes in Scripture. Others integrated historical-critical methods with idealistic philosophy, especially based on the work of Georg Hegel (1770–1831).[79] And then there were a variety of "conservative" or "moderate" theologians who resisted the rising tide of rationalism and the application of critical methods of interpretation, which they believed were undermining biblical inspiration and authority.

Friedrich Schleiermacher's Theological Hermeneutics

As Gabler's call for a distinct, historical discipline of biblical theology was gaining a hearing among scholars in Germany at the turn of the century, a young theologian named Friedrich Schleiermacher (1768–1834) was beginning to make his mark with the appearance of his short work *On Religion: Speeches to Its Cultured Despisers* (1799). Here Schleiermacher articulated what was to become a central theme of his work, namely, that "feeling and immediate consciousness" were more central to the Christian religion than doctrines and ideas about God.[80] A prolific author, Schleiermacher's thought was situated between traditional theology—interpreted through his pietistic background—and the dominant rationalism of the late eighteenth century. His most important book, *The Christian Faith* (1821–1822), laid out the basic areas of systematic theology in terms of the universal religious feeling of absolute dependence, which finds its highest form in Christianity.[81] His writings also influenced biblical studies in at least three areas, which William Baird identifies as "hermeneutical theory, critical research, and exegetical and theological synthesis."[82] In his *Life of Jesus*, Schleiermacher understood the Gospels to present Jesus "as the one sent from God to reveal a unique God-consciousness" and "to bring people into community—the kingdom of God, which is not political but a spiritual union of believers."[83]

As for encouraging any form of wider biblical theology, Schleiermacher placed his own emphasis almost completely on the New Testament, regarding the Old Testament as inferior in its theological message and inspiration. Even though Jesus and his followers appealed to the Old Testament, Schleiermacher went so far as to suggest that the real meaning of the Bible might be better understood "if the Old Testament followed the New as an appendix."[84] The lack of interest in Old Testament theology among some early nineteenth-century scholars may go back to Schleiermacher's negative attitudes.[85] In terms of methodology in biblical theology, however, it may be said that his hermeneutical thinking had a lasting impact. Schleiermacher's understanding of the interpretive task offered an early example of how the meaning or subject matter of biblical texts can be regarded as distinct from the text itself.[86] This way of thinking offered some warrant to later scholars who wished to bracket textual or historical questions in their pursuit of the theological message. A different yet parallel track to this way of thinking arises in the next section.

G. W. F. Hegel's Idealistic Philosophy

Hegel taught philosophy at the University of Berlin from 1818 until his death in 1831, overlapping the span of time that Schleiermacher taught there. Hegel's thought has had such far-reaching implications in a wide variety of areas that it is difficult to do him justice in a few short comments, but for our purposes it was his structure of human history and progress that became the lens for biblical theologians. Hegel taught that history always moves forward as the development of spirit in time through an interplay of ideas and forces he described with the terms "thesis," "antithesis," and "synthesis." In *The Philosophy of History*, Hegel declared "that Reason is the Sovereign of the World; that the history of the world, therefore, presents us with a rational process."[87] History reveals that the dialectical nature of spirit's movement "assumes successive forms which it successively transcends; and by this very process of transcending its earlier stages, gains an affirmative, and, in fact, a richer and more concrete shape."[88] It was this basic, dialectical pattern that some biblical theologians picked up on as they sought to trace religious developments in both testaments.[89]

In Old Testament theology J. K. W. Vatke (1806–1882) wrote a work entitled *The Religion of OT Presented according to the Canonical Books* (1835), which used Hegel's model to describe the development of Israelite religion. He divided the religious history of the Old Testament into eight periods, but the overall portrait reveals a reliance on Hegelian notions of "successively transcending forms." From the earliest stages of their history, Israel had learned about Egypt's form of nature religion, which (in Hegelian fashion) might be regarded as the "thesis" against which Israelite religion responded over time in various ways. The "antithesis" constituted the Hebrews' more spiritual form of religion, which culminated in exilic prophets such as Second Isaiah and eventually in the law. The historical development produced a new synthesis in the more universal religion of Christianity.[90] Other applications of this Hegelian philosophy were possible, as manifested in a work by Bruno Bauer (1809–1882) that appeared three years after Vatke's and argued that the law stood earlier than the prophets, much like the canonical order of the biblical books themselves.[91]

By far the most outstanding example of the integration of historical method with Hegelian thinking in New Testament thought was in the work of D. F. Strauss (1808–1874). The book for which he is most famous, *The Life of Jesus Critically Examined* (1835), caused such an uproar that just a few months after it was published Strauss lost his teaching post at Tübingen. One reviewer described the work as "the most pestilential book ever vomited out of the jaws of hell."[92] But Strauss was not intentionally antagonistic toward Christianity, and even though his research undercut the historicity of biblical miracles, he still believed that they taught eternal truths. His rigorous, critical analysis may be illustrated by the way he treated the accounts of Jesus' ascension. Comparing and contrasting the three passages that mention the ascension, Strauss pressed the narratives for rational and historical explanations, with questions such as, "how can a palpable body, which has still *flesh and bones*, and eats material food, be qualified for a celestial abode? how can it so far liberate itself from the laws of gravity, as to be capable of an ascent through the air?"[93] His method then led him to consider mythical aspects of the ascension stories that could have drawn on a variety of biblical and extrabiblical sources as well as the belief that the now exalted Jesus "will at some future time return from heaven in the clouds, so he must surely have departed thither in the same manner."[94]

Strauss concluded his work with a dissertation on "the dogmatic import of the life of Jesus," in which he discussed and then dismissed both orthodox and rationalist attempts to understand the person and work of Christ.[95] In their place, he articulated a distinctly Hegelian Christology which denied that the dialectical movement of Absolute Spirit was expressed in one historical person for all time. Rather, he asked, "is not the idea of the unity of the divine and human natures a real one in a far higher sense, when I regard the whole race of mankind as its realization, than when I single out one man as such realization? is not an incarnation of God from eternity, a truer one than an incarnation limited to a particular point in time?"[96] Thus, when the church pointed to a historical Jesus as the God-man, the real spiritual truth, for Strauss, was that he served as a symbolic representative of the human race.[97] In this way, the real, timeless truths of the biblical message were made relevant to modern times, a goal reminiscent of Gabler.

The application of a dialectic to other portions of the New Testament occurred in the work of one of Strauss's teachers at Tübingen, Ferdinand Christian Baur (1792–1860).[98] A brilliant church historian, Baur adopted Hegel's view of historical process in his magnum opus, entitled *The Church History of the First Three Centuries*. For Baur, "God lives in history, and history is the life of God."[99] In order to understand God's work in human history would thus require nothing less than the most rigorous historical criticism, since the church's beginnings were clearly owing to historical causes and movements. The same historical factors at work in the history of Christian thought were already at work in the content of the New Testament writings themselves, making New Testament theology "the essential presupposition of the history of dogma."[100] Baur employed his thoroughgoing historical and exegetical approach to discern the theological intentions of the New Testament authors, an approach called "tendency criticism."[101] While Baur tried to ground his conclusions about the historical development of New Testament thought in this rigorous method, he nevertheless used a Hegelian framework for organizing the historical tensions at work in first-century Christianity, and he believed that the unfolding of Absolute Spirit was expressed in the historical process.[102] He identified dialectical tensions at various stages of the early church's development, mainly between Jewish elements and later Gentile elements to form the beginnings of Catholicism in the postapostolic period.[103]

Conservative Reactions to Higher Criticism of Scripture

There was no unified "conservative" response to the rationalist or idealist currents of the early and mid-nineteenth century. There were moderating voices that saw some value in the use of higher critical methods, while others rejected such tools as antithetical to the Bible's inspirational character.[104] We have seen that von Hofmann and Hengstenberg had more traditional views on the matter of Old and New Testament unity, but these men also criticized each other on their respective methods. Von Hofmann thought that Hengstenberg erred "by emphasizing exclusively the unity of the truth of salvation supplied by Scripture, [giving] too little attention to the historical background and the historical form of Scripture."[105] For his part, Hengstenberg charged von Hofmann for clothing his rationalistic thought with "orthodox dress" because he only saw the prophetic character of history and not all of the messianic figures in the Old Testament.[106] If Hengstenberg's Old Testament Christology was regarded as too much based on a confessional approach to the Bible,[107] von Hofmann's advocacy of the so-called *Heilsgeschichte* (salvation history) interpretation of the Bible is significant for the way it looked back to the progressive revelation and inner unity of the Bible in federal theology as well as anticipated developments in the twentieth century among neo-orthodox theologians and others. Grasping the unity of the story meant that "event and interpretation are logically distinct but not separately available. The meaning of a realistic passage is the event and its interpretation."[108]

The works of Gustav Oehler (1812–1872) are regarded by some as having the most long-term influence of the nineteenth-century conservative movement.[109] Adopting an approach similar to von Hofmann's, Oehler's *Theology of the Old Testament* (1873–1874) defined that discipline as "the historical exhibition of the development of the religion contained in the canonical books of the Old Testament."[110] Oehler is clear throughout his work that he regards the subject matter of biblical theology to be divine revelation, thus giving his otherwise historical and descriptive approach a normative tone: "Hence, Old Testament theology must embrace the chief facts in the history of the divine kingdom, since it must present the Old Testament religion not only as doctrine, but in the whole compass of its manifestation. But because it ought to report what men in the Old Testament believed, in what faith they lived and died, it has to exhibit the history *as Israel believed it.*"[111] While standing between Schleiermacher's negative view of the Old Testament and Hengstenberg's overemphasis on the unity of the testaments, some scholars have thought that Oehler's concern for progression and genetic development of ideas is contradicted by the relatively small attention given to prophetic and Wisdom literature compared to the fuller treatment of the Mosaic era.[112]

Summary

Judging from the intense reactions to Strauss's *Life of Jesus*, it is probably safe to say that in the first half of the nineteenth century, the vast number of European Christians continued to hold a very high view of biblical inspiration and authority, even as critical thinking began to dominate academic study of the Bible. Amidst the rising tide of historical criticism, there continued to be a sizeable minority of moderate or conservative scholars who tried to work within a traditional framework of biblical studies that kept in mind what the church's doctrine taught about Scripture. They may have been at different points on the spectrum of openness to the newer methods of exegesis, but they understood the Bible to be a record of God's revelation to Israel and the church. Nevertheless, by the latter third of the nineteenth century, biblical scholarship's embrace of the historical method was coming into full bloom. The advances made in the early Enlightenment as well as Gabler's focus on a historical, biblical theology were reaching their logical conclusion. It was only a matter of time before the concern for history, represented by F. C. Baur and others, would usher biblical theology into a new chapter, one quite far from the dream of Gabler.

WHAT IS THE DIFFERENCE BETWEEN THE HISTORY OF RELIGIONS AND BIBLICAL THEOLOGY?

From the late nineteenth century and well past the opening decade of the twentieth century, many biblical scholars adopted a perspective and methodology which came to be called the history of religions school. Building on the advances in historical research achieved by the long line of scholars who came before them, the representatives of this school studied the Bible not so much for its theological message as for what it could tell us about Israelite or early Christian religion. Ascendancy of this movement was accompanied by a corresponding decrease in scholarly attention to biblical theology in any of its previous manifestations, be they rationalistic, Hegelian, or conservative in expression.

To highlight some of the major differences between the history of religions approach and other nineteenth-century forms of biblical theology, one could mention at least these three characteristics. First, in terms of their *goal*, history of religions approaches focused far more on the religious beliefs and practices of the people within the Bible than on the theological content of their testimonies about the words and deeds of Yahweh or Jesus. There is a fine line here, to be sure, because the study of the Bible's theology is inextricably intertwined with its history. However, the concern generally came to be only with the historical side of this pair. Second, the *method* of this school was developmental and comparative, insofar as scholars sought to understand the evolution of both the cultic practices and the biblical sources that described them. In order to achieve the most accurate understanding of Israelite sacrifices, for example, it was necessary to compare and contrast them with the actions of Israel's ancient Near Eastern neighbors, requiring more serious attention to extrabiblical sources than before. Third, the *purpose* of such research was far more descriptive than it was normative, which meant that any remaining form of biblical theology would at best merely describe, say, what the early church believed about God. There was little interest in considering how these beliefs spoke to modern people, much less how such beliefs laid a theological claim on them.

It is easier in hindsight to discern how and why the shift from biblical theology to history of religions occurred. The seeds were sown long before the nineteenth century, so that almost before biblical theology had a chance to establish itself as a distinct discipline an author such as G. L. Bauer adopted a developmental and comparative emphasis.[113] The situation was obviously far richer and more complex than the following overview would imply, given the fact that the late nineteenth century witnessed the powerful interaction of scientific, theological, and socioeconomic concepts in the works of people such as Charles Darwin (1809–1882), Albrecht Ritschl (1822–1889), and Karl Marx (1818–1883).[114] The following discussion lifts up representative examples of scholarship in both testaments, since that division itself was consistent with the historical focus on religion.

Old Testament Theology and the History of Religions

Throughout the nineteenth century, scholars had been studying the Old Testament as a source of information about the development of Israelite religion. In addition to Vatke's work mentioned earlier, W. M. L. De Wette (1780–1849) and K. H. Graf (1815–1869) wrote important studies in this area, but their theories were resisted by conservative scholars and only weakly embraced by those open to critical methods. It was in the work of Julius Wellhausen (1844–1918) that earlier insights coalesced in the now classic expression of the Documentary

Hypothesis. Wellhausen's *Prolegomena to the History of Ancient Israel* (1878) studied the development of various offices and institutions of Israel's religion, offering a coherent chronology for the theory that the first six Old Testament books derive not from Mosaic authorship but from four other sources (Yahwist [J], Elohist [E], Deuteronomist [D], Priestly writer [P]) that spanned the centuries from the early monarchy to the postexilic period. Wellhausen did more than simply affirm individual sources; he proposed a scheme whereby one could "render them intelligible as phases of a living process, and thus to make it possible to trace a graduated development of the tradition."[115] The basic movement in Israel's understanding of its relationship with God may be represented by a threefold process. First, in the combined JE narratives there is a focus on matters pertaining to nature and the land; second, in the Deuteronomic materials (D) the focus shifts to history and Israel's struggle with the nations; finally, with the Priestly writings (P) the focus becomes the law and its religious rituals.[116] Wellhausen's conclusions, while not necessarily destroying all forms of biblical theology, so rearranged the history of the biblical traditions that it weakened any theological interpretation which assumed Mosaic authorship of the Pentateuch and took at face value the history presented in the Old Testament books of Genesis through Kings. In the decades immediately after Wellhausen's *Prolegomena* was published, it became extremely difficult, if not impossible, for biblical theologians to let the message of Scripture depend directly on now obsolete historical understandings.

Wellhausen's presentation was not necessarily without its flaws, particularly in his acceptance of developmental methodologies characteristic of that time. While he might be able to show that a specific source reflected a monarchical setting, for example, it was surely possible "that significant elements of the source may go back to an earlier period."[117] It was this weakness, in part, that was addressed in the work of Hermann Gunkel (1862–1932). In books such as *Creation and Chaos* (1895) and important studies on *Genesis* (1901) and the *Psalms* (1926), Gunkel compared the Bible's literature with ancient Near Eastern sources that had been unavailable at the time of Wellhausen's *Prolegomena*. Gunkel argued that one needs to press back beyond the written traditions to earlier, oral forms on which later documents or sources depended. Wellhausen had claimed, for example, that the written sources from later times would create and "unconsciously project" their features upon the ancestral stories, thus making the figure of Abraham "a free creation of unconscious art."[118] Gunkel, however, believed that many of the ancestral stories grew out of a much longer process of tradition. In light of the antiquity of many personal names (e.g., Reuben, Simeon, and Levi), he concluded that some of the ancestral stories were "very ancient" and the names were those of "ancient peoples and tribes older than historical Israel."[119] Nevertheless, Gunkel's concern was not for the

Bible's theology per se, but for the way Old Testament literature offered access to the development of Israel's religion within its ancient Near Eastern context.

From the side of Old Testament studies, therefore, the writing of histories of Israelite religion eclipsed the production of theologies of the Old Testament. Scholars continued to use "biblical theology" or "Old Testament theology" in their titles, but these were basically histories of religion.[120] There remains a close relationship between the concepts of religion and theology, and Gunkel continued to defend his historical methods and interests against criticisms that what he produced was "a dragging down of what is Biblical to the level of the non-Biblical as to obliterate all difference between them." When he wrote those words in 1927, the tide had already turned back toward a recovery of theological interpretation, but Gunkel defined the scope and purpose of theology differently from his opponents. He wrote that the study of biblical religion was "one of the most urgent tasks of theology" in his day, a sentiment reflecting his awareness that many scholars were no longer content defining the theological subject matter of the Bible strictly in terms of the religious practices described in its literature.[121]

New Testament Theology and the History of Religions

There were parallel developments in New Testament studies during this same period, as scholars who adopted a rigorously historical-critical method argued that Gabler's call for a "purely historical" biblical theology had yet to be fully realized.[122] The emphasis on a historical theology of the New Testament, exemplified by F. C. Baur, was amplified by William Wrede (1859–1906), who embraced Baur's historical method while rejecting his Hegelianism.[123] In an important essay written in 1897, Wrede explained biblical theology not merely in terms of the thoughts or theological intentions of the biblical writers (as Baur proposed), but instead looked to the historical events and circumstances behind the writings. He rejected the belief that "the world of ideas hovered above external history as a world of its own. . . . The early Christian world of ideas is very strongly conditioned by external history, and this must be made quite clear."[124] In order to understand this history, it meant that New Testament theology must search out all available information from the extrabiblical writings of the time, since the division between canonical and noncanonical books was, in Wrede's view, a later historical development that exhibited fluctuation in that boundary during the early centuries of Christianity.[125] For these reasons, Wrede also rejected the name "New Testament theology" for this discipline. He wrote, "The appropriate name for the subject-matter is: early Christian history of religion, or rather: the history of early Christian religion and theology."[126] Wrede himself was not able to follow through on developing a full-fledged history of religion, but other scholars, whose works appeared in the first two decades of the 1900s, were heavily influenced by his outlook and methods.[127]

One finds strong resistance to a strict history of religions approach in the writings of Adolf Schlatter (1852–1938), who insisted that biblical theology, while necessarily involving historical research, demanded a consideration of the theological elements of the New Testament that speak beyond their own setting. His 1909 essay, "The Theology of the New Testament and Dogmatics," touches on a number of issues raised by the ascendancy of historical-critical methods, in particular, the problem of subjectivity in historical research, the scope and subject matter of New Testament theology, and the relationship of biblical theology to dogmatic theology.[128] Although the next chapter will address these issues, it is important to highlight here Schlatter's role as one who tended to work independently from the major modes of research, be they regarded as liberal or conservative.[129]

Schlatter believed that New Testament theology could not simply be called a historical discipline because historians can never achieve an absolute objectivity free from the influence of their own ideas, nor can they avoid the fact that the development of dogma is part of historical study in the first place.[130] Having said this, it is a vast oversimplification to see Schlatter as "nonhistorical," given his skills and interests.[131] For him "the independent development of historical science gives a measure of protection, admittedly not infallible, against arbitrary reconstructions of its object. It secures us against producing a mixture of what scripture says and what the church teaches, or a mixture of the Bible and our own religious opinions, in which neither the one factor nor the other is correctly grasped and fruitfully applied."[132] Thus, it could be said that Schlatter developed something of a "true New Testament theology" along the lines of Gabler's definitions, and like Gabler, Schlatter also distinguished between biblical theology and dogmatics. However, he did not wish to separate them completely or see the movement only in one direction (from biblical toward dogmatic theology) but rather to see them in a "dialectical" or "reciprocal" relationship, with dogmatics informing theological interpretation.[133] Finally, with respect to the scope of the discipline, Schlatter disagreed with Wrede's view of the role of extrabiblical sources and was adamant that "New Testament theology has as its subject-matter the New Testament, and nothing else."[134]

Summary

It should come as no surprise that the assessment of the history of religions approach offered by biblical theologians has been largely negative. When characterizing the impact of this period on biblical theology, some scholars have used terms such as "decline," "stalemate," and "destructive influence."[135] Even if one concludes that the late nineteenth century did not "advance" the discipline of biblical theology, it certainly contributed to an ever sharper focus on the role history plays in biblical theology. The history of religions school pressed the issues of the uniqueness of biblical faith, the way in which one organizes the concepts of biblical theology (historically, doctrinally), and the connection between biblical religion (its institutions, observances, leaders) and a biblical theology that accounts for that religion.[136] The dawn of the twenty-first century has its own debates over history, religion, and theology, and it remains to be seen how new historical methods and evidence will lead to greater understanding of the Bible's religious beliefs and practices and the ways they should form and inform theological interpretation. But before addressing the current scene, another question must be addressed.

WHY IS THE MIDDLE OF THE TWENTIETH CENTURY THOUGHT OF AS A GREAT AGE OF BIBLICAL THEOLOGY?

Scholars who have surveyed the history of biblical theology describe the discipline in the middle of the twentieth century with glowing terms such as "flowering," "golden age," "rebirth," "revival," and "new beginnings."[137] While the primary focus in this section is to ask why this era is seen in such a positive light, another question must first be asked. Given the previous dominance of the history of religions approach, with its negative reputation, what accounts for this change in the fortunes of biblical theology? Finding an answer means, of course, acknowledging the complexity of factors that occasioned a transition in methods, emphases, or directions for biblical theology. The intellectual, political, and religious climate of the early twentieth century calls for more comment than this book is able to give, but we can examine a few factors that contributed to a lessening confidence in the results of historical study and an increasing desire to ascertain the theological message of the Bible. We will then be in a better position to understand the impact of this "golden age."

A Recovery of the Theological in Biblical Theology

When terms like "recovery" are used for this era, one must clarify that this is in reference to the academic community, since there have always existed communities of faith—and scholars from them—that have upheld traditional views of the Bible's authority, inspiration, and historicity. These groups and their

adherents never gave up what Gunkel called "the ancient doctrine of Inspiration."[138] Moreover, English-speaking scholarship tended to lag behind its
Continental counterpart and was still wrestling with many of the results of
higher criticism.[139] That being said, by the year 1920, German scholarship was
feeling the residual effects of the history of religions approach, where the focus
on the Bible's historical development and religious concepts left a vacuum of
theological relevance and meaning. Scholars and church leaders alike had
already begun to question whether the emphasis on the historical was adequate
to provide a true and complete expression of the Bible's meaning, beyond the
analysis of linguistic and historical insights provided in most of the biblical
commentaries of the day.[140] On a greater scale, these advocates of biblical theology were struggling to sort out the failure of liberalism and evolutionary nat-
uralism, given the horrors of World War I, with its devastating effects on
Germany's political, social, and economic life.

The Debate over Old Testament Theology

Old Testament scholars, generally working from a Christian perspective, dealt
with the issue of the relevance of the Old Testament for the Christian faith,
since the history of religions school called into question its status as inspired
Scripture. To be sure, there remained several points on the spectrum, from a
positive call to see the Old Testament once again as revelation (equal to the
New Testament) to the negative rejection of the Old Testament altogether,
either as a source for Israelite religion or a precursor to the New Testament
and Christianity.[141] Between these positions were scholars like Gunkel who,
while denying the inspiration of the Old Testament, believed that the historical approach had confirmed it to be "a very great treasure."[142] But for Old
Testament theology at least, there were several prominent scholars, such as
Rudolf Kittel, Eduard König, Willy Staerk, and Carl Steuernagel, who raised
serious questions about the history of religions methods and presuppositions
while also advocating for Old Testament theology as an independent discipline. For example, Kittel's book *The Religion of the People of Israel*, while studying the development of religious ideas and ceremonies, focused equally on
theological themes of God's revelation and Israel's response of faith. He called
on Christians who would accept Jesus as Messiah to also "recognize that the
Old Testament and the religious history of his people was like himself, God's
own work."[143] These scholars sought a renewed Old Testament theology, one
that would explore the truth content of the First Testament on its own terms
and with its own categories, not merely as part of the mix of comparative religions or solely as background for the New Testament.[144]

   Two scholars who carried on an important debate over the relationship of
Old Testament theology to the history of Israelite religion were Otto Eissfeldt

and Walter Eichrodt, both of whom believed in the revitalization of Old Testament theology but came at that goal from different directions. Eissfeldt's 1926 essay "The History of Israelite-Jewish Religion and Old Testament Theology" argued that there was a real difference between these two disciplines, since scholars tended to subsume either the historical to the theological or vice versa, making one or the other the sole means for grasping "the essence of the subject completely." But Eissfeldt was not arguing for their separation merely on the basis of scholarly habits or experience; he claimed that the two approaches belonged "on two different planes. They correspond to two differently constituted functions of our spirit, to knowing and to believing." By "leaving both approaches in their unrestricted independence and tolerating the tension that arises between them," the two disciplines will actually "enrich each other," with historical knowledge helping to distinguish elements foreign to Christian faith.[145] In response, Eichrodt's 1929 essay "Does Old Testament Theology Still Have Independent Significance within Old Testament Scholarship?" refused to accept such separation and instead claimed that Old Testament theology was itself historical and one could not separate knowing and believing as Eissfeldt suggested.[146] In order for it to develop "the systematic task of a cross section" of Old Testament religion, "Old Testament theology has no tools other than history of religion." Eichrodt summarizes: "Thus, according to both its object and its method, Old Testament theology has its place entirely within empirical-historical Old Testament scholarship."[147]

The Debate over New Testament Theology

A similar tension between the historical and theological led to a lively debate among New Testament scholars as well, though it was ignited by the work of a Swiss theologian and pastor named Karl Barth (1886–1968). As Barth reflected on and responded to the liberalism that characterized his own academic training, he began to see the need for recovering the Bible's theological content, especially for its use in the church. His work *The Epistle to the Romans* (1918), thoroughly revised in 1921, sought to provide a theological interpretation of Paul's letter that let the apostle speak directly to people of the twentieth century. Written with minimal references to technical matters or the work of other scholars, the commentary spoke with conviction about the power and love of a God who is altogether different from humankind but was graciously revealed in both judgment and salvation through the cross of Jesus Christ. This contrast between the divine and human lay at the heart of Barth's so-called dialectic theology (also referred to as neo-orthodoxy), and it taught the absolute dependence of humans upon God. In commenting on Paul's presentation of the gospel in Romans 1:16, Barth wrote, "In announcing the limitation of the known world by another that is unknown, the Gospel does not enter into competition with the many attempts to disclose within the known world some more or less unknown and higher form of existence and to make it accessible to men. The Gospel is not a truth among other truths. Rather, it sets a question-mark against all truths."[148] While not rejecting the usefulness or necessity of historical exegesis for theological interpretation, Barth nevertheless saw historical criticism as "prolegomenon," as "preliminary work" to "genuine understanding and interpretation."[149]

Barth's impassioned call to be claimed by "the strange new world within the Bible" created no small controversy among scholars,[150] as they sometimes seized upon the tone as much as the content of statements that seemed to eliminate any historical distance between the past and the present.[151] Adolf Jülicher was one such critic who scathingly reviewed the first edition of Barth's commentary, contrasting its "practical exegesis of Scripture" with "strictly scientific exegesis." There was a great deal in Barth's commentary to aid in "understanding of our age, but scarcely anything new for the understanding of the 'historical' Paul." Jülicher also saw grave theological danger in Barth's method of ascertaining the spiritual message of the gospel in opposition to all efforts of human culture, making Barth appear like Marcion with a "dualistic approach of enmity to all that comes from the world, culture, or tradition."[152] With such a response, one can see the truth in Karl Adam's famous line about Barth's commentary exploding like "a bomb on the playground of the theologians."[153] Apart from the rhetoric of the debate, however, was the important fact that Barth redefined the boundaries between historical and theological inquiry, acknowledging the necessity of both while exalting the latter. He was trying to get on with the theological task that Schlatter called for, but even Schlatter thought that Barth had passed over the historical context of Paul's letter.[154]

The Golden Age of Biblical Theology

Having now gained some sense for how scholars wrestled with the theological implications of the history of religions approach to biblical theology, we are in a position to ask again why the middle of the twentieth century is almost universally regarded by scholars as something of a golden age for the discipline. To state the matter briefly, during this period biblical theology benefited from a shift away from the history-theology debate to the production of major works of both Old and New Testament theology—particularly by Walter Eichrodt (1890–1978), Gerhard von Rad (1901–1971), and Rudolf Bultmann (1884–1976)—as well as a great many studies that appeared in response to the work of these three figures, whose books exhibited not only a command of the biblical and extrabiblical materials but also a governing principle and methodology for organizing their theologies. The following chapters on issues, methods, and themes will develop salient points from their work, but here we can at least paint with broad strokes the contribution made by each author.

Walter Eichrodt's *Theology of the Old Testament*

Eichrodt's magnum opus was published in three volumes, reflecting the three parts of his outline of the theology of the Old Testament: God and the people (1933), God and the world (1935), and God and man (1939).[155] His work is perhaps best known for its central, organizing theme, namely, the idea of covenant: "The concept in which Israelite thought gave definitive expression to the binding of the people to God and by means of which they established firmly from the start the particularity of their knowledge of him was the covenant."[156] Eichrodt believed that the covenant, particularly in the Mosiac or Sinai traditions, was the best way to express the fundamental relationship between God and Israel. The best method for developing this idea in a systematic and comprehensive way was neither purely historical-developmental nor systematic-doctrinal; rather, "this can only be done by taking a cross-section of the realm of OT thought."[157] As he had argued in his debate with Eissfeldt, so here also Eichrodt stated that Old Testament theology "presupposes the history of Israel,"[158] though his work has been criticized by some as not really attending to historical matters.[159] The same might be said about his intention to understand the Old Testament in conversation, with the ancient Near Eastern context on one side and the New Testament on the other.[160] More attention will be given to Eichrodt's cross-section method and his emphasis on the theme of covenant, but a brief, representative assessment of his significance for Old Testament theology is this by Werner Lemke: "In spite of legitimate criticisms and acknowledged shortcomings, Eichrodt's work so far remains unsurpassed in comprehensiveness, methodological thoroughness, and theological acumen."[161]

Gerhard von Rad's *Old Testament Theology*

Many scholars over the next twenty to thirty years followed Eichrodt's work with Old Testament theologies of their own, usually following his systematic and thematic approach.[162] Gerhard von Rad's two-volume work (1957, 1960), however, challenged the adequacy of central themes for the diverse theological content of the Old Testament and also proposed that the structure of an Old Testament theology should follow the development of the biblical witness itself.[163] Thus, the theologian's "subject-matter" was "simply Israel's own explicit assertions about Jahweh." The real challenge lay in the "unfolding of the witness of the Old Testament," since it has no "center" like the New

Testament's witness to Jesus Christ. By studying this witness through time (i.e., a diachronic method rather than Eichrodt's synchronic cross-sections), one could begin to describe God's action in Israel's history by means of "confessional formulae"—brief, ancient expressions about Yahweh—that eventually led to longer "summaries of the saving history, covering by now a fairly expansive span of the divine action in history."[164] For von Rad, the most important and perhaps the oldest of these summaries was Deuteronomy 26:5–9, which traces Israel's story from the wandering of the ancestors, through the slavery and deliverance from Egypt, to the entrance into the new land.[165] Von Rad's two volumes basically describe Israel's theology in the historical traditions— primarily the Hexatuech (i.e., Genesis–Joshua), with the Psalms and Wisdom literature being called Israel's answer—and the prophetic traditions.[166] His treatment of the Old Testament goes further in two areas that Eichrodt claimed were important for his own theology, that is, historical matters and the connection with the New Testament. Von Rad began volume 1 with a lengthy, critical reconstruction of the historical portrait of Yahwism and concluded volume 2 with a section that discusses the relationship of the Old and New Testaments. In retrospect, the appearance of von Rad's theology created what has been rightly described as an impasse or stalemate between his approach and that of Eichrodt.[167]

Rudolf Bultmann's *Theology of the New Testament*

Through biblical commentaries, exegetical studies, methodological essays, and his *Theology of the New Testament*, Bultmann secured his reputation, in the minds of many, as the most important New Testament scholar of the twentieth century.[168] Much of his significance comes from his ability to draw on and integrate several key influences. First, in the tradition of F. C. Baur and others, Bultmann was committed to a thorough and rigorous use of "historical investigation" as "the way to grasp the truth of Christian faith."[169] Second, given our historical distance from the biblical text, Bultmann drew on the existentialist terminology of Martin Heidegger as the best tool for understanding the human condition, especially the basic need to live authentically in the world.[170] In order to grasp what the New Testament says about human existence, Bultmann used a method called "demythologizing" (recall D. F. Strauss) to express the essential message that lay within its mythical worldview.[171] Third, along the lines of Schlatter and Barth, Bultmann endeavored to interpret the theological subject matter of the New Testament.[172] Thus, for him, New Testament theology was essentially the descriptive task of "setting forth *the theological thoughts of the New Testament writings*, both those that are explicitly developed (such as Paul's teaching on the Law, for example) and those that are implicitly at work in narrative or exhortation, in polemic or consolation." This task meant paying attention more to the variety than the unity of the material and consequently not offering any kind of "normative Christian dogmatics."[173]

The four-part structure of his theology is as follows: (1) presuppositions of New Testament theology, which includes the message of Jesus and the proclamation of the early church; (2) the theology of Paul; (3) the theology of John's Gospel and the Johannine letters; and (4) development toward the early church. Bultmann regards *the message of Jesus* [as] a presupposition for the theology of the New Testament rather than a part of that theology itself,"[174] and he therefore offers, according to some scholars, a "pure biblical theology" of Paul and John that gets at their essential theological subject matter.[175] For example, he explains what concepts such as "flesh," "heart," and "righteousness" mean throughout the Pauline letters, particularly in relation to the life of faith. We will revisit Bultmann's approach in subsequent chapters, but for now it is fair to say that in spite of serious questions that can be asked about the relative importance of the Gospels in New Testament theology, the categories of history and myth, and the implications of some of his theological interpretations, Bultmann remains the great standard for a comprehensive New Testament theology in the twentieth century.[176]

Roman Catholic Scholarship and the Golden Age of Biblical Theology

Earlier we briefly surveyed the long tradition of classical and medieval theological interpretation, identifying the vibrant encounter with the Bible in pre-Reformation Christianity. When the events of the Reformation polarized Catholics and Protestants over matters of biblical research, the path to modern biblical theology led mainly though the churches of the European Reformation, tending to confirm the depiction of biblical theology as a Protestant Christian discipline.[177] It would not be entirely true, however, to say that all Roman Catholics after the Reformation avoided or rejected the type of critical biblical study that accompanied the Enlightenment. Indeed, Catholic scholar Richard Simon (1638–1712) may rightly be regarded as a "founder of modern biblical criticism," though it seems fair to say that until the twentieth century he was not considered such a pioneer by the Roman Catholic Church.[178] There were also individuals in eighteenth- and nineteenth-century Catholic scholarship who were deeply committed to historical interpretation, but in general scholars who were "loyal to the church . . . adopted the new methods cautiously, seeking to enlist them in support of the ancient and enduring faith."[179] The doctrine of papal infallibility, espoused in the Vatican I Council of 1870, centered the authority for biblical interpretation firmly in the pontiff's "office of shepherd and teacher of all Christians."[180] By the turn of the century, however, some individuals took part in the movement called "Catholic modernism," perhaps best exemplified by the work of the French New Testament scholar Alfred Loisy (1857–1940).[181] These modernizing efforts were kept in check both by Pope Pius X's encyclical in 1907 that condemned many tenets of historical-critical interpretation and by the "antimodernist" oath that was required of all priests starting in 1910.

In his 1943 encyclical *Divino Afflante Spiritu*, Pope Pius XII opened the way for Catholic scholars to engage in critical biblical interpretation by carefully nuancing the strictures of the antimodernist oath.[182] He stated, "Equipped with knowledge of languages and skill in the tools of the critical method, the Catholic exegete should undertake as his most important task to ascertain and to explain the true meaning of the sacred books."[183] The effects were not immediately felt in the field of biblical theology at large,[184] but "a number of Roman Catholic exegetes believed some sort of liberation was taking place."[185] With the impetus of the Vatican II Council in the early 1960s, Catholic scholars were even more encouraged to employ the "rules" of historical research in Scripture study.[186] In its statement on "the Divine Inspiration of Sacred Scripture and its Interpretation," the council seemed to encourage a biblical-theological outlook: "In order therefore to discover the correct meaning of the sacred texts, no less serious attention must be paid to the content and unity of the whole of Scripture in light of the living Tradition of the whole Church and of the analogy of faith."[187]

By the 1970s, Hasel wrote that "one can hardly speak of any differences in the application of the methods of Biblical criticism between non-Roman Catholic scholars and Roman Catholic scholars."[188] An example of a major contribution along these lines is John L. McKenzie's *A Theology of the Old Testament* (1974), which argues that "the Old Testament is not a rational system but a basic personal reality, Yahweh, who is consistent as a person is, not as a rational system." As McKenzie discusses the topical arrangement of biblical theology, he even alludes to the changing setting for Catholic scholars, such that they are not constrained to write about the Old Testament with explicit doctrinal interests: "Up to this time it has been difficult for a Catholic to write a theology of the Old Testament without an explicit section on messianism. . . . Messianism is a Christian interest and a Christian theme . . . [and] in a theology of the Old Testament, as I have described thus far, messianism would appear neither in the chapter headings nor in the index."[189] Looking back on the work of McKenzie and others, one could still argue that the level of Catholic participation in biblical theology did not yet equal that of Protestants, but the main point here is that their involvement bolsters the reputation of the mid-twentieth century as the golden age of biblical theology.[190]

The "Biblical Theology Movement": Its Rise and Decline

The works of Eichrodt, von Rad, and Bultmann were becoming known to the English-speaking world through translation in the 1950s and '60s, but during the immediate post–World War II years there was also a development in America that tapped into some of the same currents of renewal in biblical theology. In spite of such enthusiasm, this development—called the "biblical theology movement"—was nevertheless short-lived, owing to several factors relating to its own methods and presuppositions as well as to changing intellectual and social contexts. Brevard S. Childs's book *Biblical Theology in Crisis* (1970) is considered the best account of this movement, despite protests from some that it was not a "movement" nor was it in "crisis."[191] The sharp differences in opinion over the terms used to describe this era point to the number and variety of influences on and interests of those scholars with whom American biblical theology was associated in the 1940s and '50s. Among the influences, Childs mentions the recovery of theological dimensions of exegesis, especially in Karl Barth's neo-orthodoxy, and the effort to mediate the tensions that existed in the American fundamentalist-modernist debates of the 1920s and '30s.[192] Some of the key characteristics that describe the movement are its emphasis on the unity of the whole Bible, God's revelation in history through his mighty acts, and the distinctiveness of biblical revelation and concepts over against the environment in which they arose, both ancient Near Eastern and Greco-Roman.[193] One of the names most associated with the movement is G. Ernest Wright, whose book *God Who Acts: Biblical Theology as Recital* summarizes his understanding of the discipline as "*the confessional recital of the redemptive acts of God* in a particular history, because history is the chief medium of revelation." Wright's book identifies Israel's exodus from Egypt and its experience at Sinai as "the basis or core of Biblical theology," and then goes on to broaden the scope to account for other events in both testaments.[194]

This focus on historical events as the medium of revelation seemed to ground the Bible on a firm foundation in history that might actually be recoverable using the tools of archaeology and historical research. In the end, however, serious questions were raised as to the adequacy of the movement's description of what constituted both revelation and history, as well as the ability of scholars to get behind the text to the events themselves.[195] On another front, James Barr criticized the emphasis on the distinctiveness of the Bible's concepts in light of linguistic evidence to the contrary.[196] With such criticisms leveled against the movement, its advocates seemed unable or unwilling to sustain the particular form of biblical theology that had marked their earlier work. One sympathetic reviewer has written, however, that the movement should be remembered for those aspects in academic biblical studies against which it protested, namely, "excessive attention to historical analysis, a lack of theological interpretation, and misunderstanding of the religious nature of biblical texts." He adds, "Proving that the solutions the Movement offered were wrong did not make the reasons for the protest disappear."[197]

Summary

The tumult of the 1960s in society at large seemed to be mirrored in the uncertainty over what might happen next for biblical theology. When James Barr wrote his entry on biblical theology for the supplementary volume of the *Interpreter's Dictionary of the Bible* in 1976, he spoke of the great "convulsions [and] changes" in biblical theology's status since the dictionary was published in 1962.[198] That edition's article on contemporary biblical theology, by Krister Stendahl, was written just before the onslaught of arguments against the biblical theology movement and thus made no comment on the issues with which Barr begins his article. But the fall of this movement did not bring an end to the discipline of biblical theology, for with the same book in which he reviewed the movement's demise, Childs also proposed a new approach to biblical theology. And his contribution would be just one of many proposals that have appeared since the early 1970s to reassess the nature, purpose, and methods of biblical theology.

WHAT NEW DEVELOPMENTS AROSE IN THE CLOSING DECADES OF THE TWENTIETH CENTURY?

Biblical theology during the last few decades of the twentieth century faced the challenge of moving forward in light of the apparent impasse over methodology in Eichrodt and von Rad, the implications of Bultmann's synthesis of history and hermeneutics, and the disillusionment caused by the fall of the biblical theology movement. As we now consider the closing decades of the twentieth century, we will encounter scholars who remain active in the discussion today through books, articles, and papers presented at conferences on the Bible and theology. Because they represent the current state of the discipline, I will use the next three chapters to explore their insights into key issues, their methods for structuring biblical theology, and their presentation of the Bible's major themes. In this section, I will not present a detailed account of their contributions but instead identify five new developments that arose out of the preceding era: new choices for structuring a biblical theology, new methods for interpreting the biblical text, new insights into biblical history, new participants in the theological conversation, and new opportunities for relating biblical and systematic theology.

Structure: New Choices in the "Unity and Diversity" Debate

When considering how to structure a biblical theology, a helpful rubric today is the tension of unity and diversity in the Bible.[199] Most biblical theologians recognize that the Bible has elements that unify its message and others that seem to work against the grain. The debate arises over what those elements are, the relative weight given to either unity or diversity, and the manner in which they are related. Beginning in the 1970s scholars who wanted to emphasize unity of structure and purpose returned to the nature of the biblical canon, so that whatever diversity may exist "does not dissolve the canon," which holds all views together.[200] Scholars who saw the main goal as listening to the various biblical testimonies or witnesses searched for new ways to emphasize the diversity of Scripture in their structure of biblical theology.[201]

Canon as Structural Principle

Brevard Childs's new approach proposed "the thesis that the canon of the Christian church is the most appropriate context from which to do Biblical Theology." I will address the canonical approach in the following chapters, but a few specifics should be mentioned here. For Childs, biblical theology in a canonical context meant, first of all, letting the final shape of the Christian Bible serve as the object of our study instead of the "history of development that lies behind the formation of the canon."[202] A second focus of the method was on the ways that the community of faith, whether Israel or the church, received the books as authoritative and normative Scripture.[203] Over the next twenty-five years Childs produced commentaries, introductions to both testaments, and two major works of biblical theology, all developing his emphasis on canon as the organizational paradigm for biblical theology.[204] His magnum opus, *Biblical Theology of the Old and New Testaments* (1993), first considers the "discrete witness" of each biblical book (though the canonical order he follows is the Hebrew canon, not the English Bible) and then explores several major theological themes (e.g., creation, covenant, election) that arise in both testaments. Other scholars have followed this emphasis on canon, introducing their own methodological and thematic adjustments, as in the Old Testament theologies by Paul House and Rolf Rendtorff, a New Testament theology by Frank Thielman, and a biblical theology by Charles Scobie.[205]

In New Testament theology, according to James Dunn, the existence of the canon provides the limits of diversity and "*bears consistent testimony to the unifying center. Its unity canonizes Jesus-the-man-now-exalted as the canon* within the canon."[206] Peter Balla provides a slightly different approach by arguing that while none of the proposed "centers" of New Testament theology can be *the* center, the existence of these "'centers' may point to important themes which may have played some significant role in (at least part of) early Christianity," in particular through some kind of early Christian creed.[207] Thus, positions that emphasize unity tend to do so by suggesting that diverse elements can be incorporated into a coherent theological framework.

Testimony as Structural Principle

As he assessed the impasse of Eichrodt and von Rad, Walter Brueggemann came to see what he called a "convergence in recent theologies." He noticed in the works of Claus Westermann, Paul Hanson, and Samuel Terrien an awareness that the Bible's theological message might exist within the balance of paired themes or the dialectical tension of ideas.[208] Initially developing his own description of the tension between "structure legitimation" and "embrace of pain,"[209] Brueggemann built on those ideas to propose the metaphor of "testimony" as "the largest rubric under which we can consider Israel's speech about God."[210] With this metaphor in mind, Brueggemann structures his discussion around four points: Israel's core testimony, Israel's countertestimony, Israel's unsolicited testimony, and Israel's embodied testimony. Thus, because it is impossible for "any single governing category . . . [to] accommodate all the material," the structure of biblical theology must be guided by diversity rather than unity.[211]

Other scholars, working in both testaments, have followed the path of this diversity in their own theological interpretations. Erhard Gerstenberger traces various "levels of testimony in the Old Testament" through changes in social location (family, clan, tribe, etc.) and over time, concluding that "we can in no circumstances expect a unitary theology of the kind that would correspond to our ideas, namely a coherent thought structure about the being and action of God and God's claim on human beings."[212] Likewise, many New Testament theologians have followed Bultmann's concern for the variety of theological thoughts in the New Testament.[213] Although not following Bultmann on matters of history, Ernst Käsemann believed that the New Testament contained contradictory theological views, leaving a fragmented presentation that could be unified only "by an early catholicizing and more or less orthodox Church's interest in normative doctrine, in discipline for congregational and everyday life, and in its own historical beginnings."[214] More recently, Heikki Räisänen doubts the possibility of arriving at "a theology 'of' the early Christian sources, for these sources contain divergent theological standpoints."[215]

Hermeneutics: New Methods for Approaching Biblical Theology

Among the many aspects of Bultmann's legacy is that biblical studies cannot help but address hermeneutical questions that arise from our philosophical presuppositions and the language we use to express the theological thoughts of the Bible. Both Old and New Testament theologians share these concerns while also emphasizing different aspects of the discussion.

New Testament Hermeneutics after Bultmann

The debate over the most appropriate hermeneutical approach began when some of Bultmann's own students argued that their teacher downplayed matters of history, particularly the historical Jesus. Ernst Käsemann and other "post-Bultmannians"[216] believed that the historical Jesus was important for Christian faith because the Gospels portray "the abiding presence of the exalted Lord precisely within the framework of a history of the earthly Jesus."[217] Some scholars in the 1950s and 1960s, therefore, advocated a "new quest of the historical Jesus,"[218] one that sought to incorporate Jewish and early Christian sources in developing a portrait of Jesus and often used linguistic criteria for determining the authenticity of Jesus' sayings and deeds in the Gospels.[219] Historical Jesus studies remains a vibrant field, as scholars of the "third quest" employ a variety of approaches and create a variety of portraits of Jesus in his first-century Galilean and Jewish setting.[220]

A second stage in the debate, related to the first, was the so-called new hermeneutic, which obviously built on Bultmann's concern for hermeneutics but also shifted the focus from the text as an object for interpretation to language as the "word-event" that interprets the readers of the text or hearers of its proclamation.[221] Thus, the task of biblical interpretation would not be to identify universal themes and let them speak to our situation but rather to begin where people are with their expectations of the message and see how the proclaimed Jesus is a witness to faith. The complex philosophical and linguistic underpinnings of the new hermeneutic are beyond our scope here, but the method was discussed and criticized for confusing the knowledge we might gain from historical research with the faith-knowledge we have from proclamation.[222] Another direction has been suggested by Peter Stuhlmacher, who opts for neither a Bultmannian nor a "new" hermeneutic but rather a "hermeneutics of consent," which employs the critical reading of the Bible but also asks that the Bible be read in light of the claims it appears to be making upon humankind.[223]

A third direction was typified by authors of New Testament theologies that corrected Bultmann's treatment of Jesus and the Gospels. Hans Conzelmann's

An Outline of the Theology of the New Testament (1969) made the "Synoptic Kerygma" a major part of his work. Rather than addressing the problem of the historical Jesus—which Conzelmann argued was "not a theme of New Testament theology"—he described Jesus' teachings in order to present the "overall theological conception" of the Synoptic Gospels, against Bultmann's belief that "one cannot speak of theology as early as the synoptic gospels."[224] Soon after, Werner Kümmel's *The Theology of the New Testament* (1969) also reaffirmed Jesus' role as a "major witness" to New Testament theology.[225] There have since appeared important studies related to the Gospel writers themselves as theologians who handled their own sources in order to shape and present the ministry of Jesus Christ.[226]

As a fourth development, the hermeneutical debate continues in full force today with a burgeoning interest in the implications of postmodernism for biblical interpretation.[227] A term that inherently resists absolute definitions, postmodernism in biblical studies basically refers to interpretive approaches that reject any certainty about what can be known through the traditional, historical research of the modern era. In place of overarching narratives or central themes that purport to explain all the evidence, a postmodern biblical theology might, in A. K. M. Adam's view, simply seek to "make sense" of the Bible, focusing as much on the interpreter as on the texts being interpreted. Postmodern biblical theologians would therefore do their work "by establishing theological (or ideological, or psychological) warrants, and reasoning from them" rather than relying only on historical warrants.[228] It remains to be seen what a thoroughgoing postmodern biblical theology might look like, if it were attempted on the scale of an Eichrodt, von Rad, or Bultmann.[229]

Old Testament Hermeneutics and the Challenge of Literary Criticism

In Old Testament scholarship, hermeneutical issues arose not so much in reaction to Bultmann's approach as in response to the increasing interest in literary criticism and its many expressions. Ever since the work of Hermann Gunkel in the early twentieth century, Old Testament studies had benefited from the literary sensitivity inherent in form criticism, but a fresh initiative came from James Muilenburg's proposal that rhetorical criticism become an interpretive tool for close readings of the Old Testament. The goal of this method was to understand the "nature of Hebrew literary composition, in exhibiting the structural patterns that are employed for the fashioning of a literary unit, whether in poetry or in prose, and in discerning the many and various devices by which the predications are formulated and ordered into a unified whole."[230] Along with rhetorical criticism, literary methods have tapped into a renewed interest in narrative and story, which in many ways is indebted to the salvation-history model but now finds new expression on a variety of theological fronts.[231] Numerous other approaches gained followers in the late twentieth century— semiotics, structuralism, deconstruction, ideological criticism, and other post- modern methods—all of which shun the aura of objectivity that tended to accompany the historical-critical methods of modern biblical scholarship.[232]

History: New Insights into the Role of History for Doing Biblical Theology

Along with structure and hermeneutics, another challenge for contemporary biblical theology is whether a consistent use of the historical method can yield theological results. The great theologies of the golden age—by Eichrodt, von Rad, and Bultmann—all understood their work as beginning with and being grounded in the insights of historical-critical research. One debate has been about the way historical study relates to theological interpretation; another debate concerns the impact of history of religions approaches on bib- lical theology.

A Critical Biblical Theology

Over against views that make the literary nature of the Bible the primary con- text for interpretation, John Collins calls for a "critical biblical theology," one that offers a "critical evaluation of biblical speech about God. . . . Biblical the- ology should not, however, be reduced to [Wrede's definition of] 'the histori- cal fact that such and such was thought and believed' but should clarify the meaning and truth-claims of what was thought and believed from a modern critical perspective." Collins would place critical biblical theology under the discipline of historical theology, but his approach does more than merely dis- cern "sociological and historical functions" of the text. Instead, it claims that "the biblical texts must also be recognized as proposals about metaphysical truth, as attempts to explain the workings of reality."[233] This is by no means a call for developing a normative biblical theology based on such claims; rather, it asks that the theological elements of the biblical texts be taken seriously for their rhetorical function.[234]

A related question that could be raised here is the role of social science crit- icism in historical research. I broach the subject here, instead of later under "perspectives," because such criticism is a method that can be employed by historians, sociologists, and anthropologists to get at how the social order influences the way Israel or the early Christian community is depicted in the Bible. As Leo Perdue says it in more detail, "The biblical writings are con- sidered social products written by and reflecting the interests of groups who interacted with both institutions and significations of communal life, including the family, economy, government, legal system, military, education, and religion."[235] Given the scientific nature of such study, Collins acknowledges sociological insights as augmenting the critical enterprise, and others concur that this approach "complements rather than replaces historical-critical work."[236] We have already seen the use that Gerstenberger makes of a social science approach to illuminate the diverse theological expressions of ancient Israelites. Norman Gottwald is well known for his reassessment of the origins of Israel in a movement of liberation, a conclusion he bases on a sociological analysis of Israel's history and biblical literature.[237] In New Testament theology, Philip Esler has recently presented a "socio-theological model" in order to study the way cultural differences affect interpersonal communion and thus our ability to grasp the message of New Testament texts. Esler sees his method as part of the historical enterprise and boldly asserts that "the results of such historical investigation are, *in and of themselves*, the bearers of theological truth."[238]

History of Religions and Biblical Theology

The golden age of biblical theology did not eliminate all interest in the history of religions. Perdue has described the competing historical and theological interests in Old Testament theology during the twentieth century as a pendulum moving back and forth,[239] while Hayes and Prussner suggest that, in actual practice, "the two approaches frequently overlap."[240] But even if Perdue is correct in his diagnosis of a "collapse of history" in the latter part of the twentieth century, there remain voices that call for the reintegration, if not the identification, of the history of religions with biblical theology. A major proponent of giving the history of religions priority over biblical theology has been Rainer Albertz, whose *A History of Israelite Religion* (1994) argues that compared to Old Testament theology, "the history of religion [is] the more meaningful comprehensive Old Testament discipline."[241] I will assess the strengths and weaknesses of his proposal in the next chapter, but there is no denying that in the last two decades major theological questions have been raised about the religious history behind the "official" worship of Yahweh in Israel's monotheistic faith. Mark S. Smith has argued that "the contours of the distinct monotheism that Israel practiced and defined in the exile" were the result of two major processes of "convergence" and "differentiation."[242] Convergence refers to the "coalescence of various deities and/or some of their features into the figure of Yahweh," while differentiation points to the rejection of "numerous features of early Israelite cult . . . [as] 'Canaanite' and non-Yahwistic."[243] A lively debate is also being carried out on the meaning of inscriptional and iconographic discoveries that, according to some scholars, depict Yahweh with a divine consort, namely, Asherah.[244]

In New Testament studies, it is difficult to find a precise parallel to the type of debate held among Old Testament scholars of the twentieth century. At the turn of the century Wrede had pushed for a strictly historical understanding of biblical theology and thus typified the history of religions approach. Bultmann saw his own presentation standing "within the tradition of the historical-critical and history-of-religion schools," but he also tried to "avoid their mistake" of failing "to recognize the intent of theological utterances."[245] Stendahl certainly separated the descriptive, historical task from the hermeneutical enterprise done by systematic theologians. There continue to be voices who would emphasize historical investigation as the primary aspect of biblical theology, while others use historical study in order to obtain theological results.[246]

Attention to matters of historical development plays a key role in Elisabeth Schüssler Fiorenza's treatment of the early Christian community. While rejecting the supposed value-neutrality in historical investigation and its ability to get at "what actually happened" in the past, Schüssler Fiorenza nevertheless sees a continuing role for historical criticism. Applying a "critical evaluative hermeneutic" to texts such as the household codes of Colossians 3:18–4:1 and Ephesians 5:22–6:9, she argues that "the New Testament testifies to an early Christian ethos of co-equal discipleship."[247] More recently, Bart Ehrman's *Lost Christianities* has taken another look at the various expressions of Christianity that were "lost" because their writings were not included in the New Testament canon.[248]

Context and Perspective: New Participants in the Field of Biblical Theology

If the new developments discussed above have been significant, an even greater difference over previous eras is, in John Collins's words, "the changing demography of the field" of biblical studies.[249] The discipline of biblical theology has been advanced by the participation of persons and groups that had not traditionally been involved in the discussion. By emphasizing context now, I am not saying that questions of personal or social perspective were absent in nineteenth- and early twentieth-century debates. Rather, what marked the late twentieth century was a widening of the conversation to include feminist scholars, Jewish scholars, and those who study the Bible from a non-Western perspective. Moreover, unlike at early points in the history of the discipline, the matter of context and perspective is now considered as important as methodology, indeed as a part of methodology. The concern for many scholars is not that perspective and context create an unavoidable influence on our assessment of the data, but rather that these should be affirmed and embraced as one does biblical theology. The rapidly changing scene is illustrated by the

absence of these newer developments in the major surveys of the field published before 1990.[250] Given the number and diversity of such changes, all that
can be done at this point in our historical survey is to highlight a few of the
major new perspectives from which biblical theology is being practiced,
namely, feminist, Jewish, and postcolonial.

Feminist Perspectives

Inspired in large measure by the insights of liberation theology,[251] feminist
theologians have studied the Bible from the perspective of advocacy for
women, especially in response to androcentric and patriarchal tendencies,
whether in the Bible or among scholars themselves.[252] Schüssler Fiorenza, for
example, states that "feminist critical interpretation of the Bible cannot take as
its point of departure the normative authority of the biblical archetype, but
must begin with women's experience in their struggle for liberation."[253] Within
the larger program of advocacy for women there exists a considerable amount
of diversity pertaining to the question of biblical authority vis-à-vis women's
experience, the types of methods used to interpret biblical texts (historical, literary, sociological), and the perspectives from which women read the Bible. In
particular, there is increasing sensitivity to the impact that changes in geo-
graphical and socioeconomic location, as well as matters of race and national-
ity, make in one's approach to and understanding of the Bible, including
womanist (African American) and mujerista (Latina) theology among others.
With respect to biblical texts, feminist studies often focus on the problem of
inclusive language (for God and humans), the role of women in Israelite society or early Christian communities, and the kinds of historical and literary
readings that offer a countertestimony to traditional biblical interpretations.

Jewish Perspectives

This chapter has mainly studied the history of Christian biblical theology. One
reason for this approach is that the discipline itself was forged within Western
European, predominantly Protestant, Christianity. In such a context, the kinds
of concerns motivating biblical theologians in the nineteenth and twentieth
centuries were often explicitly Christian, such as the relationship between the
testaments, or were driven by higher-critical methodologies unacceptable to
more orthodox Judaism. In the 1980s, however, a lively debate arose around
the question of whether a Jewish biblical theology was a real possibility.[254]
We will examine the particulars in the next chapter, but the primary issues
revolve around the definition of terms (especially "biblical" and "theology"),
various methodological questions, and the charge of supersessionism in some
Christian biblical theology. Moshe Goshen-Gottstein has seen some possibility for a Tanakh theology, growing out of critical, academic inquiry into "what

Tanakh is all about—in what emerges as its structural totality as well as in its subcorpuses." He adds, "The overall theme of God's ways with Israel and Israel's ways with God would possibly emerge as dominant."[255] However, Jon Levenson raises serious doubts about Jewish involvement in biblical theology as it has been practiced in Christian circles and proposes instead that Jewish scholars engage in theological reflection on their tradition.[256]

Postcolonial Perspectives

While liberation theology surfaced in a Latin American context of economic, social, and political injustices against the poorest members of society, voices from the two-thirds world have provided biblical-theological analysis against the backdrop of Western Europe's history of colonization of other nations. Postcolonialism, as an intellectual perspective, finds its roots not first in biblical or theological scholarship but in other fields, in works such as those of the late literary critic Edward Said, who addressed the ways in which Western colonization and imperialistic tendencies misrepresented "the Orient" through a false, mythic discourse.[257] According to R. S. Sugirtharajah, postcolonial biblical interpretation offers a means for "Asians, Africans and Latin Americans [to overcome] the strangeness and remoteness of biblical texts by galvanizing their own cultural resources to illuminate biblical narratives."[258] By reference to peoples on three different continents, Sugirtharajah's comment points to the reality that postcolonial theology will have a variety of different expressions, depending on the unique "experiences, worldviews, and ways of understanding."[259] Thus, in India one finds Dalit theology, written from the perspective of the lowest persons in the caste system, in Korea, minjung theology, from the perspective of socially and politically oppressed people, and many more forms of theology.[260] The liberation theology that informs many of these approaches is not without its critics, and we will explore the matter further in later chapters. But for all such developments, Walter Brueggemann astutely observes that students of biblical theology today "must attend to the centrist voices that represent a long-established consensus in ecclesial and academic communities" and "to the insistent voices of those at the margin who are able to see things in the text that centrist interpretation, either by doctrinal conviction or Enlightenment restraint, is not able to discern."[261]

Biblical and Systematic Theology: New Opportunities in Developing Their Relationship

We began this journey through the history of biblical theology with the observation that theological reflection is as old as the Bible itself. This act of reflecting on the Bible's witness to God has, from the beginning, created a close bond between Bible and theology and therefore between the study of each subject. In chapter 1, I briefly observed the similarities and differences between biblical theology from the biblical scholar's perspective and theological interpretation from the systematic theologian's perspective. For much of the twentieth century, the fields of biblical theology and systematic theology were seen as distinct—if not completely separate—tasks, in large part owing to Gabler's legacy. In some respects, the distance between the fields was compounded by increasing specialization within every field of religious and theological studies, to the point that biblical scholars and systematic theologians perceived that they lacked the necessary knowledge, skill, and sophistication to comment on the other's discipline.

There is now a strong interest on the part of both sides in building bridges and creating conversations that might allow each discipline to learn from the other. One factor contributing to this developing relationship is the desire on the part of scholars not to separate—as Bultmann put it—"the act of thinking from the act of living."[262] With a postmodern openness about their own contexts, biblical theologians are more free to acknowledge their confessional or ecclesiastical traditions. Likewise, systematic theologians recognize that their subject matter is not limited to a set of doctrines based on the Bible but includes the Bible itself. As Patrick Miller has correctly observed, "Systematic theologians do not wait for biblical theologians to hand them the theology of the Bible or a theological interpretation of the whole or parts before they begin their task. Nor do biblical theologians refrain from taking their theological exegesis as far as it will go, often engaging the tradition, particularly its high points, such as Augustine, Luther, Calvin, and Barth."[263]

Another factor that has encouraged renewed conversation is the expertise of theologians and biblical scholars whose works ably cross over the bridge as well as interact with a variety of other academic disciplines. For example, theologian Michael Welker's *God the Spirit* presents a biblical theology of the Spirit even as it interacts with classic and contemporary doctrinal traditions.[264] Likewise, biblical scholar Francis Watson's works interact with contemporary theologians as he calls for biblical interpreteters to give theological concerns a primary role.[265]

CONCLUSION

The broad overview contained in this chapter provides a framework as well as some of the content for the major issues, methods, and themes of biblical theology. Although I have organized the discipline's history around seven key questions, it has been abundantly clear that the challenges of one era often have carried over into the next or resurfaced in a later form. This is not to argue for any kind of uniformity through the ages or to suggest that the new developments of our time are merely echoes of past challenges. There are truly unique circumstances that will call for serious and sensitive engagement with new approaches to and perspectives on the Bible. But while the present context is full of diversity, there is a real sense in which "the diversity was already there at the beginning."[266] It remains for us now to explore the issues, methods, and themes that reflect not only the variety of views but also the ongoing confluence of different currents into the larger stream of biblical theology.

3

The Issues Raised in Biblical Theology

Having now gained some sense of the historical contexts of people and schools of thought, this chapter aims to study several of the major issues of biblical theology. While the definition of "issue" may be a matter of debate, I am using the term here to refer to significant questions and points of disagreement that have surfaced at various times in the history of biblical theology.[1] Moreover, in keeping with the literal meaning of "issue" as something that "comes forth," the issues discussed in this chapter do seem to arise from the challenges inherent in defining biblical theology in the first place. That is to say, all of the major issues relate in some way to the controversial aspects of defining the discipline: the scope of its subject matter, the nature of its methods, and the personal and cultural influences on theological interpretation. The following chart depicts the way that aspects of definition give rise to specific theological issues.

Aspects of the definition	Issues related to this aspect
Scope of biblical theology	Relationship of Old and New Testaments Use of biblical and extrabiblical sources Unity and diversity of the Bible's message
Methods of biblical theology	Descriptive and normative approaches Relationship of history and theology Biblical theology and other disciplines
Influences on biblical theology	Modern and postmodern influences Communities and contexts

The following discussion employs as an organizing rubric the notion of *relationship*, that is, the awareness of *options* within these issues of theological interpretation. While granting the danger of forcing a rigid conceptual framework upon these matters, it is nevertheless fair to say that the issues listed above can be expressed by terms or concepts that seem to balance or, in some cases, oppose each other. What becomes a matter of debate is *how* the concepts are understood to balance, be held in tension with, or be in complete opposition to each other along a spectrum of choices. For example, when one wrestles with the question of the scope of biblical theology, the issue naturally arises of how the Hebrew Bible relates to the Greek New Testament and how they in turn relate to extrabiblical sources. Should the Old and New Testaments be studied more in terms of their unity or their diversity, and what kinds of continuities and discontinuities exist between them? For each of the issues, then, I will try to find ways to organize the different perspectives that exist and to offer examples of how these viewpoints are understood by those who hold them.

Some words of caution are in order before wading into the discussion. First of all, these issues are complex, and the most that can be done in a textbook is to introduce the thoughts of the scholars who have addressed them. Second, and growing out of the first point, my approach is intended only to acquaint readers with some of the major perspectives, providing an example or two of how a particular viewpoint is expressed. Not all scholars would choose these examples as the best representatives of a given position, but my hope is that these brief comments will be suggestive of the issues students will face and the questions they can ask when studying the work of biblical theologians.

ISSUES ARISING FROM THE SCOPE OF BIBLICAL THEOLOGY

The Relationship of the Old and New Testaments

The field of biblical theology has been subdivided into the disciplines of Old Testament theology and New Testament theology for the last two hundred years. While we have seen that the immediate causes for this division lay in the scholarship of the late eighteenth and early nineteenth centuries, two more centuries of historical research have served only to reinforce the vastly different contexts of the two testaments. After all, it is proper to ask how one could do justice to the theological message of the testaments without accounting for their different "worlds"—cultures, languages, histories, societies, faith communities, and so on. Thus, the continued separation of Old Testament and New Testament theology arises primarily from a question of the appropriate subject matter of theological interpretation. Students who study Old and New Testament theology distinctly or under the unifying rubric of biblical theology will find a number of different approaches to this issue as well as several proposals for explaining the nature of the relationship.[2]

General Approaches to the Relationship of the Testaments

The Validity of a Biblical Theology of Both Testaments

In chapter 2 we saw that in spite of the relative lack of scholarly works devoted to a biblical theology of the entire Christian Scriptures, many scholars continue to work from this perspective. For them, the relationship of the testaments is not merely one issue among others, but rather it is *the* issue. An illustration of this emphasis comes from H. G. Reventlow's *Problems of Biblical Theology in the Twentieth Century*, which devotes three-fourths of its content to one chapter: "The Relationship between the Old Testament and the New." As another example, Craig Bartholomew has recently written, "Utterly central to biblical theology must be the question of the Old Testament–New Testament relationship, and this needs to be carefully nuanced."[3] His discussion refers to Brevard Childs's assertion that the relationship of the testaments is "the heart of the problem of Biblical Theology."[4] Childs believes this relationship can be clarified by first studying the "discreet witness" of each testament, followed by "theological reflection on the Christian Bible."[5]

The Validity of a Theology of the Old Testament on Its Own Terms

Authors of theologies of the Old Testament generally defend the necessity and validity of doing Old Testament theology on its own terms, and in some cases, they have given the Old Testament the primary role as the "Scripture" to which the New Testament basically testifies as good news.[6] Wilhelm Vischer's *The Witness of the Old Testament to Christ* declared, "Strictly speaking only the Old Testament is 'The Scripture,' while the New Testament brings the good news that now the meaning of these writings, the import of all their words, their Lord and Fulfiller, has appeared incarnate."[7] He believed this because "the Old Testament tells us *what* the Christ is; the New, *who* he is."[8] Although some have argued that Vischer's actual position was quite nuanced and should not be dismissed out of hand, it is easy to see why this view can be interpreted as reducing the entire Old Testament witness merely to matters of Christology.[9] As Hasel warns, "They telescope and virtually eliminate the varieties of the Biblical testimonies. They suffer from a reductionism of the multiplicity of OT thought, which merely becomes a pale reflection of the Messiah to come."[10]

Many others see more equality and balance in the relationship, while insisting on what Bernhard Anderson calls the "relative independence of the Old

Testament."[11] Along these lines, John Goldingay seeks "to write on the Old Testament without looking at it through Christian lenses or even New Testament lenses."[12] Thus, for him, "Old Testament Theology" consists "of what we might believe about God and us if we simply use the Old Testament or if we let it provide the lenses through which we look at Jesus."[13]

The Validity of a New Testament Theology on Its Own Terms

Authors of works in New Testament theology explore the relationship of the testaments to varying degrees. Some of these comment briefly about the importance of Old Testament "background" for New Testament theology,[14] while others may study the Old Testament context of particular ideas, as Philip Esler has recently done with the theme of the communion of the saints.[15] It is true that Rudolf Bultmann spoke of the Old Testament story as "a miscarriage of history" and "history of failure," whose value was thus primarily as a promise of what would be fulfilled in the New.[16] By and large, however, most New Testament theologians articulate a more positive view of the Old Testament while still focusing on New Testament theology as a legitimate enterprise in its own right.

Particular Proposals for the Relationship of the Testaments

In light of these general approaches, what specific content have scholars given to the relationship between the testaments? How have they described the dynamics of moving from Old to New, or vice versa?[17] If we set aside those perspectives that deny any true relationship between the testaments—and would thus not offer a constructive proposal—what we find is a variety of proposals that seek to account for the continuity and discontinuity, or unity and diversity, between Old and New Testament. Students of biblical theology will therefore need to negotiate between and among these proposals, being sensitive to ways they might complement or conflict with each other. The following list neither exhausts all of the possibilities nor provides in-depth analysis of them, but these examples are offered as some of the major ways the testamental relationship is described.

Prophecy and Fulfillment

Within the New Testament itself, one finds frequent examples of the writers identifying specific events as fulfillment of Old Testament prophecies. Matthew's well-known "formula quotations" (e.g., 1:22–23; 2:15) provide one of the best examples of this phenomenon. The focus for biblical theologians has often been on messianic prophecy, that is, the way in which Old Testament sayings (divine oracles, psalms, prophetic sayings) point to the life, ministry, death, and resurrection of Jesus.[18] E. W. Hengstenberg saw the Old Testament as a source of prophecies and types of Jesus, in large measure because Jesus himself said the law and the prophets spoke of him (Luke 24:27, 44).[19] But since the actual amount of New Testament material devoted to the *explicit* fulfillment of prophecies from the Old is relatively small, this proposal has also been described in terms of a similar, yet more fluid category, namely, "promise and fulfillment."[20] Walther Zimmerli described the Old Testament as "a great history of movement from promise toward fulfillment," but he added that "one cannot calculate from the Old Testament a smoothly developing summation of all promises."[21] For Zimmerli, Christ is the fulfillment of the Old Testament promise—its "end"—not in Bultmann's sense of a failed history, but rather as one that affirms the necessity of its message for interpreting the New Testament proclamation.[22]

Christological Interpretation

A particular expression of the prophecy-fulfillment rubric is Vischer's proposal of christological interpretation, which was strongly influenced by Barth's theological work. Vischer believed that "the Christian Church stands and falls with the recognition of the unity of the two Testaments" and that the key to expressing this unity is the Bible's simple knowledge of "Jesus the Christ to whom it bears a double witness in the Old and New Testaments."[23] Since Vischer was deeply concerned that the Old Testament not be disparaged or discarded by Christians, he could uphold its role as "the Scripture" by seeing it as equally testifying with the New Testament to Jesus Christ. More recently, Francis Watson has advocated a view that sees Jesus Christ as the focus of both testaments.[24] In some ways, the christological proposal is one means of understanding Jesus' words in Luke 24:44: "These are my words that I spoke to you while I was still with you—that everything written about me in the law of Moses, the prophets, and the psalms must be fulfilled." But others might respond that Jesus is not claiming that everything in the Old Testament was written about him, but rather that its books contain things written about him which must be fulfilled.[25]

Progressively Developing Themes

Fuller treatment of theological themes must wait until later in this text, but we can at least state here that some biblical theologians have highlighted one or more themes as interpretive keys to the relationship between the testaments.[26] One noteworthy example would be the theme of *covenant*, which even during and after the Reformation was the focus of biblical-theological unity for thinkers such as Calvin and Cocceius. In the twentieth century, Geerhardus Vos organized his *Biblical Theology* around progressive revelation in God's covenants (testaments) with people, that is, the idea that God's revelation "unfolded itself in a long series of successive acts."[27] Walter Kaiser, an Old Testament scholar, proposed that the theme of *promise* might serve as a key to understanding the Bible, though he avoided forcing the concept upon every biblical book or text.[28] Still others have focused on the *kingdom of God* and the various manifestations of God's sovereign rule in the biblical story.[29] Whatever the specific theme or themes might be, this perspective invites biblical theologians to trace the connections and developing trajectories through the Old Testament and on into the New. This can become problematic when a single theme is declared to be *the* overarching idea of the whole Bible.

Salvation History

This proposal draws on strengths in the previous two models, insofar as they rely on the concept of forward movement through time and also highlight salvation as a central theme. A salvation history approach, however, does not see salvation merely as a *concept* that unfolds in history; rather it is the biblical *history itself* that ties the testaments together in a common, though unfolding, story of salvation. I will develop other aspects of this proposal in chapters 4 and 5, but here the concern is with the way this framework for biblical theology connects the Old and New Testaments. As we have seen, von Hofmann gave this approach its classic expression in the nineteenth century. In the twentieth century, von Rad's thesis was that the Old Testament's story of salvation and its fundamental future orientation helps us to see how the saving event in Jesus Christ, while certainly being a new thing, is also a continuation of the Old Testament's traditions and prophecies.[30] Several New Testament scholars have been attracted to this concept for relating the line of tradition and history in the Old Testament to that of the New.[31] Although it is not always clear exactly how one relates historical events to the Bible's interpretation of them, this approach cannot be faulted for attempting to relate historical matters and the message of salvation in the larger biblical story. What concerns some critics of this approach is that it seems to make the Old Testament "a horizontal stream of tradition from the past whose witness has been limited to its effect on subsequent writers."[32]

Typological Relationships

We saw in chapter 2 that typological interpretation was employed by Paul in the New Testament and that classical, medieval, and even Reformation theologians continued to relate people, events, and institutions in the Old Testament to those in the New. Although this method declined in academic circles with the advent of critical scholarship, both Eichrodt and von Rad advocated its usefulness within careful guidelines.[33] Eichrodt argued that typology was only one of several, valid exegetical tools employed to interpret "the history of salvation in the Old Testament."[34] Von Rad, of course, saw the primary testamental connection in terms of salvation history, but he also believed the Old Testament was "a history of the creative Word of God" in which Christian typological interpretation would also find a witness to Christ.[35] Hans Walter Wolff also suggests that "the New Testament offers the analogy of a witness of faith to the covenant will of God." This analogical relationship does not supplant the basic historical sense of the Bible but rather assists in understanding the historical sense.[36]

New Testament Quotations of the Old

While similar to other proposals, this method seeks to limit its scope to the language of New Testament texts in those places where the biblical authors were clearly quoting Old Testament passages.[37] Thus, not only is the perspective from the New Testament looking back to the Old, but the interrelationships are meant to be those explicitly made by the writers. However, there has in recent years been a broadening of the issue from the New Testament's *explicit* use of Old Testament texts to include *implicit* "allusions and echoes" of the Old Testament.[38] Moreover, scholars have been studying the New Testament writers' methods in light of the first-century contexts of Jewish interpretation. Thus, whether it is Paul's use of "exegetical paraphrase" in his letter to the Romans or Stephen's speech in Acts 7, the overall impression would be, as Moody Smith argues, that "the Old Testament is the indispensable theological-historical background for reading and understanding the New."[39]

Canonical Unity

In this proposal the focus is less on biblical content, such as quoted texts or developing themes, and more on the historical fact of the biblical canon, namely, that the Christian community arrived at a place where writings now referred to as the New Testament were placed alongside the Hebrew Bible as sacred Scripture. In chapter 2 I briefly surveyed the contribution of Brevard Childs in this regard, but I should also mention James Sanders's concept of canonical criticism, which builds on critical study into the traditions behind and editing of sacred texts in order "to ask what the *function* or *authority* was of the ancient tradition in the context where cited."[40] This question means that Sanders emphasizes the *process* of canonization within religious communities. He calls for the continued critical exploration of "comparative midrash," studying "the sociopolitical context" in which biblical texts were thought by early Jewish and Christian communities to have been fulfilled.[41] Childs, on the other hand, sees the canon more as the theological *context* from which one seeks to discern the ultimate "subject matter" of the whole Bible, namely, Jesus Christ.[42] The form of the canon as Old and New Testaments has "hermeneutical implications" for biblical theology. "The two testaments have been linked as Old and New, but this designation does not mean that the integrity of each individual testament has been destroyed. The Old Testament bears its true witness as the Old which remains distinct from the New. It is promise, not fulfillment. Yet its voice continues to sound and it has not been stilled by the fulfillment of the promise."[43]

The People of God

If canonical approaches consider a religious community's handling of its sacred traditions in order to probe intertestamental relationships, this final proposal places even more emphasis on the existence of God's people in order to understand the biblical and theological relationship of Israel and the church.[44] Perhaps this proposal could be listed among the developing themes above, but it warrants a category of its own by virtue of the complexity of questions surrounding it: the dynamics of Palestinian Judaism in the first century, the interpretation of Paul's argument about Israel in Romans 9–11, different conceptions of scriptural authority,[45] and contemporary Jewish-Christian dialogue after the Holocaust, to name only a few topics. For those scholars who do wrestle with these questions, their conclusions often express the historical, biblical, and theological tensions involved in describing the people of God. For instance, N. T. Wright concludes that what eventually became the New Testament was the product of a "subversive community of a new would-be 'people of god,'" but it was "a story rooted in Israel's past, and designed to continue into the world's future."[46] Bernhard Anderson also seeks to establish the integrity of each community while maintaining the mysterious coexistence of both Jewish and Christian communities as belonging "to Israel, the people of God."[47]

Summary

All of the above proposals have their strengths and weaknesses, and none of them can claim to have exhausted the possible connections between the testaments. When all is said and done, the best plan may be for the "multiplex approach" suggested by Gerhard Hasel, drawing on several of the above proposals.[48] There will also be a need to wrestle with the diversity of voices in Scripture, what Brueggemann has called the "polyphonic openness" of the Old Testament witness.[49] The precise nature, scope, and significance of such openness continues to be a matter of debate that will surface again when we address matters of unity and diversity.

The Relationship of Biblical and Extrabiblical Sources in Biblical Theology

Alongside the debate over whether and how to conceive of the relationship between the Old and New Testaments stands the wider issue of whether and how to make extrabiblical sources the subject matter of biblical theology. It may be difficult for some students of the discipline to grasp why this is even an issue in the first place. Are we not talking about a field called *biblical* theology, with its subdisciplines of *Old Testament* and *New Testament* theology? How could the biblical books not be the source material for this discipline? Understanding the nuances and history of the scholarly debate over these matters may make these questions seem naive, but the issue of sources is not precisely one between seasoned academics and novices. Biblical theologians themselves wrestle with the fundamental presuppositions at work behind the issue of sources, finding that the questions are not completely naive nor the answers patently obvious.

For one thing, numerous classic works of Old and New Testament theology proceed with a goal of describing what these sources say about God: "a complete picture of OT realm of belief" (Eichrodt), "the 'coherent whole' of what the Old Testament says about God" (Zimmerli), "the theological thoughts of the New Testament writings" (Bultmann), and "the diverse forms of the New Testament proclamation" (Kümmel).[50] At the same time, these works usually call for as complete an understanding as possible of the wider context in which the Bible arose. For instance, Eichrodt goes on to say, "No presentation of OT theology can properly be made without constant reference to its connections with the whole world of Near Eastern religion."[51] Thus, while Jewish and Christian faith communities revere their scriptures as unique authorities, they also take it for granted that the more background information they have on the Bible, the better equipped they are to understand its message. New Testament authors, for example, incorporated Greco-Roman literature into their works (Acts 17:28) and even quoted them favorably (Titus 1:12–13). On a broader scale, archaeological, historical, and literary research has shown that books in both testaments employed thought forms similar to those of cultures outside the immediate scope of life and religion in Palestine. Comparative studies reveal affinities between biblical literature and ancient Near Eastern traditions on a number of fronts, making it imperative that we learn as much as possible about them.[52] Finally, Jewish and Christian interpreters through the centuries have on the whole eagerly mined the wealth of knowledge that was available for their respective times and places, all in the name of illuminating the inspired Bible. It is true that some have set biblical revelation over against extrabiblical sources (e.g., Tertullian's question "What has Athens to do with Jerusalem?"), but many classical and Reformation authors were well-versed in extrabiblical literature and used it favorably. It is, therefore, only proper to ask in what ways extrabiblical sources of information should become part of the subject matter of the discipline.

The Bible's Uniqueness and the History of the Discipline

Perhaps the first aspect of this issue for beginning students of biblical theology pertains to doctrines of the Bible's inspiration and unique authority, often summarized by the eloquent testimony to the Hebrew Scriptures in 2 Timothy 3:16–17. Putting aside different theological models of inspiration, this doctrine (when applied to both testaments) seems to exalt the Bible itself as the primary, if not the only, source for biblical theology. The rationale goes that since only these books are to be regarded as inspired Scripture, then only they can offer a sure source for grasping the Bible's theological message, especially in a normative sense.[53]

Closely linked to the issue of inspiration is the question of canonicity. One example of this connection is the way some Reformation and post-Reformation traditions decided to specify which biblical writings were inspired, that is, what constituted the scope of the canon. Both the Belgic Confession (1561) and the Westminster Confession of Faith (1648) explicitly list the sixty-six canonical books of the Old and New Testaments, thus lending ecclesiastical authority to what had become the predominant mood among the Reformers, namely, to exclude the Apocrypha and Pseudepigrapha from the biblical canon.[54] In an extended treatment of this matter, James Barr argues that the Reformation's rationale for excluding the apocryphal books was "weak and internally contradictory," and that regardless of what books have been accepted as canonical, these extrabiblical written sources—like the Dead Sea Scrolls—contain theological developments that interacted with earlier canonical texts. These sources "must be part of the 'canon' for biblical theology."[55] Against this view, Goldingay argues that these extracanonical books are not properly sources for biblical theology because the Old Testament canon we have is the only one we know Judaism accepted as authoritative.[56]

The discipline of biblical theology began with a presupposition of inspiration, if one considers J. P. Gabler's affirmation "that the sacred books, especially of the New Testament, are the one clear source from which all true knowledge of the Christian religion is drawn." In order to identify the universal themes of the biblical writings, his first stage of historical inquiry included an awareness of an author's "time and place" and "the language then in use."[57] This concern played into rationalist desires to avoid letting church dogma determine the proper interpretation of ancient texts, thus placing the Bible on the same level as any ancient writing. Conservatives such as Hengstenberg and von Hofmann reacted sharply to the rising tide of rationalist thinking and continued to assume the doctrine of inspiration for their own theological interpretation. For much of the academic community in Europe, however, the ultimate rejection of inspiration opened the way for using any and all ancient sources in order to understand the religion of Israel and the early church.[58]

The comparative approach of the history of religions school took this development to its logical conclusion. The works of Gunkel on the Old Testament and Wrede on the New, by essentially redefining the discipline, are good examples of how the biblical canon could no longer be the only source under investigation. While Gunkel affirmed that the "special significance of Holy Scripture is the real and actual basis of all Biblical scholarship," he also argued that employing sources beyond the canon was "merely applying well-known principles of historical study to an epoch of ancient history."[59] Likewise, while Wrede called the canon "a collection worthy of all praise," he believed that the canonical limits of the New Testament were finally something imposed by much later church authorities, so that the New Testament books are viewed "simply as early Christian writings."[60] Countering Wrede's position was Schlatter's claim that although background information ("knowledge of the borderland") was essential, "New Testament theology has as its subject-matter the New Testament, and nothing else." For Schlatter, a merely historical approach to the New Testament would mean trying to handle it in a neutral way, something not only impossible to do but also against its own intentions.[61]

Proposals for the Status of Extrabiblical Sources in Biblical Theology

The general impression we gain from this brief survey is that scholars tend to agree on the necessity of other ancient sources to assist in biblical interpretation but disagree on their status and function in discerning the theological message of the Bible. The disagreement can be traced in large part to different definitions of biblical theology. Those that limit the scope to the canonical books usually define biblical theology in terms of the *theological content* of the writings, while those urging the inclusion of extrabiblical sources tend to think of the discipline more as a *history of religion*, with the Bible being one (perhaps the primary) source among many. But stating the matter in these terms remains problematic. For one thing, it frames the debate as if there has been little or no advance since the work of Wrede one hundred years ago. To be sure, there continue to be those who call for a history of religions approach to biblical theology, as well as those, such as Hartmut Gese, who suggest that intertestamental literature can provide the link in the history of tradition from Old to New Testament.[62] A second problem with framing the issue in terms of the history-theology impasse is its implication that the positions are so well-grounded and mutually exclusive as to leave us with two unassailable positions. Therefore, some observations are in order if we are to understand current approaches and any new proposals for handling the issue.

Using Sources to Demonstrate the Uniqueness of Biblical Faith

One approach should be mentioned that does not directly take up the debate over sources but in an indirect way offers something of a "hybrid" approach, namely, the biblical theology movement. In chapter 2 I identified criticisms of the movement, but it is helpful here to see how its proponents, somewhat like those of the history of religions school, employed historical methods to study the Bible's religious institutions and its testimonies to God's acts in history. At the same time, building on a renewed appreciation of theological interpretation, these scholars wanted to demonstrate the uniqueness of Israel's experience of God's revelation in the ancient Near East and of the early Christian community's experience of Christ within first-century Judaism and Hellenistic culture. G. Ernest Wright's book *The Old Testament against Its Environment*, and Floyd Filson's study of like name on the New Testament, emphasized the distinctive content of the biblical message about God.[63] Challenging the evolutionary principles of some historians of religion, Wright criticized the exclusive use of a developmental model to explain Israel's faith. He believed that Israel's experience of God could not simply be explained as a natural outgrowth from more primitive religious concepts and practices. In a similar vein, Filson sought to show that while the New Testament owes far more to Judaism than to the Hellenistic world, the early church's central theme—the Lordship of the risen Christ—was antithetical to first-century Judaism. For both Wright and Filson, therefore, extrabiblical sources were vitally important in order to demonstrate the uniqueness of biblical faith.

Critiquing the History of Religions Approach

Another avenue of scholarship would be to suggest that the conflict over sources is not a true impasse because of weaknesses in the presuppositions of the history of religions approach. Schlatter had already raised objections to Wrede's arguments from the standpoint of methodology, since the latter's goal (a history of early Christian religion) is closely tied to its embrace of historical-critical methods. In response, Schlatter argued that "the goal of perfect knowledge is just as unattainable for the dogmatician as it is for the historian." In almost postmodern-like fashion, Schlatter stated that all sorts of personal convictions affect historians in their work.[64] Another aspect of Wrede's argument was that being limited to the canon was to place oneself under the authority of much later church councils rather than to let all pertinent first-century documents speak for themselves. But here, too, one might ask whether the concept of the New Testament canon, for example, should be defined so much by the first attestations to the current list of twenty-seven books. If canonization is understood more in terms of a long and dynamic process rather than the eventual result in official ecclesiastical councils, then Wrede's argument becomes less persuasive.[65] The choice, therefore, can never simply be the one Wrede made it to be, namely, between scientific historians and dogmatically motivated theologians.

Distinguishing between Canonical Source and Extratextual Subject Matter

A further nuance arises from the fact that scholars who would limit their attention to the biblical canon as a source may be striving at something other than the theology of the biblical texts themselves. Wrede, of course, went beyond the text out of interest in the history of religions, but as Dan O. Via has observed, even New Testament theologies that focus on the canon may have as their subject matter "something outside of the text" that offers "access to the real subject matter of the New Testament."[66] He includes Wrede in this group but also adds works by Oscar Cullmann and Joachim Jeremias for their respective interests in history's revelatory events and the historical Jesus. The recent interest in sociohistorical research of the ancient world and its material culture has provided another source of background information. Erhard Gerstenberger is open to using social science methods as well as "the cautious and appropriate interpretation of [archaeological] finds" to learn about the "theologies of the Old Testament." He is interested in the actual faith of everyday Israelites in their various social settings, but he does not envision this interest as a "going behind the written testimonies" of the Old Testament.[67] Brueggemann also articulates the nuance in the source/subject matter distinction and offers this balanced position. While the "primal subject of an Old Testament theology is of course God," we finally have access only to the witnesses or testimonies to (and of) God in the Bible, thus making this "our proper subject."[68]

Affirming the Background/Content Distinction

Several recent biblical theologies employ the distinction between the *background* of the biblical books and their *content* in order to separate their work from the interests of a history of Israelite or early Christian religion. For example, Paul House believes that "historical studies undergird Old Testament theology" and that external "data informs Old Testament theologians," but the focus remains what "the Bible's authors believed."[69] The existence of the canon is often used as the ultimate warrant for this approach; to go beyond canonical literature would lead to confusing biblical content with extrabiblical witnesses to the broader religious environment.[70]

In New Testament studies, Francis Watson's book *Paul and the Hermeneutics of Faith* uses "the Pauline letters, the scriptural texts to which they appeal, and the non-Christian Jewish literature from the Second Temple period which appeals to the same scriptural texts." Watson hopes this "three-way dialogue" will help us understand Paul's reading of the Torah rather than merely explore the wider religious milieu.[71] N. T. Wright has argued that "though we must of course use the New Testament as our main evidence for our own description and analysis of first-century Christianity, since there is no better evidence available, we must do so in the knowledge and recognition that it was not designed primarily for this use." What he is reminding us of is that the writing of the New Testament documents was just one of many activities in the "daily life of the early church."[72] So, too, Leonard Goppelt points out how extrabiblical sources that might inform our understanding of Jesus also have limitations because of their selectivity and rhetoric, so "that we should draw the theological substance of the earthly ministry of Jesus essentially from the synoptic tradition."[73]

Summary

The above contrast between biblical theology and the history of religions should not be interpreted as an attack on the legitimacy of historical research for its own sake and on its own terms. There is surely a discipline of the history of religions, and its practitioners rightly study the historical development of the Bible's theological message as part of their subject matter. However, many Old or New Testament theologians are not persuaded that biblical theology should be defined as a study of the history of religion. If the different sides of this debate may not come to a complete agreement in terms of definition, perhaps they might appreciate the other's emphases and interests. That is, when one envisions biblical theology mainly in terms of the *content in the written sources*, then it makes sense to think of the Bible as the primary source, with all other sources providing "background." However, if the emphasis is on the *context of the biblical writers* as theologians, then greater emphasis may be placed on other sources of information to understand the writers themselves. As with so much of biblical theology, there is a fine line here as well, but continued, careful study of both the context and content of the Bible can only serve scholarly and faith communities.

The Relationship of Unity and Diversity in Biblical Theology

As we have just seen, the scope of biblical theology can be debated in terms of sources within and outside of the Bible, but there is another issue that arises when one asks about the scope or range of biblical material, namely, how we approach the content *within* the Bible. The biblical sources themselves present us with a vast and diverse set of literary forms, written across many centuries, with multiple themes and purposes. Can the theological message of the Bible be described in ways that articulate both its unifying features and its diverse elements, whether it be within each testament individually or for the Bible as a whole? Almost everyone recognizes some form of diversity in the Bible and its constituent parts, but many also believe that significant unifying elements exist, and quite a few scholars have attempted to identify a "center" of the Old or New Testament or of the whole Bible.[74] Before considering specific proposals for relating unity and diversity, we need to reckon with the matter of the biblical data themselves.

The Basic Question of the Data

We have noted that the use of the singular term "the Bible" obscures the fact that it derives from the plural Greek form for "books." To be sure, we can still say this is one *collection* of books, but the notion of a collection makes no claim about the content within its books. The history of biblical interpretation reveals that Jewish and Christian scholars traditionally operated under a belief in the divine inspiration of Scripture, so that what Enlightenment scholars would begin to label as contradictions, these earlier interpreters would regard as only apparently contradictory. Gabler himself worked with the presupposition of the Bible's inspiration, but he also believed it was necessary to deal with the issue of diversity by comparing and contrasting biblical content in order to ascertain the most general and universal ideas.[75] Today it is generally accepted that even when one holds to the inspiration of the Bible or affirms some kind of unity in its basic message (or history, themes, trajectory, and so forth), there remain numerous examples of major and minor tensions within and among the biblical books. In Old Testament studies one might mention the different literary and theological approaches of Genesis 1 and 2, the various documentary strands of the Pentateuch, the Levitical and Deuteronomic views of the law, or the relationship of Wisdom literature to the rest of the Bible. In the New Testament, there is the Synoptic problem and efforts to harmonize the Gospels' content,[76] the relationship of narrative in Acts to the letters of Paul, the classic debate over Paul and James on justification, or even the tensions within the Pauline letters themselves.[77]

How then are biblical theologians to negotiate the similarities and differences in the biblical texts? Hartmut Gese has stated the problem this way: "The basic task of biblical theology consists in facing the multiform complex of texts, which differ sharply in their history and subject matter, and attempting to describe the theology of this complex." He goes on to call this task one of "comprehending unity in plurality," adding that this "fundamental problem of biblical theology" is found both in the whole Bible and even in individual texts.[78] But does the sheer fact of multiple sources, texts, and settings mitigate against any kind of unity, theological or otherwise? Can *a* message or *the* message be found? Or, if one speaks of many messages or themes, do these appear as a harmony of compatible voices or a cacophony of unrelated noises? The following discussion reveals that this issue is usually handled by emphasizing one element more than the other (e.g., unity over diversity), whether one has only one testament or the whole Bible in mind.

Perspectives That Stress Unity as the Stronger Element

There Is an Overarching Unity That Could Be Called a "Center" of Old Testament, New Testament, or Biblical Theology

Many biblical theologians have asked whether the unity of the Bible (or either testament's) theology expresses itself as a "center," a translation of the German term *Mitte*. For biblical theology, this term does not necessarily imply some "central" location in the Bible or that there is one and only one central theme. The concept of center is not only a central idea but perhaps also a "center of gravity" for either testament or the whole Bible.[79] Thus, affirming that there is a center does not necessarily mean that every passage or biblical book is explicitly related to that concept, but rather that each part of the canon is attracted to this concept by canonical, historical, or other thematic influences. But to some scholars who regard this matter as important, it functions as the standing or falling article of the discipline. Speaking of Old Testament theology, Walter Kaiser writes, "If no such key can be demonstrated inductively from the text, and if the writers were not deliberately writing out of such an awareness, then we shall have to be content with talking about different theologies of the OT. Consequently, the idea of an OT theology as such must be permanently abandoned."[80]

I have already alluded to some unifying approaches in the discussion of the relationship between the testaments, since a strong connection between the testaments is usually founded upon a belief in their essential unity, be it literary, historical, or theological. In his surveys of Old and New Testament theology, Hasel identifies and briefly describes several proposals. For the Old Testament, he includes "covenant," "the holiness of God," "God as the Lord," "Israel's election as the people of God," and "rulership of God," to name only a few.[81] For the New Testament, he lists among others, "anthropology," "salvation history," "covenant," and "Christology," or some specific aspect of it, such as the cross.[82] Several of the central themes mentioned for the Old Testament are also affirmed for the New, which therefore makes them "centers" of the whole Bible. A classic example is the idea of covenant, first expounded by Cocceius and later by Vos, who spoke of "the covenant of grace"as the uni-fying factor for the progressive stages of biblical revelation.[83] While not wish-ing to minimize "the complexity of the Bible," John Bright affirmed that "there nevertheless runs through [the Bible] a unifying theme which is not artificially imposed." He identified a collection of concepts revolving around "the idea of a people of God, called to live under his rule, and the concomi-tant hope of the coming Kingdom of God."[84] Quite a few scholars believe that the plethora of proposed "centers" in and of itself undermines the possibility that there is any center at all. Although some may believe that this plight describes the Old Testament more than the New, they would obviously doubt the possibility of a central biblical theology. Von Rad argued that the Old Tes-tament "seems to be without a centre which determines everything and which could give to the various separate acts both an interpretation and their proper theological connexion with one another. We can only describe the Old Testa-ment's revelation of Jahweh as a number of distinct and heterogeneous reve-latory acts."[85] But others see the numerous proposals as evidence that von Rad's position is unsatisfactory.[86] Even so, instead of arguing for a central *con-cept*, many scholars have sought a different expression of unity.

There Is Some, Perhaps Even Significant, Diversity, but It Can Be Understood through a Unified Structure or Scheme

This approach to the problem grows out of the concern that the rich diversity of biblical concepts would never allow us to choose one of them as the most important of all. At the same time, choosing some unifying terminology from outside the Bible is also unacceptable to the vast number of biblical theolo-gians. Thus, Elmer Martens prefers to speak of the "design of God as a unify-ing and organizing principle of the Old Testament material." He believes there is a basic plan "to bring deliverance, to summon a people who will be pecu-liarly [God's] own, to offer himself for them to know and to give them land in fulfillment of his promise."[87] Another proposal is to take a developmental cat-egory such as "tradition history" as what holds the biblical canon together, something that von Rad's student Hartmut Gese has done: "A unity of the Bible is not to be established artificially through exegetical cross references between the Old and New Testaments. A unity exists already because of tra-dition history." He adds, "There is no opposition in content or in tradition his-tory between the Old Testament and the New Testament."[88] This approach is picked up by Peter Stuhlmacher, who looks back on the Old Testament from a New Testament perspective and sees a clear connection of tradition, leading to "the message of reconciliation [as] the determining center of Holy Scrip-ture as a whole."[89] Along these lines, Frank Matera has recently suggested, "The unity of the NT is more profitably sought in the story or narrative world to which the various writings witness and in which they are now embedded. It is found in the narrative of how the God of Israel revealed himself in Jesus Christ for the salvation of Israel and the nations."[90]

Another scheme of holding diverse material together would be through the balancing of "polarities and tensions," as in the proposals of Claus Westermann, Samuel Terrien, and Paul Hanson.[91] These authors in no way minimize the diversity but recognize the presence of more than one key theme or principle. In Old Testament theology, Ronald Clements described the balance of "law" and "promise," reflecting the two major sections of the Hebrew canon: Torah and Prophets.[92] Peter Balla, as we have seen, recognizes the diversity of themes in the New Testament but still believes that their presence within one canon points to the possible existence of "a basic, creed-type theology to which all those Christians adhered, whose writings are gathered in the New Testament. Their allegiance made it possible for them to express their belief in different ways, because they all thought—about themselves and the others—that they are within the boundary of that 'creed' that may (at least partly) be reconstructed by us from 'creedal elements' in the New Testament."[93] A somewhat related notion to the diversity of sources is what G. B. Caird calls an "apostolic conference" model, with the major witnesses sharing insights of early Christianity. He believes that "every book, in so far as it has something to contribute, should be allowed a hearing." If there be any unity, it will not be a matter of "whether these books all say the same thing, but whether they all bear witness to the same Jesus and through him to the many splendoured wisdom of the one God."[94]

Perspectives That Stress Diversity as the Stronger Element

Limitations with various theories of "unity"—that they are either too selective or too abstract—lend some weight to a "diversity" perspective. And while scholars often appeal to the existence of the canon as a great unifying factor in biblical theology, others point to the canon's multiple books, literary forms, historical settings, and themes as an argument against unity. Add to this the postmodern critique that we are unable to recover the "intention" of the original biblical writers, and it seems as if unity is a lost cause. Still, biblical theologians may express varying understandings of just how theologically diverse the Bible is.

Diversity Is the Result of Contradictory Theologies in the Bible

Some biblical theologians do not point to mere tensions or multiple books and so forth; they suggest that the existence of contradictions in the Bible makes a unified theology impossible. We saw in chapter 2 that Ernst Käsemann doubted the prospects of a unified theology: "The New Testament as we have it is a fragmentary collection of documents from the earliest period, while the bulk of the material has vanished for ever. By and large there is no internal coherence. The tensions everywhere evident amount at times to contradictions."[95] For examples of this phenomenon, he pointed to the way the Gospels criticize each other's theology, particularly their Christology, the differences between Paul and James over the theme of justification, and the conflicting reports about Paul's apostolic ministry as recorded in the book of Acts and Galatians, to name a few.[96]

It is, of course, possible to search for ways to resolve these differences, explaining less clear texts in light of the clearer ones, or describing them as tensions rather than contradictions.[97] Frank Thielman, who is inclined to see a larger unity of the New Testament message and thus prefers the term "tension," nevertheless says there are times when "the best historical reconstruction of the text seems to yield a meaning that is contradictory to the canon's dominant theological tendency. When this happens, it is necessary to view the apparent divergence as theologically significant." He later adds, "Although the basic insight of faith can warrant the conclusion that the theological emphases of the New Testament documents are not ultimately contradictory, that same conviction prohibits solving the problem of theological diversity either by reducing the witnesses of the texts to a harmonious core or by offering implausible harmonizations."[98]

Diversity Creates Necessary Tensions, Even If the Result Is a "Canon within a Canon"

Not all scholars on this side of the argument lament diversity in terms of irreconcilable differences. Erhard Gerstenberger does not "regard the plurality and the clearly recognizable syncretism of the Old Testament tradition as a disaster, but as an extraordinary stroke of good fortune. The diversity of theologies opens up for us a view of other peoples, times and ideas of God; it relieves us of any pressure to look for the one, unhistorical, immutable, absolutely obligatory notion and guideline in the ups and downs of histories and theologies."[99] In like manner, Walter Brueggemann, whose earlier work made use of the "tensions and polarities" model, has with the newer rubric of "testimony" concluded that "the several testimonies to Yahweh, in any particular moment of Israel's life, were often in profound dispute with one another, disagreeing from the ground up about the 'truth' of Yahweh." He goes on: "Old Testament theology must live with that pluralistic practice of dispute and compromise, so that the texts cannot be arranged in any single or unilateral pattern."[100]

This embrace of diversity in New Testament theology may be adjudicated through the concept of a "canon within the canon," which essentially refers to an individual's or whole faith community's preference for particular biblical writings over others, say, the Gospels over the Letters or the Prophets over the Law. James Dunn observes "that no Christian church or group has in the event treated the NT writings as uniformly canonical. Whatever the theory of canonicity, the reality is that *all Christians have operated with a canon within the canon.*" Some may beg to differ with Dunn's sweeping claim, but for all practical intents and purposes there is truth to what he says. As we saw in chapter 2, Dunn proposes "a common faith in Jesus-the-man-now-exalted" as "*the unifying centre . . .* the canon within the canon."[101] I will address canonical issues and methods below, but it should be said here that Dunn's proposal is not that we actively eliminate the books that seem to be outside his "canon within the canon." To the contrary, he argues that the whole canon continues to have a significant function in preserving both the unity and diversity of the New Testament.[102]

Summary

It is difficult to find a way forward in the unity-diversity debate. On the one hand, the choice of a single theme to unify either testament or the Bible becomes too specific to handle the manifold witness of the individual biblical books. On the other hand, while the choice of an overarching concept—such as Hasel's proposal that "God/Yahweh is the dynamic, unifying center"—has the advantage of accounting for different perspectives, its unity may remain too general to be of any constructive help.[103] Moreover, a structural rubric like "history" or "the canon" essentially leaves us where we started: with the biblical story in its canonical form. Identifying these more obvious problems with the search for unity, however, does not necessarily imply that the pendulum should swing completely over to an incoherent disunity. Thus, Charles Scobie's recent work of biblical theology, *The Ways of God*, seeks to avoid "distorting the biblical material," but it also proposes to identify "a limited number of major biblical themes, grouping around them associated subthemes, and tracing each theme and subtheme through the OT, then through the NT, following the scheme of proclamation/promise: fulfillment/consummation."[104]

It is not, of course, a matter of adding up the competing elements to determine relative amounts of unity and diversity, but it may be possible to maintain the necessity of listening to all voices in the Bible while also acknowledging the natural human tendency to bring a sense of order to the biblical data. In this regard, James Barr's assessment seems balanced, namely, that the concept of a "center" has a valid function, not only because of the demands to publish an organized book of biblical theology but also as a "hypothesis" that is proposed for consideration by others.[105] Offering constructive proposals for relating diversity to unity, though these may be roundly condemned by some scholars, seems to be a more promising way forward than endlessly discussing the methodological risks of such efforts.

ISSUES ARISING FROM THE NATURE
OF THE TASK OF BIBLICAL THEOLOGY

If what constitutes the source material for biblical theology remains a debated topic, so too are issues that arise from uncertainty over the task of the discipline. Chapter 1 introduced some of these matters, and chapter 2 went on to discuss how they have played out in the history of biblical studies. It is now incumbent upon us to focus on what is at stake in the positions and proposals presented by biblical scholars. The three broad areas of consideration are the relationship between descriptive and normative aspects, between history and theology, and between biblical theology and other theological disciplines.

The Relationship of Descriptive and Normative Aspects
of Biblical Theology

The above subheading speaks of descriptive and normative *aspects* of the discipline, but it should be made clear at the outset that there have been times when biblical theologians understood these concepts not as compatible aspects but as mutually exclusive *alternatives* for defining the task of biblical theology. The balance or tension here has also been identified using other word pairs—meant/means, descriptive/prescriptive, and nonnormative/normative—all of which Gerhard Hasel sees as growing out of the dichotomy of what he calls "the Gabler-Wrede-Stendahl approach."[106] Whatever terms are used to describe this issue, what is at stake is whether the descriptive and normative tasks are mutually exclusive or are in some way compatible with each other. Or to push the matter further, does determining what a text *meant* in the biblical setting necessarily imply specific answers to what it *means* today?

A particularly clear example might be a passage that makes some claim about the exclusivity of Yahweh or of Jesus. One may conclude that the declaration of Isaiah 45:5—"I am the LORD, and there is no other; besides me there is no god"—most likely *meant* that the postexilic community understood Yahweh to be the sole deity. But does one then move to the claim that this *means* Yahweh is the sole deity for all peoples today? Or if it be determined that Jesus' words in John 8:58—"Very truly, I tell you, before Abraham was, I am"—*meant* a claim to share in divinity, does this *mean* that Jesus has a legitimate claim upon people's faith and obedience today?[107] Of course, if one argues that a complete and accurate description is out of reach, the normative move may be put off indefinitely. But the question here is not whether sound exegetical methods will always yield conclusive interpretive results but whether the text's meaning for today is controlled by those results when individuals or faith communities deem them to be conclusive for themselves. To gain some perspective on how we arrived at this juncture it will be helpful to recall the path that led here.

Background of the Question in the History of the Discipline

Biblical scholars are nearly unanimous in their belief that the roots of the descriptive-normative question lay in J. P. Gabler's foundational distinction between biblical theology and dogmatic theology, the former of which he intended to be a historical and exegetical task that described the theological thoughts of the biblical writers. Dogmatic theology was surely a legitimate task, but for Gabler it was a later step and one left to theologians who could draw out the philosophical implications and applications of the Bible's teaching.[108] With this division of labor intact, biblical theologians would be free to do their work without being constrained by particular doctrinal systems. We have seen that modern discussions of biblical theology have been strongly influenced by Krister Stendahl's agreement with Gabler's distinction, expressed by Stendahl's contrast of "what it meant" and "what it means." Finally, as noted above, Gerhard Hasel's widely used introductions to the field continually connect the "descriptive" definition of the discipline with the rubric "Gabler-Wrede-Stendahl."[109]

In his discussion of modern New Testament theology, A. K. M. Adam agrees with Hasel's claim regarding these three scholars and states the relationship this way: "Their considerable influence—or, to be more exact, the considerable influence of Wrede's appropriation of Gabler, reconfigured through Stendahl—constitutes a definitive characteristic of a distinctively modern New Testament theology." Adam's judgment seems to be accurate, insofar as most Old and New Testament theologians today would embrace *the best* of modernism, namely, the critical tools it offers for biblical research.[110] Nevertheless, there is also much variation in the way this descriptive task is explained, undertaken, and supplemented by concerns that go beyond mere description of biblical content. As Paul House wrote in 1998, "There is a growing conviction that theology must address the world in some normative fashion. Totally descriptive theology is waning at the moment."[111] This is not to claim, of course, that a "totally normative theology" is arising in place of the "totally descriptive theology." Some thinkers qualify the level of normativity one might derive from the Bible. Robert Morgan, for example, states, "Christian scripture does not yield a normative theology but suggests a doctrinal norm," which for him is christological in nature, "that in having to do with the crucified and risen Lord Jesus Messiah they have to do with God, the one God of Israel who loves the world as its Creator, Redeemer, life-giver."[112] It is helpful, therefore, to consider some of the ways biblical scholars have made and are making the interpretive move from description of the Bible to its normative meaning.[113]

Adopting a Descriptive Approach with Normative Implications

During the past two centuries, there have always been proponents of some kind of normativity in biblical theology. Adolf Schlatter, who himself believed that New Testament theology required a historical approach, maintained the connection with normativity when he spoke of "the New Testament word, which confronts us with the claim that we should be affected by it in all our behavior and without reserve." Part of his rationale for this conclusion was that any effort by the historian to "bracket questions of faith" flew in the face of the New Testament's own purposes.[114] In their own distinct ways, both Barth and Bultmann carried on this program in Europe,[115] while in America Geerhardus Vos based his *Biblical Theology* on "the infallible character of revelation."[116] Contemporary scholars, depending on the purpose and scope of their work, tend to exhibit normative concerns by means of the community they hope that biblical theology will address. These are not, of course, absolute categories with clear dividing lines; rather, they appear to be a matter of a theologian's interests and emphases.

Thus, although some theologians continue to define their task in terms of the Gabler-Wrede-Stendahl tradition, Dan O. Via suggests that they are using their methods "in support of theological claims."[117] Via lists G. B. Caird, Peter Balla, and James Barr as examples of an outlook in biblical theology that thinks primarily in terms of the historical method but also holds some place for contemporary meaning. For example, Caird opens his work on New Testament theology by defining it as "a historical discipline" whose "purpose is descriptive."[118] But Via points out places where Caird also says things such as, "The ultimate test of a New Testament theology rests not in intellectual criteria but in the contribution it makes to the life of the Christian community."[119] As for Balla, he wants to maintain the strictly historical, descriptive nature of New Testament theology and therefore does not believe the discipline inherently has a normative aspect. However, he does not go so far as to agree with scholars who claim that no theology exists in the Bible; instead he contends that "we have to report what these writings say about their claim of being normative," but the scholars' purpose is not to convince "readers about the truth of the claim of the biblical writings."[120] Overall, Via does not deny that Caird, Balla, and others understand their work as historical or descriptive in nature, but he does show that they will generally reveal some effort to clarify the contemporary relevance of what they have described.

Speaking to the Christian community

Brevard Childs forthrightly acknowledges his perspective as a biblical theologian addressing the Christian community. He does this through his repeated references to the theological unity of the testaments of the Christian Bible, as the subtitle of his *Biblical Theology* avers: *Theological Reflection on the Christian Bible*. With Gerhard Ebeling, Childs believes that we cannot completely or objectively distance ourselves from our theology. But to this negative argument he adds the positive stance: "To speak of the Bible now as scripture further extends this insight because it implies its continuing role for the church as a vehicle of God's will. Such an approach to the Bible is obviously confessional."[121] In a similar manner, John Goldingay states, "I want to formulate a statement that is theological in the sense that it expresses what we can believe and live by and not merely one that restates what some dead Israelites believed."[122] Among recent New Testament theologians, Philip Esler is also quite clear about the New Testament being "a fundamental resource for the maintenance of the Christian life." His focus on the theme of Christian community grows out of his express intention "to promote a specifically Christian rationale for reading the New Testament that is related to its role in speaking of God's ongoing relationship with human beings and with the cosmos."[123]

Speaking Beyond *the Christian Community*

A number of other scholars, while recognizing the important role that biblical theology has for the church, have begun to look beyond it to the problems that exist in our twenty-first-century context. Walter Brueggemann, for example, has expressed his deep reservations about the supersessionism he believes is inherent in so much of Christian interpretation of the Bible. He fears that Childs's program imposes a christological reading on the Old Testament that serves "the hegemonic, triumphalistic claims of the church." In its place, he calls for greater sensitivity to the way the Bible subversively undermines such claims and urges that we attend to the "polyphonic" character of biblical testimony.[124] Our current context demands that we recognize that "the Old Testament is always addressing, belatedly, a second listening community: the larger public that is willing to host many alternative construals of reality." We must especially heed the biblical claims of justice in a context of "technological, military consumerism."[125] Among New Testament theologians, Heikki Räisänen has called for "actualizing" or addressing the present context with historical and theological insights, even while he believes that Gabler was right to separate historical from theological tasks. But "biblical studies are to serve society and mankind within their own limited resources, but not the church in particular. The task is not proclamatory, but informative and understanding." The concluding paragraph of his book *Beyond New Testament Theology* lays down the challenge that scholars either be "guardians of cherished confessional traditions" or "follow those pioneering theologians and others congenial to them on their novel paths, fearlessly reflecting on the biblical material from a truly ecumenical, global point of view."[126]

Revisiting the Distinction between "What It Meant" and "What It Means"

If it is natural that biblical theologians will feel called to write for and speak to the church, the synagogue, and the world, what then remains of the "meant/means" distinction? When one describes a certain emphasis in the theology of Israel's scriptures or the New Testament writings and then hears in them a challenge for our time, does this not imply that "what it meant" and "what it means" are extremely close, even if they are not identical? One of the ways in which Stendahl's distinctions have been amended is in scholarship that operates from a very high view of Scripture, as is the case for many evangelical Protestants. In their book *How to Read the Bible for All Its Worth*, Gordon Fee and Douglas Stuart acknowledge the difficulties of interpretation and the need for open and honest communication about hermeneutics, but they go on to say, "On this one thing, however, there must surely be agreement. A *text cannot mean what it never meant*. Or to put that in a positive way, the true meaning of the biblical text for us is what God originally intended it to mean when it was first spoken. This is the starting point."[127] Such a foundational position comes very close to saying that "what it means" *is* "what it meant." There will surely be unique, cultural implications and applications that distinguish the biblical world from ours, but the overlap, according to Fee and Stuart, is vastly greater than the differences. Instead of Stendahl's separation of tasks (fig. 1), they draw "meant" and "means" closer together (fig. 2). People may debate Fee and Stuart's presuppositions about our ability to ascertain authorial intention in the Bible (or whether there is such a thing), but what they are pointing out is that "what is meant" and "what it means" are not mutually exclusive. While acknowledging the vast differences between the Bible and our world in terms of historical, literary, and cultural understandings, Fee and Stuart are saying that there is no prima facie reason why the theological overlap cannot be large indeed.

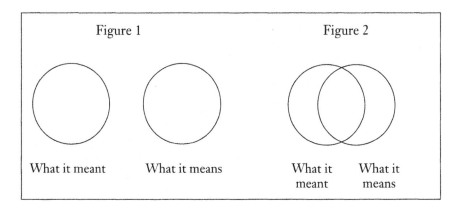

Figure 1   What it meant   What it means

Figure 2   What it meant   What it means

Several scholars offer a critique of Stendahl's distinction from quite a different angle, showing that there is no unanimity about the categories he proposed for doing biblical theology today. Ben Ollenburger's 1986 essay "What Krister Stendahl 'Meant'—A Normative Critique of 'Descriptive Biblical Theology'" argues that there are logical and methodological problems in Stendahl's claim "that historical-critical descriptions exhaust the work of biblical theology." Ollenburger contends that Stendahl's own description of the meant/means distinction is imprecise, and that the way scholarship actually works does not leave a wall of separation between biblical theologians (discovering what the Bible meant) and systematic theologians (explaining what the Bible means). To be sure, Ollenburger asks that we not find fault in the goal of "making room for the work of historical-critical description in biblical theology, and of making biblical theology accountable to that kind of distinction." Literary criticism is just such an enterprise where a scholar may use historical-critical descriptions but "is not free simply to transgress them."[128] Ollenburger's analysis of the issue has resonated with other scholars, such as A. K. M. Adam, who sees in it a call for "a more hermeneutically sophisticated vision" for biblical theology.[129] For different reasons, Walter Brueggemann also denies the meant/means distinction. For him, the biblical text with its "elusive quality . . . invites interpretation that is free, expansive, and enormously imaginative."[130] These remarks by Adam and Brueggemann do not mean that description was solely the possession of "modern" biblical theology. Nor does Ollenburger's critique charge Stendahl with having a positivistic approach that rules out "the conclusions of contemporary hermeneutic theory, or even common sense, that everyone works within the context of certain social and cognitive structures that bear upon the work of interpretation—that everyone has presuppositions." Stendahl did, however, want "common discourse" to be "historical and descriptive."[131]

Summary

The above discussion reveals that whether or not they adopt Stendahl's understanding of the task, biblical theologians will continue to offer descriptions of the Bible as well as probe into its contemporary, normative relevance. They will, perhaps for a long time, wrestle with the implications of finding another paradigm for relating historical description and normative interpretation, and the future will call for cooperation between biblical scholars, systematic theologians, ethicists, and others, in light of the division of labor long rooted in the Gablerian model. To put the matter this way reveals that the currents of other key issues are inherent in the above discussion. In particular, two task-related issues have been just below the surface of the descriptive-normative debate, namely, the relationship between history and theology and the relationship between biblical theology and other theological disciplines.

The Relationship of History and Theology
in Biblical Theology

How is this relationship different from the descriptive-normative one just discussed? After all, many biblical theologians would agree with the connection G. B. Caird made when he defined New Testament theology as both historical and descriptive.[132] But there are at least two considerations that distinguish this new question from the immediately preceding one. One is that the task of description does not have to focus on the historical aspects of the Bible; a second is that theology is not self-consciously connected with history in the way that norms are connected to description. Let me elaborate. First, it is conceivable that a person could practice biblical theology without uniting description and history, since one might limit description to nonhistorical aspects of the biblical text.[133] For example, one could describe the text's literary elements and then suggest that these yield theological meaning apart from a full explication of the historical background. Thus, the term "description" can refer to much more than the historical features of the Bible. A second consideration is the way the descriptive-normative pair is more tightly knit that the history-theology pair. Those theologians who wish to make some normative move claim that those norms are grounded in their accurate description of the text, even if that description is not very sophisticated. To claim otherwise would leave one without a "biblical" norm, seeing that it had no connection to the text. But when history and theology are in view, the connection is not so firm. A person might undertake theological interpretation of a passage apart from any concern for the history behind or in the text. Many would argue, of course, that such an approach is impossible, but the point is that they could conceivably claim such a separation. Thus, persons who draw normative conclusions will be self-consciously dependent on some sort of descriptive task, whereas it is possible that persons doing theological interpretation of the Bible may not be self-consciously dependent on the results of historical research.

But can we ever truly avoid some sort of historical interpretation when practicing biblical theology? Even if we self-consciously avoid the exegetical matters attended to in historical-critical study, is it not the case that we will subconsciously be making historical assumptions? One such assumption would be that our theological interpretation is accurate because it is consistent with, for example, what Isaiah or Paul thought about God. But the moment one makes this sort of connection between the past and the present, the matter of historical distance is implicitly raised, if not explicitly admitted. People who engage in biblical theology because they believe in a God who has been involved in human history and continues to speak today have already broached the history-theology relationship whether or not they intended to. The issue, therefore, is not *whether* theological interpretation is related to historical research but rather *how* they are related to each other. Since this question has long been asked in the discipline, we need quickly to review the key contributions in order to formulate an answer today.

The Relation of the "Historical" and the "Theological" in the History of the Discipline

Sensitivity to historical matters in biblical studies owes much to the Reformation's desire to understand the Bible as a book rooted in its own time and place. Reflecting what was by then a long tradition of seeking the "plain or literal sense," the Reformers believed the Bible's theological meaning and message were not dependent on the interpretation of the religious authorities of the sixteenth century.[134] In his own way, Gabler made historical research central to his proposal for biblical theology by outlining the criteria whereby one could accurately interpret the biblical writers in light of their particular historical circumstances. Only then could one hope to draw out the kinds of universal ideas upon which to build a pure biblical theology. Gunkel, Wrede, and others in the history of religions school pushed all concern for the Bible's theological meaning completely over to dogmatics, making biblical theology a thoroughly historical discipline. Their great fear, of course, was that the failure to separate the historical and theological tasks would necessarily lead to a "distortion of the results of historical investigation."[135] There were, of course, those like Schlatter who questioned the possibility of historical research untouched by theological dynamics, but part of the debate arose from different definitions of "religion" and "theology." As Boers wrote, "The real difference is that the *Religionsgeschichtliche* school approached the New Testament from the outside as the object of critical historical scrutiny, whereas Schlatter approached it from the inside as one who participated in the primitive Christian religion would have done."[136]

It would be two decades before serious discussion of the relationship of history and theology resumed. The 1920s essays by Eissfeldt and Eichrodt, as well as the debate over Barth's Romans commentary, brought theological interpretation back to the scholarly arena, forcing theologians to wrestle with the role that historical study played in biblical theology. What arose in the middle of the twentieth century were a series of proposals, each of which connected history and theology on different grounds. The biblical theology movement privileged history by seeking to ground the Bible's theology in its confession of the actual events through which God acted in history. One expression of reliance on historical research was that "archaeology was the necessary key to unlock the mysteries of the biblical world and to place the Bible within its proper historical and cultural context."[137] Von Rad offered a somewhat different approach by placing the emphasis not on historical events but rather on the development of Israel's traditions and confessions about Yahweh. In New Testament theology, Bultmann used the historical method to interpret the biblical writings, but he is remembered just as much for the hermeneutical stance by which he produced a "pure" biblical theology.

All of these approaches—relating theological and historical methods in various ways and to various degrees—form the context in which Stendahl proposed a return to a fully descriptive and historical biblical theology. Although I have spoken of the dominance of the Gabler-Wrede-Stendahl approach, there is some truth in Barr's observation that talk of dominance should be tempered by the reaction against Stendahl's ideas in many quarters.[138] In some respects, by distinguishing between descriptive, historical study on the one hand and hermeneutical reflection on the other, Stendahl thought he was going against the grain of practice in the late 1950s and early 1960s. Forty years later, the scholarly landscape reveals a continued struggle to relate history and theology in the practice of biblical theology.

Major Approaches to the History-Theology Relationship Today

Throughout this chapter I have summarized important proposals for handling issues in biblical theology. There is always danger in such summarizing, because it necessarily tends to generalize specific proposals that are presented with much more nuance than an introductory treatment can cover. Thus, the following three approaches should not be taken to reveal the full complement of methodological similarities and differences among scholars. With that caveat, I suggest that we consider a spectrum of positions, from those that tend to give priority to the theological side of the relationship to those that reverse the priority, with other positions balancing the elements in various expressions of tension.

Theology as the Primary Category

This perspective does not envision the theological aspect of biblical theology as completely independent of historical research or interests, but it does stress their differences and contend that giving the historical element priority leaves one unable to make biblical theology relevant to our contemporary context. Some of the particular concerns in this perspective are the necessity of faith and the inadequacy of history for biblical theology.

Some biblical theologians have been explicit about *the necessity of faith* for a complete and accurate approach to the discipline. Alan Richardson's 1958 work *An Introduction to the Theology of the New Testament* sees biblical theology as a "science" that has its own hypotheses and methods to corroborate the facts, with faith as a necessary standpoint for the task: "A proper understanding of Christian origins or of New Testament history is possible only through the insight of Christian faith."[139] In a different way, Childs's proposal for canonical interpretation raises the matter of faith by calling on biblical theologians to view "history from the perspective of Israel's faith-construal." This sensitivity to the faith communities that produced the Bible is enhanced when the theologian "takes his stance within the testimony of Israel and struggles to discern the will of God. Fully aware of his own frailty, he awaits in anticipation a fresh illumination through God's Spirit, for whom the Bible's frailty is no barrier."[140] In response to the emphasis on faith, Barr acknowledges that "few are likely to embark on biblical theology without a faith commitment." What he asks, however, is that such faith "be only a commitment to discover what is really there in the Bible, even if what is found disagrees with our present faith-commitments, extends them in a quite unexpected way, or goes in a quite different direction from them."[141]

If one were to articulate a scholarly approach to the role of trust in biblical interpretation, it might look something like what Peter Stuhlmacher has called "a hermeneutics of consent." To employ such an approach, Stuhlmacher would argue, does not thereby eliminate any and all critical reading of the Bible but rather asks that the Bible be read in light of three aspects that the historical-critical method has either rejected or overlooked. The first is an "openness to transcendence," whereby we not only ask "how *we* relate to the texts" but also "ask what claim or truth about man, his world, and transcendence we hear from these texts." Second, this approach requires "methodological verifiability," that is, it "must as far as possible be verifiable as to method, reasoned out, and capable of correction." Third, there should be an "effective-historical consciousness" through which this practice "reflect[s] on its own locale of interpretation as well as on the fact that a history of effects and of interpretation lies between us and the texts to be interpreted."[142] A hermeneutics of consent offers itself as an alternative to a "hermeneutics of suspicion," aspects of which I will address later in light of postmodern and contemporary approaches. For now we may say that application of Stuhlmacher's proposal, also in postmodern fashion, calls for a certain amount of empathy for the object of study (the Bible) if we are to understand it on its own terms as well as in terms of the questions raised by modern, critical methods.[143]

Another emphasis among those giving priority to theology over history is *the inadequacy of historical study* to exhaust the Bible's theological meaning. Commenting on the contribution of Karl Barth, New Testament scholar Gregory Dawes writes, "The historical criticism of the Bible has a valuable role to play in helping us understand the biblical proclamation of the action of God, but it loses all theological significance when it attempts to reach behind that witness in an attempt to discern the hand of God at work in human history."[144] There has been no shortage of critics of Barth's perspective, as some fear that it "all too easily becomes an indifference to history totally incompatible with the belief that God revealed himself in events which happened *sub Pontius Pilato*."[145] Barth of course denied the charge, even in the first edition to his commentary: "The historical-critical method of Biblical investigation has its rightful place: it is concerned with the preparation of the intelligence—and this can never be superfluous." He was happy not to have to choose between the historical method and belief in the Bible's inspiration, yet he declared, "But, were I driven to choose between it [historical method] and the venerable doctrine of Inspiration, I should without hesitation adopt the latter, which has a broader, deeper, more important justification. The doctrine of Inspiration is concerned with the labour of apprehending, without which no technical equipment, however complete, is of any use whatever."[146]

In various ways throughout his career, Brevard Childs has also found that the historical-critical method is "sorely deficient" and does not do "justice to the theological dimensions" of Scripture. Agreeing with David Steinmetz, Childs writes that "historical critics share a proclivity to defer the question of truth endlessly. Historical description is not enough, but it belongs to the central task of exegesis to move from the witness to the reality of which Scripture speaks."[147] Childs believes that his canonical approach enables the scholar not only to undertake the most technical aspects of linguistic and historical exegesis but also to ask about the theological function of those findings in light of the process that brought the biblical texts to their current canonical shape.[148]

One other angle on the inadequacy of purely historical approaches is that of Walter Brueggemann, who comes to the question not out of a concern finally to get at the "truth," either about human history or God's existence, but rather to ascertain precisely what the biblical texts themselves are attempting to affirm about God and the world. Brueggemann knows there is no retreating from the gains of the historical-critical approach to biblical interpretation, but he rejects the methodological certainty that accompanied much of it in the nineteenth and twentieth centuries. He hopes that his understanding of biblical theology can steer a course between a *fideism* that lets faith determine the outcome of critical investigation and a *skepticism* that might be hostile to any theological claims in the text.[149]

History as the Primary Category

Rainer Albertz sees the history of Israel's religion to be a more meaningful category than Old Testament theology for biblical studies. This is not because Albertz has some naive belief in history as a purely objective task or that he thinks one should never raise theological questions based upon critical biblical study. Rather, he states that the history of religions approach is superior for these reasons: It "corresponds better to the historical structure of large parts of the Old Testament"; it reckons with the fact "that religious statements cannot be separated" from their historical background; it is not tempted to bring any contradictions down to the level of abstraction; it also provides a much safer ground for Jewish-Christian dialogue today by avoiding a view that gives the Old Testament its meaning solely through Christian appropriation; and it avoids all claims to absoluteness.[150] There are, of course, different expressions to a history of religions approach, such as the British and Scandinavian "myth-ritual" schools that explored common themes of kingship and celebration of the New Year among cultures of the ancient Near East.[151] There are also ways of studying Israelite religion that do not have to make its historical development the primary category of organization.[152] But for those who may be wary of letting theological convictions distort historical findings or cover over tensions in the Bible, Albertz's proposal for a history of religions approach will continue to have a strong appeal.

The primary emphasis on history is not necessarily the sole possession of the history of religions approach since, as we have seen, a goodly number of biblical theologians define their discipline as strictly historical but do not focus only on Israelite or early Christian religion. One expression of this outlook is John Collins's "critical biblical theology." Wary of the "dogmatic considerations, à la Childs, on the one hand, and the Bible without theology, à la Gottwald and [Robert] Oden, on the other," he calls for an alternative definition of biblical theology "as an area of Historical Theology." From this perspective, biblical theology would be like the history of religion insofar as it concerns itself with "the portrayal of God in one group of texts, the Bible. While the material to be explained is canonical, the context of interpretation is not restricted, as it is in Childs's canonical approach. Biblical Theology can make full use of historical, sociological, and literary research, and so can be integrated fully into the mainstream of biblical research." Collins admits that there are potential problems with this approach, but as long as one "regards theology as an academic discipline, which is analytical rather than confessional," he contends that this critical biblical theology can make positive contributions for the "academy rather than for the church."[153] Collins has made a helpful contribution not only by articulating an "alternative" approach but also by acknowledging that the differences among scholars may be owing as much to their definitions of theology and the identity of their audiences as to the methods they employ.[154]

In the post-Bultmannian era, some New Testament theologians wished to ground theology firmly on some kind of a historical reconstruction, such as Jesus' authentic sayings (Jeremias).[155] With the advent of the so-called "third quest for the historical Jesus," scholars seem far less concerned with reconstructing verbatim quotations of Jesus' teaching or absolute descriptions of his actions. The focus instead has been on developing a more complete portrait of the setting that would have formed and shaped Jesus' life as a first-century Galilean peasant. In fact, Ben Witherington has said that what we really have is "the quest for the historical Galilee" rather than of Jesus himself.[156] But even where sociohistorical research is concerned, Dan Via has shown how most, if not all, of those scholars using these methods have some sort of theological concern.[157] If this is indeed the nature of the discipline—if scholars have deep historical *and* theological commitments—can these be held in tension to produce sound results without compromising the essential concerns of either side of the spectrum?

History and Theology Compatibly Serving the Same Goal

Walking a tightrope is a demanding task, even when attempted by a seasoned veteran under perfect conditions. In biblical theology, it may be that no one can find a way to articulate the hoped-for compatibility without leaning, ever so slightly, toward one side or the other. If there is a possibility of walking that line, it will probably have to be attempted on the level of definitions, particularly of what constitutes historical method and theological interpretation.[158] This has been the approach taken by Peter Balla, who defends "retaining the historical character of the enterprise of New Testament theology" while arguing that "a definition of history is preferable which leaves room for discussing reports about God's acts in human history." He writes that this "wider" definition of history "may be fruitful in the study of a field that has the talk about God as its main characteristic."[159] While Balla himself does not opt for making the results of such investigation normative, he has attempted to find a consensus position that does not rule out either history or theology out of hand.[160]

Perhaps the most comprehensive, continuing project in New Testament theology over the past fifteen years has been that of N. T. Wright, represented in his multivolume work on *Christian Origins and the Question of God*.[161] Wright's project is both historical and theological, their relationship nuanced in a variety of ways. He writes, "We need to do both history and theology: but how?" The approach to the problem, for Wright, involves redressing the assumptions in modern Western culture, one of which is "that 'history' and 'theology' belong in separate compartments. The challenge is now before us to articulate new categories which will do justice to the relevant material without this damaging dualism—and without, of course, cheating by collapsing the data into a monism in which one 'side' simply disappears into the other." In Wright's view, the dualism between history and theology can be avoided when a third component, literary study, is brought more seriously into the picture, pointing to a "creative synthesis of all of them. We must try to combine the pre-modern emphasis on the text as in some sense authoritative, the modern emphasis on the text (and Christianity itself) as irreducibly integrated into history, and irreducibly involved with theology, and the postmodern emphasis on the reading of the text." The next chapter will explore some of the specific ways that Wright sees these three working together, but the theoretical assumption is that they are not contradictory. Neither the historian nor the literary critic can avoid consideration of theology, that is, "the question of God."[162]

Summary

If biblical theology has as its goal the identification and understanding of the theological message of the Bible, then regardless of how well we succeed at expressing and practicing the sought-for compatibility of approaches, there will always be efforts at historically sensitive, theological interpretation. As we draw the discussion of this issue to a close, some observations are in order about the prospects for the ongoing relationship of history and theology. A first consideration is the matter of *purpose*. Although I alluded to different "audiences" for those who place the interpretive priority on one element or the other, it is only fair to acknowledge that no one should be faulted for wishing to speak to their particular communities, be they academic, ecclesial, or some other group. This acknowledgment does not give anyone permission to disparage those methods others choose to employ; it should rather be an invitation to incorporate the insights of others to inform one's explication of critical, confessional, or even political biblical theologies. Second, there is the matter of *definition*. The history-theology debate might be advanced if scholars could articulate the impact that "narrower" or "wider" definitions of history and theology would have on their conclusions. Of course, no single definition of historical method or theological content will ever be acceptable to everyone, even if there are broad areas of agreement over fundamental elements of either aspect. But these definitions can be invitations to further conversation and mutual correction on the way toward a holistic biblical theology. Finally, there is the matter of *variety*. Lurking behind my approach in this chapter has been the assumption that pairing different relationships would illuminate the key issues of biblical theology. This approach has admittedly been for the sake of organizing the issues in a manageable way, not to limit the possibilities with respect to their solution.

On this issue in particular, however, it must be emphasized that limiting the image to a simple pair of concepts in tension with each other misrepresents the very Bible whose theology is being explored, as Wright suggested. There are surely a variety of considerations that impact the relationship of history and theology. For example, language and literature are the channels whereby the Bible's theological testimony is communicated and connections with history can be sought.[163] Then, too, one might choose to say, with Ulrich Mauser, that historical criticism is "neither the friend nor the foe of biblical theology."[164] Finally, Joel Green believes it is possible to move forward by acknowledging that "theology and history are not the polar opposites they have been made to be in recent centuries."[165] His proposal for the way forward brings us to the next issue under consideration.

The Relationship of Biblical Theology to Other Theological Disciplines

From the outset of this book, one of the challenges I identified for the discipline of biblical theology was the problem of comprehensiveness: Could biblical theology rightly claim to be the sole means for identifying and understanding the message of the Bible? Are there not several legitimate conversation partners, among them systematic theology, pastoral theology, theological ethics, political theology, and so on? The one discipline that has received the most attention has of course been systematic theology, and thus it will be the primary focus here. Still, many of the same observations made here about its relationship to biblical theology will also be relevant to the latter's connection with the others.

In the late 1940s, Geerhardus Vos distinguished biblical theology from systematic theology mainly in terms of their *principles of organization*: "In Biblical Theology the principle is one of historical, in Systematic Theology it is one of logical construction."[166] To Vos, it was not as if biblical theology had a greater claim on the Bible or transformed its message less than systematic theology. Closely related to the concept of organization is their difference in the *methods and tools* they use to understand the biblical text, with biblical theology employing a full range of historical methods in its research. A third difference pertains to the *purpose and scope* for which each discipline uses the Bible. Trevor Hart has recently written, "Perhaps the chief difference lies in the way in which systematic theology deliberately and extensively seeks to engage the distinctive priorities and emphases of Scripture (discerned at least in part through the work of biblical theologians) with those which confront it in wider intellectual concerns, the insights, claims, and assumptions of other disciplines, and of the wider world."[167] Although this seems to make biblical theology a "descriptive" counterpart to a "normative" systematic discipline, Hart insists that the descriptive-normative distinction cannot be applied in that way, for all of the reasons I noted earlier.

The Relationship between Biblical and Systematic Theology since the Eighteenth Century

A great many surveys of the discipline point out that among Christian thinkers prior to the Enlightenment there was no separation between the study of doctrines and the study of the Bible.[168] In chapter 2 we explored ways in which people were doing theological interpretation as a precursor to what became biblical theology, but there is no problem with acknowledging that prior to Gabler there had been no attempt to offer an ordered account of the relationship between critical, biblical interpretation on the one hand and the development of doctrines on the other hand. Whereas Gabler wanted to "rightly establish the use in dogmatics of these [biblical] interpretations and dogmatics' own objectives," Wrede was far more wary of letting dogmatic theology reach back and influence biblical theology.[169] In their own way, the twentieth-century debates over Barth's theological interpretation or the confessional concerns of the biblical theology movement wrestled with matters of distinguishing the proper sphere of each discipline.

Against this background we saw how the last thirty years has seen a burgeoning interest on both sides to engage in dialogue. Gerhard Hasel believes biblical and systematic theologians should work together in a complementary fashion, because each has unique strengths and emphases. For example, while the "Biblical categories, themes, motifs, and concepts" are "less clear and distinct" than those of the systematic theologian, those categories "are more suggestive and dynamic ones for expressing the rich revelation of the deep mystery of God."[170] In spite of the serious efforts on the part of scholars to work together, important questions remain about how to overcome the problems that have tended to separate them from each other. Any proposals today will need to account for challenges to cooperation from both directions.

Major Approaches to the Biblical Theology–Systematic Theology Relationship Today

Reasons for Biblical Theology to Keep Its Distance from Systematic Theology

The long history of biblical interpretation has shown that suspicion of "dogmatics" or "theology" has run deep and comes to the surface at various times in various ways. Dennis Olson has identified "four recurring objections or problems" that other scholars have for integrating the disciplines. First, the diversity in the Bible should not be conformed to any systematic, theological unity. Second, biblical study should be objective and neutral, a goal best maintained in the academic area rather than in the church. Third, Christian theology will inappropriately influence or direct the findings of biblical theology and especially of the Old Testament. Finally, the patriarchal Bible with its violent God cannot be allowed to form a basis for contemporary theology.[171]

Scholars may certainly raise one of these objections without accepting the others. For example, Heikki Räisänen is insistent about the merits of Wrede's purely historical approach, even if he would push beyond description to "actualize" interpretation to address the "problems of the present-day significance" of that descriptive work. This may even involve a kind of "theologizing *about*" early Christian sources, but Räisänen is clear that he does not use the term "theology" in what he calls the "narrow, authoritarian, traditionalist sense" of some biblical and systematic theologians, especially for ecclesiastical use.[172] Thus, although once again we see that one's definitions affect how one relates the disciplines, there is still a strong suspicion about joining biblical theology with systematic theology, particularly as it is conceived of in church settings. Of course, churches and their seminaries are precisely the contexts in which and from which most of the scholars desiring cooperation do their work.

Reasons for Systematic Theology to Chart Its Own Course Apart from Biblical Theology

Classically, the doctrine of Scripture was an essential part of the prolegomena to any systematic theology, so we should not expect the kind of animus toward the Bible that has been expressed at different times by biblical scholars toward theology. Still, church theologians (and some biblical scholars) have shared their displeasure over the state of biblical studies, describing its approach as "bankrupt" and claiming that biblical scholarship "holds the Bible captive and makes it inaccessible to ordinary folk."[173] The critics are not calling for a complete separation of the disciplines, but they have passed judgment on the supremacy of the historical-critical approach. In its place they propose a return to earlier methods of interpretation "that created and sustained the communal faith and identity of the early Church." These would especially include a canonical approach that sees the Bible as telling a unified story, one that can be understood in terms of its own inner, narrative logic.[174]

In chapter 1, I explained how I use the terms "biblical theology" and "theological interpretation" in a somewhat synonymous fashion, and as I define them I believe that it is possible to do so. But Stephen Fowl has argued that the "dominant tradition in the discipline of biblical theology" (that is, the Gabler-Wrede paradigm) "is deeply at odds with the type of theological interpretation" that he envisions.[175] Fowl contends that biblical theologians have focused too much on the debate over unity and diversity in the Bible, assuming "that the 'theologies' of the Bible are simply specific examples of properties contained in texts of the Bible which can be extracted by means of a general method available to anybody regardless of their larger interpretive aims." Not only does Fowl deny that texts have some "determinate meaning" that can be discovered using specific methods; he also argues that biblical theologians have failed to consider the different theological contexts from which interpreters work and the variety of aims they have in seeking meaning in the text.[176]

One of the boldest statements has come from New Testament scholar Luke Timothy Johnson: "If Scripture is ever again to be a living source for theology, those who practice theology must become less preoccupied with the world that produced Scripture and learn again how to live in the world Scripture produces."[177] The article in which he wrote that is less about the independence of systematic theology from biblical theology and more about the context in which and the purpose for which one studies the Bible. He states, "The intellectual curiosity driving the scientific dissection of past cultures is entirely legitimate," but in biblical studies, this attempt "to secure the otherness of the text" increasingly occurs in academic settings unrelated to the church. "The community of readers who might have embodied the imaginative world of Scripture became themselves more disembodied, as the analysis of ancient texts took place in a context apart from the practices of piety." Johnson attacks biblical theology because "it suggests the possibility of a theology that is not biblical, and a study of the Bible that is not theological." His solution to the problems inherent to biblical theology is "to encourage the development of theologians with scriptural imagination within the structures of the church itself."[178] Thus, biblical theology is left behind as faith communities develop their own habits of reading the Bible that are more conducive to recovering the world Scripture imagines.

Biblical Theology and Systematic Theology in Constructive Dialogue

Even if one rejects Johnson's argument as a whole, it starkly raises the question of whether biblical theology can—on its own—be the discipline that identifies and understands the Bible's message and meaning. Several biblical theologians sense the kind of disconnect that Johnson diagnoses and are trying to forge a new path of constructive dialogue with systematic theology. Two aspects of this dialogue have emerged in recent years, the first answering objections to the compatibility of the disciplines and the second proposing constructive models for reframing their relationship.

Asserting the compatibility between biblical theology and systematic theology is not in itself a recent phenomenon, since fifty years ago Gerhard Ebeling envisioned a "close co-operation on the part of the various theological disciplines."[179] But some biblical theologians have now addressed the serious attacks on such cooperation with arguments of their own. In response to the four problems he surveyed, Olson offers these reflections. First, the Bible's diversity does not rule out "a Christian systematic theology if the notion of a 'system' is broadened beyond a single or root concept or metaphor."[180] Both disciplines have to recognize the provisional nature of their observations of a Bible that declares humankind's inability to completely comprehend the divine.[181] Second, biblical theology cannot claim to have some neutral or objective approach over against the confessional approaches of systematic theology. "Every interpretation of the Bible, God, and reality presupposes a complex set of presuppositions, prejudices, and interests which originate from many, often untraceable, sources." Third, far from separating biblical interpretation from the Christian tradition of creeds or other confessional documents, "the notion of *sola scriptura* sought always to place current institutional church teaching and practice under the scrutiny and judgment of the orally proclaimed gospel of Jesus Christ whose primary witness is Scripture and whose secondary but important guide is church tradition."[182] Fourth, we can and should read "negative" elements in the Bible in light of the larger witness of Scripture.

If these reasons can be marshaled to persuade biblical theologians of the need for dialogue on their part, is there some theoretical basis for constructive dialogue with systematic theology that differs from Johnson's call for the church to chart its own course? One proposal for constructive dialogue is to understand biblical theology as a "bridge" discipline, or what Charles Scobie calls "an intermediate biblical theology." This definition avoids the problems of earlier models that either overly integrated biblical theology into systematic theology or kept them completely independent from each other. Following Childs and others, Scobie thus places biblical theology between, but also in conversation with, "historical study" of the Bible on one side and the "faith and life [of the church] on the other." Scobie is well aware that "the bridge has to be constructed in such a way that it will carry heavy traffic, and traffic moving in both directions."[183]

Another model has been proposed by Elmer Martens, who also wants to overcome a false dichotomy between biblical and systematic theology. He describes the "traditional model" of their relationship in terms of two separate structures. On one side is biblical theology, which forms the synthetic capstone that is built upon exegetical, textual, and historical analysis. On the other side is systematic theology, which serves as a second level discipline between historical theology on the bottom and practical theology on the top. The only connection between biblical and systematic theology is the one-way movement whereby the former may provide a descriptive summary of the biblical data for systematicians to incorporate in formulating normative doctrine in light of the contemporary context. He finds this model seriously flawed for many of the same reasons discussed above concerning dichotomies between descriptive and normative, historical and theological concerns. In its place, Martens proposes an alternative model whereby biblical and systematic theology are partners between the biblical text in its context on one side and the church within society on the other.[184]

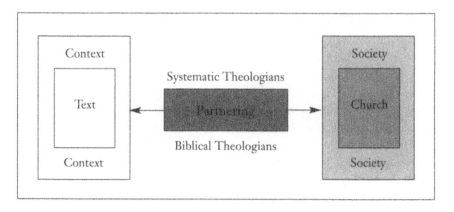

As partners, both disciplines work with Scripture and both speak to the church in the world. Their emphases will of course differ. Biblical theology "will take the lead" in "[sorting] out the question of biblical norm," and systematic theology will give the cues as their work points to "the modern (or postmodern) society and culture."[185]

Summary

And so it appears, once again, that beginning with the heuristic device of a two-sided opposition pushes us beyond traditional boundaries and limits. There are other theoretical models for conceiving the relationship of biblical and systematic theology, ones which place them in dialogue or partnership with each other. Moreover, neither of these disciplines exists entirely independently of other disciplines, be they philosophical, scientific, or religious in nature. Commenting on how Christian communities might listen to "an effective constellation of voices" from Scripture and tradition, Dennis Olson reminds us that "other Christian and non-Christian voices may also be creative dialogue partners."[186] Perhaps the crucial issue for scholars is what constitutes "theology," and the various answers given seem to reflect the contexts out of which scholars do their work. With this realization, we come to the last set of major issues in biblical theology.

ISSUES ARISING FROM THE CONTEXTUAL INFLUENCES ON BIBLICAL THEOLOGY

Debates over the sources for biblical theology as well as the nature of its task do not occur in a vacuum. If anything has characterized the last quarter-century of biblical scholarship, it is the growing awareness of and sensitivity to the role that context plays in every intellectual pursuit. I am here not speaking about *the Bible's* various social, historical, literary, and canonical contexts, all of which have been pursued to various degrees for centuries and have provided valuable insights into biblical theology. Rather, I mean *our own contexts*, that is, all of the ways in which our location in space and time affects who we are, how we think, and what we believe. Chapter 1 introduced this factor as a challenge in defining biblical theology, and chapter 2 concluded with a brief comment on new participants in biblical theology, representing different contexts from which people may interpret Scripture. In what follows, we will first explore a larger and more general discussion about the impact of postmodernism on the modern discipline of biblical theology and then focus on a few particular contexts that have provided a fertile ground for theological interpretation.

The Relationship between Modern and Postmodern Outlooks in Biblical Theology

Before I can comment on the relationship between these two outlooks, it is necessary to address the problem of defining postmodernism.

What is Postmodernism?

For a book on biblical theology, the concept of postmodernism is far too broad to introduce, much less be able to offer a comprehensive assessment of its intellectual and academic influence. In fact, the notion of a comprehensive definition would be inherently resisted by postmodern thinkers, who would question whether such a task is either possible or desirable. But in spite of the fact that defining postmodernism is fraught with difficulties, A. K. M. Adam has written, "Even if postmodernity is not any one thing, it is some things more than others."[187] What things, then, ought we say about it? First, the term itself has been employed since the early twentieth century in a variety of fields, including art, literature, history, philosophy, and social theory, usually to indicate a transition in techniques, methods, and perspectives that could be distinguished from those of the immediately preceding era. While the word "postmodern" does not seem to have a common usage in its early stages, increasing reference to postmodernism in the 1960s and 1970s brought it into the mainstream of academic life, where it has attracted attention from scholars in every discipline.[188] In light of the multiplicity of uses, Hans Bertens writes, "If there is a common denominator to all these postmodernisms, it is that of a crisis in representation: a deeply felt loss of faith in our ability to represent the real, in the widest sense. No matter whether they are aesthetic, epistemological, moral, or political in nature, the representations that we used to rely on can no longer be taken for granted."[189] Thus, Adam observes that postmodernism is "a movement of resistance," such that the "post" implies not only a chronological shift (i.e., *after* modernism) but also a conceptual one (i.e., *over against* modernism).[190]

Second, there seem to be certain key notions that characterize postmodernism as a movement of resistance against modernism. Many scholars highlight postmodernism's "rejection of 'objectivity,' or of the distinction between the subjective and the objective."[191] That is to say, if modern science and historical reasoning assumed that humans have the capacity to study people, things, and events apart from any personal, subjective influences, then postmodern thought argues that we can never keep our own perspectives, habits, and preferences out of our research. Postmodernism, says Leo Perdue, "places the source of understanding within the interaction of the mind of the interpreter, his or her multiple locations, networks of identities, and the linguistic-cultural expressions of the text."[192] For these reasons, Adam (following the work of Cornel West) states that postmodernism is marked by three tendencies: antifoundational, antitotalizing, and demystifying. That is to say, postmodern thinkers tend to be suspicious of modernity's claims to provide absolutely certain starting points for knowledge (antifoundational), to offer universal rules that explain or apply to every specific event (antitotalizing), and to appeal to the unquestionable nature of reason itself (demystifying).[193]

A third consideration, however, builds on the very uncertainty to which postmodernism points, namely, just how different it finally is from modernism. At first glance, this claim seems absurd, given the way postmodernism sets itself over against modernism in some rather significant ways. Nevertheless, as Dan Via observes, not a few scholars have raised this very issue. For one thing, postmodern thinkers exhibit a great deal of variety in their respective emphases and concerns, and many of them prefer not to use the term or admit that the differences with modernism are marginal.[194] Moreover, the exercise of suspicion and skepticism that characterize postmodern methods of interpretation are either amenable to the modern, critical enterprise or represent its logical conclusion. Practically every advance in knowledge has been marked by questioning the predominant thought-forms and methods, and modern historical critics should be pleased to exercise an even greater critical stance in their work.[195] The mention of historical criticism leads us to consider postmodernism's impact on biblical studies itself.

Biblical Theology and the Postmodern Challenge

Among the many facets of this issue, two areas of special interest for postmodernism's relationship to modern biblical theology stand out, and though they are interrelated, they can still be distinguished in the following manner. The first pertains to methodology and problems with the historical-critical paradigm. The second focuses more on the role of human beings as interpreters of the biblical text.

Questioning Modern, Historical-Critical Methodology

Although postmodern biblical scholars sometimes complain about the dominance of the historical-critical method over the past two hundred years of biblical studies, attacks on its hegemony and the privileged position of its adherents in the academy are secondary to more serious implications of their position. Because postmodernism denies both the existence of absolute foundations for human knowing as well as the ability of human reason to attain certainty of knowledge, it also contradicts "the claim that biblical texts have a single determinate meaning created by their authors and accessible to later generations through the use of scholarly interpretive models."[196] The problem of isolating "a single determinate meaning" in biblical texts forms the essence of "deconstruction," one of the predominant postmodern methods of interpretation. Often associated with French philosopher and literary critic Jacques Derrida (1930–2004), "deconstruction is primarily a complex, close exegesis of texts—often the very texts identified and evaluated as the primary texts of Western thought. A close reading serves to disclose the *aporia*, the unresolved tensions, conflicts, and contradictions within the text that are often ignored by non-deconstructive exegetes."[197] While we should not simply equate deconstruction with postmodernism or equate Derrida with either of those terms, it is true that Derrida's reading of biblical texts such as Genesis 11—the story of the tower of Babel—looks for aspects of the story that point to disruption of meaning.[198] Derrida writes, "The 'tower of Babel' does not figure merely the irreducible multiplicity of tongues; it exhibits an incompletion, the impossibility of finishing, of totalizing, of saturating, of completing something on the order of edification, architectural construction, system and architectonics."[199] Adam also reminds us that there are various ways in which deconstructive critics read texts, from close readings that seek how a "text undoes the arguments it is ostensibly making," to showing how "the rules of a given discourse . . . cross one another, cancel each other out, and obstruct the presumed goals of the operation."[200]

Modern biblical studies is not unaware of hermeneutical complexity or problems with determining meaning in a text. As one committed to historical-critical interpretation, John Collins asserts, "Historical critics may also appreciate ambiguity in texts, but often argue that one meaning is primary—either the author's intention or what the text would have meant in its original setting."[201] Thus, while he may accept "some formulations of postmodernism," Collins avers, "Even if determinate meanings are determined by the critic's reading strategy, for meaningful communication to occur there is need of some basic consensus on the limits of valid interpretation, some shared sense of the text that constrains the free play of imagination."[202] But this leads us to consider the role of the reader in interpretation.

Questioning Our Role as Readers

If postmodernism questions how biblical texts have meaning, it also raises the issue of what readers themselves bring to the Bible. Following the twentieth century's growing awareness of the role of hermeneutics in biblical study, there is no going back to a view that completely excludes or even discounts the involvement of the reader in interpretation. As Perdue puts it, "Meaning is the interaction of text, interpreters, and contexts. Interpreters participate fully in the 'meaning' of texts."[203] But this raises the question: What sort of role are we envisioning for interpreters? Surely it is impossible to quantify percentages of involvement in the equation of biblical interpretation and theology, but how do readers participate, as Perdue puts it? Here again, postmodernism has offered a wide range of methods and perspectives. For example, a "reader-centered" approach contends that whatever the original authorial intention or circumstances of a biblical book were, "the text began to be read differently almost immediately after its initial reception, even by the first readers." Although various types of reader-response criticism are caricatured as affirming "whatever the text means to me," Edgar McKnight argues that "the reader is the touchstone for meaning and validation" in biblical interpretation. He goes on to explain that "when a reader says that the text means thus-and-so for her or him . . . the reader has come to a satisfying synthesis on the basis of the various textual and extratextual factors that play a part in reading and interpretation. Other readers are not obliged to agree; therefore, the interpreter has to persuade others that the synthesis is in accord with the various factors."[204] This process obviously involves a community of readers who must arrive at meanings that seem most valid and persuasive to them.

Another hermeneutical factor that has resonated with postmodernism is the emphasis on human imagination, "the power of the human psyche (conscious and unconscious) to form mental images, either immediately or indirectly derived from perception or sensation, that lead to the attainment of meaning."[205] In some ways, Arthur Walker-Jones rightly asserts that "imaginative theological judgment" has always been a part of the *modern* enterprise of biblical theology. In a study of Gabler, Eichrodt, and von Rad, he argues that their methods show that a "synoptic, theological decision influences which patterns in scripture are interesting and thus constitute biblical theology."[206] In today's usage, the concept of imagination implies creativity and a certain stretching of "the limitations of epistemology," but Perdue states that "there are norms and criteria of evaluation that may be articulated, including tradition, reason, experience, coherence, compelling engagement, humaneness, and even results."[207] In biblical studies, Walter Brueggemann has explored the power of prophetic speech in terms of imagination, the creating of alternatives to dominant cultural models.[208] The recovery of a scriptural imagination by faith communities was central to Luke Timothy Johnson's proposal for a theological interpretation that simply cannot be achieved by purely academic study of the Bible.[209] There are, to be sure, many dangers that can beset this emphasis, and in some of its forms imaginative reading of the Bible draws on the very dichotomy between reason and image prevalent in modern, critical thinking. But advocates of a positive role for the imagination in biblical theology are especially persuaded of its usefulness for "moving between the biblical text and the church's theological tradition."[210]

Evaluating the Role of Postmodernism in Biblical Theology

Regardless of whether postmodernism represents a completely new and different stage in the history of biblical interpretation, it is still possible to make some general observations of its impact on modern biblical theology. There may be no example of a thoroughgoing "postmodern biblical theology," but scholars such as Brueggemann and Adam share many postmodern concerns. Putting aside all the reservations about its vague and indeterminate status, in what ways has biblical theology been strengthened or weakened by the postmodern moment?

Positive Contributions

For one thing, postmodernism has increased our sensitivity to the potential excesses of historical criticism. What is in view here are, for example, claims of absolute (or near) certainty in reconstructions of biblical history, or denigration of nonhistorical methods as completely unviable means for interpretation. Whenever historical critics operated with a notion of historicity as "what can be proved as fact" or "what actually happened" (a view often connected with Leopold von Ranke, 1795–1886), too much faith was placed in the human ability to grasp the past.[211] But even though a positivistic sense of history has been undercut, one need not describe the status quo in terms of an either-or dichotomy, as if postmodern concerns ruled out any and all modern methods of biblical interpretation. Adam does not deny the usefulness or applicability of many modern *methods* of biblical criticism; rather, he challenges the modern *mind-set* that presupposes the absolute correctness of historical, rational, and scientific analysis as a means to obtaining the truth about the Bible's origins, contexts, and meaning. This decentering of strictly historical approaches has also encouraged an interest in so-called precritical modes of theological interpretation.

A second contribution of postmodernism is what some have referred to as a recovered "empathy" for the Bible as a theological document, one that serves as sacred Scripture for communities of faith.[212] Paul Lakeland suggests that in this postmodern moment, scholars must cultivate the virtues of both "critique and empathy." While critique has been the generally accepted, modern mode of learning, "requiring as it does the disciplined analysis of the particular object of inquiry," the habit of empathy requires a "suspension of judgment" and precludes "premature analysis or critique and does battle against the strong urge of the academician to place the object of inquiry in some preapproved taxonomy, system, or metanarrative." To be sure, empathy should not become "sentimentality," where we are unwilling to analyze the Bible for fear of losing its beloved, authoritative status. Nevertheless, in some ways, the scholar must "*love* the object of inquiry," a perspective that will allow him or her to "reach the object of inquiry" rather than letting it "remain within the labyrinth of the inquirer's mental pathways."[213]

Ongoing Concerns

A major concern cited by some scholars, representing both academic and ecclesiastical perspectives, is what becomes of the question of "truth" if human knowing is bereft of all its foundations. As Perdue writes, "Perhaps the most debilitating [loss] is dispensing with any affirmation as true in any sense of the word."[214] To be sure, postmodernists would reply that the concept of truth is open to different understandings, not all of which are in conflict with traditional historical or theological concerns.[215] But it is likely that biblical theologians who try to connect their work with matters of faith will experience a tension between a hermeneutics of suspicion and one of trust. Thus, Richard Hays claims that "in order to read scripture rightly, we must trust the God who speaks through scripture. . . . Like Abraham, like Mary, like Jesus, like Paul, we stand before God with empty and open hands. That is the posture in which the reading of scripture is rightly performed."[216] He goes on to cite approvingly Stuhlmacher's notion of a "'hermeneutics of consent'—a readiness to receive trustingly what a loving God desires to give us through the testimony of those who have preceded us in faith."[217]

An illustration of this principle is R. W. Moberly's treatment of Exodus 34, where Moses' personal involvement with and intercession for Israel precedes the revelation of God's character in verses 6–7: "The implication is that self-involvement makes possible an encounter with, and fuller knowledge of, God that a self-distancing would impede; in other words, certain kinds of 'objectivity,' in which the knower tries to keep distance and distinctness from what is known, rule out the kind of knowing of God which is the foundation of biblical and Christian faith."[218] Thus, many people of faith approach the Bible expecting some sort of personal experience of God. They welcome aspects of the "postmodern turn" that seem to encourage such an approach, even as they wrestle with postmodern methods and perspectives that might question concepts of truth and authority associated with the Bible.[219]

A second concern is what to do with the historical method in a postmodern setting. The balance between a subjectivity we cannot completely escape and an objectivity we cannot fully achieve seems difficult to find, insofar as the results of studying the Bible in the midst of that tension remain elusive. Not only are biblical texts complex in their nature; we as human beings are fallible in our understanding. While not wishing to be overly credulous about biblical history nor unnecessarily dismissive of its reports of miracles, Gregory Dawes affirms that there is still an ideal of objectivity, one that means wrestling with how different our assumptions are from those of the Bible.[220] Nevertheless, when speaking about the historical Jesus, for example, John Meier is unwilling to give up on the goal of objectivity altogether and believes that any portrait of Jesus should "be open to verification by any and all persons using the means of modern historical research." So how do we balance our contextual subjectivity with the goal of methodological objectivity? Meier proposes a *provisional objectivity* that involves "knowing one's sources, having clear criteria for making historical judgments about them, learning from other questers past and present, and inviting criticism of one's peers." We can at least "try to exclude [our standpoint's] influence in making scholarly judgments."[221]

Summary

If some aspects of postmodernism are compatible with some aspects of modern biblical theology, then we again see that the contrast is one of tension, not contradiction. Biblical theologians negotiate and adjudicate between different emphases and methods, seeking ways of coherence but also appreciating differences. Walter Brueggemann envisions a "new post-hegemonic situation [that] both permits and requires biblical theology to be done differently," which for him is to recognize that "the text is saturated with disjunctions and contradictions that mark it as an endlessly deconstructive enterprise."[222] Regardless of whether others follow him in describing the new situation as postmodern, what really matters to him "is a *pluralistic* interpretive community that permits us to see the polyphonic character of the text, and the *deprivileged* circumstance whereby theological interpretation in a Christian context is no longer allied with or supported by dominant epistemological or political-ideological forces."[223] Although disagreeing with much of Brueggemann's analysis, Collins would agree with the sentiment of inclusion: "The main gain of postmodernist criticism, in my view, is that it has expanded the horizons of biblical studies, by going out to the highways and by-ways to bring new 'voices from the margin' to the conversation."[224]

The Relationship between Different Contexts and Communities

As we near the end of our journey through the issues of biblical theology, there is a temptation to make this last area a catch-all for a host of topics yet to be treated. The vagueness of terms such as "contexts" and "communities" would seem to support this impression. Even so, there is some rationale in approaching this final issue precisely in these terms. Earlier I described what Collins calls "the changing demography of the field," namely, the inclusion of new theological voices, especially those at or outside the margins of the modern enterprise of biblical theology. While Collins is right that postmodernism has supported this expansion, these new contexts are not necessarily postmodern in themselves. In fact, we could make a case that the examples below originated within the orbit of modern, critical reflection that was informed and energized by nonmale, non-Christian, or non-Western experience.

Thus, the issue here is one of community and experience: How might biblical theology be practiced from a sense of belonging to a community that has been formed and shaped by particular experiences? And how does one's identity with such a community relate to potential connections with those who interpret the Bible from within other contexts? For reasons of space, I will limit the discussion to feminist biblical theology, Jewish biblical theology, and postcolonial biblical theology. While they have in common a lack of "history" within the modern discipline of biblical theology, each highlights different aspects of context and community. Also for reasons of space, I will limit each area to a particular question rather than attempting to survey all known perspectives, methods, and scholarly contributions. The perspectives, as well as the many I have not even mentioned, deserve fuller treatment, something that has been ably supplied by other sources. This chapter is about key issues for biblical theology, and so my discussion may seem reductionistic in its attempt to focus on specific aspects of a larger and more complex situation.

Feminist Biblical Theology and the Issue of Women's Experience

The question that is put to the discipline of biblical theology by the methods of feminist scholars is this: How does one's experience influence biblical-theological reflection? Feminist theologians like Elisabeth Schüssler Fiorenza claim that biblical interpretation "must begin with women's experience in their struggle for liberation."[225] For much of Christian history, experience usually came last on the list of sources of revelation and theological thought, well behind Scripture, tradition, and reason. This is not to say that personal experience was never emphasized in connection with the Bible, since pietists considered experience essential to proper and faithful interpretation. Nor is the matter of starting from the human point of view original even in the modern period, given the emphasis on existence and anthropology in Bultmannian hermeneutics. But what feminist theology has done is to highlight *women's* experience, especially in light of a long history of patriarchy, discrimination, and oppression, and how that experience relates to the Bible's status as authoritative teaching. There were certainly many streams of thought that flowed into the feminist movement of the 1960s as one expression of the larger civil rights movement. The events of that decade formed the immediate historical context for feminist theology in America, but its concerns also dovetailed with those of the liberation theology emerging in Latin America in the early 1970s, with both focusing on the struggle for freedom from oppression.[226] Mary Ann Tolbert, therefore, defines feminist hermeneutics "as a reading of a text (or the writing of an analysis, or the reconstructing of history) in light of the oppressive structures of patriarchal society."[227]

In a 1988 survey of feminist biblical scholarship, Katharine Sakenfeld identified "the place of women's experience (and the proper definition of 'experience') in appropriating the biblical witness [as] . . . the central issue around which feminist discussion of approaches to biblical authority revolves." Even then, Sakenfeld was able to identify at least three different understandings of women's experience in relation to the Bible: (1) experience playing a central role in biblical interpretation, determining what in the text is liberating; (2) a more traditional view in which experience is subordinate to Scripture; and (3) a position where the Bible has authority because its liberating message "makes sense of" women's experience.[228] The same kind of variety existed with respect to feminist interpretive strategies in the 1970s and '80s.[229] Since those initial efforts to critique all theological approaches to the Bible "that did not take women's issues and experiences seriously, . . . [a] second generation [of feminist theology] moved beyond critical evaluation to a more systematic presentation," primarily employing either historical or literary methods of interpretation.[230]

Bringing Women's Experience to Bear on Biblical Theology

There can be no debate over the claim that the discipline of biblical theology did little or nothing to consider women's experience prior to the end of the twentieth century. As Francis Watson puts it bluntly, in spite of numerous methodological developments, "one thing has changed hardly at all, and that is that the debate is carried on over the centuries almost exclusively by men.

Biblical scholarship has been a matter of men arguing with men."[231] It may seem like a mere academic exercise to ponder how the past two hundred years of biblical theology would have been different had women's perspectives been integral from the beginning. But while such a question is replete with anachronism, there is still some value in contrasting the seven issues we have already discussed in this chapter with this new focus on women's experience. As we looked at the traditional perspectives on the issues, most of the major positions had been laid out by male scholars who rarely focused on women in the Bible or on the Bible's patriarchal tone. However, feminist scholars have discussed the issues (e.g., history and theology, descriptive and normative), while also bringing completely new perspectives to the way these issues are negotiated and new attention to the role of women in the biblical text.[232]

Therefore, regardless of how we might answer hermeneutical questions about the impact of gender on biblical interpretation, the facts related to publishing and treatment of issues speak for themselves. Feminist scholars continue to contribute new insights and raise new questions about the Bible that were virtually unseen and unheard of for centuries. Having said that, the hermeneutical issue is still pertinent. Some of my students are inclined to believe that their being men or women has almost no impact on their interpretation of the Bible, while others would rank their denominational affiliation, family background, or other areas as far more influential than any sex- or gender-related perspective. Those students who do see at least some direct correlation almost invariably are women who identify themselves as feminists or men who affirm women's concerns.[233] But all of the students admit that they will never again look at Genesis 1–3 in quite the same way after reading Phyllis Trible's *God and the Rhetoric of Sexuality*, or be able to overlook the character of Hagar in Genesis 16 and 21 after working through Trible's *Texts of Terror*.[234]

Since I have spoken in general terms about feminist theology, another factor that must be mentioned is the diversity of perspectives that go beyond the confines of American scholarship in the past thirty years. As Sakenfeld notes, "Recognition of the importance of differing contexts has led many women who are not North Atlantic whites to reject 'feminist' as an umbrella term." They instead speak of "'womanist' theology to refer to black American women's work, *'mujerista'* theology to refer to the work of Hispanic women (with recognition of the existence of many different contexts among these women), and 'Asian women's' theology for work done in Southeast and East Asia (again with recognition of many national and regional subgroupings)."[235] For example, Renita Weems states that her interest in biblical depictions of and references to violence against women arises in part from her "identity as a woman—an

African American woman," one who is sensitive to "biblical imagery that condones violence against socially marginalized women."[236]

Prospects for a Feminist Biblical Theology

What would a thoroughgoing biblical theology from a feminist perspective look like? What about an Old or New Testament theology? These are questions that remain to be answered, but if we are witnessing what Perdue calls a "second generation" of feminist theology, then we will likely have our answers in the near future. One expression could work along the lines of Trible's proposal in 1989. She envisions a theology that would attempt three things: the exegesis of biblical texts that use feminine language for God, discussion of biblical women who have been neglected in scholarship, and rereading patriarchal texts in order to recover a liberating message. Then, building on such work in the text, Trible would trace "contours and content" starting with the creation stories and working to issues of Israelite religion and questions of biblical authority.[237] Other proposals might be less literary and more sociohistorical, along the lines already pioneered by Carol Meyers and Schüssler Fiorenza. Still others might be written from womanist, *mujerista*, or other contexts.

In terms of the whole history of biblical theology, the phenomenon of feminist scholarship is quite new, meaning that expectations for and assessment of its contributions should be measured. Nevertheless, there have been several positive developments for biblical theology either proposed or encouraged by the feminist emphasis on experience, touching on major issues such as methods, hermeneutics, and the nature of the descriptive task. First, through the use primarily of literary criticism, new and powerful readings of individual biblical texts or books highlight the place of women in the Bible. The intent may not always have been to describe or construct the theology of such biblical passages, but Brueggemann's assessment of Old Testament research is fair and accurate: "The outcome of Trible's work, as with the work of some other feminist readers, is to make available to us a troubled world of faith where Israel had to live."[238] Second, we clearly see how powerfully different communities shape and nurture biblical interpretation and theology, a truth that has long been assumed or accepted but now comes to the forefront. The experience of belonging and solidarity is evident, for example, in *mujerista* theology, as it works for the liberation of all oppressed peoples at the margins of society.[239] Third, dovetailing with postmodern insights, Tolbert points to the growing awareness within biblical scholarship that "no value-neutral position exists nor ever has."[240] Interpretation cannot merely be a private, spiritual exercise; it will involve some kind of advocacy, either expressed or implied, pushing interpreters to listen for criticisms of their own presuppositions and methods.

Along with these contributions come ongoing challenges for the category of women's experience of oppression as it impacts biblical interpretation. First, the very strength of doing theology within particular communities may make it difficult for constructive or systematic presentations of biblical theology that transcend boundaries and engage other alternatives. The vital task of finding one's voice, especially if that search is conducted against the background of oppressive circumstances, may consume one's interpretive attention. And in relation to the Bible, the perennial problem of how to assess our "distance" from such an ancient text can be more acute for those employing exclusively literary interpretation.[241] Second, and related to the first point, is the continuing need to determine how different experiences relate to each other. If another person's experience of suffering is far greater than my own, can I even begin to read the text as he or she reads it? Is it possible for oppressors and oppressed to find a shared language that embraces their particular situations while also going beyond both of them to a narrative of reconciliation? Sakenfeld alludes to a potential problem for the category of experience that arises when we do not fully understand another's context. Referring to encounters she had with many Asian women both at a 1993 conference and in less formal settings, Sakenfeld was struck by the way women in different social, economic, and national circumstances drew different conclusions on the message of the book of Ruth.[242] Third, and perhaps more for biblical *theology*, is what we shall do with language for and conceptions of God, both in the Bible and in our own discourse. Brevard Childs has questioned gender inclusive language for God because of its implications for the classic creedal statements about the Trinity or incarnation.[243] In spite of the fact that scholars have criticized Childs's "anti-feminist" stance, the challenge remains of how proponents and critics of inclusive language can carry on a constructive dialogue that remains faithful to different communities while it assesses the rhetoric and authority of biblical language about God.[244]

Jewish Biblical Theology and the Issue of Biblical Theology as a "Christian" Discipline

The prospect of having major contributions to biblical theology by Jewish scholars calls for clarification. The issue here is not about some completely new phenomenon, for the unbroken chain of Jewish biblical study predates any form of Christian biblical theology and has provided a vibrant interaction with the Hebrew Bible for Jewish faith communities around the world. Rather, the issue is prompted by the relationship of that long and venerable tradition of interpretation and theological reflection with the modern discipline of biblical theology as practiced in a mainly Protestant Christian environment. The late 1980s witnessed important discussion over the possibility of and prospects for a Jewish biblical theology. Although the issue here has several facets, the basic question is whether modern biblical theology is inherently a Christian discipline, leaving Jewish scholars unable to participate.

At the beginning of a third millennium of Jewish-Christian relations, it should be obvious that the issue is not only about interests and methods. Christian biblical theologians have to confront the history of misunderstandings and persecutions, from Marcion's rejection of the Old Testament to the horrors of the Holocaust. For our present context, it is especially this latter reality that surrounds and conditions whatever dialogue might occur over technical matters of biblical interpretation. As Marvin Sweeney has written, "Both Jewish and Christian theologians . . . have argued that the *Shoah* has forever changed the way in which the Hebrew Bible is to be read theologically."[245] Is the specter of history too great to overcome, or are there ways for Jews and Christians to read Scripture together and learn from and be challenged by each other's insights? In what follows I discuss three basic perspectives on the issue.

Jewish Biblical Theology and Christian Old Testament Theology Are Essentially the Same Discipline

In an effort to renounce all forms of supersessionism "as morally and theologically bankrupt," many Christian biblical theologians have sought common ground between Jewish reflection on the Hebrew Bible and Christian reflection on the Old Testament.[246] Numerous scholars decry statements in the classic Old Testament theologies by Eichrodt and von Rad that described Judaism as having a "torso-like . . . appearance in separation from Christianity," or "that the way in which the Old Testament is absorbed in the New is the logical end of a process that is initiated by the Old Testament itself."[247] It is, therefore, understandable that Christian biblical theologians would look for all available common ground on which to stand with Jewish scholars, and one of the ways this has been done is to emphasize similarities between the subject matter of the Old Testament and the Hebrew Bible, while minimizing any differences between respective biblical canons and understandings of theology.

When addressing the prospects for including Jewish scholarship in Old Testament theology, Werner Lemke writes that "there is nothing in the essential nature and character of this discipline which would compel us to continue to define it as an exclusively Christian theological enterprise." Lemke does not believe terminology such as "Old Testament" is problematic, since by whatever name one calls that collection of literature, "we are essentially talking about the same entity." Moreover, "Old Testament theology can be done without reference to the New Testament or early Christian theology."[248] Other Christian scholars see hope for dialogue based on the many common theological themes shared by Jews and Christians, such as revelation, redemption, covenant, and promise.[249]

A different angle on the essential similarities is to maintain that the *academic* exploration of the literature of the Old Testament can be conducted by Jews and Christians, but the work must be merely descriptive and *not theological*. Matitiahu Tsevat claims that a Jewish biblical theology is not possible or necessary since "it is nothing other than the theology of the Old Testament which, as has been stated, is a branch and a task of the study of literature." For Tsevat, using adjectives such as "Jewish" or "Christian" with "theology" implies "that the theologian programmatically transfers his base outside of the Old Testament and lets himself be guided by convictions that originate in foreign realms," such as the Talmud or the New Testament.[250] Thus, even if the content of the two canons is the same, does the concept of theology prohibit a common task?

Jewish Biblical Theology and Christian Old Testament Theology Are Antithetical to Each Other

Jon Levenson has presented the most eloquent argument against Jews and Christians sharing in the theological interpretation of the Hebrew Bible. He not only points to the deeply rooted Christian history of the discipline, with its examples of anti-Semitic rhetoric; he also identifies numerous methodological challenges, such as the limitations of the historical-critical approach of modern biblical theology and its propensity "to construct a systematic, harmonious theological statement out of the unsystematic and polydox materials in the Hebrew Bible."[251] If the subject of study is limited to individual passages, Levenson grants that "Jews and Christians can work together, just as they can on modern historical investigation." Even with "larger contexts" there is potential for cooperation "as each identifies imaginatively with the other's distinctive context. But imagined identities are only that, and if the Bible (under whatever definition) is to be seen as having coherence and theological integrity, there will come a moment in which Jewish-Christian consensus becomes existentially impossible."[252]

This strong statement from a Jewish perspective is matched by Brevard Childs's conviction "that the discipline of Old Testament theology is essentially a Christian discipline, not simply because of the custom of referring to the Hebrew Scriptures as the Old Testament, but on a far deeper level." The depth of this level is illustrated by a variety of factors, first of which is viewing the Old Testament "as a completed entity which is set at a distance in some sort of dialectical relationship with the New Testament and the ongoing life of the church." Other key differences are the implicit assumption in Old Testament theology that a relationship exists "between the life and history of Israel and that of Jesus Christ." Childs's overall treatment tends to agree with

Levenson's arguments about historical criticism, the openness of the Hebrew Bible toward later traditions, and a different understanding of the authority of oral tradition.[253] These reasons move Childs toward his canonical approach which, in spite of criticisms to the contrary, remains very attentive to Jewish biblical interpretation.[254] Given Levenson and Childs's argument that the purposes and contexts of Jewish and Christian biblical theology are mutually exclusive, is there any hope for cooperation in more than just limited ways?

Jewish Biblical Theology and Christian Old Testament Theology Are Distinct Tasks but Can Inform Each Other in Constructive Ways

At the very least, Levenson and Childs have shown that there is simply no way to equate the *theological* elements of Jewish and Christian biblical study, and thus any hope for constructive dialogue must maintain the integrity of Jewish and Christian distinctiveness. Moreover, any proposal for mutual cooperation must address the other serious problems they raise. At the same time, Sweeney's call for interaction is persuasive, in that "modern theological reflection is crucial to the well-being of both Christianity and Judaism." Not only would Christians "address a moral problem" of rejecting the theological relevance and independence of Judaism and learn ways to "reappropriate [the Old Testament] as sacred scripture"; Judaism would have "the opportunity to articulate a distinctive theological understanding of the Hebrew Bible over against that of Christianity."[255] Brueggemann shares this hope and conviction but acknowledges that "the process of redress will be long, difficult, and costly for Christians."[256]

One response to the antithetical position is through the broadening of theological approaches beyond the historical ones that Levenson criticized twenty years ago. Then, too, Brueggemann has a point that Levenson's position on the "polydoxic" character of the Hebrew Bible seems inconsistent with his position about the finality of difference between Jewish and Christian interpretation.[257] Christian theologians today are far more inclined to accept the rich diversity of perspectives within the Hebrew Bible than they were a few decades ago.[258] And while there are important rhetorical differences in the names our faith communities use for their scriptures and how they shape the canon, the similarity—indeed, the *identity*—of textual content suggests a commonality that can still embrace the distinct perspectives.[259]

In light of these arguments, Moshe Goshen-Gottstein's proposal for a distinct "Tanakh theology" comes into play, since he believed it was important to articulate a Jewish biblical theology that "can take Tanakh in its absolute canonical finality." He thinks it is possible to address the message of the Tanakh by looking at the biblical sayings "on the relationship between God, people, and land, and how such a base line might contrast with later Jewish theologies." Goshen-Gottstein died before he was able to produce a comprehensive work of that nature, but his proposal sought to maintain the integrity of Jewish biblical study along with the benefits of trying to say "'what Tanakh is all about' . . . not as a static picture but in the constant dynamics of ambivalence and dilemma."[260] If such a proposal could be articulated, then there would be a more complete content for the dialogue than just the smaller passages of which Levenson speaks. It would make possible James Dunn's assessment, "At the heart of biblical theology is the interface between a Jewish biblical theology and a Christian biblical theology—the interface that is the New Testament itself."[261] Recognizing the necessity and possibility of the goal neither ensures a smooth journey nor clearly describes the destination, but it does move us beyond wishful thinking to hopes for Jewish-Christian cooperation in biblical theology in the future.

Postcolonial Biblical Theology and the Issue of the Ideology of Liberation

We saw in chapter 2 that postcolonial biblical theology involves the efforts of Christian communities in Africa, Asia, and Latin America to draw on their own cultural experiences of colonial or imperial oppression as they read and interpret the Bible. R. S. Sugirtharajah defines "postcolonial criticism as a textual and praxiological practice initially undertaken by people who were once part of the British, European, and American Empires, but now have some sort of territorial freedom while continuing to live with burdens from the past and enduring newer forms of economic and neo-colonialism."[262] Appreciating the diversity of national, racial, and social situations embraced by postcolonialism, as well as its critique of earlier, colonial perspectives, one might be inclined to identify it with postmodernism. Postcolonialism and postmodernism do share some important characteristics, but there is at least one critical way in which they differ, and it lies in their understanding of the Bible's great narrative of liberation. Thus, Sugirtharajah writes, "Unlike postmodernism, which sees the end of grand narratives, postcolonialism views liberation as a meta-story which still has to play out its full potential." He goes on to add other differences, such as postcolonialism's attraction to the potential for economic liberation in the modern world and its rejection of postmodernism's reticence to draw ethical conclusions about human behavior and society.[263] Biblical theologians in the West have also begun to see postcolonial biblical theology as a fruitful partner in the ongoing conversation about the Bible's message. Erhard Gerstenberger calls on Westerners to exercise a theological awareness that we "live in an area of the world which has been unilaterally favoured by the history of colonialization and imperial conquest."[264] In what follows, I will first compare and contrast a general liberation biblical theology with postcolonial emphases and then go on to engage the issue of ideological criticism of the Bible's liberation narrative according to postcolonialism.[265]

Liberation Theology and Postcolonialism

We have already seen how the various expressions of feminist theology today share a common concern with liberation theology, namely, the struggle against oppression and for equality and justice.[266] Liberation theology is generally traced to the work of Latin American priests and theologians in the late 1960s and early 1970s, as they testified to the struggle of the poor for social justice and freedom. Gustavo Gutierrez helped to define liberation theology's basic approach in his book *A Theology of Liberation* (1973). For Gutierrez, theology is "critical reflection on praxis," by which he means that theology is not only the seeking of spiritual wisdom or rational knowledge but also being critically aware of our "active presence in history." Moreover, individuals and the church must move beyond the level of personal knowledge "to a clear and critical attitude regarding economic and socio-cultural issues in the life and reflection of the Christian community." Thus, the goal is to develop "a theology of the liberating transformation of mankind," expressing itself "in the protest against trampled human dignity, in the struggle against the plunder of the vast majority of people, in liberating love, and in the building of a new, just, and fraternal society—to the gift of the kingdom of God."[267]

What then is postcolonial biblical interpretation and what does it share with a liberation hermeneutic? According to Sugirtharajah, there are three main tasks of postcolonial interpretation. First, it studies the Bible to uncover its "colonial entanglements," that is, the ways in which it contains formerly unexamined assumptions of the colonial contexts in which it arose. Second, it "engage[s] in reconstructive readings of biblical texts" to ascertain liberation themes and a focus on diverse and excluded people groups. Third, it "interrogate[s] both colonial and metropolitan interpretations" to expose the ideologies of earlier biblical commentators. In sum, "it seeks to puncture the Christian Bible's Western protection and pretensions, and to help reposition it in relation to its oriental roots and Eastern heritage." Thus, while sharing some of liberation theology's perspectives and themes, especially a concern for "the Other," postcolonial interpretation would reject the way liberation theology "remains within the bounds of Christianity and its construction is informed by Christian sources." One example of the difference is that while liberation theology grasps the power of the exodus for an enslaved people, postcolonial interpretation points out the effects that act of freedom had on its victims, namely, the Egyptians and Canaanites, and "discerns the parallels between humiliated people of biblical and contemporary times."[268]

Assessing the Claim of Ideologies in the Bible's Liberating Narrative

How, then, is the liberating metanarrative—which is significant to both liberation and postcolonial interpretation—to be read? Within the complexity of perspectives, two important questions emerge for biblical theology. First, we must ask about the centrality and interpretation of the so-called liberation metanarrative of the Bible. Postcolonial readers are not the only ones to question liberation theology's reading of texts like the exodus story. From a modern, critical perspective, Jon Levenson explores George Pixley's treatment of the exodus and finds it wanting on several counts.[269] Along with the historical problems of interpreting the exodus as primarily a class struggle between peasants and their Egyptian or Canaanite rulers, Levenson is particularly concerned "that the hermeneutics of suspicion that [Pixley] applies to the biblical text—at least when it fails to endorse his social ideal—is never applied to the ideal itself and the modern political tradition that has tried the hardest to implement it." He admits that the "'preferential option for the poor' is a central element of the Hebraic social ethic. But it does not in any way suggest classlessness or primitive communism as either a reality or an ideal. The condemnation of the oppression of the poor by the rich in the Hebrew Bible cannot be construed as a rejection of the very existence of the two classes." The real focus is "the miraculous escape to their native and promised land of foreigners who had been impressed into state slavery," and the meanings of "enthronement, covenant, and dedication" are predominant.[270]

Levenson's reading has had its share of critics, such as John Collins, who contends that in spite of its acknowledged particularity (for Israelites) and its theological focus on the covenant with Yahweh, "social and political liberation is a fundamental part of the Exodus story, as Levenson also admits." But rather than embracing a liberation hermeneutic, Collins cautiously observes, "In the full biblical story, liberation and colonization are two moments in the same extended process, and another, less political, moment is provided by the giving of the law. One may, as many have, choose to focus on only one of these moments, for the sake of effective rhetoric. But the story as a whole has an inherent ambiguity that gives rise to a plurality of interpretations."[271] In similar fashion, Brueggemann urges "that such marginated readings can see dimensions of the text that established readings of a historical-critical or theological-dogmatic kind have missed."[272] Thus, even if Levenson's exegetical arguments are granted, it is still fair to question the impact of the whole exodus-conquest tradition on non-Israelites. But this returns us to the diversity of perspectives from which one might explore that impact, the concern at the heart of postcolonial biblical criticism.

A second question pushes the matter of ambiguity and plurality further, asking about the nature and efficacy of interpreting the Bible ideologically. Postcolonial readings do not consider the biblical narratives "as a series of divinely guided incidents or reports about divine-human encounters, but as emanating from colonial contacts." As an example of this practice, Sugirtharajah says that a postcolonial approach might "wish to revisit the Book of Esther, in order to unveil its ideological and cultural assumptions," which include acceptance of patriarchy, the luxury of royal families, and the system of imperial rule. Far from being a liberating text, the book of Esther could be seen as urging its readers who live as aliens in a foreign land to conform and assimilate into the dominant culture. The driving force behind postcolonial biblical study, therefore, involves questions about power: "Who has the power to interpret or tell stories? To whom do the stories/texts belong? Who controls their meaning? Who decides what texts we choose? Against whom are these stories or interpretations aimed? What is their ethical effect? Who has power to access data?"[273]

These questions relate to matters of ideology and advocacy. Whether the category of ideology can be applied to *texts themselves* has been disputed by Stephen Fowl. If ideology is loosely defined "as a consensual collection of beliefs, attitudes, and convictions that is related in certain specifiable ways to a whole range of social, political, and material artifacts and practices," then Fowl claims that ideology cannot be a property of a text. While he grants that "the production and interpretation of texts are part of the means by which individuals and groups can further their social, political and theological agendas," Fowl argues that the ideologies of these individuals and groups are their own and "not things they uncovered in the text." When one confuses the text itself with the ideologies of its writers and readers, a whole host of other questions arise about authorship, textual history, and why—if the text has an ideology—there have been "various and incompatible ideological uses of a text over time."[274]

Even if we accept Fowl's argument about texts, we are still left with the problem of ideologies past and present. One might, with Leander Keck, say that "it is time to apply ideology criticism to the ideology critics themselves, and to ask about the power quotient in their own scholarship and career patterns," but surely the ideology critics know the self-referentiality of their method.[275] Another approach would be for faith communities to reach consensus on their own reading, perhaps concluding that whatever position they advocate, they will seek to subsume their own story to the Bible, to see it as "*the* story. . . . And within *this* story, as narrated or anticipated by the Bible, there is at work the God whose mission is evident from creation to new creation."[276] Although postcolonial theologians will not see this strategy as an option, there will be common ground on the importance of "the story" and that it functions in significant ways for each and every community that reads the Bible.

CONCLUSION

As we look back on this journey through the issues that arise in biblical theology, it is clear that some issues will remain open-ended for some individuals and groups, while others might have a different list of issues that need further clarification. And within each set of commitments often comes a large range of options by which to express those commitments. For example, while a great many people of faith have settled for themselves the matter of making the biblical canon the sole basis for biblical theology, others are less certain about such an approach. Perhaps bridges between positions can be built, but some appear so far apart that the chasm cannot be bridged. Moreover, there is no single, neutral standpoint from which to assess the issues. Even if there were, how could we find a completely disinterested arbitrator? The amazing reality, however, is that the abiding nature of these differences has not kept people from practicing theological interpretation or writing comprehensive works of Old and New Testament theology, or even of biblical theology.

For this reason, it seems more fruitful to employ the analogy of an intersection than a bridge. Bridges serve one road at a time, direct the traffic in only two directions, and make it difficult to turn around. An intersection, especially one for more than two roads, is a place of great activity as well as great caution. The issues of biblical theology do not function as road blocks here, but they are stop signs. They call attention to the intersection of conflicting proposals and presuppositions, which require more than a mere slowing down to nod at another's position. For the benefit of all travelers, we might do well to see the intersection as a place of commerce for biblical theology, where we truly stop to reflect on the issues in the company of others. If we can do this sincerely, the biblical-theological intersection can be a place to share backgrounds and perspectives, serious questions and tentative answers. On the journey of this book, it is time to move on to a consideration of methods, but we will not leave the issues completely behind us. They will come with us and reappear in various ways as we meet the biblical theologians who have ventured proposals for how we go about understanding what the Bible says about God.

4

The Methods Used
in Biblical Theology

Biblical theologians devote considerable time and space to questions of method, and many of the major theologies of the Old or New Testament begin with an extended rationale for the approach they take. These discussions are valuable because they enable us to see various methodological trends, advances, and problems that arise over time, but the amount of energy scholars invest in methodology can also seem daunting to the beginning student of the discipline. My goal in this chapter, therefore, is not to probe the historical and theoretical underpinnings of these methods but rather to ask practical questions, such as how scholars try to discern the message of the Bible and what organizing principles they use to structure that message. Of course, attention to practical matters always runs the risk of generalization and misrepresentation, leading readers to the incorrect conclusion that each scholar uses only one method or that methodology is the most important part of biblical theology. The reality is clearly more complex than my summary treatment in this chapter, since each biblical theologian draws on a wealth of experience and comes to the Bible with a distinct constellation of interests and concerns.

Given that caveat, some preliminary observations are in order. First, the methods we will explore arose mainly during the past two hundred years, that is, within the modern discipline of biblical theology. There are, of course, good reasons for this choice, not the least of which is to maintain some control over an otherwise enormous amount of material. Moreover, it has only been during these two centuries that scholars have thought self-consciously about biblical-theological method in the tradition of Gabler's first musings. Nevertheless, quite a few scholars appreciate so-called precritical approaches, like those discussed in chapter 2, which seek in various ways to apprehend a spiritual sense to the Scriptures.[1] Second, my plan is to cut across the usual testamental boundary, seeing that Old and New Testament scholars can be reasonably grouped together when it comes to their methods. While their terms may differ, those who survey the discipline of biblical theology generally identify basic categories of methods, and these seem to apply fairly well to both testaments.[2] Third, for the purpose of synthesis, this chapter follows other studies in using the concepts of approach and method somewhat synonymously, but these terms may at least be distinguished. *Approach* is a broader category, embracing both the methods one uses to study the Bible as well as one's perspective on and motivations for doing the task. The term *method* tends to focus on techniques and tools for getting at the Bible's message. Before we begin to discuss their variety, however, a word about the difficulties of organizing the different methods is in order.

THE CHALLENGE OF ORGANIZING THE METHODS OF BIBLICAL THEOLOGY

Students of biblical theology will find several lists of methods in the scholarly literature, lists that differ in the number of and names for the types of methods. For example, in Gerhard Hasel's introductory works, the longest chapters deal with methodology, and he lists as many as ten methods for Old Testament theology and four for New Testament theology.[3]

Old Testament	*New Testament*
1. Dogmatic-didactic	1. Thematic
2. Genetic-progressive	2. Existentialist
3. Cross-section	3. Historical
4. Topical	4. Salvation history (*Heilsgeschichte*)
5. Diachronic	
6. "Formation of tradition"	
7. Thematic-dialectical	
8. Recent "critical" OT theology	
9. "New biblical theology"	
10. Multiplex canonical	

Hasel's examples are somewhat dated, but more recent works tend to use similar terms while slightly amending the lists or the representative theologians for each type.[4] Whatever system of organization we choose, Reumann was correct when he wrote in the early 1990s that scholars can "honestly disagree over past trends, recent history, and predictions of what will ensue."[5] As long as we avoid misrepresenting a scholar's explicit concerns, several different organizational patterns can emerge. Longer and more detailed lists have merit because they highlight distinctions and shades of emphasis, and the unique categories become important precisely because they do not fit into this or that typology.[6] At the same time, if there are similarities to be found among the methods, then the discipline might benefit from an organization that relates some methods to others in terms of their fundamental focus. For example, one might see how in Hasel's list, dogma, themes, and topics all emphasize something about the content of the Bible's theology. The eventual number of approaches may be the same as in other listings, but overarching connections will emerge this way.

Another challenge is raised by Hasel's list of New Testament methods, namely, his "historical" category. For Hasel, this term served as a rubric for works such as that of Werner Kümmel, which distinguished themselves from Bultmann's program of a theological anthropology. But when it comes to the methods of biblical theology, there is broad acceptance of the tools of historical criticism for biblical interpretation. Indeed, we saw in the debate over "history and theology" that scholars equally committed to the methods and (most) results of critical research come down in different places theologically. For these reasons, it is not possible to identify one, distinct "historical" or "descriptive" method of biblical theology. To be sure, John Collins has spoken of a "critical biblical theology," but he places its key task—"the critical evaluation of speech about God"—in the field of "historical theology," with a strong history of religions accent. He also sees the study of biblical genres as "the primary contribution of historical criticism to biblical theology," leading to his affirmation of the category of "story," a type of method that will be discussed later.[7]

Thus, returning to the problem of organization, I have chosen to arrange the most prevalent methods by what I believe to be the primary methodological contributions of biblical theologians. At the risk of oversimplifying what Reumann calls the "kaleidoscopic" nature of the field, the methods and approaches of biblical theology can be grouped by three main foci: (1) *what* the Bible's theology is, that is, its content; (2) *how* scholars express that theology, especially the shape it takes in the Bible; and (3) *where* we enter into dialogue with it, that is, our perspectives on the Bible and its message. With these categories I am asking not only about the eventual structure or outline individual works of biblical theology have but also about the concerns theologians have as they approach the Bible. All of them address the content of the Bible's theology, but for some their primary emphasis is to explicate biblical themes and topics. Then, too, all scholars are implicitly aware of the way the Bible has given shape to its message, but some scholars believe this emphasis is overlooked in the search for unified themes, and so they develop their theological reflection in terms of the shape of the biblical material. More recently, all biblical theologians understand that we enter into conversation with the text from different perspectives, but for some this is their overriding concern. Let us proceed, then, with a survey of these three major foci and the ways in which scholars work with them. Here is an overview of what follows:

Major Focus	Particular Expression
Content	Systematic/doctrinal Cross-section/central theme/topics Story/narrative
Shape	Tradition history Canonical authority Witness/testimony
Perspective	Existential Experiential Social/communal

METHODS THAT FOCUS ON THE BIBLE'S THEOLOGICAL CONTENT

In this first major area, we find works that describe and explain the Bible's theological content in terms either of its connections with doctrinal concepts, central themes that emerge throughout the core of the biblical material, or the content of the primary narrative or story line in the Bible. There will, of course, be ways in which these three expressions of content relate to each other, but they also represent distinct theological methods.

Systematic or Doctrinal Arrangement

The modern discipline of biblical theology developed in part because of the close connection between theological interpretation of Scripture and the doctrinal systems of Protestant orthodoxy. Although Gabler hoped that his method of historical investigation would yield results beneficial to the work of dogmatic theologians, he nevertheless criticized the "inappropriate combination of the simplicity and ease of biblical theology with the subtlety and difficulty of dogmatic theology."[8] Even so, the earliest attempts to produce biblical theologies were patterned on basic doctrinal concepts, such as in G. L. Bauer's focus on theology, anthropology, and Christology.[9] Their successors eventually focused on the development of religious ideas, bringing about the ultimate ascendancy of the history of religions approach. With the advent of the golden age of biblical theology, however, some scholars returned to various arrangements of their work that were clearly related to a systematic, doctrinal framework.

Classic Doctrinal Approaches

Old Testament theologians in the 1920s were, according to Hasel, "to a larger or smaller degree dependent on the Theology-Anthropology-Soteriology arrangement of systematic theology."[10] These efforts were criticized by Eichrodt as unsatisfactory simply because they derived their "treatment of the realm of OT thought" from dogmatics rather than "along the lines of the OT's own dialectic."[11] But in his *An Outline of Old Testament Theology* (1949), Th. C. Vriezen found himself rejecting both of these options. He stated, "It is not really possible to press Old Testament theology into a systematical survey" because it "implies some measure of arbitrariness," yet he also claimed that Eichrodt's outline of the "existential relationship . . . between God and people, or God and the world," had its limitations.[12] When all is said and done, however, Vriezen's own outline is clearly dependent on the order and logic, if not the precise titles, of the classic loci of systematic theology (revelation, theology, anthropology, Christology, soteriology, ecclesiology, and eschatology). His six chapter headings for "the content of Old Testament theology" were: (1) the nature of the knowledge of God, (2) God, (3) man, (4) the intercourse between God and man, (5) the intercourse between man and man (ethics), and (6) God, man, and the world in the present and the future.[13] Vriezen spoke of Old Testament theology "as a part of Christian theology" and described "the message of the books and their authors [as] the *doctrines* of the Old Testament with respect to certain special subjects."[14] Even so, it is fair to say, with Hayes and Prussner, that little of his "strong Christian emphasis" actually "appears in his discussion of the contents of the theology."[15]

New Testament theology in the second half of the twentieth century also had representatives who followed a systematic or doctrinal arrangement. In 1958, Alan Richardson openly advocated an approach to the Scriptures that would involve "the committed Christian . . . [in] the unrelenting effort at restatement of the faith of the Church of Jesus Christ." While defining the discipline of New Testament theology in such a way as to use historical and critical tools, he was convinced that Christians could write a New Testament theology beginning "with apostolic faith," as opposed to the perspective of "liberal humanists" that emphasized human achievement.[16] Thus, starting with a confessional approach, Richardson organized his work in sixteen chapters that reflect a systematic-theological development similar to that in Vriezen's text. Two chapters relating to faith, knowledge, and revelation open the work, followed by three dealing with theology (the power of God, the kingdom of God, and the Holy Spirit). Christology comes next with six chapters on a variety of topics (e.g., messiahship, the life of Christ, resurrection, atonement), and the last five focus on various topics appropriate to ecclesiology (ministry, baptism, and Eucharist).

An even more explicitly doctrinal organization is Donald Guthrie's *New Testament Theology* (1981). Describing his method as "thematic"—as opposed to one that merely takes up the books of the New Testament according to their literary groups (Gospels, etc.)—Guthrie acknowledges that there are implicit dangers, such as relying on proof texts to support one's themes. Thus, for every theme he treats, he systematically discusses in canonical order what the New Testament books say about it. But the overarching organization of the massive volume is clearly based on systematic theology's loci: (1) God, (2) man and his world, (3) Christology, (4) the mission of Christ, (5) the Holy Spirit, (6) the Christian life, (7) the church, (8) the future. These chapters are followed by two more, one on ethics and the other on the New Testament doctrine of the Scriptures. Guthrie is sensitive to criticisms that his "divisions [parallel] . . . those of historic dogmatic theology," but he responds that these "major areas of spiritual enquiry are essentially timeless" and they will be of more help to readers who seek answers to "what the NT teaches" about specific matters.[17]

How ought we to assess the use of doctrinal categories to organize the theological content of the Bible? A traditional criticism of this approach is that it imposes a set of ideas that are external to the Bible on its theology, rather than letting the categories arise from the biblical text. Thus, although Hasel admits that Richardson avoids the dogmatic structure of "theology-anthropology-soteriology," he still thinks that the latter has a "superimposed structure from without."[18] In the same vein, Bernhard Anderson sees the task of biblical theology "to go behind the later incrustations of doctrine to the living experience of faith with all of its ambiguities, temptations, and struggles," and G. B. Caird states that the "whole tenor of the New Testament is opposed to dogmatism and authoritarianism."[19] There is no doubt that there is wisdom in keeping extrabiblical categories from *controlling* the interpretation of biblical ones, and Caird points out several other problems with a dogmatic approach: (1) "category"—that is, confusing biblical revelation with human doctrines; (2) "interest"—theologians can wrongly assume the biblical writers were interested in the same questions as they; (3) "reference"—we too easily think dogmatically when we see references in the Bible to categories such as law and gospel; (4) "authority"—our natural desire to equate our doctrines with biblical expressions, so that our beliefs are "in harmony" with the Bible.[20]

These seem to be reasonable and valid concerns from the side of biblical theology, but the real question is whether they apply to the theologies of

Vriezen, Richardson, and Guthrie, seeing that the *actual content* of their works stays close to the biblical texts. For example, in his treatment of "the law in the Christian life" (an area highlighted by Caird as problematic), Guthrie constantly assesses what the term means for biblical authors, and his scholarly references are almost always to biblical, not systematic, theologians.[21] He does not appear to mention Christian doctrine in general, nor Reformation perspectives in particular. Guthrie wants his work to be a useful reference for readers who want to know "what the NT teaches," something even Caird sees as the one strength of a dogmatic approach. The fact of the matter is that biblical theologians must choose some arrangement of their material, and poorly organized presentations will be helpful to no one. Thus, Barr's sympathetic treatment of the question points out that there is nothing uniquely Christian about categories such as "God-man-sin." Moreover, he suggests that if biblical theologians are to develop a structure of any kind, it *"ought to be and must be . . .* brought from without and inserted into the material." Instead of seeking an arrangement based on ideas, however, Barr proposes "a set of headings such as 'stories-practices-institutions.'"[22] Whether Barr's categories are more helpful at describing theological meaning in the Bible than doctrinal categories can be debated; both may be equally useful depending on one's purposes and one's community of interpretation. Thus, if one is sensitive to Caird's valid concerns, it may yet be possible to produce "systematic" biblical theologies that open the door for conversation not only with theologians in specific confessional traditions but also with those doing constructive theology in nontraditional settings at the margins.

Theological Interpretation

Since we are speaking of doctrinal categories for ordering a biblical theology, it seems fitting to mention how systematic theologians approach biblical texts. We saw in chapter 3 how some biblical scholars join in the critique of the modern discipline of biblical theology, which Stephen Fowl claims is "systematically unable to generate serious theological interpretation of scripture."[23] Accepting this verdict, Francis Watson proposes a different model of interpretation from the ones traditionally associated with biblical theology, as suggested by the subtitle of his 1997 work, *Text and Truth: Redefining Biblical Theology*. The redefinition understands "biblical theology [as] a theological, hermeneutical and exegetical discipline, and its hermeneutical and exegetical dimensions are placed at the disposal of its overriding theological concern." Watson believes this definition relativizes the current "lines of demarcation" between three communities: theologians, Old Testament scholars, and New Testament scholars. He readily acknowledges that the individual studies in *Text and Truth* "do not outline any detailed programme for the practice of a future biblical theology." He believes his own *"ad hoc* procedure . . . [is] the most fruitful and promising way to practise contemporary 'biblical theology.' The time does not seem ripe for grand syntheses."[24] But methodologically speaking, Watson works with several principles: the historical and theological integrity of biblical narrative; texts having a "'literal sense' dependent on 'authorial intention'"; "that the truth of God is textually mediated"; and a negative criterion that opposes "the erasure of textuality for distinctively theological reasons," an error he calls "neo-Marcionism." In part 2 of his work he considers "the Old Testament in Christian Perspective," focusing especially on its teachings about creation and humankind made in the image of God. He states, "From the standpoint of Christian faith, it must be said that *the Old Testament comes to us with Jesus and from Jesus, and can never be understood in abstraction from him.*" Watson's point of view thus "rejects all interpretive programmes that assume an autonomous Old Testament."[25]

For his part, Stephen Fowl affirms much of Watson's project of theological interpretation, stating that "in many respects Watson and I are plowing the same field," but he also wants to distinguish his own concerns from Watson's. In particular, Fowl wants to point out that his own project is much more intent on understanding "the purposes for which Christians engage scripture." He writes, "I treat scriptural interpretation as a practice which both shapes and is shaped by Christian convictions and practices and which both calls forth and relies upon the presence of a community manifesting a certain sort of common life." It is important for Fowl to address the practices of reading the Bible within Christian community, since (as we saw in chapter 3) he denies that texts have some determinate meaning or ideology. What, then, can "counter Christians' tendencies to read the Bible in order to underwrite their own sinful habits and practices"? In his chapter on "vigilant communities and virtuous readers," Fowl argues that readers must practice "truthful, critical self-reflection" toward themselves and their communities, not as "an end in itself" but rather to become "better able to attend to God."[26]

It is difficult to compare and contrast the above approaches to theological interpretation with the more comprehensive and systematic treatments of the Bible's theology offered by Vriezen or Guthrie. To one like John Collins, who operates with a "critical biblical theology," the christological approach of Watson will be "a peculiarly narrow and dogmatic view of Christianity."[27] But the real difference is not so much one of narrowness or dogmatism as it is the fact that these scholars operate with different definitions of biblical theology. If Collins believes his own view to be less narrow than Watson's, he has still chosen to define the discipline in a way that regards Watson's definition as an unreasonable alternative for biblical theology. Even with these sharp disagreements, there is no denying that serious theological reflection is taking place on both sides of this debate. We can surely hope that those who disagree over definitions, methods, and purposes can still learn from each other's interpretive results. One constructive way forward may be the work of Michael Welker, who has proposed that systematic theology and biblical theology can help "to correct reductionistic forms of thought with forms and styles of thought that are both more exegetically grounded and more powerful as well in their time- and cultural-diagnostic capabilities.[28] Welker distinguishes his project of "realistic theology" from "biblical theology" insofar as the latter "does not at present make sufficiently clear the systematic and constructive concern that is directed not only to past experiences and expectations of God, but to present and future ones as well."[29] Welker affirms "the self-referential nature of scripture . . . [as] a living whole, in that it points from a variety of perspectives giving witness to God and divine agency in and for the creation, through which it itself becomes a source of living water."[30]

Cross Sections, Central Themes, and Multiple Topics

Another major way of getting at the content of the Bible is by employing methods either to seek the "inner structure" of the biblical canon or to identify "a textually derived center."[31] Although they are not identical, these methods share some important similarities and thus may be studied together. First, in principle they are both efforts to account for unifying elements in the Bible, for without some unity there can be no "*systematic examination* with objective classification and rational arrangement of the varied material."[32] For some, the very idea of doing biblical theology must be abandoned if one can only discern competing theologies in the Bible.[33] Second, while the search for a central theme may wish to draw on the historical development of the biblical traditions, both the cross section and central theme approaches reject an exclusively genetic and purely descriptive understanding of biblical theology. If a form of unity may be found in either testament or the whole Bible, then there is the potential for normative biblical theology. Third, like other "content" methods, there is usually some interest in recognizing connections between the Old and New Testaments. Eichrodt saw the task as "determining to what extent . . . [Old Testament religion] ties up with the NT revelation and is analogous to it."[34] Let us now turn to a brief consideration of their distinctive contributions to biblical-theological method.

A Cross-Section Method

In chapter 2 we saw how Walter Eichrodt had employed the concept of "cross section" to determine the essential elements of Old Testament theology. We can begin to understand this method's key characteristics by the way Eichrodt distinguished it from (what he regarded to be) two erroneous approaches. On the one hand, he rejected the use of any "dogmatic scheme" whereby to arrange the theology that arose from the Old Testament realm itself, what he called "the OT's own dialectic." On the other hand, he did not think it was enough to use the historical method to determine theological developments diachronically (i.e., through time), as had been done in the history of religions approach, for this would reduce the relationship between the testaments "to a thin thread of historical connection and causal sequence." Over against the "thin" description of historical analysis and the imposed categories of dogmatic theology, Eichrodt opted for "a systematic synthesis" to interpret "the outstanding religious phenomena of the OT in their deepest significance."[35] In order to create a synthetic portrait of Israel's faith, one would have to dig deeply into the biblical sources in their historical contexts, searching for concepts that might be common from one period to the next.

Coupled with this synthetic emphasis was attention to the "double aspect" of Old Testament theology, exploring the connections between the Old Testament with ancient Near Eastern religion on one side and "the exclusive realm of NT belief" on the other. Proceeding along these lines, Eichrodt concluded, "That which binds together indivisibly the two realms of the Old and New Testaments—different in externals though they may be—is the irruption of the kingship of God into this world and its establishment here." For Eichrodt, the special way the kingdom manifested itself was through covenant relationship with God, especially God's relationship with the people of Israel, "who in his rule proves himself to be also the God of the World and the God of the Individual."[36] These "three principle categories" emerge as the structure for Eichrodt's theology: (1) *God and the people*—included here is a study of the covenant concept, the nature of the being and activity of the covenant God, the charismatic and official leaders of Israel, the prophetic messages of judgment and the hope of salvation; (2) *God and the world*—the focus here is especially on God's power in Spirit, word, and wisdom as well as God's rule over creation, be it in the visible realm of nature, history, and human being or in the celestial world and underworld; (3) *God and man*—this studies the individual in human community and personal relationship with God, with special attention to morality, sin and forgiveness, and immortality.

Eichrodt's synthesis continues to be admired by all students of the discipline for its depth and breadth, even though many have criticized specific features of his method.[37] Some criticisms pertain to the method's presuppositions, such as concerns that the search for synthesis will eventually emphasize unity at the expense of diversity. But generally scholars call into question various aspects of the execution of the method, namely, that the results do not match the method's goals. For one thing, while Eichrodt regularly compared Israel's theology to its ancient Near Eastern background, his consideration of the New Testament connections were limited at best.[38] Others point out that Eichrodt's theology exhibits a strong tension between universal and particular aspects, so that the religious thoughts behind "God and the people" and the other two spheres ("God and the world" and "God and the individual") seem to stand on their own. "Each one has its own doctrine of God, its own conception of sin, and its own interpretation of salvation." Yet another common critique is that large portions of the Old Testament, like the Wisdom literature and even the Prophets, do not often speak explicitly about covenant.[39] This problem may not be insurmountable, seeing that it was the reality of the relationship with God rather than the presence of "covenant" language itself that mattered for Eichrodt, but its absence does raise the possibility that one might employ a cross-section method to discern more explicit themes. The attraction of a system that could identify what was most central to biblical books leads to the next section.

Central Themes

When I discussed the issue of unity and diversity in chapter 3, I mentioned several proposals for a "center" as well as some of the strengths and weaknesses of the concept itself. My concern here is for *methods* that would be equipped to identify a central theme, since it is not merely a matter of counting up the number of references to a word that seems replete with theological significance or of seizing upon an idea and fitting everything into it. As Ronald Clements states, "We must, in the interests of a truly historical and critical approach, submit to becoming less systematic than this, and more open to trace the broken lines of unity where the Old Testament draws them." He goes on to describe the challenges of working with the various dimensions of faith, including the literary, historical, cultic, and intellectual.[40] Walter Kaiser is also aware of the complexity of the task in Old Testament theology, but he believes that we can discern "an inner center or plan to which each writer consciously contributed." According to Kaiser, the biblical texts themselves evidence "a principle of selectivity . . . by the rudimentary disclosure of the divine blessing-promise theme" in the book of Genesis. The method by which he identifies the central theme of blessing-promise involves several criteria, especially recognizing "interpretive statements" given by the authors, "the frequency of repetition of the ideas," and "the recurrence of phrases or terms that begin to take on a technical status." Other criteria have to do with the way important ideas are expanded for new stages of history, so that "biblical theology draws its very structure of approach from the historic progression of the text and its theological selection and conclusions from those found in the canonical focus."[41] What results from Kaiser's study is an outline of eleven "historic periods of Old Testament theology": the prepatriarchal era (creation, fall, flood), patriarchal era, Mosaic era, premonarchical era, Davidic era, sapiential era (linking wisdom with Solomon), three eras defined by their respective prophetic ministries (ninth, eighth, and seventh centuries), exilic times, and postexilic times.[42]

New Testament theology in the post-Bultmann era endeavored to recover the interest in the historical Jesus that had been of marginal importance to Bultmann's program.[43] One important voice for the validity of historical investigation in the "new quest" era was Joachim Jeremias, whose theological method was largely historical and linguistic, but it also provided a means for uniting the New Testament message around Jesus' proclamation. Jeremias first sought to substantiate the authenticity of Jesus' sayings in the Gospels by means of comparisons with the teachings of Judaism as well as an examination of their language and style. Building on this confidence in the proclamation of Jesus, Jeremias identified five major New Testament themes: the mission of Jesus, the dawn of the time of salvation, the period of grace, the new people of God, and Jesus' testimony to his mission.[44] In his work *The Central Message of the New Testament* (1965), Jeremias essentially connects the major themes of Jesus' sacrificial death, justification, and the revealing word with the proclamation of Jesus.[45]

Other Topical Approaches

Numerous other biblical theologians have tried to describe the subject matter of the Bible without focusing on one theme or claiming to have grasped the cross section of either testament's religious ideas. The themes and topics they identify exist more in relation to each other than in any kind of strict unity. Bernhard Anderson makes this distinction by saying that "the Old Testament does not have a *center* in the same sense that Jesus Christ is the center of the New Testament. Nevertheless, it is important to consider what part of the Old Testament is *central*, in the sense of being fundamental to Israel's theological understanding."[46] The "center/central" distinction may seem like a fine line, but Anderson's method is to account for "the diversity of Israel's theological expressions and at the same time show the integrity of the faith of Israel in relation to the religions of antiquity." Thus, beginning with the Torah, he discovers that "what is basic is Israel's witness to divine revelation: the self-disclosure of the Holy One (*qadosh*) so that the people may call on (worship) God by the personal name, YHWH."[47]

Other scholars have expressed the basic structure of Old Testament theology in related pairs, such as Ronald Clements's emphasis on law and promise. Clements's method involved a combination of literary, historical, and religious interests, so that one should attend not only "to the literary form and structure" of the biblical books but also "at those broad categories by which the Old Testament as a whole has been understood." According to Clements, "The most widespread and basic category which has been employed to describe the nature of the material which the Old Testament contains . . . is that of 'law,' or more precisely *tôrâh*," which constitutes "the comprehensive list of instructions and stipulations by which Israel's covenant with God is controlled." But along with the notion of law comes the category of promise, borne from "the way in which the prophets gave new hope to Israel and Judah, after the ruination of the old kingdoms had occurred in the eighth to the sixth centuries BC."[48]

One can also find discussion of multiple topics, as in Ronald Youngblood's list of nine "themes that constitute the heart of the Old Testament." His method is "to trace the development of certain key themes from one end of the Bible to the other," a task that requires one "to define each concept, describe the cultural setting in which it arose in ancient Israel, delineate the various stages through which God's people passed as they grew in their understanding of it, and discuss briefly its ultimate fulfillment in Jesus Christ."[49] The result finds the heart of the Old Testament in monotheism, sovereignty, election, covenant, theocracy, law, sacrifice, faith, and redemption.

New Testament theologians have also worked with the different witnesses in the canon in an effort to discern their major emphases. Werner Kümmel stated, "The task of a theology of the New Testament can only consist in first allowing the individual writings or groups of writings to speak for themselves, and only then to ask about the unity which is shown therein, or else to affirm a diversity which cannot be eliminated." Thus, his method does not assume at the outset a resultant unity but rather works with what he calls the "major witnesses" (Jesus, Paul, and John) to see how they all combine "the belief in the presence of divine salvation through the sending of Jesus and the expectation of the consummation of salvation through the coming of Jesus Christ in glory." This similarity among the New Testament's major sources, combined with "the message of God's condescension in Jesus Christ," forms "the two-fold message" of New Testament theology.[50]

Another kind of twofold relationship is found in James Dunn's study of "unity in diversity" and "diversity in unity." Highlighting his method is the question that drives his study, namely, "Was there ever a single orthodoxy within primitive Christianity, within the New Testament?" Since terms like "orthodoxy" and its counterpart "heresy" tend to be emotionally charged, Dunn suggests that the more useful terminology is that of unity and diversity: "What was the unity, the unifying element, the uniting force in earliest Christianity? And what breadth of diversity existed in Christianity from the first?"[51] Dunn then proceeds in part 1 ("Unity in Diversity") with a careful, historical-critical study of several theological concepts—kerygma, confessional formulae, the

New Testament's use of the Old, and subjects such as ministry and sacra-
ments—each time surveying elements of unity and diversity. In the last chapter of part 1 ("Christ and Christology"), for example, he concludes that "*there
was no one christology in first century Christianity but a diversity of christologies.* . . .
Within this diversity however a unifying element is regularly discernable:
namely, *the affirmation of the identity of the man Jesus with the risen Lord.*" Dunn's
method for part 2 takes its cue from the structure of late second-century Christianity and its four main expressions he calls "Jewish Christianity," "Hellenistic Christianity," "apocalyptic Christianity," and "early Catholicism." These
four help to determine what boundaries might have existed to the diversity of
first-century Christianity. The upshot of this analysis is that "*the integrating
centre* for the diverse expressions of Christianity . . . was the unity between the
historical Jesus and the exalted Christ."[52]

On a grander scale there is the project of Charles Scobie, whose work of
biblical theology *The Ways of Our God* (2003) encompasses both testaments and
traces major themes "following the scheme of proclamation/promise: fulfill-
ment/consummation." An interesting aspect of his method is how he incor-
porates proposals that "subsumed under *one* key theme" the complex and
diverse theology of the Bible. Scobie believes these themes "obviously have a
lot of merit and, taken together, form the most useful guide to a multithematic
approach."[53] He groups these themes into four main areas: (1) God's order—
dealing especially with matters of nature and history; (2) God's servant—here
Jesus Christ is understood as the fulfillment of the whole complex of messianic
and servant themes; (3) God's people—Israel exists in covenant relationship
with God, who is also at work with all peoples and who creates the eschatological community of the church; and (4) God's ways—mainly biblical ethics
as expressed in the Torah, Prophets, and wisdom teachings.[54] These areas all
have numerous subthemes that develop the theological content of pertinent
passages from both testaments in an overall framework that understands the
Old Testament as promise and fulfillment while the New Testament is fulfillment and consummation.[55]

The above discussion has offered a range of emphases on "centrality" as well
as choices for structuring theological concepts that were traced through the
Old and New Testaments. The adequacy of any given theme or set of categories will continue to be debated, with some being too limited to account for
the diversity and others being too general to serve as a "center."[56] This unity-
diversity tension seems to be a problem especially for methods that explore
content in terms of *ideas* or *concepts*, but another content-focus is possible,
namely, the *current form* in which they are found. This method identifies the
content of biblical theology with the narrative or story of the Bible.

Narrative and Story

This third "content-type" of method shares some features of the "tradition-history" approach that we will examine shortly. They both focus less on religious ideas or theological themes and more on the sweep of the larger biblical (or testamental) narrative. But where the methods in the next section concern themselves with the development and shaping of the traditions into their current canonical form, the narrative/story method studies the current form itself and identifies the theological content with that form. Biblical theology thus becomes a narrative theology, with its method being informed by literary criticism of the "story" rather than by historical criticism of the origin and form of its sources.

The Rise of Narrative Methods

As part of the larger and more general developments in literary criticism during the twentieth century, the possibility of a biblical theology of narrative or story gained sharper focus in the 1970s and 1980s, associated especially with the work of Yale scholars Hans Frei and George Lindbeck. Frei diagnosed the Enlightenment's concern for whether the Bible's "realistic narrative" was historical, a problem that in Frei's opinion had "remained unresolved in the history of biblical interpretation ever since."[57] For his part, Lindbeck acknowledged the gains made by historical criticism, but he also believed that Scripture could be studied in "its own interpretive framework . . . as a whole in its canonical unity." When asking what holds together the "diverse materials" contained in the Bible (poetic, prophetic, historical, etc.), he answered, "These are all embraced, it would seem, in an over-arching story which has the specific literary features of realistic narrative as exemplified in diverse ways, for example, by certain kinds of parables, novels, and historical accounts."[58] For biblical theology, says Darrell Jodock, this literary emphasis understands that "the narrative form is an indispensable feature of what is being said . . . [and it] is indispensable because the story cannot be reduced to or translated into a proposition without significant loss of meaning."[59] In his own study of the method, George Stroup observed that narrative exists as "a primary genre in Scripture" not only because individuals and communities tend to relate their experience through stories but also because "the faith of Jews and Christians is radically thisworldly and historical."[60]

Biblical theologians themselves have been cautiously optimistic about a method that would approach the Bible as narrative or story, though the verdict is by no means unanimous. Barr carefully distinguishes the biblical "story" from "history" for several reasons, not the least of which is the range of meanings for "history." Moreover, the concept of story should not be confused with history because "the way in which the story is told tells us how the past has been understood in the ancient community."[61] Barr also rejects the criticism "that 'story' is not an adequate term because not all of the Bible is narrative," for the story of any people may contain many nonnarrative literary forms. Having said that, however, Barr denies that narrative is the only form for biblical theology; there are "other modes of expressions: for instance, affirmation, questioning, argument, hypothesis, speculation, comparison, to mention only a few."[62]

Evangelical theologians have been less sanguine about the implications of a method that approaches the Bible as "story," mostly because it seems to carry with it the fictional or mythical nature of the biblical narratives.[63] They feel the rub of what Collins refers to when he says that some conservative Christians "have welcomed the category of 'story' as a means of evading the possibility of disconfirmation to which the history is subject. The freedom from disconfirmation, however, is bought at a price, since it necessarily excludes the possibility of confirmation, too."[64] Other objections have been mounted as well, from the range of nonnarrative genres to the way the category of story "undermines [the Bible's] reference to God and what he has done in and through Jesus Christ."[65] Some evangelicals, however, are more optimistic, finding hope in N. T. Wright's joining of literary, theological, and historical methods. Countering the objections listed above, they contend that "literary and rhetorical methods position biblical scholars well to attend to the biblical story with creative nuance and detail."[66] What we need to ask now is, if this method works, what is the theological content of the biblical story?

The Content of the Biblical Story

In the first volume of a projected three-part Old Testament theology, John Goldingay has offered what he calls a work of "narrative theology," describing the story of the Old Testament as "Israel's gospel." He writes, "Old Testament faith expresses itself initially in a narrative. The main bulk of the Old Testament is a narrative account of Israel's story and of God's involvement with it. Its narrative form corresponds to its substance, and theological reflection on its gospel needs to work with its narrative form."[67] Acknowledging the great variety of elements that make up that story (e.g., promise, deliverance, migration, political division, religious apostasy), Goldingay nevertheless argues that "the Old Testament tells us who God is and who we are through the ongoing story of God's relationship with Israel." Volume 1 goes on to unpack the story by following the canonical order of the primary narrative (Genesis–Kings), but rejecting the view that the Old Testament tells the story of failure, he presses on to consider the postexilic period in Ezra, Nehemiah, and Esther.[68] The theological content of the story is organized from a theocentric perspective, with God as the subject of an active verb, such as "God began" for the creation stories or "God started over" for the postflood narratives.[69] The story approach for biblical narrative will be supplemented with other methods as Goldingay interprets the theological content of the Prophets and the Writings.

Some New Testament theologians have been attracted to the "story" model for biblical-theological reflection. Over against methods that organize New Testament theology thematically or in terms of canonical "blocks of material," Frank Matera believes that "it may be more advisable to employ a narrative approach that discloses the way in which particular writings or blocks of material inscribe the story of Christ and the story of the church into the story of Israel." Matera contends that this model would "need to hear the different and sometimes conflicting ways in which the story is told, for example, as the inbreaking of God's kingdom (the Synoptic Gospels), as the revelation of the Father to the world (the Fourth Gospel)," and others.[70] N. T. Wright's multivolume project works with a three-pronged historical, literary, and theological approach to the New Testament, especially with respect to Jesus and Paul.[71] The literary task for Wright is part of a complex approach to knowledge and reality which holds that "stories form an essential part" of the worldviews that are the framework for all our knowledge of the world.[72] His method for biblical theology requires the "discernment and analysis, at one level or another, of first-century stories and their implications," and the meaning these stories give to events, understood in their historical context, help to uncover what the biblical texts are saying about God.[73]

Recently a group of six scholars led by Marvin Pate published a whole-Bible theology that fits this methodological emphasis, appropriately titled *The Story of Israel: A Biblical Theology*. After describing the story of Israel's disobedience and rejection of the prophets against the background of the Deuteronomistic framework of obedience/blessing and disobedience/curse, they argue that this story "is a pervasive theme throughout the Old Testament, Second Temple (less appropriately labeled 'intertestamental') literature, and the New Testament, allowing for both unity and diversity."[74] The authors structure the story based on the major sections and canonical order of the Bible.[75] Although they devote twice as much material to the New Testament as to the Old, an important feature is their theological interpretation of Second Temple literature that seeks to demonstrate "a thematic bridge" between testaments, namely, "Israel's sin—exile—restoration." This bridge reflects the "refrain [that] runs throughout the biblical canon, encompassing such motifs as people of God, new covenant, promise/fulfillment, wisdom, kingdom of God, gospel, and new creation."[76]

Summary

As we reflect on the above methods, we may affirm their common interest in describing the theological content of the Bible, a goal that all biblical theologians hold as part of their task, even if other methodological factors (such as perspective) take on greater importance for them. Thus, when I tentatively defined biblical theology as identifying and understanding what the Bible says about God, the "what" in that definition was highlighting the *content* that scholars work with in doing biblical theology. Each of the "content" methods have drawn criticism for some actual or potential weakness: doctrinal approaches for importing categories external to the Bible; thematic and topical approaches for leveling the Bible's theological diversity; and the narrative method for needing to clarify historical and theological referents. Even if some criticism misses the mark here or there, the potential problems indicate that biblical-theological method cannot finally avoid dealing with matters other than the ideas themselves or the story itself. We need to address the relationship of diverse concepts or narrative elements to each other and to the whole biblical portrait or story.[77] This issue of relationship was addressed above in Dunn's work on unity and diversity, but now we must turn our attention to fuller treatment of those methods that are more developmental and concerned with the shape and shaping of the biblical text as we have it.

METHODS THAT FOCUS ON THE SHAPE OF THE BIBLE'S THEOLOGICAL WITNESS

The methodological question we highlight here is *how the Bible presents its theology*. The methods that follow are concerned in one way or another with the development of theological views and the forces that went into shaping the Bible's theological witness. Three major expressions of this methodological focus arise in considering the Bible's history of tradition, its nature as authoritative canon, and the diversity of its theological witnesses and communities.

Tradition History

This general category of method has itself developed over the course of the discipline's history, with significant expressions in both the nineteenth and twentieth centuries.

Salvation History Approaches

In chapter 2 we saw how in the mid-nineteenth century J. C. K. von Hofmann advocated the unity of the testaments in one "salvation history" (*Heilsgeschichte*), so that "the Biblical proclamation of salvation originated step by step in the course of Holy History."[78] A number of factors influenced von Hofmann's work, among the most important being Cocceius's idea of progressive revelation in history and the empirical, historical methods he learned from his teacher, Leopold von Ranke.[79] Von Hofmann's theological method was based on the necessity of Christian faith and experience. He forthrightly stated, "The prerequisite of Biblical study is not a theoretical doctrine of inspiration but a belief in Holy Scripture as that which Christians know it to be through experience."[80] With this foundation, he laid out several steps for a correct understanding of each testament, including a knowledge that "the history of the Old Testament is the provisional stage of that salvation which in the New Testament is realized and moves towards its consummation." From there the theologian must (1) "know the facts of this process and their intrinsic connection," (2) "perceive the respective place which each fact occupies in that process," (3) "appraise the typological significance which each fact possesses with reference to the New Testament,"[81] (4) investigate "in what respect is the New Testament witness affected by the fact that it is expressed in terms borrowed from the Old Testament," and (5) determine "in what respect is the meaning of that terminology modified by the fact that it serves to give expression to the New Testament witness."[82] Sensitivity to literary and historical context was one other ingredient in this method, where the interpreter understands "the viewpoint in Holy History from which the narrative has been told" and is able to relate the meaning of a passage for the whole process of salvation.[83]

Von Hofmann's program was not able to reverse the rising tide of idealistic interpretation in the nineteenth century, but the notion of salvation history experienced a rebirth in the neo-orthodox theology of Karl Barth and later in the work of New Testament scholar Oscar Cullmann.[84] Although he distinguished his work from von Hofmann's, Cullmann nevertheless believed the term *Heilsgeschichte* helpfully expresses the fact that "biblical history" is revelatory and redemptive, making it "the heart of all New Testament theology."[85] A key factor that contributes to this view is Cullmann's understanding of "the Christ-event . . . as the temporal *mid-point* of the entire historical process," making the "center of [Christian] proclamation . . . the Christian conception of time and history," especially history as linear rather than circular in nature.[86] As Cullmann developed his approach, he concluded that "salvation history" was similar to "what we call history (*Historie*)" in its character of a related set of events, but "a radical distinction exists between salvation history and history, since salvation history does not have an *uninterrupted* sequence of events. According to New Testament faith, God selects only specific events bound together by a developing connection."[87] Aware of this salvation history, the people of God experience a tension between what God has already accomplished in Christ and what is not yet completed. For Cullmann, biblical interpretation today is closely linked to our having faith in salvation history, thus giving his program a normative application for exegesis, proclamation, and theology in the church.[88] The closest Cullmann comes to setting forth the substance of a New Testament theology of salvation history is in a chapter called "The Main New Testament Types," which in four parts discusses its beginnings with Jesus, followed by developments in primitive Christianity, the letters of Paul, and the Gospel of John.[89]

In terms of biblical-theological method, what a "salvation history" model offers is a focus not only on the theological content of the Bible but also on the structure by which all of the biblical story can be understood. Thus, Cullmann saw much similarity between what he was doing and the tradition-historical methods of Gerhard von Rad.[90] What continues to be the greatest point of contention is the relationship between salvation history and what might be called universal history. The precise nature of their similarities and differences is difficult to explain, but some biblical scholars and theologians still find the categories useful.[91]

Tradition-History Approaches

Gerhard von Rad's impact on twentieth-century biblical theology was enormous. As part of the golden age of that century, von Rad's work offered a compelling alternative to Eichrodt's more systematic and thematic presentation. I have already mentioned several details of his place in biblical theology (see chapter 2), so here I will only highlight a few methodological elements. His two-volume *Old Testament Theology* approaches the Bible not merely with the tools of the historical-critical method; it uses the very notion of historical development as the key to identifying Israel's theology. According to von Rad, the scholar must "interrogate each document . . . as to its specific kerygmatic intentions," but instead of searching for a central theme among these diverse documents, von Rad explored the history of different literary traditions behind the final form of the text to identify "Israel's own explicit assertions about Jahweh." These "explicit assertions" were found in what he termed "confessional formulae," originally brief, historical summaries of Yahweh's actions on Israel's behalf, the oldest being Deuteronomy 26:5–9.[92] Drawing on his ground-breaking study "The Form-Critical Problem of the Hexateuch" (1938), he studied other such formulae (e.g., Josh. 24:2–13; Neh. 9:6–31; as well as poetic elaborations such as Pss. 78, 105, and 136) and thus identified distinct "Sinai" and "exodus" traditions that emphasized, respectively, justice (or law) and redemption (or gospel).[93] These various "confessions" represented Israel's theological reflection at distinct moments in its history, where for example, a prophet might bring together old traditions with his new situation to create "something completely actual and an entity in itself."[94] This "actualizing" function is one of the ways von Rad linked the Old and New Testaments together in promise and fulfillment. When considered as a whole, his theology falls into two main parts: one that deals with "the theology of Israel's historical traditions" and another that covers prophecy.

Von Rad's method returned a sensitivity to the matter of "continuing divine activity in history." And similar to Cullmann's emphasis on time, von Rad claims that by creating "a historical sequence" for God's saving acts, Israel had "broken through to the concept of a linear historical span." But, unlike Cullmann, von Rad was not concerned with actual historical events; rather, he claimed that "in principle Israel's faith is grounded in a *theology of* history."[95] Various criticisms have been leveled at von Rad's method: (1) he seems to privilege the Deuteronomistic historical and theological perspective, finding the most important confessional formulas in Deuteronomy; (2) by placing greater emphasis on the exodus and ancestral traditions, he tends to downplay the role of creation theology in the shape of Old Testament thought; and (3) while he resists the notion of a "center" of Old Testament theology, one could argue that he ultimately replaces Eichrodt's thematic center with his own, namely, history.[96]

Tradition History and the Whole Bible

The far-reaching legacy of von Rad has been picked up and extended by other scholars who see it as a means of connecting the traditioning process of the entire Bible, thus allowing a return to a truly biblical theology. Hartmut Gese and Peter Stuhlmacher share a common methodological vision of the process whereby biblical traditions were eventually formed into their canonical shape and status. For Gese, "the fundamental problem of biblical theology [is] comprehending unity in plurality," and the method that best accounts for and assesses that relationship is one which studies the "preliterary antecedents" of texts, "the development of the text as literature," and "the growth of the text tradition into a corpus embracing the whole." In light of this process, therefore, "the gulf supposedly between the Old and New Testaments does not exist traditio-historically at all, and no dubious bridges are needed to span it." The key historical requirement for this position is that there was "no closed Old Testament prior to the New Testament," which allows for the events of the New Testament to be taking place as the final Old Testament traditioning process occurs.[97] Stuhlmacher shares Gese's basic views about the canonical formation of the testaments, though he differs on other issues, such as the role of historical-critical method and the existence of a theological center to the New Testament.[98] Stuhlmacher emphasizes the legitimacy of "assent" to the theological claims of the Bible, even as one employs a historical approach,[99] but in terms of overall method, New Testament theology cannot be an independent discipline apart from consideration of the Old Testament.[100]

Those who have taken issue with Gese and Stuhlmacher's method—what Hasel called "the formation-of-tradition method"—have not only pointed to the perennial problems of relating the testaments but have also asked whether the New Testament writers thought self-consciously about their use of the Hebrew Scriptures in the way Gese asserts.[101] Then, too, Räisänen criticizes Stuhlmacher for paying "too little attention to the internal differences in the New Testament on the one hand and those between the testaments on the other."[102] Any attempt to develop a complete biblical theology will face the challenge of unity and diversity, but the instinct in these "tradition" methods rightly calls attention to the historical and developmental (i.e., diachronic) dimensions of the Bible's formation. As Dunn writes, "A biblical theology conceived exclusively or even primarily in synchronic terms cannot hope to cope fully with the diverse and changing emphases of the biblical texts whose scriptural force was always context-related to one degree or other."[103] Thus, we are moved again to consider the shape and shaping of the biblical texts as they were received as authoritative Scripture for communities of faith.

Authoritative Canon

I have mentioned the impact of the canonical approaches associated with Brevard Childs and James Sanders as they impinged upon new developments in the discipline and on the relationship of the testaments. Each of these scholars has contributed to biblical-theological reflection through their distinct emphases—Sanders on the process of canonization in faith communities and Childs on the canonical shape as context for biblical theology (see chapter 3). Our attention here will be especially with Childs, insofar as he developed his program through several major publications in the 1980s and 1990s.[104] Since our concern in this chapter is methodological, the main question is how his canonical concerns offer a proposal for doing biblical theology.

Brevard Childs's Canonical Method

Childs's *Biblical Theology of the Old and New Testaments* represents the culmination of his thinking about the canonical approach to the Bible, and thus it will serve as a guide for the discussion that follows. He understands the discipline of biblical theology to embrace both descriptive (including "philosophical, historical, and literary analysis") and normative (addressing "the content testified by the witness") tasks as "two parts of the one enterprise which remain dialogically related." Thus, the primary goal of biblical theology for Childs is "to understand the various voices within the whole Christian Bible, New and Old Testament alike, as a witness to the one Lord Jesus Christ, the selfsame divine reality." To reach this goal, Childs considers it to be "the fundamental task of Biblical Theology . . . to describe the theological functions of the great revelatory events in Israel's history and their subsequent appropriation by the tradition," followed by a description of "the New Testament's witness to God's redemption through Jesus Christ in the context of the early church."[105] This is what Childs means by attending to "the discrete witness" of each testament before addressing unifying elements of the Bible's theology. But as he studies the biblical texts, he does not merely consider the "final form" as one might expect a "canonical" method to do; rather, drawing on von Rad's tradition-historical concepts, Childs seeks to recover "a diachronic dimension within the canonical form," grasping the depth of theological reflection among the different witnesses.[106]

The outline of a biblical theology takes shape first with "the discrete witness of the Old Testament," which follows the tripartite structure of the Hebrew canon: Torah (four chapters), Prophets (Former, five chapters, and Latter, one chapter), and Writings (three chapters).[107] The "discrete witness of the New Testament" is then laid out in a more diachronic, historical order than a canonical one, for example, discussing the early church proclamation and Paul's gospel before the four Gospels. Part of Childs's justification for a different approach to the two testaments is that the "New Testament tradition developed from its primary witness to the exalted Christ which is clearly demonstrated in Paul, to a theological concern to relate the witness to the earthly Jesus with the resurrected Lord."[108] The final stage of the theology is "theological reflection on the Christian Bible," which takes up ten topics or themes, such as "the identity of God" and "God the creator."[109] Before we can begin to assess the strengths and weaknesses of Childs's program, we need to consider more recent attempts to build on his work and write canonical biblical theologies.

Recent Canonical Theologies

Paul R. House's *Old Testament Theology* (1998) works with a primarily canonical approach that is joined to a thematic, book-by-book presentation.[110] House states that "Childs's approach works best when he follows a book-by-book format," since to do otherwise "hampers his efforts to explain the inner structure and vital facets of the canon as it unfolds." He also takes issue with other features of Childs's method, like not equating text with revelation and not giving the Writings significant attention.[111] Thus, House is also attracted to an amended form of Hasel's "multiplex" method but with his own distinctives, such as rejecting any critical reconstruction of the sources behind the Pentateuch but also being open to a type of thematic center. He writes that his book "uses the Old Testament's insistence on the existence and worship of one God as a major, normative, theological and historical emphasis."[112] What results, then, are twenty-four chapters that match the order and numbering of the Hebrew canon, each with a thematic title focused on some aspect of God's activity (e.g., "the God who creates" for Genesis or "the God who saves" for Isaiah) or God's nature (e.g., "God is holy" for Leviticus or "the God who keeps promises" for the book of the twelve minor prophets), though others have a more responsive feel to them, such as "the God who expects faithfulness" (Numbers) and "the God who is worth serving" (Job).

Another canonical approach is Rolf Rendtorff's *The Canonical Hebrew Bible: A Theology of the Old Testament* (2005), which brings to full expression the proposal he presented in *Canon and Theology: Overtures to an Old Testament Theology* (1993). Like Childs, Rendtorff owes much to von Rad's principle of "retelling" for the form of biblical theology, but he also "develops it a step further, not only assuming the canonical basis of the Hebrew Bible but also making the texts themselves, in their present 'canonical' shape, the point of departure for the account."[113] Because modern biblical criticism, in a sense, "lost" the texts in their final form, the "primary task" for Rendtorff is "in allowing the intentions of those who gave the texts their present shape to come into their own."[114] The structure he gives his work, again much like Childs, treats the books in their canonical order by major groups (Pentateuch, Former Prophets, Latter Prophets, and Writings), followed by "themes of the Old Testament," with eighteen chapters of varying length.[115] This second, thematic part is necessary to appreciate those ideas that transcend "the boundaries of the individual books in their contexts," but he treats them in the order they arise in the Bible.[116] In a nutshell, what Rendtorff finds in the basic structure of the three-part Hebrew Bible is that in the Torah "*God acts,*" in the Prophets "*God speaks,*" and in the Writings "*people speak* to God and of God."[117]

A recent New Testament theology by Frank Thielman (2005) represents a variation on the canonical method, as indicated by its subtitle: "a canonical and synthetic approach." Recognizing the importance of both historical and canonical methods, Thielman's goal is "to produce a theology of the New Testament rather than a theological history of early Christianity" and "to describe the theological concerns of each New Testament book, and of the New Testament as a whole, from the perspective of the times and circumstances in which each text was written."[118] Thus, while he treats each book individually (the sole exception is Luke-Acts), he does so in three major groupings— Gospels and Acts, Pauline letters, and non-Pauline letters and Revelation— within which the books are arranged in chronological order and given a thematic title (e.g., "Mark: The Death of God's Son as Good News," or "Galatians: The Grace of God and the Truth of the Gospel"). With this method, Thielman is able to call attention to elements of unity *and* diversity:

> The large measure of common theological ground among the four [Gospels], and between the four and the apostolic witness contained in the rest of the New Testament, shows that their antiquity is matched by their fundamental theological unity. Their diversity attests to the richness of the gospel. It reminds Christians that the gospel is . . . more profound than human schemes to harmonize it and manage it are able to comprehend.[119]

Assessing Canonical Approaches

The amount of literature on various aspects of the canonical approach, especially Childs's distinctive articulation of it, is vast and growing all the time. To do justice to the debate would take a book of its own, but we can at least call attention to some of the arguments that deal especially with methodology. There are clearly many ways in which canonical approaches offer a bold and innovative proposal for integrating historical, literary, and theological interests in a biblical theology.[120] Childs himself sees problems in a positivistic use of historical criticism and thus readily uses a broad range of sources, including "precritical" scholars, in his interpretive work.[121] He almost single-handedly reintroduced into scholarly circles a concern for canonical matters in general (he shares this with James Sanders), and his particular interest in the final shape of the text moved critical methods beyond the source, form, and tradition criticism of the previous decades. Finally, although Childs's confessional interests are much decried by his critics, his understanding of Old Testament theology as a Christian discipline does encourage a dialogue between the Old Testament and Christian theology.

There is no shortage of critics of this method. At least four general areas of concern have been raised. First, some scholars raise a question about the *clarity of the method* itself, that is, what precisely is this method and how does it bring the Bible's theology to bear upon our contemporary settings?[122] Part of the problem here is that Childs has produced several works—commentaries, introductions, and theologies—bearing the "canonical" label but each emphasizing different aspects of his method. In some settings he focuses more on a history of interpretation of texts than on their final, canonical form. His *Biblical Theology of the Old and New Testaments* thus provides two applications of "exegesis in the context of biblical theology" as a way of showing how he handles texts.[123] A second concern deals with the *nature of the final form* and declares "that no concluding final form exists, since the transmission of the oldest manuscripts and the ancient translations shows that many texts were not finally fixed at all, but that there were different versions in circulation."[124] Rendtorff's response to this argument is to downplay the significance of these deviations and stress that "the final form" concept serves mainly as an alternative to some "critical 'reconstruction'" of the text.[125] Such a response then shifts the debate slightly, so that the issue becomes a matter of why one gives more "theological value" to either earlier strands of tradition or later canonical texts.[126] Third, numerous questions are raised about the *confessional nature of this method*, at least as Childs has presented it, as understanding both testaments as a witness to Christ. He has been criticized by people such as Collins, who rejects the approach as a whole, and Goldingay, who acknowledges the value of the final form while denying that the Old Testament serves as a witness to Christ.[127] Francis Watson, for his part, claims that Childs has an idealized picture of the "community of faith and practice" that receives the final form, whereas the reality throughout history regularly reveals "conflict-ridden situations."[128] Finally, some scholars raise an *ideological question*, saying that granting religious authority to the canonical form of the Bible runs aground on those places where there are "gross immoralities" or other objectionable aspects to the biblical text.[129]

The debate over this method is not going away soon, seeing that major works of canonical biblical theology continue to appear. Disagreements over the existence and nature of a final form notwithstanding, broad agreement exists over the writings that Jewish and Christian communities historically accepted as sacred Scripture. And these collections hold together many different voices, themes, and concerns, some of which can be related for their similarities while others resist any unifying force. Thus, Rolf Knierim has stated:

> The canon has finalized the problem. In the process of canonization, authoritative theological traditions from many generations and diverse settings were condensed into close juxtaposition on the same synchronic level. . . . In generating this problem without resolving it, the canon itself calls for the discernment of a theological criterion for the purpose of its own proper theological understanding.[130]

If the canonical method has leaned in the direction of unity, there have been other methods that highlight the diversity.

Diverse Testimony and Witness

Recognizing diversity is nothing new in the modern discipline of biblical theology, or in the long history of theological interpretation for that matter, and attempts to give shape to that diversity were seen especially in the "polarities and tensions" school of thought in works from the late 1970s and early 1980s. In the section on "content" methods just above, I addressed the phenomenon of balanced, thematic pairs, but those proposals did not focus so much on the dynamic and dialectical nature of the tensions as did the works of Claus Westermann, Paul Hanson, Samuel Terrien, and Walter Brueggemann, whom Hasel studies under the category of "thematic-dialectical method."[131] Briefly stated, these authors sought "to move beyond the dominance of a single center, recognizing that no single motif can contain all of the elements."[132] For example, Westermann believes the diversity in the Old Testament can only be expressed in the story of divine action and word, coupled with human response; these "are the elements forming the constant basic structure of this history."[133] Terrien's *The Elusive Presence* (1978) argued that "the motif of divine presence" can account for "historical complexity without ignoring coherence and specificity."[134] However, "presence is a surging which soon vanishes and leaves in its disappearance an absence that has been overcome."[135] For his part, Hanson speaks of twin polarities, one that is "visionary-pragmatic" (or vision-revision) that also can be expressed in terms of "form-reform," with the first half of these poles being more "cosmic" in its vision of reality and the second pole more "teleological" (i.e., temporal and diachronic).[136] Taking his cue from these works, Brueggemann published a pair of articles in 1985 that explored the tension between the common theology of the Old Testament—which legitimated the structure not only of human governance but of divine creation and providence—and "the embrace of pain," which was a "minority voice" represented mainly by laments and protests made to Yahweh.[137] It was out of this sense of necessary tension that Brueggemann began to develop his major proposal for Old Testament theology.

Walter Brueggemann's Method of Testimony

Brueggemann has been a leader in the field of biblical theology for thirty years, always resisting unitary schemes that would drown out voices at the margins, either of Scripture, the church, or society. His theology has sometimes been described as "postmodern" or "nonfoundational,"[138] but Brueggemann is most concerned with a pluralistic community that is capable of hearing the diversity of voices in the Bible.[139] Thus, it is fitting that his massive *Theology of the Old Testament* (1997) moves beyond the bipolar tension of his earlier work to a more complete expression of the diverse forms of testimony in Scripture.[140] Of course, his concern for and openness to the diversity go hand in hand with a rejection of the exclusive use of historical criticism on one hand and an embrace of literary and sociological approaches on the other. In an important move, he therefore chooses to focus only on what the text says about God, apart from any concern with what lies behind the text in the way of ontology (say, the actual existence of the God to whom testimony is given) and historicity (such as confirmation of events).[141] Likening the task of biblical theology to that of assessing testimony in a trial, Brueggemann explains that the only available reality for the court is the testimony given on the stand. The court "cannot go behind the testimony to the event, but must take the testimony as the 'real portrayal.'

Indeed, it is futile for the court to speculate behind the testimony."[142] With this decision in place, Brueggemann uses a literary-theological approach to study "Israel's characteristic speech about God," that is, "the speech to which Israel reverted when circumstance required its most habituated speech." The best examples of this speech occur in full, active verbal sentences, of which Yahweh is the subject bound to "the object—variously, individual persons, Israel, creation, or the nations." Thus, statements like "The LORD has done great things for them" (Ps. 126:2) or "The LORD brought you out from there by strength of hand" (Exod. 13:3), are examples of the primary theological testimony about Yahweh.[143]

Brueggemann's massive work is divided into four parts, which discuss the main types of "characteristic" utterance: (1) Israel's core testimony—describing God's creative and redemptive actions as well as the qualities attributed to God; (2) Israel's countertestimony—like a courtroom cross-examination, these utterances testify to the hiddenness of God and the human experience of pain, evil, and negativity; (3) Israel's unsolicited testimony—here Yahweh is understood always in relation to various partners, especially Israel, but also individuals, the nations, and creation itself; and (4) Israel's embodied testimony—Israel's relationship with Yahweh was concretely mediated through the Torah, the priestly cult, as well as the leadership of king, prophet, and sage. Given this diversity of witnesses, theological tensions are bound to arise within the larger canon of Scripture,[144] and even after the exile there is "no ready convergence of sovereignty and solidarity" in steadfast faithfulness to Israel.[145] Brueggemann concludes his work by reflecting on several issues that challenge the discipline of biblical theology and the way its results might speak to the pressing problems of our time.[146]

Other Diversity Approaches

Erhard Gerstenberger's work clearly stresses theological diversity in the Old Testament. After acknowledging how "the epistemological, social, economic, and gender-specific conditions of our time are so different from those of antiquity" Gerstenberger proceeds to distinguish his approach especially from "canonical" methods.[147] Much like Brueggemann, he is "not so much going behind the written testimonies from the ancient Israelites of those times as attempting as far as possible to recognize the faith that they were practising in their everyday life and social group, in order to be able to enter into conversation with such expressions of faith." Since their actual faith and practice is in view, Gerstenberger welcomes the use of archaeology, particularly the way it may reveal "the counter-voices to the 'official theology' (which never existed as a uniform view)." He thus sets out "to demonstrate the typical ideas of God and the other theological configurations in each of [five] social contexts and to demonstrate their consequences for social ethics": family and clan, village and small town, tribal alliances, the monarchical state, and confessional and parochial communities.[148] His study of the ever widening circles of Israelite society leads Gerstenberger to conclude that "official" religion was never able to completely change "family faith," though conflicts did arise and other societal practices supplemented those of the smaller circles.[149] Again, like Brueggemann, he concludes with a chapter relating the theological insights of the Old Testament in terms of "effects and controversies" in our time.

In New Testament theology, there has been no precise counterpart to Brueggemann's program, but I have mentioned scholars (e.g., Dunn) who have employed methods to ensure the hearing of different voices. G. B. Caird's *New Testament Theology* (1994), completed by L. D. Hurst, aims to hear the diversity of witnesses through his apostolic "conference table approach," somewhat along the lines suggested by a meeting that Paul, Barnabas, Peter, John, and James had in Jerusalem (Gal. 2:1–10).[150] For Caird, the task of writing "a New Testament theology is to preside at a conference of faith and order," with at least the following twelve participants: the four Gospel writers, Paul, the Pastor (i.e., the presbyter of the letters of John), John the seer (i.e., the author of Revelation), and the authors of the books of Hebrews, James, 1 Peter, 2 Peter, and Jude. Although Caird acknowledges difficulties and historical questions about the model, he insists (much like Brueggemann does) that "the past is not accessible to us by direct observation, only through the interrogation of witnesses." Jesus himself, while not participating in the conference, remains the focus, and developing a portrait of him is the goal. "Research must begin with the documents and their theology and arrive only at the end of its course at the teaching of Jesus."[151] If "conference" be the *model* for Caird's theology, "divine salvation" is its *theme*, with the seven main chapters devoted to different aspects of its plan, necessity, experience, and so forth. These insights coalesce—they are not harmonized—in two chapters that study and summarize the "theology of Jesus," since for Caird "the historical Jesus is a deeply theological figure in the same sense as Paul, John, and the others."[152] Jesus is God's appointed agent to fulfill Israel's destiny, but he would also come to be understood "first as the fulfiller of the destiny of the human race, and then, in consequence, as the bearer of a more-than-human authority and the embodiment of a more-than-human wisdom."[153]

Assessing the "Diversity" Approaches

The approach to biblical theology espoused by Brueggemann and others seeks to move beyond the impasse of "unifying theme" versus "history of tradition" but also to offer a constructive alternative to canonical approaches on the matter of theological diversity. Thus, aspects such as countertestimony are not aberrations or mere minority voices; they become a fully integrated part of biblical theology. Brueggemann's structure accounts for Wisdom literature and lament traditions, not as an afterthought or mere human response but as "speech about God" on the same level as the core testimony. Yet another strength of this approach is its use of newer scholarly methods, drawing on sociological and literary analysis for theological insight. Finally, both Brueggemann and Gerstenberger are committed to nonsupersessionist approaches to the Old Testament and oppose any efforts to Christianize Israel's scriptures.

How have the above methods been criticized? For one thing, Brueggemann's emphasis on the exclusive role of speech in biblical theology seems to rule out appeals to extrabiblical "testimony" or "evidence" from history.[154] If one is suspicious of the merits of historical criticism or its positivistic excesses, then this criticism may not matter. But then one may ask whether the trial metaphor is completely apropos insofar as a court does admit nonverbal evidence (e.g., DNA testing or other physical "exhibits") within the context of a witness's testimony.[155] This would not be a problem for Gerstenberger, who is open to artifactual evidence to inform the social setting of Israelite religion. Second, while both Brueggemann and Gerstenberger bracket concern for going "behind the written testimonies," Gerstenberger has a history of religions focus on Israel's practice of the faith or how the social structures influenced Israel's theology. In other words, the ultimate subject matter is the religion of Israel rather than the theological testimony of the Old Testament. A third issue for some scholars is Brueggemann's embrace of postmodernism, particularly whether he consistently holds to its rejection of metanarratives. Collins points out that Brueggemann does not reject all metanarratives on principle but rather sees a conflict between "Israel's Yahwistic construal of reality" and Western society's "military consumerism."[156] Hence, Collins argues that since Brueggemann obviously opts against the modern metanarrative, he "wants to exempt the sacred text from the suspicion to which all other metanarratives are subjected."[157] To be fair, if Brueggemann is inconsistent on application of the metanarrative concept, it seems mainly for the purpose of granting the Old Testament some voice "as *a subversive protest* and as *an alternative act of vision* that invites criticism and transformation."[158] Finally, Brueggemann's understandings of ontology, history, and revelation have been challenged for various reasons. To be sure, Brueggemann in no way denies God's existence or that of ancient Israel, but his tendency to avoid these matters does seem to stand outside of traditional Jewish and Christian biblical interpretation.[159] With respect to revelation the issue is similar. While traditional theology may tend to use "the scholastic categories of inspiration and revelation," these terms were meant to express the mystery that the words of Scripture were of human origin even as they were God's word. But for Brueggemann the main thrust of his assertion that "testimony becomes revelation" is that human imagination establishes the reality of that to which biblical speech points.[160] This understanding does justice to the human element of Scripture but leaves little room for dialogue with systematic theology on the question of whether and how *God* is speaking today.

METHODS THAT FOCUS ON OUR PERSPECTIVES AS READERS OF THE BIBLE

The third methodological focus arises from the perspective of human existence, experience, and social reality. Scholarly contributions in the areas of biblical-theological content or the shape of biblical theology are here joined by those which place the starting point for the task with ourselves: Rudolf Bultmann's anthropological method, feminist and postcolonial theologies, and sociological approaches that assume some analogy between past and present communal existence. In grouping these methods together, I am not suggesting that they share significant theological interests or arrive at similar places when the task is accomplished; those criteria look at the end-product of biblical theology. Rather, because the focus here is on the beginning, the place from which one starts to do biblical theology, these methods open up new possibilities for the discipline. In one way or another, they all go beyond an exclusively historical-critical approach that moves only *from* the Bible and *toward* the reader. Bultmann's focus on existence required him to start with an awareness of the fundamental human condition of anxiety and the need for authenticity. Feminist and postcolonial theologies commence from their experiences of oppression arising from patriarchal or colonial structures and worldviews. Finally, a recent sociological approach considers our life in human community and the connections that makes between our situation and the world of the Bible.

Human Existence

Rudolf Bultmann's Theological Anthropology

Certain features stand out in Bultmann's work, such as his concern for the "variety" of theological thoughts as opposed to their unity, and his focus on the theologies of Paul and John. For Bultmann, the overall purpose of New Testament theology "consists in the unfolding of those ideas by means of which Christian faith makes sure of its own object, basis, and consequences."[161] If this is the goal, we must ask about the specific methodological interests that illustrate his starting point in human existence.[162] In a 1957 essay entitled "Is Exegesis without Presuppositions Possible?" Bultmann answered his question by saying that while we must avoid "presupposing the results of exegesis" at all costs, "no exegesis is without presuppositions, because the exegete is not a *tabula rasa* but approaches the text with specific questions or with a specific way of asking questions and thus has a certain idea of the subject matter with which the text is concerned."[163] For Bultmann, this idea of "the subject matter" meant having a true "life relation" to the text, something he called a "preunderstanding," and existential philosophy offered the best vocabulary for expressing our relationship to the biblical message.[164] Bultmann argued that Martin Heidegger's existential analysis was essentially "the New Testament view of who we are [as] beings existing historically in care for ourselves on the basis of anxiety, ever in the moment of decision between the past and the future, whether we will lose ourselves in the world of what is available and of the 'one,' or whether we will attain our authenticity by surrendering all securities and being unreservedly free for the future." What the New Testament thus declares is that "human beings as such, before and outside of Christ, are not already in their authentic being—in life—but are rather in death."[165]

Since humankind lives in this historical, existential predicament, only a scientific and historical method can be used to ascertain the Bible's theological message for our existence. If the biblical writings are to be understood as "witnesses of faith and proclamation . . . they must first be interpreted historically, because they speak in a strange language, in concepts of a faraway time, of a world picture that is alien to us."[166] At this point Bultmann called on the method of demythologizing, since "the early Christian community thus regarded [Jesus] as a mythological figure," employing language about him as "a great, pre-existent heavenly being who became man" or as "the Son of Man [returning] on the clouds of heaven to bring salvation and damnation as judge of the world." Bultmann believed we should "abandon the mythological conceptions precisely because we want to retain their deeper meaning," and the method of recovering that meaning is what he called "*de-mythologizing*. . . . Its aim is not to eliminate the mythological statements but to interpret them." Demythologizing is not merely a method Bultmann employed to translate the message of the early church for the modern world; "the process of demythologizing began, partially with Paul, and radically with John." Thus, for example, eschatological language about a future return of Christ was, for Paul, no longer merely the expected Parousia but now was "with the resurrection of Christ the decisive event [that] has already happened."[167]

The above description of Bultmann's method is reflected in the arrangement of his New Testament theology on several levels. For one thing, the major emphases on Paul and John make sense in light of their more extensive demythologizing of the proclamation about Christ. A second factor, and related to this first point, is Bultmann's decision to regard "the message of Jesus [as] a presupposition for the theology of the New Testament rather than a part of that theology itself."[168] Not only did Bultmann place less emphasis on the historical Jesus; he had a correspondingly greater emphasis on our historicity, that is, on our place in the present, existential moment. Third, since human existence is the crucial starting point for biblical theology, it is not surprising that Bultmann's major sections on Paul and John deal especially with "anthropological concepts" and the human condition of living in a world under sin, death, and judgment. For example, he develops the significant concept of faith in existential terms when he writes, "'Faith' as man's relation to God also determines man's relation to himself; for human existence, as we have seen, is an existence in which man has a relationship to himself. 'Faith' is the acceptance of the kerygma not as mere cognizance of it and agreement with it but as that genuine obedience to it which includes a new understanding of one's self." Hence, Bultmann can look back on his project in the "Epilogue" and state that he was trying "to interpret the theological thoughts of the New Testament in their connection with the 'act of living'—i.e. as explication of believing self-understanding."[169]

Post-Bultmannian Theological Methods

In chapter 2 I summarized different ways in which New Testament theologians responded to Bultmann in the 1950s and 1960s. Owing to its scope and influence, his work drew critical attention from different groups. Several of his own students (the "post-Bultmannians") as well as so-called right-wing critics challenged Bultmann's views of history, myth, and the role of the historical Jesus in biblical theology. There were also "left-wing" critics who charged that he had "not gone far enough in his program of demythologizing," while still others adopted a "new hermeneutic" focusing less on the human existential condition and more on the "word event" that claims us as hearers of proclamation.[170] No one has produced a New Testament theology that followed Bultmann's methods in all respects, but some, like Herbert Braun, followed his "theological and philosophical content criticism consistently, applying it relentlessly also to the notion of the existence of a 'reified' God 'in himself.'"[171] Braun's affinity to Bultmann's method also appears when he states, "I can speak of God only where I speak of man, and hence anthropologically."[172] On questions of faith, knowledge, and history, Norman Perrin stood with Bultmann over against his critics on the right and left. This "center" position held to a threefold distinction regarding types of knowledge modern people can have toward Jesus Christ: (1) "empirical historical knowledge," which comes from using the tools of critical research and through which we can have some limited knowledge of the historical Jesus; (2) "historic knowledge," which deals with the significance of someone as a historical phenomenon who "speaks to us" and has some existential contact with us; and (3) "faith-knowledge," which arises when the historic knowledge we have of someone's general significance moves to "the level of religious faith, belief or commitment." For Bultmann and Perrin, the object of faith-knowledge is "not the historic Jesus, he is the Christ, the eschatalogical Jesus."[173]

A major work that shares several of Bultmann's theological interests is Hans Conzelmann's *An Outline of the Theology of the New Testament* (1969). In his preface he admits his "indebtedness" to Bultmann for the basic outline of his theology, but he also acknowledges the changing scholarly landscape since Bultmann's work appeared and the resultant need for a "new account." In particular, whereas Bultmann essentially limited discussion of the Synoptic Gospels to the realm of "presuppositions of New Testament theology," Conzelmann devotes a special section to the theology of the Synoptics in their own right. Moreover, to correct the impression that Bultmann's existential interpretations of Pauline and Johannine texts were a "pure distillation" of their theology, Conzelmann emphasizes their historical contexts and how, for instance, Paul's thought "was conditioned by the period in which he lived."[174] The outline of Conzelmann's theology has five main parts: (1) the kerygma of the primitive community and the Hellenistic community, (2) the Synoptic kerygma, (3) the theology of Paul, (4) the development after Paul, and (5) John. The largest and central section on Paul also echoes Bultmann's anthropological categories and his interest in translating mythical categories for today. For example, when Paul speaks of Christ as the "second Adam" over against the "primal man" (Rom. 5:12–21; 1 Cor. 15:21, 45–49), Conzelmann writes, "As a myth it [the primal man] cannot be proclaimed, but only interpreted in existentialist terms. It therefore needs not only correction (which Paul, in fact, makes), but also expansion: Paul must be able to draw the line from the saving event to the preaching."[175]

Assessing Existential Approaches

Bultmann's work deserves to stand alongside the works of Eichrodt and von Rad as part of the golden age of biblical theology, and all the more so seeing that he rose above his contemporaries and predecessors in New Testament theology. For one thing, he endeavored to move beyond the debates of Wrede and Schlatter by integrating historical method with hermeneutical sensitivity in order to achieve both a "true" and a "pure" biblical theology.[176] Bultmann's use of Heidegger's philosophical terminology about human existence was a counterpart to Baur's nineteenth-century use of a philosophical framework for human history.[177] Robert Morgan thus writes, "Baur and Bultmann made themselves philosophical theologians because they wished to interpret the NT theologically, for example, as speaking a truth that invited a religious response. Their theological convictions about the NT demanded philosophical sophistication as well as historical scholarship to express them."[178]

Second, by starting with human existence, Bultmann brought anthropology more fully into biblical theology where it had been hitherto overshadowed by other thematic and historical concerns. He took seriously our existential location as persons confronted by anxiety and uncertainty, who come to Scripture with some kind of "preunderstanding" that makes interpretation possible. As Via describes this hermeneutical circle, "An interpretation will always incorporate the prior understanding that derives from the context of the interpreter's existence. This means that there is no exegesis without presuppositions."[179] A third and closely related strength of Bultmann's method was his determination to face the implications of biblical language. In spite of the criticism his demythologizing program received from several quarters, he at least reckoned with the nature of the biblical language instead of simply assuming that all its categories easily compared to those used in modernity. As Via writes, Bultmann's definition of myth "delineates or distinguishes myth from other kinds of symbolic language and shows that myth in essence undermines the transcendence of God."[180]

Bultmann's theological method has been the subject of scrutiny for decades, and over this time scholars have raised several concerns. First, they have criticized the structure of his New Testament theology in that it focused most of the attention on Paul and John and comparatively little on the Gospels and the historical Jesus.[181] Whether one interprets his emphases as "a significant shortfall" of a theology of all the New Testament books, or as "a bit thin and . . . unlikely to satisfy other Christians whose faith depended more on the Synoptic Gospels," Bultmann's successors (such as Kümmel and Conzelmann) were determined to include the theology of the Synoptics in their work.[182] Second, for all of Bultmann's embrace of historical-critical method, his stress upon how the kerygma addresses us in our existential situation tended to downplay history.[183] But the problem here is more than a matter of choice or emphasis; it points to an "almost complete silence of the *Theology* with respect to details of situation of New Testament writers and audiences, particularly as to contextual problems and responses."[184] This oversight goes hand in hand with Bultmann's narrow view of Judaism, which Räisänen describes as "a vicious caricature [that] causes his New Testament theology to be incurably lop-sided."[185] And when we consider Bultmann's low view of the Old Testament (see chap. 3), one can see why Francis Watson speaks of Bultmann's "neo-Marcionite position."[186]

Third, several scholars have criticized the anthropological and existential approach to the Bible as preoccupied with the individual instead of the communal, the spiritual instead of the political.[187] In surveying representative critiques of this individualism, Via suggests that "the emphasis on the individual must give way to an emphasis on the social group . . . [and] the hermeneutical vantage point for interpreting the New Testament should be sociopolitical as well as philosophical (existentialist)."[188] Finally, Bultmann's particular handling of mythological language came under fire from theologians who saw it as "narrowing the witness of the NT writers by an interpretation that eliminated (contrary to Bultmann's stated intentions) essential dimensions of the theology contained in the mythical language."[189] In like manner, Bultmann's appeal to what represents the "modern" scientific view of the world also speaks more for his early to mid-twentieth-century setting and could possibly be informed by more postmodern understandings of science.[190] The recent literary methods have given us a renewed appreciation for story, symbol, and myth on their own terms, without having to set them aside for some "pure" meaning.[191]

Human Experience

Contemporary biblical theology has many practitioners whose methods presuppose a necessary starting point in human experience, that is, in the complex interaction of an individual's and society's languages, history, cultural heritage, and so forth. In chapters 2 and 3 I surveyed the phenomenon of and issues raised by new participants in the field of biblical theology, especially feminist and postcolonial scholars, and I highlighted their preference for experiential approaches to Scripture. When we consider the category of experience as it pertains to method, however, a number of factors complicate a typology of these approaches. First, it seems to be a characteristic of more recent work in biblical theology that an individual scholar might employ several methods to discern the message of Scripture, and given the diversity within the new perspectives themselves, there simply is no single method that typifies a feminist or postcolonial engagement with the biblical text. A second factor arises from their methodological relationship to postmodernism. These scholars tend to think of knowledge as "perspectival, relational, contingent, engaged—not, even as a desirable ideal, simply a matter of a knowing self 'in here' disinterestedly laying hold of an external object 'out there.'"[192] But while they appreciate the insights of postmodernism, they do so for different reasons, being attracted to its critiques of foundationalism, historicism, colonialism, or various forms of hegemony in the church, the academy, or society at large. Third, "human experience" perspectives have different understandings of biblical authority, which means that they may wish either to hear how the Bible speaks to their experience or to learn how certain readings of the Bible empower them to critique oppressive social structures within and outside of the Bible. Fourth, the methods I will mention are not unique to the newer, experiential perspectives. To a greater or lesser degree, they have all been used by scholars who see themselves as representative of traditional forms of biblical theology. For all of these reasons, therefore, I will simply offer a few examples of some of the methods used by scholars who begin their work from the standpoint of their experience.

Literary-Critical Methods

The field of literary criticism is multifaceted and has been surveyed in a number of excellent works that reveal its broad appeal in many corners of academic biblical studies.[193] Literary criticism has contributed enormously to biblical theology over the past thirty years, such that a major project like Brueggemann's Old Testament theology can make rhetorical criticism a centerpiece of its method.[194] But given the fact that biblical scholars apply the term "literary criticism" to a variety of methods, finding a precise definition can be challenging. Robert Alter provides a helpful description in his now classic book *The Art of Biblical Narrative*:

> By literary analysis I mean the manifold varieties of minutely discriminating attention to the artful use of language, to the shifting play of ideas, conventions, tone, imagery, syntax, narrative viewpoint, compositional units, and much else; the kind of disciplined attention, in other words, which through a whole spectrum of critical approaches has illuminated, for example, the poetry of Dante, the plays of Shakespeare, and the novels of Tolstoy.[195]

Thus, one of the features that makes literary criticism attractive to a wide variety of perspectives is its accessibility and adaptability. Readers can draw on their experience studying other works of literature besides the Bible and on that basis begin to make connections with the biblical text. By using the kinds of "close reading" techniques mentioned by Alter, people bringing fresh perspectives and experiences to bear upon biblical interpretation can gain new theological insights into the text.

Phyllis Trible's practice of rhetorical criticism represents a consistent application of literary methods from a feminist perspective. Her approach understands biblical texts to exist as "an organic unity (form-content)," since biblical literature is never a set of ideas separated from their literary form; nor do forms exist in some abstract sense but always with their content. For this reason, rhetorical criticism necessarily attends to "the very words, phrases, sentences, and larger units" of the biblical text. Moreover, rhetorical criticism generally "begins and ends with the final form of a text, though it is not limited to that form" but may consider the literary and tradition-historical developments behind the form. As Trible approaches the Bible to ascertain its meaning, she is not so much looking merely for the intention of the original author but understands that "the total act of communication" also involves the reader and the text itself. She prefers "a text-centered" approach wherein the "reader holds responsibility for articulating the meaning, an activity that happens in the presence of other readers (friends, foes, and foils) and other texts." In terms of specific things to look for in any biblical passage, Trible lists these: beginnings and endings of passages, repetitions of words and phrases, narration and dialogue, overall structure of a passage, the development of plot, the portrayal of characters, syntax, and particles such as conjunctions.[196]

Although Trible has not written a comprehensive work of biblical theology, she has applied this method to numerous biblical passages and books (e.g., the creation narratives in Genesis 1–3, the book of Jonah, and "texts of terror" in Old Testament narrative). Along with these, her programmatic essay "Five Loaves and Two Fishes: Feminist Hermeneutics and Biblical Theology" (1989) envisions doing exegesis of "neglected texts and reinterpreting familiar ones" as the foundation of a feminist biblical theology. The second stage would try to articulate the theological "contours and content" by focusing "upon the phenomenon of gender and sex in the articulation of faith." She states six proposals for a feminist biblical theology that develops this focus: (1) begin with the canonical text, at Genesis 1–3, and how "creation theology undercuts patriarchy," (2) working off this base, "the presence or absence of the female in Scripture" would be studied, (3) "Israelite folk religion would become a subject for theological reflection," (4) consider language for God in an effort to expose idolatry, (5) "recognize that, although the text cannot mean everything, or anything, it can mean more and other than tradition has allowed," (6) "wrestle with models and meanings for authority."[197] These proposals bring us full circle to the starting point of experience, for one can see how the issue of women's experience of patriarchy forms the conceptual frame of reference for this biblical theology.

Literary approaches have also become an important part of New Testament theology, as we saw particularly in N. T. Wright's method of relating history and theology to the literary character of the biblical story.[198] This threefold approach does not seek theological content through literary analysis alone, since as Robert Morgan observes, "there is nothing inherently theological about literary study of religious literature, such as the Bible. In fact it is quite likely to be less theological than historical study, because it is usually less interested in the original authors and their subject matter." Nevertheless, Morgan goes on to acknowledge that "these new approaches offer new possibilities for [New Testament theology] because some literary theories about reading are similar to some Christian belief in how the revelation of God in Jesus Christ is mediated through biblical literature." Moreover, he believes that "the literary frame of reference . . . is hospitable to a greater variety of plausible readings of the biblical text than historical study, and so maximizes the possibilities for [New Testament theology]."[199]

If there has been criticism of literary methods in biblical theology, it has often turned on the danger of readings with no relation whatsoever to historical context or theological content. With respect to history, Leo Perdue expresses concern over the lack of "distanciation" that can exist if one reads the Bible as literature completely apart from its historical context. While clearly not dismissing literary methods, Perdue states, "In any theological enterprise, there needs to be a detailed explication of the world and community of the implied audiences of the texts. In doing this, dialogical interaction with the narrative worlds of the Bible would be facilitated." Like Wright, Perdue sees no fundamental conflict between literary and historical analysis; by doing both well, one can gain "entrance into the linguistic worlds of the Bible . . . leading to the intersection of life and faith."[200] A second challenge is the relation of literary methods to theology, as Morgan observed above. John R. Donahue writes, "The new literary criticism has been a detour along the way of New Testament theology since its practitioners often are reluctant to move from questions of structure and form to questions of theological meaning." But while pointing to problems of literary "skepticism" or a focus only on "the autonomous world of the text," Donahue believes that literary methods are "a necessary step toward theological reflection" and can lead us to "the threshold of new theological constructs."[201] Along these lines Francis Watson sees important points of contact between literary approaches and theological interpretation: a common interest in the "final form"of the text, the desire to integrate "the parts of a text into the whole in which they are embedded," and "a critical awareness of the structure of the act of reading or interpretation itself," thus allowing for the insights of a community's history of interpretation.[202]

In other words, while literary methods may allow one to avoid historical context or theological content, there is nothing inherently antithetical in the relationship of these three aspects of biblical study. Indeed, reading biblical literature *as literature* seems both unavoidable and absolutely necessary to ascertaining any theological message it may yield. Different faith and academic communities will handle the intersection of history, literature, and theology according to different commitments and sensibilities. They will also negotiate matters of biblical authority and the balance between descriptive and normative aspects of biblical theology. Those who privilege their experience as a starting point for the journey will continue to bring to that intersection distinctive ways of understanding both the task and the goal of biblical theology.

Historical Methods

In the introduction to this chapter I made a disclaimer about the broad use of historical methods among biblical theologians, such that no one approach deserved to be called "historical." In singling it out for attention now, I am merely pointing to the fact that historical concerns are not antithetical to the newer, experiential perspectives, and that the latter do not necessarily take refuge in imaginative literary readings that appeal only to their own, inner rationality. For all of its limitations debated in the previous chapter, the historical-critical method has been used by some feminist theologians to interpret what the biblical texts may reveal about the social conditions of ancient Israel or the early church. Two prominent examples are the works of Carol Meyers and Elisabeth Schüssler Fiorenza.

In her book *Discovering Eve: Ancient Israelite Women in Context* (1988), Meyers builds on archaeological and sociological studies of Iron Age Israelite highland villages to argue that in those settings "males may appear autonomous, but in fact can no more act or survive on their own than can females."[203] Meyers's study of Genesis 2–3 leads her to see Eve as a symbol for "Everywoman" in ancient Israel, a character who represents all the concerns for daily life and sustenance in the Israelite highlands. Of particular interest are the words of judgment in Genesis 3:16, which she interprets as being more about pregnancies and agricultural work needed to sustain the society than implying any mandate of women's submission to men.[204] Thus, she states, "Genesis 3, as a wisdom tale, addresses the conditions to which the highland settlers had to adapt. It deals with elementary questions about life and its hardships, about the endless and unremitting efforts it requires." By integrating biblical exegesis with sociohistorical research, therefore, Meyers proposes that the Genesis narratives basically present a portrait of gender equality in which men and women worked hard to survive.[205] The texts of the Bible may be androcentric, but they reveal an egalitarian household for early Israel.

Elisabeth Schüssler Fiorenza has worked along a parallel track insofar as she has investigated the New Testament documents and other writings "to explore the problem of women's historical agency in ancient Christianity in light of the theological and historical questions raised by the feminist movements in society and church and to do so in terms of critical biblical studies." Her 1983 work *In Memory of Her: A Feminist Theological Reconstruction of Christian Origins* set as its goal "to reconstruct early Christian history as women's history in order not only to restore women's stories to early Christian history but also to reclaim this history as the history of women and men." For Schüssler Fiorenza this task "requires a feminist hermeneutics that shares in the critical methods and impulses of historical scholarship on the one hand and in the theological goals of liberation theologies on the other hand."[206] To be sure, she denies that historical research can ever tell us "what the text meant" or provide "an accurate description, objective reflection, and value-free report of the past"; instead her work is truly one of *reconstruction* that depends a great deal on the rhetorical qualities of the biblical text.[207] Her work thus proceeds to study "the Jesus movement" (focused mainly on Jesus' proclamation of the kingdom), "the early Christian missionary movement" (a study of house churches and their missionary call to service in the Spirit), "Pauline modifications" to the vision of women and men serving in a "discipleship of equals," "the patriarchal order in the household," and the question of ministry within a patriarchal church. From this study, Schüssler Fiorenza concludes that early Christian communities practiced an equality of men and women in leadership, prophetic teaching, and matters of marriage. Based on this analysis, Scripture can speak normatively "as a resource in the liberation struggle of women and other 'subordinated' people" only when it is interpreted using feminist hermeneutics.[208]

There is no need here to rehearse all the strengths and weaknesses of historical method, but what can be said is that the work of feminist scholars such as Meyers and Schüssler Fiorenza reveals a joining of more traditional historical tools with insights from sociology or hermeneutics, respectively. Historical approaches that begin with and are informed by women's experience make their most valuable contribution, methodologically speaking, by raising questions about the place of women in Israelite society or early Christian community. This initiative, as Phyllis Bird points out, "exposes a defect in traditional historiography," which typically neglected women's roles and focused on the activities of men in the Bible. The aim, therefore, is not merely to add "a new chapter on women" but rather to undertake reconstructions of the history in order to discover the roles of men and women in relation to each other, not in isolation from each other.[209]

Acknowledging the necessity of these questions, however, still calls for a consideration of *how* one "reconstructs" various aspects of society in antiquity. Scholars will still have to relate methodological presuppositions to the range of interpretations that biblical texts seem able to sustain. In assessing Meyers's work, John Collins writes that she "relies to a great degree on sociological and anthropological studies of peasant and 'frontier' societies that are assumed to be comparable to ancient Israel. There is always some doubt as to whether the society in question is the appropriate background for a particular biblical text." He goes on to state that her translation and interpretation of Genesis 3:16 seem "unduly dependent on her hypothesis that the story reflects life in the highland settlements."[210] Likewise, with respect to Schüssler Fiorenza's understanding of the original Jesus movement's preference for "Sophia-God" in the Q traditions, Francis Watson claims that not only are the references she uses based on "the hypothesis of Q," but that there are still more references to God as Father than to Sophia in the Gospels.[211] The details of any proposed historical reconstruction will be debated, but the method—in use since the advent of the history of religions school—will not be abandoned in the near future in spite of the challenges. Every new piece of linguistic or material data will be sifted for what it might imply about the past, and biblical theologians will keep asking about the theological content of texts in relation to each reconstruction.

Ideological Criticism

Among the newer methods in biblical studies at large is ideological criticism, an aspect of "the sociology of knowledge, which engages in the analytical assessment of philosophies and their epistemologies." I have already mentioned the debate over where ideologies are embedded (in texts, in authors of texts, or in both?), but regardless of where scholars locate them, the concept to which they are referring presupposes that "all understandings and views have developed out of human experiences of life and the interests of the self or group to which one belongs."[212] Thus, some biblical scholars ask questions about what the texts reveal about the society that produced them and how those who produced them were seeking to maintain or challenge prevailing views, customs, and structures.

Womanist theologian Renita J. Weems did not explicitly aim to write a work solely of ideological criticism, but she does probe how aspects of Israelite prophecy perpetuated the abuse of women. Weems's book *Battered Love: Marriage, Sex, and Violence in the Hebrew Prophets* (1995), though not a complete biblical theology, exemplifies a theological method for studying how the prophets use marriage as a metaphor for God's judgment on Israel (see, e.g., Hos. 1–3). Building on historical and literary study of the marriage metaphor, Weems explores the metaphor's power in order "to illuminate the relationship between biblical literature and its social setting."[213] As the prophets politicized "women, sex, and marriage" in their speeches, they integrated "three separate but interrelated commentaries on Israelite society: the social world of Israel, the political fortunes of Israel, and the religious life of Israel." Using marriage as "a trope for contemplating God's power and Israel's punishment," the prophets' repeated correlation between "divine judgment and husbands battering their wives is haunting and telling. It suggests that as far back as the days of biblical writings women in love were women in trouble."[214] The upshot of Weems's argument is that such metaphors would not work effectively unless they reflected reality and fit "with a web of emotional, social, political, historical, institutional data." The prophetic message would resonate with men's expectations for the behavior of their wives and with their desire not to be perceived as adulterous or unfaithful.[215]

Postcolonial biblical scholars are much more explicit in their critique of ideologies, though as we have seen there is considerable variety among the types and concerns of postcolonial biblical interpreters. Sometimes these scholars will "draw attention to the inescapable effects of colonization and colonial ide-

ologies on interpretive works such as commentarial writings, and on historical and administrative records which helped to (re)inscribe colonial ideologies
and consolidate the colonial presence."[216] A study by Samuel Rayan, for example, looked at how many European commentaries written between 1850 and
1980 treated the story of Jesus being asked about paying taxes to the imperial
Roman government (Matt 22:15–22). Those commentaries written during the
time of colonial rule tended to take "an anti-Zealot and pro-Roman position
which endorsed Caesar's rule and Jewish subjugation and, by extension, legit-
imized the then current colonial rule and supported the tax demands of the
ruling authorities." Conversely, those commentaries written after colonial rule
had passed avoided political interpretations and studied the narrative for its
personal, moral application, particularly seeing it as reflecting a post-70 CE
milieu where followers of Jesus "were encouraged to dissociate from political
and revolutionary causes and to pay their respects and taxes to the state authorities, who were appointed by God as an instrument to defeat evil."[217]

Postcolonial scholars, however, can also critique the way some Third World
theologians continue to use Western methods to interpret the Bible on behalf
of indigenous peoples. In other words, says R. S. Sugirtharajah, their works
"are based on and rework Western reading methods."[218] According to Wonil
Kim, minjung theology's appropriation of the exodus narrative works with
"the methodological primacy of history, event, and narrative over conceptual
analysis," an approach Kim labels as typical of Western rather than Korean
hermeneutics.[219] He charges that "just as Korean Marxists do not give a second
thought to the fact that Marx was German or Bolsheviks were Russian, Minjung theologians do not consider it problematic that their methodology of biblical interpretation depends so heavily on that of the West." But their attraction
to the liberating narrative of the exodus "unwittingly sidesteps the history,
event, and narrative of the impending plight of the other 'Minjung'; on the
other side of the Reed Sea." Thus, Kim calls for us to "keep searching for the
God of Minjung in, through, and beyond the god of the Exodus, and that we
search for that God dialectically in, among many other places, the Bible."[220]

The next few decades will provide a setting for long-term evaluation of the
methods and results of postcolonial criticism, especially if these scholars produce comprehensive works of Old Testament, New Testament, or biblical theology. The field of biblical theology should continue to debate the meaning
and function of ideological criticism. There is potential to go beyond the
charge that every scholarly presupposition or method is ideological to the
core, if such charges are not used to end all debate but rather to advance it by
asking *how* our self-interest influences our theological interpretation.[221] Getting to this point does not, by any means, settle the differences between perspectives. In a recent article, Jacqueline Lapsley refers to a conference of

Reformed scholars in South Africa at which a discussion arose over interpretations of the tower of Babel narrative in Genesis 11. When an American scholar interpreted the account as divine support for cultural diversity, this was countered by some South African scholars who "observed that a very similar interpretation of that text was one of the central biblical foundations for apartheid[,] . . . [that] Gen 11 teaches that God does not want different cultural and linguistic groups to live together." The incident highlighted the way "that the interpreter's cultural context (American concern for diversity; South African concern for unity) is crucial for making interpretive judgments." Lapsley proposes that not only do we need to ask how interpretations explain biblical texts and how cultural context leads to different interpretations but that we also need to ask, "How might specifically theological reflection help the exegete to interpret Scripture better?" The story of Balaam, to which Lapsley refers, points to important principles of doing biblical theology: shunning any self-serving interpretation while at the same time grasping the larger context of God's work of creation and redemption.[222] These important steps of the process must also be accompanied by the hard work of wrestling with those portions of the story (such as the impending destruction of the peoples of Canaan) that move some readers to distrust the very God whose story is recounted in Scripture.

A Social-Communal Approach

The appeal to and use of sociological methods to discern the theology of the Bible has already been seen in those approaches that focused on the diversity of witnesses (e.g., Gerstenberger). As we complete our survey of methods that highlight our perspective as readers, however, we need to acknowledge a recent application of sociotheological method in the work of Philip Esler. His *New Testament Theology: Communion and Community* (2005) is not a "theology" in the traditional sense but rather a proposal of an "entirely different model for New Testament theology," one that is inspired by, among other intellectual currents, social identity theory. Esler's goal is "to promote a specifically Christian rationale for reading the New Testament that is related to its role in speaking of God's ongoing relationship with human beings and with the cosmos." In order to avoid the problems that arise with strictly thematic or doctrinal methods of study, his approach appeals to the "oral and dialogical character of communication" such that Christians today may "engage with the authors of these [biblical] texts on an interpersonal and intersubjective basis that involves hearing their voices as much as reading their words."[223] Thus, Esler's project is at its heart ecclesiological, not in the sense of being one locus among several in systematic theology, but rather as the indispensable context for and means of doing New Testament theology.[224] Among the theoretical foundations of Esler's method are Martin Buber's ideas of interpersonal communication and Schleiermacher's understanding of the dialogical character of communication.[225]

This framework prepares the way for Esler's study of early Christian fellowship as members of the body of Christ and how Christians today may in some real way share that communion through the New Testament writings. Chapters 8–10 form the core of his theological presentation of "the communion of the saints": its biblical and doctrinal origins and development (chap. 8); various models for understanding this communion, such as "collective memory theories" (chap. 9); and Esler's rationale for adopting a form of "integrative dualism" as an explanation for existence after death in an intermediate state (chap. 10). For him, communion of the saints means "that (1) the New Testament authors are alive with God and, in an important sense, with us in the period preceding the parousia and the resurrection of the just, and that (2) in reading their works we engage in not just ethical, symbolic, or anamnetic communion, but in actual communion with them." We experience this communion in and through the writings of the New Testament canon, not in Childs's sense—which Esler takes to obliterate "the personal presence and memory" of the ones who wrote the biblical documents—but rather in Bakhtin's sense of dialogical truth. "To introduce the canon into the discussion reminds us of the rich plurality of voices with whom this process is possible and compels us to attend to issues that flow from their unmerged but nevertheless combined coexistence."[226]

Esler's innovative method holds much promise, as his brief application to Paul's letter to the Romans shows (chap. 12). There are several benefits from this approach, perhaps first and foremost among them being the rightful establishment of community, with all its implications for communication and communion, as a major element of biblical theology. In other words, while most of the above models in this chapter implicitly assume or explicitly acknowledge the social context of biblical interpretation, Esler has proposed and worked out a thoroughgoing integration of such context. A second strength of this method is its determination to hold on to the integrity of the original historical particularities of biblical literature while also appreciating their canonical form as Scripture for faith communities. As Esler writes, "We wish to understand [the New Testament authors] in their otherness, perceiving their horizon where it should be, separate from ours, with a separation that persists in spite of our conversation." Third, his emphasis on the dialogic nature of communication and truth, à la Bakhtin, is one way to measure the diversity of voices within Scripture without erasing the comm-*unity* that holds text and readers together.[227]

Until there is a more complete application of this method to the biblical canon, we will be unable to assess its workability, but there are a few questions that might be raised about the project. For one thing, while it is Esler's sole purpose to reestablish the ecclesial context for biblical theology, one senses early on a mild disparagement of systematic theology. The weaknesses of Gabler's distinctions notwithstanding, it does not seem necessary to lessen the connections systematic theology has with biblical theology in order to support an ecclesiological approach. Both theological disciplines—biblical and systematic—may be in service of faith and academic communities. Second, finding his discussion of Christian communion and the New Testament compelling, I was moved to ask how this method might apply to the Christian practice of Old Testament theology. All other things being equal, would Esler's method only serve Jewish theological engagement through "communion" with the authors of the Hebrew Bible? Do Christians have a right to claim the same sort of communion with the "saints" of the Old Testament as they do with the New? Finally, given Esler's explicit purpose to bring the contemporary Christian community into conversation with the Bible, some will surely charge that faith convictions will influence the results of Esler's otherwise critical and historical exegesis. In a recent article, Michael V. Fox declares, "Faith-based Bible study is not part of scholarship even if some of its postulates turn out to be true." He continues, "The best thing for Bible appreciation is secular, academic, religiously-neutral hermeneutic."[228] That position is difficult to reconcile with Esler's project in spite of the latter's nuanced theoretical position. Of course, Fox's position is grounded in its own "community" that seeks to know the intent of the biblical authors. It is of the very essence of our methodological survey to recognize that students of the discipline will have to make choices as to which perspectives and communities offer readings of Scripture that seem most consistent with its content, context, and intention.

CONCLUSION

My previous paragraph may have presented alternatives more starkly than necessary, for a great many biblical theologians wish to write on behalf of academic and faith communities, trusting that there is no final contradiction between the two endeavors. But more to the point for this chapter, one might also wish to seek the very best insights of each method in order to fashion some kind of "multiplex" approach, to borrow Hasel's term. There is certainly some merit in this sentiment, and one of the goals in this chapter was to distinguish the special emphases or contributions of scholarly methods, not to deny their compatibility. The "experience" perspectives themselves revealed an appreciation for the same kinds of approaches discussed much earlier in the chapter. Having said that, however, we should not smooth over differences too quickly. Agreeing with Leo Perdue, Burke Long has written that "biblical theology has a future, but only insofar as it can recognize pluralism *within* (the diversity of biblical traditions, the contestatory construction of the canon, the history of pluriform interpretations of the Bible) and pluralism *without* (the increasingly interconnected world of not always reconcilable methods of biblical criticism and its social locations)." However, Long takes issue with Perdue, not for the latter's openness to methods at the margins, but for his "prescribing the terms for conversation and limiting its potential for irreconcilable differences."[229] It does seem reasonable, however, that not every aspect of a method or perspective will be irreconcilable with all others. Distinctions can and should be made between areas of greater and lesser compatibility. Perhaps some positions in biblical theology are irreconcilable, but there will always be lessons we can learn from the insights and methods of others, no matter how different from our own they may be.

5

The Themes Developed
through Biblical Theology

Our encounter with the history, issues, and methods of biblical theology leads us now to consider the themes that arise from theological interpretation of the Bible. Although this is the last major chapter, the real journey of this book is only beginning, since the ultimate goal of biblical theology is not merely to talk about its history, issues, and methods—as vital as these areas are—but rather to read and engage the biblical text itself and draw some conclusions about its theological subject matter. In one sense, of course, there is no final destination when one is doing biblical theology; the conclusions we draw are tentative for several reasons, not the least of which is that we continue to grow in our knowledge of the Bible and of the manifold ways that people have interpreted it. In another sense, however, scholars should try to make their conclusions about the Bible's theology as clear and as sound as possible, in order to facilitate substantive conversation with other theological disciplines as well as to provide resources for those who see a legitimate place for normative applications to contemporary contexts. Thus, whether one understands biblical theology as the foundation of a doctrinal and confessional theology for particular faith traditions or one wants to address pressing matters in national or global communities, encountering the themes of biblical theology is both a serious and exciting enterprise. But before we begin this encounter, we should address the difficulty of organizing the content of the Bible's theology.

THE CHALLENGE OF ARRANGING THE THEMES

All of the preceding chapters have hinted, in one way or another, at the challenges that beset any attempt to order the contents of biblical theology, but here

169

we may briefly identify at least three major problems that arose in those sections and how we might respond to them.[1] First, the sheer number and diversity of themes that biblical theologians have identified and discussed makes it difficult to do justice to the breadth and depth of the Bible's theology. Even if one limited the scope only to the proposed "centers" or major themes, the amount of material would be quite large indeed. In a book of this type, of course, limits must be placed on the thematic subject matter, but an arrangement should be chosen that will embrace the most frequent and important themes. Second, the multiplicity of methods also affects the choice and arrangement of themes. I previously discussed the strengths and weaknesses of the three major types of methods (content, shape, and perspective) and found that all of them offered some valuable insight for the question of organization. Biblical theology aims to identify and understand the theological subject matter of Scripture, but it is necessary to be sensitive to the distinctive historical and canonical shape it was given. Then, too, several contemporary perspectives offer new ways to interpret biblical themes in light of the influences that led to their scriptural presentation. Third, the relationship of the testaments becomes acute when we address biblical themes, because very important categories do not easily carry over between the Old and the New Testaments. For example, the messianic identity of Jesus, the nature of the resurrection, and the worldwide scope of the church's mission are significant in the New Testament message, but where should they be considered in relation to Old Testament themes? Moreover, a biblical theology in a Christian context seeks to apprehend the "discrete witness" of each testament before seeking connections between Old and New.

In light of these challenges, I set forth the following principles of organization. First, with a great many scholars, I believe biblical theology should endeavor to understand the relationship of diverse themes to each other. This leads me to identify some major rubrics for the presentation and not merely list a dozen or more different themes. Second, in order to name these major rubrics, I build on the three major methodological approaches and reflect their emphases. A concern for the *content* of biblical theology leads to a focus first and foremost on the God to whom biblical testimony is given. Many of the biblical theologies we studied call attention to the Bible's statements about God's character, words, actions, and ways with creation. Next, appreciating the diverse influences that shape the biblical witness calls us to focus on the *developmental aspect* of humankind's relationship with God. And then, the emphasis on *context and perspective* suggests the horizontal plane, namely, our relationship with other human beings. Third, since thematic approaches have been accused of disregarding important historical and canonical concerns, I generally discuss the themes with an eye toward their development in time or in the canon, especially distinguishing the Old and New Testaments. Finally, the major rubrics should reflect some significant theological interests of each testament and, for Christians, of the whole Bible. I have chosen the two great commandments—love of God and neighbor—which are set forth early in the Old Testament and reaffirmed in the New Testament. They reflect the basic vertical and horizontal dimensions of the Ten Commandments and are both dynamic rather than static ideas. These dimensions dovetail with the three methodological interests, to form the following thematic outline.

The God attested in biblical theology	God is: the character of God God speaks: the words of God God acts: the works of God
Living in relationship with God	Through history and story Through creation and covenant Through worship and life
Living in relationship with human beings	Nation and nations Need and justice Community and calling

THE GOD ATTESTED IN BIBLICAL THEOLOGY

We begin here because God is "the primal subject" of biblical theology.[2] Even when one includes New Testament theology's emphasis on Jesus Christ as "the image of the invisible God" (Col. 1:15) and "the reflection of God's glory and the exact imprint of God's very being" (Heb. 1:3), the ultimate referent remains the God whom Jesus makes known. It is thus appropriate to unfold what Paul House calls "a definite portrait of God" by summarizing the main themes of the biblical witness to God.[3] The discussion below makes a systematic move—separating out for the moment certain observations about God's being and attributes—but acknowledges with many scholars that the biblical witnesses do not present a divine portrait apart from God's words and actions.[4] Even so, biblical theology has as part of its task the relationship of these different statements, creating legitimate space for naming some general divine characteristics that grow out of the portrait of God's speaking and acting.

God Is: The Character of God

This first section briefly comments on God's existence and a few of the many qualities or characteristics attributed to the person of God. Of course, the

Bible's witness to God's existence is so fundamental that every statement made about God necessarily assumes and affirms divine reality. It is nevertheless necessary to begin here because the content of this witness does more than lay a foundation for everything that follows; it highlights from the start one of the crucial differences between the Old and New Testament's language about God, causing us immediately to confront the matter of New Testament theology's distinct understanding of God.

Old Testament Witness: Yahweh Is the One and Only Living God

As the subject of the first sentence of the Bible, God ("Elohim") becomes and continues to be the main character of the biblical drama. The exclusive use of Elohim as the divine title in Genesis 1:1–2:3 is balanced by the name "LORD God" ("Yahweh Elohim") in the parallel creation account of Genesis 2:4–25.[5] Thus, although God's revelation of his personal name "Yahweh" is alluded to in places such as Exodus 6:3—"I appeared to Abraham, Isaac, and Jacob as God Almighty, but by my name 'The LORD' I did not make myself known"—the use of "Yahweh" numerous times in Genesis already makes the canonical identification of Israel's deliverer in Exodus with the world's creator in Genesis. At significant moments in Israel's history, such as the covenant renewal ceremony with Joshua, the nation is therefore challenged to affirm its exclusive devotion to Yahweh: "[Joshua] said, 'Then put away the foreign gods that are among you, and incline your hearts to the LORD, the God of Israel.' The people said to Joshua, 'The LORD our God we will serve, and him we will obey'" (Josh 24:23–24).

These affirmations, occurring throughout the narrative of the Old Testament, should not mask the complex historical, sociopolitical, and religious development of Yahwism among the individual tribes or, later, the united and divided kingdoms,[6] but as Patrick Miller correctly observes, "That other deities were worshiped at different times or by different groups or that syncretistic movements took place from time to time cannot undermine the centrality of the worship of Yahweh throughout the course of ancient Israel's history," and, we might add, throughout the Old Testament.[7] The repeated association of the plural form ("Elohim") with a singular verb also points to the way in which the Bible's theological witness to Yahweh not only related to the witness Israel's neighbors gave to their gods; it also subsumed the characteristics of these many gods in Yahweh as the one, true, and living God.[8] Thus, while there is wisdom in avoiding what Gerstenberger calls a "unitary theology of the kind that would correspond to our ideas, namely a coherent thought structure about the being and action of God and God's claim on human beings," the predominant rhetoric of the Old Testament is to call Israel to the exclusive worship of Yahweh, the "great King above all gods" (Ps. 95:3).[9] This is the one whose power elicited the worshipful confession from Israel in Elijah's day: "The LORD indeed is God; the LORD indeed is God" (1 Kgs. 18:39).

All of this helps to explain the importance of the Shema of Deuteronomy 6:4: "Hear, O Israel: The LORD is our God, the LORD alone."[10] This verse, writes Miller, "seems to have been an implicit polemic against the notion, whether specifically articulated or not, that there was more than one Yahweh."[11] In addition to the claim of Yahweh's unitary status affirmed in the first commandment—"You shall have no other gods before me" (Exod. 20:3)—the Old Testament likewise affirms that Yahweh does not exist in physical form as an idol and is not to be worshiped through such symbolic representations; hence the next commandment, "You shall not make for yourself an idol. . . . You shall not bow down to them or worship them" (Exod. 20:4–5).[12] Critiques of idol worship were particularly popular among the prophets, who were known to ridicule the incongruous use of the same tree for firewood and for idol making (Isa. 44:9–20; see also Jer. 10:1–11 and Ezek. 8:7–18). Rather than having some physical manifestation, Yahweh was present and operative in the world through his spirit, which influenced judges, kings, and prophets (e.g., Judg. 14:19; 1 Sam. 10:10; Isa. 61:1) but was also an expression of his personal comfort and presence, as David prayed, "Do not cast me away from your presence, and do not take your holy spirit from me" (Ps. 51:11).

New Testament Witness: God Revealed as the Father, by the Son, through the Spirit

A biblical-theological witness to the Christian doctrine of the Trinity is far beyond the scope of this study, and it may seem out of place so soon in the discussion of themes.[13] Still, having set forth something of the Old Testament's insistence on the uniqueness and oneness of Yahweh, one cannot address the New Testament's understanding of God without reckoning almost immediately with its frequent references to Father, Son, and Spirit, all three of which are found in most New Testament documents.[14] To be sure, the New Testament writings also presuppose and affirm the existence of one, true God, whether through Jesus' own testimony to the greatest commandment (Matt. 22:37–38), associated directly with the Shema, Paul's testimony to the Athenian philosophers on Mars' Hill (Acts 17:23–34), or the exhortation in the letter of James, "You believe that God is one; you do well. Even the demons believe—and shudder" (2:19).[15] However, one cannot escape the impression that, in various ways and to various degrees, the New Testament authors shift the theological center of gravity from the confession of God's oneness to the confession that "God has made [Jesus] both Lord and Messiah" (Acts 2:36). Richard Bauckham argues:

> Early Christians presupposed Jewish monotheism of the late Second
> Temple period and its monotheistic reading of the Hebrew Bible. . . .
> With the inclusion of Jesus in the unique identity of YHWH the faith
> of the Shema is affirmed and maintained, but everything the Shema
> requires of God's people is now focused on Jesus. Exclusive devotion
> is now given to Jesus, but Jesus does not thereby replace or compete
> with God the Father, since he himself belongs to the unique divine
> identity. Devotion to him is also devotion to his Father.[16]

The frequent testimony to the risen Christ as "Lord," a translation of the
Greek *kurios*, used in the Septuagint to translate *Yahweh*, forms the heart of the
earliest Christian confession of faith, that "Jesus is Lord" (Rom. 10:9; 1 Cor.
12:3).[17] The Gospel writers often indirectly pointed to Jesus' divine identity
by his miraculous deeds and self-authenticating words. Endowed with power
to control nature—"Who then is this, that even the wind and the sea obey
him?" (Mark 4:41)—and claiming a unique relationship with God—"Father,
glorify me in your own presence with the glory that I had in your presence
before the world existed" (John 17:5)—Jesus is presented in the Gospels as
sharing in divine existence and character. He takes the very name of God for
himself when he says, "Very truly, I tell you, before Abraham was, I am" (John
8:58), and the letter to the Colossians expresses the highest incarnational
Christology when it declares of Jesus, "For in him all the fullness of God was
pleased to dwell" (Col. 1:19). The opening words of John's prologue, "In the
beginning was the Word, and the Word was with God, and the Word was
God" (John 1:1), and the Christ hymn in Paul's letter to the Philippians
(2:6–11) are part of the fuller testimony that leads Ulrich Mauser to affirm, "It
remains central to the proclamation of the NT that a specific, historically iden-
tifiable, human being is acknowledged as the Word, the Son, the Image, the
Glory and Imprint of God, with such power that in him one of human form
and likeness is invested with the name of God (Phil 2:7 and 10–11), and hence
with divine identity."[18]

In still other ways the New Testament writers drew the Spirit of God into
the dynamic of the Father-Son relationship, such as by describing events like
Jesus' baptism: "And he saw the Spirit of God descending like a dove and
alighting on him. And a voice from heaven said, 'This is my Son, the Beloved,
with whom I am well pleased'" (Matt. 3:16–17). The baptismal formula, "in
the name of the Father and of the Son and of the Holy Spirit" (Matt. 28:19),
and some epistolary benedictions have a Trinitarian ring to them: "The grace
of the Lord Jesus Christ, the love of God, and the communion of the Holy
Spirit be with all of you" (2 Cor. 13:13). In still other places, the Spirit operates much as in the Old Testament, manifesting God's power for witness (Acts
2:4, 17), to bring new birth (John 3:5–8), to guide and teach (John 14:17, 26;

15:26; 16:13), and to confirm within human hearts their status as children of God (Rom. 8:15–17). With respect to the Father-Son relationship, Mauser asks, "What does the language of the spirit of God add to this unity in duality? Put into the simplest form, the Spirit of God is the transforming power of the one act of God in Christ which effects in human recipients of the gospel a wealth of benefits through which their lives are renewed, justified, made holy, and ordered for service."[19]

Nothing in the New Testament authorizes biblical theologians to work backward from the New to the Old and pour a developed Christology or Trinitarian theology into every messianic reference or text about the spirit. But these New Testament references do reveal that their authors were working in the other direction, affirming that God's spirit was still at work in Israel and that what was true of Yahweh in the Old Testament was true of Jesus in the New.[20]

Old and New Testament Witness to the Character of God

Affirmations about the "character" of God tend to generalize God's words and actions, as well as words spoken to and about God in the Old and New Testaments. There are several ways in which the content of this section could be unfolded, such as through a focus on the titles and names of God, or through overarching metaphors, as in Tremper Longman's treatment of God as covenant king, divine warrior, and immanuel.[21] Since the sections on God's words and actions below will provide more references to the biblical-theological witness, the following paragraphs will briefly touch on a few word-pairs relating to God's character.

Knowing and Wise

Running as a deep undercurrent in the Old Testament literature is the confidence that Yahweh is a perfectly wise and all-knowing God. Yahweh's wisdom and knowledge are not so much abstract qualities as expressions of relationship, of the belief that God knows Israel personally and will lead them wisely. God does, of course, know about events and even human thoughts, a feature that often surfaces in narratives. In Genesis, for example, God knows that the man and the woman have disobeyed (chap. 3), what Cain thinks and does against his brother (4:6–10), and what the general human condition is prior to the flood (6:5). But other writings speak of Yahweh's relationship with Israel as one in which he has "known" them (Deut. 9:24); indeed, as Amos declares, "You only have I known of all the families of the earth" (Amos 3:2a).[22] The psalms also probe the intimate and personal knowledge God has of individuals: "O LORD, you have searched me and known me. You know when I sit down and when I rise up. . . . Even before a word is on my tongue, O LORD, you know it completely" (Ps. 139:1–4) and "The LORD knows the days of the blameless, and their heritage will abide forever" (Ps. 37:18). All of this is set within this conviction: "O LORD, how manifold are your works! In wisdom you have made them all; the earth is full of your creatures" (Ps. 104:24).

The New Testament writers also express confidence in the full extent of God's wisdom and knowledge, as Paul's doxological conclusion to his discussion of Israel shows: "O the depth of the riches and wisdom and knowledge of God! How unsearchable are his judgments and how inscrutable his ways!" (Rom. 11:33). For Paul, God's wisdom may be manifest in the world in ways that seem counterintuitive, such that the cross reveals Christ to be "the power of God and the wisdom of God" (1 Cor. 1:24). There are texts that suggest divine knowledge on the part of Jesus during his ministry—"He knew what they were thinking" (Matt. 12:25)—or through the letters to the seven churches of Asia: "I know your works, your toil and your patient endurance. I know that you cannot tolerate evildoers" (Rev. 2:2). But the New Testament, like the Old, often speaks of knowing on a relational level: "I am the good shepherd. I know my own and they know me" (John 10:14). The personal aspect is maintained even when the relationship is rejected, as in Jesus' saying, "Then I will declare to them, 'I never knew you; go away from me, you evildoers" (Matt. 7:23; see Luke 13:27). Paul affirms the same basic truth when he writes that "anyone who loves God is known by him" (1 Cor. 8:3), and the Pastoral Letters concur: "The Lord knows those who are his" (2 Tim. 2:19).[23]

Loving and Providing

The previous section hinted at the fact that knowledge is just one expression of God's abiding, compassionate relationship with human beings.[24] The exodus story connects God's love for Israel with the covenant he made with the ancestors and later with Moses' generation, from Yahweh's compassionate concern at the first revelation to Moses—"I have observed the misery of my people" (Exod. 3:7–10)—to the profound declaration on Mount Sinai: "The LORD, the LORD, a God . . . abounding in steadfast love and faithfulness, keeping steadfast love for the thousandth generation" (Exod. 34:6–7). This "steadfast love," or *hesed*, is essentially Yahweh's "covenant loyalty" toward Israel as a people, but it can also be shown toward individuals (e.g., to Davidic kings, 2 Sam. 7:15) and between individuals (Ruth 1:8).[25] The prophets communicate Yahweh's passionate devotion to Israel, even at the point of judgment—"How can I give you up, O Ephraim? . . . My heart recoils within me; my compassion grows warm and tender" (Hos. 11:8)—and this love becomes a motive for their return from exile: "I will bring them back because I have compassion on them" (Zech. 10:6).[26] Israel experiences God's love in numerous ways, but an especially significant metaphor is the provision of God, which Juliana Claassens shows has several manifestations: manna in the wilderness (Exod. 16; Num. 11), "the bread" of instruction (Deut. 8:3), food for all creation (Ps. 104), the banquet of woman wisdom (Prov. 9:1–6), the restoration of Israel and creation (Jer. 31:12–14; Amos 9:13–15; Joel 2:18–19), among others.[27] In these places, biblical writers explore God's provision with feminine imagery, revealing that the qualities of God are not presented in exclusively male terms.[28]

In the New Testament, God's love and provision surface in several, often implicit ways. For example, while the Synoptic Gospels do not "state clearly that God loves human beings,"[29] Jesus reveals his deep compassion when he weeps over Jerusalem (Luke 19:41–44) and portrays God's provision through his miraculous feedings (e.g., Matt 14:13–21) as well as the Passover meal with his disciples (Matt. 26:26–29).[30] The Johannine traditions are more explicit about God's love in Christ, who expresses the "greatest love" by sacrificing his life for his friends (John 15:13). Of this theme Geoffrey Grogan writes, "God's love is singularly expressed in the atoning work of Christ . . . [and] the New Testament uses rich vocabulary of love quite prodigally in relation to the cross."[31] John declares, "God so loved the world that he gave his only Son" (John 3:16), and in 1 John, love practically becomes the defining attribute of God: "Whoever does not love does not know God, for God is love" (1 John 4:8).[32] For Paul, the strength of God's love is shown in the fact that nothing can "separate us from the love of God in Christ Jesus our Lord" (Rom. 8:39). Moreover, the Old Testament teachings on God's provision are echoed in Paul's assurance to the citizens of Lystra that God has given them "rains from heaven and fruitful seasons, . . . filling you with food and your hearts with joy" (Acts 14:17). In particular, Paul assures believers in Philippi, "And my God will fully satisfy every need of yours according to his riches in glory in Christ Jesus" (Phil. 4:19).

Merciful and Forgiving

The magnificent revelation in Exodus 34:6–7 closely associates the compassion of God with mercy and forgiveness: "The LORD, the LORD, a God merciful and gracious, slow to anger, . . . forgiving iniquity and transgression and sin." In spite of Israel's repeated cycles of rebellion (e.g., Judg. 2:11–23) and the threat of ultimate destruction and scattering of Israel's remnant (Deut. 4:26–28), the Deuteronomistic literature always held out hope for restoration and forgiveness: "Because the LORD your God is a merciful God, he will neither abandon you nor destroy you; he will not forget the covenant with your ancestors that he swore to them" (Deut. 4:31; see also 1 Kgs. 8:46–51). The prophets foretold an ending to the exile (Jer. 29:10–14) and then exulted in its conclusion (Isa. 40:1–5), because God's very nature is to be forgiving: "Who is a God like you, pardoning iniquity and passing over the transgression of the remnant of your possession? He does not retain his anger forever, because he delights in showing clemency. . . . You will cast all our sins into the depths of the sea" (Mic. 7:18–19). Even as the destruction of Jerusalem provided the occasion of the Old Testament's deepest grief, the poet was reminded that "the steadfast love of the LORD never ceases, his mercies never come to an end" (Lam. 3:22). The repentant psalmist could plead for himself, "According to your abundant mercy blot out my transgressions" (Ps. 51:1), and among the reasons for the psalmist's praise in Psalm 103 is the truth that Yahweh is the one who "forgives all your iniquity, who heals all your diseases, who redeems your life from the Pit, who crowns you with steadfast love and mercy" (vv. 3–4).

The New Testament teachings on forgiveness certainly have a horizontal, ethical dimension, but this was closely related to the assurance that one could pray to God, "Forgive us our sins" (Luke 11:4; see also Col. 3:13, "just as the Lord has forgiven you, so you also must forgive"). Jesus himself set the example from the cross, with his first words there being, "Father, forgive them; for they do not know what they are doing" (Luke 23:34).[33] While it is fully in God's nature to be merciful, Paul draws on Exodus 33:19 to reaffirm the freedom of God's forgiveness: "I will have mercy on whom I have mercy, and I will have compassion on whom I have compassion" (Rom. 9:15). The Pastoral Letters connect the expression of God's mercy with the purpose of Jesus' life and death: "Christ Jesus came into the world to save sinners—of whom I am the foremost. But for that very reason I received mercy" (1 Tim. 1:15–16). The Johannine letters also relate God's forgiveness with Jesus' atoning death as well as his ongoing intercession for sinners: "If anyone does sin, we have an advocate with the Father, Jesus Christ the righteous; and he is the atoning sacrifice for our sins, and not for ours only but also for the sins of the whole world" (1 John 2:1–2).

Holy and Righteous

We saw how "the self-disclosure of the Holy One" was, for Anderson, part of Israel's basic witness to God's revelation,[34] and Vriezen writes that "the transcendence of God is expressed most clearly by the word holiness. . . . The idea of holiness is the one most typical for the Old Testament faith."[35] Exodus and Leviticus are especially replete with references to God's holiness, whether Moses stands upon "holy ground" (Exod. 3:5) and Yahweh commands him to "keep [Mount Sinai] holy" (Exod. 19:23), or Levitical laws are followed by the refrain, "For I the LORD your God am holy" (Lev. 19:2). God's holiness underlies the expectation that Israel will be a sanctified people: "Be holy, for I am holy" (Lev. 11:44). The name Yahweh, too, is set apart in Israel's worship, that they might "glory in his holy name" (Ps. 105:3) and "give thanks to [his] holy name" (106:47). The book of Isaiah invokes Yahweh's title at least two dozen times as "the Holy One of Israel" (e.g., Isa. 1:4; 5:19), often in a context that explains why judgment must come upon the sinful nation, and Isaiah's vision of

Yahweh's heavenly abode was punctuated by the call of the seraphs, "Holy, holy, holy is the LORD of hosts; the whole earth is full of his glory" (Isa. 6:3). Like holiness, God's righteousness is also inherent to the divine nature, but it manifests itself particularly in relationship to Yahweh's people who are to live in just and upright ways.[36] For this reason, the psalmist can pray, "Lead me, O LORD, in your righteousness because of my enemies; make your ways straight before me" (Ps. 5:8), but through the prophet God can involve his people and the world: "Listen to me, my people, and give heed to me, my nation; for a teaching will go out from me, and my justice for a light to the peoples" (Isa. 51:4).

With respect to the New Testament writings, Donald Guthrie writes, "It is clear that the basic assumption of God's holiness is taken over from the OT" and that "this conviction that God is holy forms an important element in the NT account of salvation."[37] The same call to holiness is issued for believers, and on the same grounds as in the Old Testament: "Like obedient children, do not be conformed to the desires that you formerly had in ignorance. Instead, as he who called you is holy, be holy yourselves in all your conduct; for it is written, 'You shall be holy, for I am holy'" (1 Pet. 1:14–16).[38] When the righteousness of God is brought into view, however, Guthrie argues that in the New Testament, "this is basic to the whole plan of salvation."[39] While I will say more about this concept later in relation to justification, it is Paul's letters that make the revelation of God's righteousness foundational to understanding both the need for salvation as well as the means of salvation: "But now, apart from the law, the righteousness of God has been disclosed, and is attested by the law and the prophets, the righteousness of God through faith in Jesus Christ for all who believe" (Rom. 3:21–22).

Mighty and Glorious

In a very real sense, the Bible understands the act and existence of creation as a display of God's glorious might: "The heavens are telling the glory of God; and the firmament proclaims his handiwork" (Ps. 19:1). Yahweh's power and glory are celebrated in one of the oldest examples of Hebrew poetry, the song of the sea (Exod. 15), where Israel sings "to the LORD, for he has triumphed gloriously. . . . Your right hand, O LORD, glorious in power—your right hand, O LORD, shattered the enemy" (vv. 1, 6). The plagues and the parting of the Red Sea are, of course, manifestations of Yahweh's might, but even the giving of manna was understood by Moses to reveal "the glory of the LORD" (Exod. 16:7). God's special presence with Israel in the tabernacle and the temple is depicted as a cloud of glory (Exod. 40:34), which may depart in judgment (Ezek. 10:18) but also return in restored fellowship (Ezek. 43:4). It is indeed "the LORD, strong and mighty, the LORD, mighty in battle," who enters Jerusalem as "the King of glory" (Ps. 24:8–10), but Yahweh's glory is not only for Israel to experience. He wants Israel to "declare his glory among the nations" (Ps. 96:3), and even the celestial powers will be judged in a display of his glory (Isa. 24:23), for he says, "I am the LORD, that is my name; my glory I give to no other" (Isa. 42:8).

The Synoptic Gospels all testify to Jesus' transfigured glory (Matt. 17:2; Mark 9:2–3; Luke 9:29), an event apparently alluded to by John: "And we have seen his glory, the glory as of a father's only son, full of grace and truth" (John 1:14; see a parallel recollection in 2 Pet. 1:17–18). In his apocalyptic discourse, Jesus foretells that the world "will see 'the Son of Man coming on the clouds of heaven' with power and great glory" (Matt. 24:30), an event Jesus directly relates to Daniel's vision of the Son of Man being received in heaven and "given dominion and glory and kingship" (Dan 7:14). But a vision of Christ's glory is also intended for believers even now, who "with unveiled face, seeing the glory of the Lord as though reflected in a mirror, are being transformed into the same image from one degree of glory to another" (2 Cor. 3:18). They also have the hope, like Stephen (Acts 7:55), of seeing the glory of God, whether in death or at the Lord's return (1 Pet. 4:13). The New Testament resounds in benediction—"to the only wise God, through Jesus Christ, to whom be the glory forever!" (Rom. 16:27; see Phil. 4:20)—and in the praise of the whole cosmos: "To the one seated on the throne and to the Lamb be blessing and honor and glory and might forever and ever!" (Rev. 5:13; see 4:11; 5:12).

Summary

This brief description of some of the themes of God's being and character truly scratches but the surface of the biblical testimony. While the topics above serve as a representative cross section of Old and New Testaments, there are many others that might have been discussed. Brueggemann lists numerous "metaphors of governance" for Yahweh (judge, king, warrior, and father) as well as "metaphors of sustenance" (artist, healer, gardener-vinedresser, mother, and shepherd) that could rightly have been considered in my own treatment.[40] In addition to some of the characteristics I have listed, Guthrie adds concepts such as goodness, faithfulness, uniqueness, and unity.[41] But for now we have enough of a portrait to return specifically to the words and actions that gave rise to that portrait in the first place, indicating the way in which biblical-theological readings create an ever expanding circle of interpretation.

God Speaks: The Words of God

God's speaking is, technically, also an action of God, but this particular activity and the content it engenders—namely, the words and speeches themselves—are inestimably significant for the biblical tradition and later theological reflection on the Bible, both of which have regarded these words as revelatory communication, or simply "the word of God." Here, too, we shall see that the material goes far beyond a survey approach, but we can at least highlight three representative pairs describing the content or effect of God's speech: It creates and calls, promises and blesses, and reveals and instructs.

God Creates and Calls

I will say more about God's *act* of creating, but here I want to emphasize that the word God *speaks* is truly a creative word. The most obvious passage to consider is Genesis 1, where God's words not only effect creation ("Let there be . . .") but God's speech also names ("calls") parts of the created order and then prescribes activity ("Let the earth put forth vegetation," v. 11), diversity ("of every kind," v. 11), and relationship ("to separate . . . to rule," vv. 14, 16; "I have given you every plant," v. 29).[42] As God revels over creation in his speeches to Job, there are several places where his words impact the ongoing processes of nature. Yahweh tells the sea to stay within its bounds—"Thus far shall you come, and no farther" (38:11)—and implies that he has "commanded the morning . . . and caused the dawn to know its place" (38:12). At the close of the exile, Isaiah 40–55 highlights both the inherent power of God's words and their certainty to achieve an intended outcome. Not only is it true that "the word of our God will stand forever" (Isa. 40:8), but Yahweh declares, "[My word] shall not return to me empty, but it shall accomplish that which I purpose, and succeed in the thing for which I sent it" (Isa. 55:11; see 45:23). In like manner, the creative word also *calls* persons into relationship, leadership, and service: Abraham and Sarah (Gen. 12:1), Moses (Exod. 3:10), Joshua (Josh. 1:2–9), numerous prophets (Isa. 6:9–13; Jer. 1:4–10; Ezek. 2:3–10), to name only a few. But more than having a focus on the call of individuals, God's creative word constitutes Israel as a people, by calling them and claiming them for himself: "But now thus says the LORD, he who created you, O Jacob, he who formed you, O Israel: Do not fear, for I have redeemed you; I have called you by name, you are mine" (Isa. 43:1).

New Testament writers approach the subject of God's creative and calling word from different angles. John's Gospel, by identifying Jesus as the incarnation of the eternal "word" or *logos* (John 1:14), emphasizes that "all things came into being through him, and without him not one thing came into being" (John 1:3), a sentiment echoed by Colossians: "for in him all things in heaven and on earth were created. . . . All things have been created through him and for him (1:16).[43] The creative power of God's word is accompanied by the concomitant power to transform and recreate the cosmos: "By the word of God heavens existed long ago and an earth was formed out of water and by means of water. . . . But by the same word the present heavens and earth have been reserved for fire. . . . But, in accordance with his promise, we wait for new heavens and a new earth" (2 Pet. 3:5, 7, 13). The Gospels all depict Jesus as calling disciples both to follow him and to go forth in ministry in his name (e.g., Matt. 10; 28:19–20). Paul understands this gospel to be a manifestation of God's power to save (Rom. 1:16–17), and it is a gospel that embraces human agency in proclamation: "So faith comes from what is heard, and what is heard comes through the word of Christ" (Rom. 10:17).

God Promises and Blesses

We are not long into the biblical story before we encounter God's promissory speech, usually within the context of some larger covenantal purpose. Immediately after the flood, Noah's family is embraced with all creation by God's commitment "never again [to] curse the ground because of humankind. . . . Nor will I ever again destroy every living creature as I have done. As long as the earth endures, seedtime and harvest, cold and heat, summer and winter, day and night, shall not cease" (Gen. 8:21–22). These universal promises form the backdrop for Yahweh's promises to Abraham and the other ancestors, making an intricate web of stories and settings wherein Yahweh promises descendants, land, and various blessings both to their families (e.g., presence and protection) and to "all the families of the earth" (Gen. 12:1–3, 7).[44] The Pentateuch repeatedly refers to these promises, sometimes implicitly noting how Israel has increased in spite of its circumstances (Exod. 1:7) and sometimes explicitly quoting Yahweh's own words that reveal him to be "the LORD, the God of [the] ancestors, the God of Abraham, of Isaac, and of Jacob" (Exod. 3:16; see 6:2–9). To be sure, the Israelites' enjoyment of what is promised becomes tied to their trust and obedience, whether they are delayed from entering the new land (Num. 13–14) or are poised to cross over the Jordan River (Deut. 8). But once they are in the land, writes Claus Westermann, they can tell the old stories from the perspective of fulfillment:

> The promises given to the fathers provide assurance that the God who promised in the past and fulfilled his promises of the land and of increase will remain faithful to his word, that one can rely for the future on the words and actions of this God. This makes it possible to look back and see Israel's history as a coherent whole and to look forward trusting in God's future actions.[45]

With the potential for great blessings comes the specter of potential curses (Deut. 27–28), something that the whole Deuteronomistic History aims to demonstrate through case after case of failed leadership. On a parallel track to these indictments, the narrators of the prophetic history particularly in 1–2 Kings call attention to many cases where promises (or warnings) occur "according to the word of the LORD," just as a prophet had promised they would (e.g., 1 Kgs. 13:26; 14:18; 15:29). And after the exile, Cyrus's decree to release the captives occurs, from the perspective of Ezra, "in order that the word of the LORD by the mouth of Jeremiah might be accomplished" (Ezra 1:1).

In various ways all four Gospels work with the themes of promise and blessing. They understand the ministry of John the Baptist as a fulfillment of the Isaianic portrayal of "the voice of one crying out in the wilderness" (Matt. 3:3; Mark 1:3; Luke 3:4; John 1:23). For its part, Matthew's Gospel creatively connects Jesus' life with Old Testament events and persons using several "formula quotations" (e.g., Matt. 1:23). The opening chapters of Luke employ poetry and song to celebrate the fulfillment of ancient promises to Israel: "Thus [the Lord] has shown the mercy promised to our ancestors, and has remembered his holy covenant, the oath that he swore to our ancestor Abraham" (Luke 1:72–73). Paul also sees the gospel as "promised beforehand through his prophets in the holy scriptures" (Rom. 1:2), and he is particularly drawn to the way all nations may now experience the blessing that comes through Israel (Rom. 15:8–12).[46] The Letter to the Hebrews develops at some length the nature of God's promises by citing the ancestral story and concluding, "When God desired to show even more clearly to the heirs of the promise the unchangeable character of his purpose, he guaranteed it by an oath" (Heb. 6:17). Although some promises to Israel might be spiritualized by New Testament writers (physical versus spiritual descendants of Abraham), aspects such as the land promise remain problematic.[47] Nevertheless, James Hanson argues that the pattern of the "endangered and reaffirmed promises of God," clearly shown in Israel's tension-filled history, is played out on the stage of the New Testament documents as well and can thus provide a framework for relating the Old and New Testaments.[48] Finally, though not as frequent as in the Old Testament, the communication of God's blessings also finds a home in the New Testament, from the Beatitudes with which Jesus begins the Sermon on the Mount (Matt. 5:1–12; cf. Luke 6:20–26) to those offered believers who are undergoing the intense tribulations described in the book of Revelation: "Blessed and holy are those who share in the first resurrection" (Rev. 20:6) and "Blessed is the one who keeps the words of the prophecy of this book" (Rev. 22:7).

God Reveals and Instructs

The activity of revelation is, of course, implicit in the notion of promise and blessing, since God must choose some means of revealing those promises and sharing those blessings. The fact is, however, that often no precise means of revelation is given, as in many Genesis texts where God simply "said" something to the man and the woman, to Cain, to Noah, to Abraham, and so on.[49] But one also finds God communicating with people through dreams (e.g.,

Abimelech in Gen. 20:3; Jacob in Gen. 28:12–13; Pharaoh in Gen. 41:25), though the narrator does not specify that every dream comes from God, even if we may assume this is usually the case (e.g., Joseph's dreams of dominion over his family in Gen. 37:5–11). At other times, people discern that God is working in their circumstances by setting forth options for action, as does Abraham's servant in Genesis 24. Dreams and visions continue to dot the landscape of the biblical story (e.g., Ezekiel or Daniel), but these experiences seem reserved for prophets and kings; it is the prophecy of Joel that the spirit of God, poured out on all flesh, would bring prophecies, dreams, and visions to young and old, male and female, slave and free (Joel 2:28–29).

In the formation of the Hebrew canon, prophets are the quintessential communicators of God's word to Israel. Within and following the Bible, Moses remained the exemplar of prophecy—"The LORD your God will raise up for you a prophet like me from among your own people" (Deut. 18:15)[50]—but Israel's history saw several other prophetic leaders: Samuel (1 Sam. 3:20); Nathan (2 Sam. 7:2); Elijah (1 Kgs. 17–19), and Elisha (2 Kgs. 2–9), to name only a few.[51] The Major and Minor Prophets themselves represent a move away from service primarily to kings and toward judgment upon Israelite religion, society, and leadership. Although their oracles surely foretold the coming of judgment as well as distant restoration, their main function was to declare God's indictment upon the people and call them to repentance. Typical of these statements is Isaiah's challenge to Judah: "Wash yourselves; make yourselves clean; remove the evil of your doings from before my eyes; cease to do evil, learn to do good; seek justice, rescue the oppressed, defend the orphan, plead for the widow" (Isa. 1:16–17). Inviting the people to "argue" things out with Yahweh (1:18), Isaiah declares the basic alternatives: "If you are willing and obedient, you shall eat the good of the land; but if you refuse and rebel, you shall be devoured by the sword; for the mouth of the LORD has spoken" (Isa 1:19–20). Similar indictments came from Hosea (6:1–3) and Amos (5:14–15, 23–24) in the northern kingdom prior to Isaiah, and from Jeremiah in the southern kingdom after him (Jer. 4:1–4).

Prophetic calls to repentance are set against the backdrop of God's instructions revealed preeminently in the Torah. In Exodus there are the "ordinances" of the Book of the Covenant (Exod 20:18–23:33); in Leviticus there is the Holiness Code (Lev. 17–26); and in Deuteronomy Moses commands, "So now, Israel, give heed to the statutes and ordinances that I am teaching you to observe" (Deut. 4:1). Israel is to be continually occupied with God's laws, not just keeping them in their hearts, but to "recite them to your children and talk about them when you are at home and when you are away, when you lie down and when you rise" (Deut. 6:6–7).[52] Enjoyment of the land God gave them is directly tied to their obedience, "that it may go well with you, and that you may live long in the land that you are to possess" (Deut. 5:33). Even after judgment and exile, Yahweh expected the people to worship according to the law, whether in the repopulated areas of Samaria (2 Kgs. 17:25–28) or the resettled region of Judah (Ezra 7:10–20; Neh. 8).[53] The poetic literature also exalts the place of torah, both celebrated in psalms—"Their delight is in the law of the LORD, and on his law they meditate day and night" (Ps. 1:2; see Ps. 119)—and passed down in the traditional, proverbial wisdom of family settings (Prov. 1–9).

As in the Old Testament, the concepts of revelation and instruction in the New are multifaceted. There continue to be those individual experiences of divine communication through dreams (Joseph in Matt. 1:20–23; 2:13, 19–20), angelic visitations (Mary in Luke 1:26–38), or visionary experiences (Paul in 2 Cor. 12:3–4; and John in Rev. 1:10–20). Ultimately, however, the Letter to the Hebrews understands the variety of revelatory encounters to be eclipsed by the fact that "in these last days [God] has spoken to us by a Son" (Heb. 1:1–2). Even Moses, the faithful lawgiver and prophet, is finally regarded as a servant compared to Christ, "faithful over God's house as a son" (Heb. 3:5–6). In the Gospel of John, Jesus understands himself as the definitive embodiment of the long-awaited Messiah, when the Samaritan woman says, "'When he comes, he will proclaim all things to us.' Jesus said to her, "I am he, the one who is speaking to you'" (John 4:25–26).

Jesus therefore takes the role of authoritative interpreter of torah, reinterpreting and applying it in the Sermon on the Mount (Matt. 5:21–48) but also affirming the authority of torah until all is fulfilled (Matt. 5:17–20). Jesus sets his understanding of the commandments over against Pharisaic traditions, which he sees as "making void the word of God" (Mark 7:13), and he connects his ministry with "the law of Moses, the prophets, and the psalms" (Luke 24:44).[54] In the book of Acts, the Hebrew Scriptures remained the standard by which Paul's gospel was to be judged, as eloquently stated of the Berean Christians who "welcomed the message very eagerly and examined the scriptures every day to see whether these things were so" (Acts 17:11). An extremely high view of both the God-breathed character of Scripture and its continuing usefulness is asserted in 2 Timothy 3:16–17, a sentiment not far from the conviction that "the word of God is living and active, sharper than any two-edged sword" (Heb. 4:12). To be sure, the Pauline letters raise the specter of the precise function of "works of the law" in establishing and maintaining relationship with God (Rom. 4; Gal. 4), but there is no contradiction between the law and the gospel in Paul's thinking. As Frank Thielman writes, "The Mosaic law continues to speak as Scripture for Paul, but it is sovereignly interpreted by the gospel. . . . The Mosaic law is absorbed by the gospel, but only under the transforming influence of the eschatological Spirit."[55]

God Acts: The Works of God

In previous chapters we saw how the biblical theology movement emphasized God's acts, particularly regarding "history as the arena of God's activity," making biblical theology "first and foremost a theology of recital . . . [of] the formative events of his history as the redemptive handiwork of God."[56] But even if we do not make God's actions in history the defining rubric of biblical theology, it is necessary to consider the ways in which the Bible testifies to those acts. In what follows I have chosen four word-pairs to express some major aspects of theological witness to the works of God in creation, covenant, history, and redemption.

God Creates and Recreates

Having considered the creative aspects of God's word, we may here observe that Genesis 1 narrates several other claims about creation, such as its basic orderliness in the framework of "days," the claim of totality, that is, all that exists ("the heavens and the earth"), and the essential goodness of what was made ("and God saw that it was good").[57] There is no question that when the Hebrew verb *bara'* is employed, God is portrayed as the sole creator of the structures of the world and of humans in the image of God (Gen. 1:1, 27; 2:3), but Genesis 1 and 2 also contain indications that God will share with humans the exercise of "dominion" (Gen. 1:26) and the task of caring for the garden (Gen. 2:15).[58] Nevertheless, God continues to be able to control nature, and key moments such as the great flood, the plagues in Egypt, the parting of the Red Sea, and the crossing of the Jordan River all illustrate this power. Job 38–41 is a celebration of God's intimate knowledge of and ability to influence nature's workings, even as it acknowledges "an amazingly diverse universe" and "a world that is not risk free."[59] The Old Testament also celebrates God's creative act of restoration, beginning with the way the postflood account echoes Genesis 1: "God blessed Noah and his sons, and said to them, 'Be fruitful and multiply, and fill the earth'" (Gen. 9:1). As Patrick Miller observes, "The covenant with Noah restores and secures the creation for the benefit of the creatures, animal and human."[60] The hope of natural renewal is a significant feature of the prophetic books, usually with the focus on the land of Israel and Judah (Hos. 2:21–22; Amos 9:11–15; Ezek. 47:6–14; Zeph. 3:14–20) though in places the vision embraces a wider scope and hints at cosmic restoration (Isa. 2:1–4; 11:6–9; 65:17).

I have mentioned the Gospels' testimony to Jesus' miraculous powers, and several of these narratives draw on Old Testament themes of sovereignty over nature and connect Jesus' actions with those in Israel's history: the calming of the sea and walking on water (Mark 4:35–41; 6:47–52), the multiplication of loaves and fish (Mark 6:30–44), the changing of water into wine (John 2:1–11), and so on.[61] The New Testament unquestionably affirms God's act of and responsibility for creation, sometimes assuming this truth in passing (Mark 13:19; Eph. 3:9) while at other times explicitly asserting divine creation in and through Jesus Christ: "You are worthy, our Lord and God, to receive glory and honor and power, for you created all things, and by your will they existed and were created" (Rev. 4:11). Paul's letter to the Romans reflects on human suffering within the context of creation's "groaning in labor pains until now," because "creation was subjected to futility, not of its own will but by the will of the one who subjected it, in hope that the creation itself will be set free from its bondage to decay and will obtain the freedom of the glory of the children of God" (Rom. 8:22, 20–21). This hope of restoration finds a specific expression in Christian faith in the resurrection of the dead: "Just as we have borne the image of the man of dust, we will also bear the image of the man of heaven" (1 Cor. 15:49). Ultimately, a re-creation of the entire universe is in view, perhaps most eloquently depicted in one of the visions in the book of Revelation:

> Then I saw a new heaven and a new earth; for the first heaven and the
> first earth had passed away, and the sea was no more. . . . And I heard
> a loud voice from the throne saying,
>
>> "See, the home of God is among mortals.
>> He will dwell with them as their God;
>> they will be his peoples,
>> and God himself will be with them;
>> he will wipe every tear from their eyes.
>> Death will be no more;
>> mourning and crying and pain will be no more,
>> for the first things have passed away." (Rev. 21:1–4)

God Chooses and Makes Covenant

Eichrodt's great work will always be known by the way it highlighted the theme of covenant, but other theologians, such as Vos, have traced a progressive series of covenants with people. In one sense, the entire biblical story plays itself out in terms of decisions that God makes in the spheres of creation and redemption, allowing us to see why some theologians have regarded the themes of covenant or election as central to the biblical narrative. What I have in view here, however, is God's choice to establish special relationships with individuals and groups. Immediately after Yahweh's declaration to "blot out from the earth the human beings I have created" (Gen. 6:7), we read that "Noah found favor in the sight of the LORD" (6:8). And in Noah's case, Yahweh also made a covenant that embraced Noah, his descendants, and all the animals (9:9–10). The same balance of choosing and covenant-making exists with Abraham and Sarah (12:1–3; 17:4), and that covenant is reaffirmed for each of the ancestral generations (26:2–5; 28:13–15). The matter of choice becomes especially focused in the birth of Rebekah's twin boys, Jacob and Esau, about whom we learn that God has decided before their birth which will serve the other (25:23).[62] Covenant language is explicitly used for Sinai (Exod. 24:7; 34:10), under Joshua (Josh. 24:25), with David and his descendants (Ps. 89:34–37; see 2 Sam. 7), and a new covenant with the house of Israel and Judah (Jer. 31:31–34). Following the exile, the remnant may go forth in the confidence that Yahweh has chosen them, a theme often repeated in Second Isaiah (41:8–9; 43:10, 20; 44:1–2). Two important threads run through these narratives of choice and covenant, the first being the lack of qualification and deservedness on the part of human beings. Jacob's deceptive personality, Moses' hesitancy to lead, David's sinful choices, and Israel's obstinacy all set in bold relief the completely gracious character of God's choice. The second theme involves the ultimate goal or purpose of God's choice and covenant, namely, some type of service, witness, or blessing to others. Yes, Israel benefits from being a chosen people—Yahweh calls them "my treasured possession out of all the peoples" (Exod. 19:5)—but from Abraham's initial call, the vocation was to be a blessing to the nations (Gen. 12:3), and God's expectations for individuals and the people as a whole are expressed precisely at the points where they fall short (2 Sam. 12:7–14; Amos 3:2).

In the New Testament, Matthew employs one of his fulfillment quotations from the servant passages of Second Isaiah to Jesus' ministry of healing: "Here is my servant, whom I have chosen, my beloved, with whom my soul is well pleased" (Matt. 12:18; see Isa. 42:1–4). This language harkens back to the heavenly voice at Jesus' baptism, singling him out as "my Son, the Beloved, with whom I am well pleased" (Matt. 3:17). In like manner, Jesus the chosen one calls his disciples and commissions them for service, saying, "You did not choose me but I chose you. And I appointed you to go and bear fruit" (John 15:16). In the Gospels and even during Paul's first missionary journey, the basic missional stance upholds Israel's chosen status, focusing the first ministry efforts toward them: "Go nowhere among the Gentiles, and enter no town of the Samaritans, but go rather to the lost sheep of the house of Israel" (Matt. 10:5–6; see Acts 13:5, 14; 14:1). But there is also a widening of the circle, as when Jesus speaks of his impending death—"This cup that is poured out for you is the new covenant in my blood" (Luke 22:20)—but makes no mention of the "house of Israel and Judah" or the law written on their hearts, which were integral to Jeremiah 31. Paul thinks of first-century Jews as his own people, Israelites to whom "belong the adoption, the glory, the covenants, the giving of the law, the worship, and the promises" (Rom. 9:4), but he also understands the ministry of the Spirit to embrace any believer in Jesus as an adopted child of God (Rom.

8:15–17; Gal. 4:6–7). The great passage on election (Rom. 9–11) shows that God's original plan for Israel, rooted in the ancestral promise, is still being worked out in history. According to N. T. Wright, Paul is arguing against a view "he suspects may exist in the Roman church, . . . a belief according to which God has effected a simple transfer of promises and privileges from Jews to Gentiles, so that Jews are just as shut out now as Gentiles were before." Wright adds, "As in [Romans] 11.11–15, Israel itself is 'cast away' for the reconciliation of the world, and thus can and will be 'received back again' with a meaning of nothing short of 'life from the dead.'"[63] Here, too, God's will remains a mystery of electing love that cannot be explained on the basis of any human claim (Eph. 1:3–6) but only by exclaiming, "See what love the Father has given us, that we should be called the children of God; and that is what we are" (1 John 3:1).

God Rules and Judges

As with other biblical themes, one could safely argue that God's actions of ruling and judging are assumed on every page of Scripture, but sometimes a narrative (or a character within it) will call special attention to God's providential workings, which may even use evil human intentions for good, as Joseph testifies at the end of his life (Gen. 50:20).[64] Yahweh's will interacts with Pharaoh's ever hardening heart to bring about the former's intentions to humble Egypt and ultimately deliver Israel from bondage (Exod. 4:21–23).[65] In a similar vein, God prohibits Balaam from prophesying any trouble for the tribes of Israel as they camp near Moab (Num. 22:12) and much later influences events on a massive scale to effect the release of exiled peoples through Cyrus's decree (Ezra 1:1; see Isa. 45:1).[66] Several historical psalms trace God's actions on Israel's behalf (Pss. 78, 105–107, 136), and in other places the biblical authors employ various analogies and images to affirm God's sovereignty: Yahweh works with Israel as a potter with clay (Jer. 18), and in Second Isaiah he declares, "'My purpose shall stand and I will fulfill my intention,' calling a bird of prey from the east, the man for my purpose from a far country" (Isa. 46:10–11). In the apocalyptic literature, Daniel's personal experiences, interpretation of dreams, and different visions all point to the truth that Nebuchadnezzar hears from the "holy watcher," that is, that "the Most High is sovereign over the kingdom of mortals; he gives it to whom he will and sets over it the lowliest of human beings" (Dan. 4:17).

God demonstrates ability and authority to judge humankind early in the primeval story, when he responds to the man and the woman's disobedience in the garden (Gen. 3:9–19). In many ways this scene sets the tone for Yahweh's later acts of judging, insofar as the interrogation involves humans in explaining their actions and reveals divine patience and forbearance, as do the provisions that allow the human race to live on and experience a measure of success against the serpent (3:15–19). Even when the judgments are of utmost severity—the great flood, the plagues on Egypt, or the death of the exodus generation—Yahweh endures repeated disobedience prior to definitive action. But upon their arrival, God's judgments bring desolation on Israel and Judah, their land and their hopes (Jer. 4:23–28; Hos. 13:9–16; Joel 1–2). Psalm 2 depicts Yahweh as enthroned in heaven, laughing at the way earthly kings seek to destroy the king of Israel: "Then he will speak to them in his wrath, and terrify them in his fury" (Ps. 2:5). On the individual level, traditional Israelite wisdom believed that God's discernment of the human heart meant that human actions would always be subject to his ultimate judgment (Prov. 16:1–9).

In the New Testament, the language of "the kingdom of God" (Mark) or "the kingdom of heaven" (Matthew) expresses the sphere in which God rules and reigns.[67] To be sure, the concept of "kingdom" was completely grounded in the thought of the Old Testament, for some of the earliest Israelite poetry spoke of how "the LORD will reign forever and ever" (Exod. 15:18), and the psalms celebrate that Yahweh's "kingdom is an everlasting kingdom" (Ps. 145:13).[68] But here the accent falls on Jesus' repeated use of the term from the beginning of his public ministry: "From that time Jesus began to proclaim, 'Repent, for the kingdom of heaven has come near" (Matt. 4:17). G. E. Ladd speaks of the present and future meanings of this concept: "God *is* now the King, but he must also *become* the King." He adds, "The coming of the Kingdom for which we pray in the Lord's Prayer means that God's will be done on earth, i.e., that his rule be perfectly realized (Matt 6:10)."[69] Jesus especially concentrated this language in several of his parables (Matt. 13; Mark 4) in which he both set forth his program of ministry and the unique style and shape it would take. The kingdom begins small and grows in the midst of the world, slowly and secretly, but it is of great value to those who find it. Ultimately the kingdom will be revealed, and God will discern who is truly part of it.[70]

Jesus' disciples carry out their ministry in the book of Acts, confident that they are participating in this kingdom's work and that God will sovereignly rule in order to protect them against persecution and to empower them "to heal, and [do] signs and wonders . . . through the name of your holy servant Jesus" (Acts 4:30). It was in this context that the great rabbi Gamaliel warned the Sanhedrin not to harm the early Christian community: "If this plan or undertaking is of human origin, it will fail; but if it is of God, you will not be able to overthrow them—in that case you may even be found fighting against God!" (Acts 5:38–39). Paul's typical missionary preaching in the synagogues was a rehearsal of God's rule among Israel through its history up to the life, death, and resurrection of Jesus (Acts 13:16–41), but even in Athens, Paul traced God's creative and ruling activity in the world so as to prepare the way for repentance. It is precisely here that the themes of ruling and judging coalesce for Paul, since he tells the philosophers that God "has fixed a day on which he will have the world judged in righteousness by a man whom he has appointed" (Acts 17:31). In this way, the gospel message linking kingdom and judgment parallels that of Paul. Of course, during human history God also works through human governance (Rom. 13:1–7; 1 Pet. 2:12–17), but finally the Son of Man himself will take the throne of judgment over all the nations (Matt. 25:31–46). As the heavenly chorus sings, "Hallelujah! For the Lord our God the Almighty reigns" (Rev. 19:6), the "King of kings and Lord of lords" will be revealed (Rev. 19:16).

God Saves and Restores

The Old Testament theme of salvation expresses itself primarily in material ways, as deliverance from physical harm and illness, enemies who would attack the righteous, or other nations that would exercise political, economic, and military control over Israel. The individual lament psalms crystalize the need for deliverance from every threat to life and its blessings: "Rise up, O LORD! Deliver me, O my God! For you strike all my enemies on the cheek; you break the teeth of the wicked. Deliverance belongs to the LORD; may your blessing be on your people" (Ps. 3:7–8). The same is true in the communal laments: "For not in my bow do I trust, nor can my sword save me. But you have saved us from our foes, and have put to confusion those who hate us" (Ps. 44:6–7). This regular association of deliverance with the destruction of enemies points to one of the crucial challenges in any theology of the psalms, namely, what to do about the "enemy language." It is one thing to celebrate stories of deliverance and restoration when individuals, such as Noah or Job, can receive God's protection or eventual blessing during or after some life-threatening experience. It is quite another for people of faith to appropriate the widespread cries for vindication and vengeance in the worship book of Israel. At the very least, Patrick Miller rightly notes, "the realism of the psalmist's praise of the Creator is alert to the reality of evil and wickedness in this beautiful and orderly world. . . . [The psalmist] knows that iniquity is present and capable of shattering the beauty and order and good of the world God made."[71]

The great moments of deliverance in the Old Testament are the exodus and return from exile, with the theology of the latter patterned on the former's motifs (Isa. 43:16–21). But as we saw in previous chapters, postcolonial interpretation has questioned the usefulness, or at the very least, the universal applicability of the liberation motif for the entire Third World. Without restating the arguments of that debate, we can and should acknowledge that articulating biblical-theological themes means wrestling with at least two challenges. The first is to reckon with how the biblical narrative, and theologies based on it, were misappropriated by all sorts of explorers, conquerors, and missionaries.[72] The past cannot be changed, but the errors of past interpretation might be more easily avoided when we acknowledge them. A second challenge calls students of Scripture to discern the character of the God depicted in the exodus story and relate that portrayal with all such characterizations throughout the Hebrew Bible.[73]

Given the fact that the exile had again forced Israel to deal with God's purposes (Ps. 89:38–45), the prophets foresaw a restored nation, indeed, a resurrected one that would again live with the breath of God's spirit: "And you shall know that I am the LORD, when I open your graves, and bring you up from your graves, O my people. I will put my spirit within you, and you shall live, and I will place you on your own soil; then you shall know that I, the LORD, have spoken and will act" (Ezek. 37:13–14). Apocalyptic literature even envisioned a bodily resurrection beyond earthly life, with the hope that the righteous might "shine like the brightness of the sky" (Dan. 12:3).

The Gospels' focus on the death of Jesus—leading many to speak of these books as passion narratives with long introductions—makes them stories of salvation. In all sorts of explicit and implicit ways their authors understand this salvation to be another stage in the story of Israel: The angel tells Joseph, "You are to name him Jesus, for he will save his people from their sins" (Matt. 1:21); Zechariah speaks prophetically that God "has looked favorably on his people and redeemed them. He has raised up a mighty savior for us in the house of his servant David" (Luke 1:68–69); and Moses and Elijah talk with Jesus about "his departure [literally, "exodus"], which he was about to accomplish at Jerusalem" (Luke 9:31). Luke's most celebrated parables are those in which persons are saved from destitute circumstances (the "good Samaritan," 10:30–37) or found in their lostness (the "prodigal son," 15:11–32). It is true that the book of Acts relates accounts of miraculous deliverance from danger—Peter from Herod's death sentence (Acts 12:6–17) or Paul's surviving a shipwreck (Acts 27:9–44)—but the apostolic witness is by no means preoccupied with material blessing or earthly safety. Instead, it rivets attention on salvation in Christ, who was not delivered from earthly suffering and death in order that he might achieve eternal life for others. Peter and John declare, "There is salvation in no one else, for there is no other name under heaven given among mortals by which we must be saved" (Acts 4:12), while Paul and Silas tell the jailer in Philippi, "Believe on the Lord Jesus, and you will be saved" (Acts 16:31).

The New Testament letters explore several facets of God's salvation and restoration through Christ. Paul glories in the scandal and the foolishness of "the message of the cross" (1 Cor. 1:18–25), such that he "decided to know nothing among [the Corinthians] except Jesus Christ, and him crucified" (1 Cor. 2:2). The Letter to the Ephesians extols the application of God's merciful salvation: "For by grace you have been saved through faith, and this is not your own doing; it is the gift of God—not the result of works, so that no one may boast" (Eph. 2:8–9), a thought echoed in the Pastoral Letter to Titus: "He saved us, not because of any works of righteousness that we had done, but according to his mercy" (Titus 3:5). Even so, salvation is paradoxically something *in which* to do "good works" (Eph. 2:10) and *which* to "work out . . . with fear and trembling" (Phil. 2:12). It is therefore logical that a New Testament theology like Caird's would be structured around the multifaceted dimensions of salvation (its plan, need, fact, experience, hope, and bringer). But no discussion of salvation would be complete without affirming that the ultimate vision of God's salvation in Christ includes the material as well as the spiritual. For human beings, Jesus' miraculous raising of the dead (the girl in Mark 5:41–42, or Lazarus in John 11:43–44) and his own resurrection (Matt. 28:6) point to his ultimate victory over death and the grave that Paul eloquently expounds in 1 Corinthians 15. And the gift of resurrection is enveloped in the larger plan of God to restore all creation in the new heavens and new earth (Rom. 8:19–21; Rev. 21:1).

Summary

This selective study of the God attested in biblical theology clearly has been traditional, that is, it has emphasized the "core testimony" of the biblical witness. Nevertheless, at certain points I have also broached some of the problems that arise and tensions that exist in this portrayal. My emphasis partly lies in the fact that I will address some of the main challenges, the "countertestimony," in the following section on relationship with God. But I also readily admit to interpreting ambiguity in God's portrayal within a much larger and more straightforward witness to God's character, words, and acts. To be sure, no presentation of biblical theology should fail to grapple with the voices or even impressions that someone like Brueggemann may hear and see in Scripture. That he, for example, chooses to regard the exile as testifying to the "shattered transcendence" of God can only assist the discipline by giving the strongest possible exposition of the theological tensions.[74] Having said that, however, I am persuaded by Terence Fretheim's argument that Israel's struggle to understand God's will and ways "does not mean that God has a divided will with regard to the divine purpose."[75] But that very real struggle moves us to consider its own theological context, namely, the themes that arise when considering the Bible's witness to God's relationship with human beings.

LIVING IN RELATIONSHIP WITH GOD

While biblical theology first and foremost expounds the God of the Bible, and can therefore distinguish themes about God's character or actions, this exposition can never finally be separated from all of the ways in which the biblical writers perceived their relationship with the God whose story or character they extolled. If the greatest commandment calls on people to love God above all things, then it is incumbent upon biblical theology to explore the implications of the relationship within which this love is offered and accepted. The issues and methods of the discipline indicate the benefits of different approaches to the Bible's theological content, so that along with the concepts themselves comes an appreciation of the historical dimensions of biblical theology as well as the perspectives of human existence and experience. For these reasons, the discussion below highlights three major ways of shaping the relationship Israel and the church believed it had with God, and these, in turn, will yield important themes of their own: history and story, creation and covenant, and life and worship.

Through History and Story

Many important themes in biblical theology emerge when we reflect upon the way the Bible articulates people's experience with God, in particular, the sense Israel had of the dynamic nature of their relationship with Yahweh or, likewise, of the church with the God and Father of Jesus Christ. Given the depth and breadth of the theological dimensions involved, I have chosen to consider three tenses of history and story. Not only is biblical theology a grateful remembrance of what God has done in the past; it is also faithful actualization of what God is doing now and a hopeful account of what God will do in the future.

Remembering the Past with Gratitude

The field of biblical theology has often been captivated by the Bible's own sense of history, its ways of remembering and rehearsing the key moments of God's revelation to and action on behalf of the generations of the past. Whether scholars describe this phenomenon in terms of a "history of salvation" (von Hofmann's model or the nuance given it by Cullmann), Wright's "mighty acts of God," or von Rad's "creedal formulae," the remembering was always meant to express the people's wonder and gratitude for what God had done for them.[76] Several examples of early Yahwistic poetry (e.g., Exod. 15; Judg. 5; Deut. 33; Ps. 68; Hab. 3) describe Yahweh's power to save,[77] but longer, narrative recollections exist, such as the opening chapters of Deuteronomy (1–3), which recount the events since leaving Mount Sinai. The Torah's sense of history surfaces even in the brief, historical preamble to the Ten Commandments, thus placing the Decalogue against the background of Yahweh's identity as "the LORD your God, who brought you out of the land of Egypt, out of the house of slavery" (Exod. 20:2). The books of the Deuteronomistic

History (Joshua, Judges, Samuel, Kings) not only recount the eras of leadership in light of the theology and literary perspective of Deuteronomy,[78] but they also contain confessions by non-Israelites such as Rahab of Jericho: "For we have heard how the LORD dried up the water of the Red Sea before you when you came out of Egypt, and what you did to the two kings of the Amorites that were beyond the Jordan. . . . The LORD your God is indeed God in heaven above and on earth below" (Josh. 2:10–11). The place of these books in the Hebrew canon as "Former Prophets" also helps to explain the selectivity of Israel's recollections; their telling of the past is never a detached, "objective" account but rather one within which the prophetic word reigns supreme to achieve Yahweh's purposes. The other major historical work of the Old Testament, that of the Chronicler (1–2 Chronicles, Ezra, and Nehemiah) takes yet another perspective on the past, focusing far more attention than the Deuteronomists on David's influence upon temple worship (1 Chr. 22–29) and other priestly matters.

The Babylonian exile was a low point historically speaking, but some psalms reveal its deleterious effect on the people's sacred memory: "How could we sing the LORD's song in a foreign land? If I forget you, O Jerusalem, let my right hand wither! Let my tongue cling to the roof of my mouth, if I do not remember you, if I do not set Jerusalem above my highest joy" (Ps. 137:4–6). The postexilic era provided opportunities for the people and their leaders to remember again and be grateful for Yahweh's faithfulness to Israel through the ages, even as they were moved to confession and petition for their current plight: "You have been just in all that has come upon us, for you have dealt faithfully and we have acted wickedly" (Neh. 9:33). In all of this, however, John Goldingay argues that Israel's story is still "gospel": "The good news is that bad news has neither the last word or the first word. It stands in the context of a purpose to bless that was set in motion at the Beginning, and a purpose to create that persists to the End."[79] Perhaps that is one reason why the Psalter, completed after the exile, still contained many psalms of thanksgiving and praise: "O give thanks to the LORD, for he is good, for his steadfast love endures forever" (Ps. 136:1). Indeed, in Westermann's famous expression, the Psalter itself moves "from lament to praise," making Israel's final word, literally and symbolically, "hallelujah" (Ps. 150:6).

The Gospels offer selective reflections on the meaning of Jesus' life, death, and resurrection, much like the Former Prophets selectively recounted Israel's history. Although it was Luke's purpose to investigate "everything carefully from the very first, to write an orderly account" (Luke 1:3), scholarly study of the "Synoptic problem" has pointed to the perspectives of and choices made by each Gospel. What John declared about the necessity of his own editorial activity—"Now Jesus did many other signs in the presence of his disciples, which are not written in this book" (John 20:30)—could be said of all four Gospels. The Synoptic Gospels to varying degrees form their retelling of the good news about Jesus in light of the connections they make with Israel's narrative. For its part, John's Gospel seems more consciously than the Synoptics to reflect a postresurrection perspective, acknowledging from the start that his account is of the very Word of God and pointing to Jesus' glory as "the only Son, who is close to the Father's heart" (John 1:18).[80] In its proclamation, the early church continued the Old Testament's narrative style of history, if Stephen's speech (Acts 7) and Paul's preaching (Acts 13) are any indication. And embedded in the New Testament letters are hints of this historical sense, grounding the revelation of Jesus Christ and the church's preaching in the flow of history: "his Son, who was descended from David according to the flesh" (Rom. 1:3); "When the fullness of time had come, God sent his Son, born of a woman, born under the law" (Gal. 4:4); "He was revealed in flesh, vindicated in spirit, seen by angels, proclaimed among Gentiles, believed in throughout the world, taken up in glory" (1 Tim. 3:16). By using "echoes of scripture," says Richard Hays, Paul invited "his readers and hearers to a *conversion of the imagination*. He was calling Gentiles to understand their identity anew in light of the gospel of Jesus Christ—a gospel message comprehensible only in relation to the larger narrative of God's dealing with Israel."[81] That this identity was to engender thankfulness on the part of early Christian communities is evident in the way they are called to pray: "In everything by prayer and supplication with thanksgiving let your requests be made known to God" (Phil. 4:6; see Col. 3:17; Eph. 5:20). Paul is thankful for his remembrance of churches and individuals (Phil. 1:3; Phlm. 4), and he also gives thanks for the way "Christ always leads us in triumphal procession," carrying on the story of the gospel (2 Cor. 2:14).

Living in the Present by Faith

Although Hebrew terms for "faith" and "believing" are used less frequently than their Greek counterparts in the New Testament, the notion of living in the present by faith was fully consistent with Old Testament theology.[82] In the midst of his struggle to claim the divine promises extended to him and his family, Abraham was able to express faith in Yahweh: "And [Abraham] believed the LORD; and the LORD reckoned it to him as righteousness" (Gen. 15:6). Far from having accomplished righteousness on his own, "it is stated programmatically that belief in God's promise alone has established Abraham's right relation to God."[83] Even when a narrative does not explicitly state that people believed God's "word of salvation," writes Westermann, "in reflective retrospect, from a distance, it is said that the Israelites believed the word of salvation which came to them: Exod. 4:31: . . . And the people believed . . . Ps. 106:12: Then they believed his words; they sang his praise."[84] Individual faith may be highlighted using other terms or expressions, such as the midwives' "fear of God" rather than Pharaoh (Exod. 1:17, 21), Solomon's prayer that the temple symbolize God's presence and blessing (1 Kgs. 8:23–53), or Esther's courage to act on behalf of her people in spite of the dangers (Esth. 4:16). The prophetic words of assurance, "Do not be afraid," were especially intended to elicit faith from people in a time of crisis, as Isaiah's oracle from Yahweh comforted Hezekiah when Sennacherib's army besieged Jerusalem (Isa. 37:6), or as Second Isaiah's message encouraged the exiles to trust and not fear: "Do not fear, for I am with you, do not be afraid, for I am your God; I will strengthen you, I will help you, I will uphold you with my victorious right hand" (Isa. 41:10). Habakkuk's oracle contends that "the righteous live by their faith" (Hab. 2:4), so that such a person "trusts in the reliability of God's promise contained in [Habakkuk's] vision."[85] Of course, if it is "the righteous" who trust God, then there was always the specter of unbelief, and this is cited by the narrator of Kings as one of the reasons for Israel's downfall: "They would not listen but were stubborn, as their ancestors had been, who did not believe in the LORD their God" (2 Kgs. 17:14). But like the issue of gratitude for the past, this word of judgment is not the final message regarding faith. Israel's psalms were but one of the places where people found the faith to carry on in trying circumstances, by the expression of trust found in many lament psalms—"But I trusted in your steadfast love; my heart shall rejoice in your salvation" (Ps. 13:5)—or in the "psalms of trust" themselves (Pss. 23, 91, 121, 125, 131).[86]

When Jesus comes on the scene in Mark's Gospel, his very first words are, "The time is fulfilled, and the kingdom of God has come near; repent, and believe in the good news" (Mark 1:15). Along with repentance, therefore, came faith as an essential response to the gospel of the kingdom. It is not, of course, necessary for the verb "believe" or its synonyms to be used in order for faith to be expressed. There is Peter's statement that Jesus is "the Messiah, the Son of the living God," which Jesus calls a revelation from the Father (Matt. 16:16–17). Then, too, the Gospel narratives relate many stories of faith, from Joseph and Mary's acceptance of God's plan (Matt. 1:24; Luke 1:38) to the numerous Johannine accounts of individuals who are challenged to believe: Nicodemus (John 3:1–21), the Samaritan woman (John 4:1–42), the man born blind (John 9:1–41), and the sisters of Lazarus (John 11:1–44). Faith may be weak and yet still be real—"I believe; help my unbelief!" (Mark 9:24)—and Thomas's story shows that a blessing remains for all who believe in Jesus without having seen him in the flesh (John 20:29). That story is immediately followed by the purpose of John's Gospel: "But these [signs] are written so that you may come to believe that Jesus is the Messiah, the Son of God, and that through believing you may have life in his name" (John 20:31). The apostolic preaching, like that of Jesus, called for faith and repentance, confirmed in the sign of baptism (Acts 2:38–39; 16:31).

Over the past fifty years, New Testament theology has given special attention to the Pauline doctrine of justification by faith, from Bultmann's existential interpretations to the currently debated "new perspective" on Paul, which seeks to relate Paul's work more consistently to his Jewish roots in their first-century context.[87] Theological interpretation has often turned on the meaning of the Greek in Romans 3:22, *dià písteōs Iēsou Christou*, translated by the NRSV as "through faith in Jesus Christ" but with a marginal reading, "through the faith of Jesus Christ"; this latter reading is encouraged by Richard Hays, N. T. Wright, and others. What is at stake here is that the *primary* means of God's righteousness being revealed is *Jesus' own faithfulness to God*, which is then claimed in faith by human beings.[88] Emphasizing Jesus' faith in (or faithfulness to) God rather than human faith (which is also mentioned in Rom. 3:22) does not make Luther's insights into justification passé, but it is part of a larger interpretive argument that avoids simply equating first-century Judaism's view of the law with medieval Catholicism's view of the role of works in salvation.[89] Yet another issue is the relationship between what Paul says about justification by faith in Romans and Galatians with what James says about justification by works in James 2:14–26. The matter is complex, but Paul's argument is primarily that justification is not achieved by humans through "works prescribed by the law" (Rom. 3:28), whereas James stresses that believers do good works—he especially singles out care for the poor (Jas. 2:15–17)—as an expression of their living faith: "I by my works will show you my faith" (Jas. 2:18).

Elsewhere in the New Testament, Ephesians understands faith as the means whereby we receive God's gracious salvation, adding that even the expression of faith "is not your own doing; it is the gift of God—not the result of works, so that no one may boast" (Eph. 2:8–9). Having said this, the author immediately ensures that the purpose of salvation is "for good works, which God prepared beforehand to be our way of life" (Eph. 2:10); indeed, faith is a necessary part of the "armor of God," serving as a shield "with which . . . to quench the flaming arrows of the evil one" (Eph. 6:16; see 1 Thess. 5:8). Hebrews defines faith as "the assurance of things hoped for, the conviction of things not seen" (Heb. 11:1), and then goes on to develop this thesis through many examples of Old Testament characters who lived their lives "without having received the promises, but from a distance they saw and greeted them" (11:13). This delay of the promise is explained by the larger goal of uniting the ancestors with first-century believers as corecipients of the promise.[90] But even while there may be infrequent material blessings or physical evidence for the reality of God's kingdom in the world, the Johannine letters declare, "And this is the victory that conquers the world, our faith. Who is it that conquers the world but the one who believes that Jesus is the Son of God?" (1 John 5:4–5).

Awaiting the Future in Hope

From its outset, the story of the Old Testament anticipates the future, awaiting obedience to every command of the Creator and reception of every blessing that is promised. After the judgment declared in the garden, children are named in hope, as Lamech said of his son Noah: "Out of the ground that the LORD has cursed this one shall bring us relief from our work and from the toil of our hands" (Gen. 5:29). There is, of course, often the threat of destruction, sometimes divine (Gen. 6:7) and sometimes human in its source (Exod. 1:22), but the story goes forward because faithful people hope for the restoration and fulfillment of God's promise. Joseph commanded the Israelites to carry his bones with them when they left Egypt, for he testified, "I am about to die; but God will surely come to you, and bring you up out of this land to the land that he swore to Abraham, to Isaac, and to Jacob" (Gen. 50:24). Much of Deuteronomy's rhetoric works with the hope of inheriting the land of Canaan, but there also come responsibilities to live in covenant obedience to Yahweh. In like manner, Samuel warns of the life Israel will have under the rule of kings (1 Sam. 12:1–18), and the conclusion to the Former Prophets holds out a faint glimmer of hope that, in spite of national destruction and exile, a Davidic king still lives. There may yet be an heir who can lead the people back to their land (1 Kgs. 25:27–30).[91]

When the Latter Prophets come into view, the "prophetic hope" of divine forgiveness and ultimate restoration to the land is, of course, preceded and overshadowed by the weight of judgment against idolatry and injustice. Thus, there were times in Israel's history where it was not wise to hope for "the day of the LORD," as when Amos warns: "Alas for you who desire the day of the LORD! Why do you want the day of the LORD? . . . Is not the day of the LORD darkness, not light, and gloom with no brightness?" (Amos 5:18, 20).[92] Even so, the positive dimensions of the prophetic hope cannot be underestimated, for they contain Yahweh's final word regarding both Israel's future and, with them, that of the whole world: "In days to come the mountain of the LORD's house shall be established as the highest of the mountains, and shall be raised up above the hills. Peoples shall stream to it, and many nations shall come and say: 'Come, let us go up to the mountain of the LORD, to the house of the God of Jacob'" (Mic. 4:1–2; see Isa. 2:1–4).[93] The ability to hope also serves as a feature of Israel's worship and prayers, assuring both individuals and the people that there is reason to "hope in God" (Pss. 42:5, 11; 43:5; see Ps. 71:5, 14) and seek his gift of renewal in spite of uncertainty (Ps. 90:13–17; see Hab. 3:17–19).

The Greek noun for "hope" (*elpis*) does not occur in the Gospels, and its cognate verbal form (*elpidzō*) is used in only five instances.[94] Nevertheless, the concept of attention toward the future is present in Jesus' teachings. He instructs his disciples in the Olivet discourse, "Keep awake, therefore, for you do not know on what day your Lord is coming" (Matt. 24:42; see also the parable of the wedding attendants in Matt. 25:1–13), and he certainly expresses hope for himself and the repentant thief on the cross when he promises, "Today you will be with me in Paradise" (Luke 23:43). In a far deeper way, however, the gospel proclamation of the kingdom comes with eschatological force, such that John the Baptist stands as a latter-day fulfillment of Isaiah's prophecy of the Lord's coming (Isa. 40:3–5; and in all four Gospels). John himself interpreted Jesus as the one who would decisively save and judge the people of God (Matt. 3:11–12), and Jesus, in turn, viewed John as the latter-day Elijah (Matt. 11:13–14; see Mal. 4:5–6). Put in this light, therefore, the Gospels definitely share something of the future orientation of earlier apocalyptic writings and the other writings of the New Testament.[95]

Paul's hopefulness operates on several levels. He trusts that God will complete the work God has begun in the lives of believers (Phil. 1:6; see 1 Cor. 1:8–11) and in the same context goes on to express his confidence about his own future, in this life and beyond: "It is my eager expectation and hope that I will not be put to shame in any way, but that by my speaking with all boldness, Christ will be exalted now as always in my body, whether by life or by death. For to me, living is Christ and dying is gain. . . . My desire is to depart and be with Christ, for that is far better" (Phil. 1:20–21, 23). We have seen how Paul anticipated the renewal of creation and the glory of God's children in the redemption of their bodies (Rom. 8:17–23), but he also related this hope to the Lord's return to raise the dead and meet his people at the "archangel's call and with the sound of God's trumpet . . . and so we will be with the Lord forever" (1 Thess. 4:16–17).[96] According to Richard Hays, Paul's outlook on the future was tied in with his understanding of Israel's story, "the message of eschatological salvation promised in Israel's scriptures—pre-eminently Isaiah—to the whole world."[97] Paul's message to his first-century readers, writes Herman Ridderbos, was that while "Christ's advent, death, and resurrection" had already inaugurated "the eschatological time of salvation," the full "revelation of the mystery . . . will not be completed before Christ shall have been manifested in glory with all his own."[98]

Much like the Old Testament prophets, several New Testament writings maintain that the future contains the certainty of judgment. Many of Jesus' teachings in the Synoptic Gospels refer to expressions of temporal or final judgment, often contained in symbolic and parabolic form (Matt. 7:24–27; 25:31–46; Mark 12:1–12; Luke 21:5–36) but sometimes stated directly: "Not everyone who says to me 'Lord, Lord,' will enter the kingdom of heaven, but only the one who does the will of my Father in heaven" (Matt. 7:21). The Gospel of John also refers to a judgment "on the last day" when Jesus' own word will serve as the standard (John 12:47–48; see 9:39), but it is also clear that for John, Jesus' death is the definitive judgment upon the world: "'Now is the judgment of this world; now the ruler of this world will be driven out. And I, when I am lifted up from the earth, will draw all people to myself.' He said this to indicate the kind of death he was to die" (John 12:31–33). Authors of New Testament letters often refer to the coming judgment on false teachers and those who persecute believers (2 Thess. 1:9; 2 Pet. 2:4–20; Rev. 6:16–17; 16:4–7), and there is frequent reference to the "day of the Lord" (1 Thess. 5:2–5; 2 Thess. 1:10; 2:2; 2 Pet. 3:10; 1 John 2:28).[99] But for the faithful, the focus is not on fear of a coming judgment—"perfect love casts out fear" (1 John 4:18)—but rather upon their "living hope through the resurrection of Jesus Christ from the dead" (1 Pet. 1:3). The challenge remains to persevere in this hope, knowing that "hope that is seen is not hope. For who hopes for what is seen? But if we hope for what we do not see, we wait for it with patience" (Rom. 8:24–25).

Summary

In reflecting on the "story" quality of both testaments, John Goldingay states, "The biblical story comprises a beginning and a development but no end."[100] Such description of the narrative parallels the past-present-future motif above, insofar as hope does not ascertain the exact nature of what may come or what we will be (1 John 3:2). This does not mean, however, that further reflection on the story must cease, for new insights and proposals always hold the promise of clarifying theological interpretation of the text.[101] Readings from the "margins" or the "center" will wrestle with continuity and discontinuity in the story itself and in the people of the story. In this regard, it is again true that my discussion has leaned toward the "center," perhaps closer to a core testimony. The uncertainty in the outcome of narratives, such as the problematic conclusion to the Gospel of Mark, raises questions about what we are to do with the ambiguity. No quick or easy solutions will truly and fully deepen our gratitude, increase our faith, or strengthen our hope.[102] But Ellen Charry wisely comments that "enduring unclarity is confusing and enervating. It must eventually give way to some meaning, even if that meaning is only temporarily satisfying and must later be revised. . . . The tension between an unfollowable world and a followable God must be resolved in one direction or the other."[103] The biblical story and the history out of which it grew, with all their disjointed pieces, invite mature theological response to the past, present, and future, much like Paul's celebrated triad of "faith, hope, and love" always remains part of "a still more excellent way" (1 Cor. 13:13).[104]

Through Creation and Covenant

The above discussion provides some historical and narrative sense to the theology of relationship with God, setting the context for the content below. Moreover, the first part of this chapter, on the God attested in biblical theology, described key thematic features of God's creative and covenant-making activity. In what follows, the spheres of creation and covenant will be studied to discern how the Bible witnesses to humankind's responsibility before God in these two areas. Biblical theologians have understood the relationship between creation and covenant in different ways, and several proposals have surfaced, some placing greater emphasis on one or the other concept, while others have maintained a level of tension between them. Patrick Miller highlights the importance of this relationship when he writes that the "interaction [of creation and covenant] is theologically complex but an accounting of it in biblical theology has been, and remains, a matter of no small urgency. It has to do not only with getting our theology straight, but with how to live in this world and with one another."[105] With this in mind, I will consider human responsibility within creation and covenant separately and then focus on the problem of disobedience when either area, or their relationship, becomes skewed.

Human Responsibility for Creation

God's creative word and activity set the stage for the biblical drama of human responsibility for the created order. As the very image of God on earth, humans are responsible for all other forms of life (Gen. 1:26) and, as part of God's command and blessing to multiply on the earth, are granted the right to "subdue" and have "dominion" over it.[106] Although these terms can suggest an abusive stance toward nature, these activities are included in the evaluation "very good" (Gen. 1:31), and thus Terence Fretheim states that "having dominion and subduing are understood *originally* as completely positive for the life of the other creatures."[107] Since the terms "good" and "very good" need not imply a natural state of perfection, scholars have debated the relative power and presence of "chaotic forces" at work in creation. Levenson's careful treatment of the matter takes the "persistence of evil" in the world seriously, but Fretheim is also correct that the language of Genesis 1:2 ("without form and void") is not describing evil.[108] The need for human activity is further solidified by the way Genesis 2 relates humankind to the earth from which it was formed (v. 7) and portrays humans as needing "to till and to keep" the garden (v. 15).[109] The rest of the primeval story reinforces the theology of these foundational chapters, with Noah's family maintaining responsibility in a fashion parallel to Genesis 1–2 (see Gen. 8:16–19) and God involving humans and nature in the covenant following the flood (Gen. 9:9–17).

The Ten Commandments also express concern for creation in the command to rest from work on the Sabbath, in which both humans and domestic animals are included (Exod. 20:8–11; see Gen. 2:2–3). Other legal material required that the land lie fallow every seventh year, not only for the sake of human beings, especially the poor, but also that "the wild animals may eat" (Exod. 23:10–11; see Lev. 25:2–7 and further regulations for the year of jubilee in Lev. 25:8–55). The Deuteronomic code wound a tight connection between the people and the land, so that they would never forget it was Yahweh's gift to them (Deut. 8:7–20). Their failure to remain obedient formed a part of the prophetic indictment against Israel, as Jeremiah asked God, "How long will the land mourn, and the grass of every field wither? For the wickedness of those who live in it the animals and the birds are swept away" (Jer 12:4; see Hos. 4:1–3; Amos 4:10).[110] In contrast to the sadness of these judgments, the creation psalms revel in the majesty and wonder of what God has made, and by extension call for human involvement and responsiveness to God's law (Pss. 8:5–8; 19:1–6; 104). If nature can join humans in praise of their common creator (Ps. 148), humankind should regard the world with the same love and delight that God has for it (see Job 38–41). Likewise, the Wisdom literature itself employs creation imagery, especially in the character of Woman Wisdom (Prov. 8:22–31), to teach that "the world is open to human probing and yields insight to those who ask appropriate questions and consider issues in a discriminating way."[111] Although there are not grounds for developing a complete or systematic "natural theology" based upon Wisdom literature, the Old Testament as a whole does portray what Fretheim calls "*a mutuality of vocation*; both humans and nonhumans are called to a vocation on behalf of each other in the furtherance of God's purposes for the creation."[112]

Considering their much different contexts and interests, the New Testament authors pay little attention to the topic of human responsibility for creation. Nevertheless, their writings give us no reason to conclude that the early Christian communities held a vastly different or lower view of creation. Through his example, instructions, and the imagery of his parables, Jesus assumes and communicates a clear regard for the interaction of people with nature; still he tends to place himself as the center of attention: "The sabbath was made for humankind, and not humankind for the sabbath; so the Son of Man is lord even of the sabbath" (Mark 2:27–28). Like the prophetic critique of preexilic Israel, so too Jesus' parables compare his own setting to mismanaged vineyards and kingdoms (Matt. 21:33–46; Luke 19:11–27). On the positive side, among the Beatitudes is Jesus' expectation that there will be an earth for the meek to inherit (Matt. 5:5). The tone of these teachings is matched by a similar subtlety in the rest of the New Testament. Believers are to care for their physical bodies as "members of Christ" and as "a temple of the Holy

Spirit" (1 Cor. 6:15, 19).[113] So, too, the hope of new creation is now focused on union with Christ, which makes it possible for human beings to share with creation in a glorious transformation (Rom. 8:18–25; see 2 Cor. 3:18; 5:17).

Human Responsiveness to Covenant

God's gracious initiative in covenant-making expected a faithful and obedient response regardless of the expression or circumstances.[114] In spite of their different circumstances, these covenants always had stipulations by which the human partners would demonstrate their willingness to abide by Yahweh's commands, the nature and extent of which varied greatly. Noah and his family had to respect human life and carry on the expansion of the human race (Gen. 9:4–7), while Abraham's keeping of the covenant involved the observance of circumcision for all his descendants (Gen. 17:9–14). The numerous commandments of the Mosaic covenant were clearly more detailed than those with Noah and Abraham, given that Israel was committing to a community of order and justice: "Then [Moses] took the book of the covenant, and read it in the hearing of the people; and they said, 'All that the LORD has spoken we will do, and we will be obedient'" (Exod. 24:7). Confirmed and expanded in Moab (Deut. 29:1) and Shechem (Josh. 24), there are no major developments until Yahweh enters into a special relationship with King David to ensure unconditionally that his dynasty will last forever (2 Sam. 7:12–16). While any given king may be punished for committing "iniquity," Yahweh promises never to "take [his] steadfast love from him" (v. 15). The final development in Old Testament covenantal theology comes in the form of Jeremiah's oracle that Yahweh will make a "new covenant with the house of Israel and the house of Judah. . . . I will put my law within them, and I will write it on their hearts" (Jer. 31:31, 33).

Bernhard Anderson speaks of Old Testament covenant theology as forming three primary yet parallel tracks: "the Priestly, the Mosaic, and the royal," which he describes as "the promissory covenant with Abraham and Sarah; the covenant of law with Moses, Miriam, and Aaron; and the covenant of dynastic leadership with David."[115] When taken together these major covenantal theologies contained various aspects of humankind's relationship with God as well as expectations for relationships among humans. But all of these contexts, different though they are in focus and content, share the common requirement of exclusive devotion to Yahweh, whose gracious initiative lays a claim on Israel's loyalty. Commenting on the way the First Commandment defines Israel's identity, Patrick Miller writes:

> If the Lord of Israel is the one who made us and the world of which
> we are a part; if the Lord of Israel is the only one who can take away
> our fear and save us in our trouble, if the Lord of Israel has alone
> brought us to this place and alone is our hope for the future, then all

our trust and all our obedience and all our adoration are placed there and nowhere else.[116]

On the one hand, Israel's failure to maintain such devotion clearly formed part of the biblical explanation for judgment: "They despised [Yahweh's] statutes, and his covenant that he made with their ancestors, and the warnings that he gave them" (2 Kgs. 17:15); or as Jeremiah puts it, ". . . a covenant that they broke, though I was their husband, says the LORD" (Jer. 31:32). On the other hand, Anderson shows that the biblical writers could not explain all of Israel's suffering in terms of disobedience—"All this has come upon us, yet we have not forgotten you, or been false to your covenant" (Ps. 44:17)—and such dissonance between God's word and their experience "created a crisis of covenantal theologies."[117]

While it may be true that the New Testament writers do not treat covenant as a major category,[118] its authors seem to assume its existence in the background even if it rarely comes to the forefront. The most explicit mention in the Gospels is Jesus' reference to the cup at Passover, which he calls "my blood of the covenant" (Matt. 26:28; Mark 14:24), though Luke connects this with Jeremiah 31 with the phrase "the new covenant in my blood" (Luke 22:20).[119] Stephen's narration of Israel's history recalls the ancestral covenant (Acts 7:8), but its primary rhetorical purpose there sets up his indictment of the religious leaders in Jerusalem. When we come to the book of Hebrews, Brevard Childs states that "the theology of covenant becomes a major rubric for its author."[120] For one thing, the letter sees Jesus' death as a sacrificial confirmation of a new covenant that contrasts with the first one: "For this reason [Christ] is the mediator of a new covenant, so that those who are called may receive the promised eternal inheritance, because a death has occurred that redeems them from the transgressions under the first covenant" (Heb. 9:15).[121] But a second contrast is set up between the kind of relationship envisioned under each covenant, that is, between earthly, terrifying Mount Sinai (Heb. 12:18–21) and "Mount Zion . . . the city of the living God, the heavenly Jerusalem" (Heb. 12:22).[122] Childs argues that in spite of these contrasts, "the writer of Hebrews . . . does not relegate Israel's scriptures to the past, but continues to view the biblical text as God's living voice addressing a pilgrim people who await the heavenly city (13.14)."[123]

The above contrast raises the difficult question of the New Testament's appropriation of the promises associated with the covenant, particularly in the way literal concerns such as land, descendants, and material blessing tend to be expanded if not spiritualized, while the greater focus is placed on the inclusion of the Gentiles.[124] Once again, Jesus himself became the focus of God's promises—"For in [Jesus Christ] every one of God's promises is a 'Yes'" (2 Cor. 1:20)—and the Pauline theme of "union with Christ" worked with this notion.

In Paul's thought, relationship with God in Christ was not something maintained by humans at a distance but something they experienced *in him*: "For if we have been united with him in a death like his, we will certainly be united with him in a resurrection like his" (Rom. 6:5); "for in every way you have been enriched in him" (1 Cor. 1:5); or "rejoice in the Lord always" (Phil. 4:4). The Letter to the Colossians also develops this theme: "Continue to live your lives in him, rooted and built up in him" (Col. 2:6) and later, "For you have died, and your life is hidden with Christ in God" (3:3).[125] According to Herman Ridderbos, the concept of being "in Christ" is not a mystical experience for rare occasions; rather, it speaks "of an abiding reality determinative for the whole of the Christian life, to which appeal can be made at all times, in all sorts of connections, and with respect to the whole church without distinction."[126] Thus, Paul continues the communal sense of covenant operative in the Old Testament while at the same time extending the notion of relationship with God—"I will take you as my people, and I will be your God" (Exod. 6:7)—to an even more intimate union with the Creator and Redeemer.

Human Weakness and Sin

The theme of human sinfulness is not properly a separate topic from creation and covenant responsibilities, but it calls for special attention in light of the Bible's focus on disobedience to covenant expectations and failure to care for God's gracious gift of the earth and land. This very focus, however, makes a biblical-theological study of the matter quite difficult, for literature in every genre, time period, and canonical section of the Bible explores the reasons for and the consequences of sin. Mark Biddle's recent study of this theme probes the biblical vocabulary and its various dimensions by concentrating not on legalistic definitions but on its essential aspect as "the violation of the basic relationship to God," which surfaces in human pride, rebellion, rejection of authentic freedom, and a basic lack of trust.[127] While some biblical texts refer to the weakness of human nature in and of itself ("We are dust," Pss. 90:3; 103:14; Gen. 2:7; see Eccl. 3:19–20; Heb. 4:15), other texts lay the blame on the inherent sinful nature of human beings: "Every inclination of the thoughts of their hearts was only evil continually" (Gen. 6:5; Jer. 17:9; Rom. 3:9–18).

Old Testament narratives are full of stories of individual failure among even the greatest of characters in Israel's ancestry and national history: Abraham and Sarah's use and mistreatment of Hagar (Gen. 16); Joseph and his brothers' strained relationship (Gen. 37–50), Moses' murder of an Egyptian and his lack of faith (Exod. 2–4), Miriam and Aaron's jealousy (Num. 12), David's adultery and his arranged death of Uriah (2 Sam. 11), and Solomon's idolatry (1 Kgs. 11).[128] The primeval story, of course, sets forth the foundational choice of disobedience to God's command in the garden (Gen. 2:16–17; 3:6–7), followed by the downward spiral of murder and vengeance (Gen. 4) up to the corporate sinfulness of humankind before the flood (Gen. 6:5). The behavior of Israelites delivered from Egypt was often marked by bitterness, complaining, and rebellion (Exod. 17:1–7; 32; Num. 11:1–5; 14:1–4; 16), and the entire Judges "cycle" points to their regular abandonment of Yahweh (Judg. 2:11–23), paving the way for the concluding verdict: "All the people did what was right in their own eyes" (Judg. 21:25). Along with the Deuteronomistic judgment on the northern kingdom's covenant breaking, the prophetic books describe a number of different ways that the people misconstrued their relationship with Yahweh, from the empty worship of Israel (Amos 5:21–23) and Judah (Isa. 1:11–15) to the failure of their leaders in every sector of society to shepherd the people (Ezek. 34): "their kings, their officials, their priests, and their prophets" (Jer. 2:26; 13:13). The collective nature of the people's guilt and the shared suffering of sin's effects was partly addressed by oracles such as those in Jeremiah and Ezekiel that advocated a doctrine of individual responsibility (Jer. 31:29–30; Ezek. 18:19–20), but as Biddle shows, these statements addressed the efforts of "the generation that experienced the exile . . . to displace responsibility for its fate onto its ancestors."[129] To be sure, proverbial wisdom held individuals responsible for learning, so that they might avoid a whole host of foolish errors—"the complacency of fools destroys them" (Prov. 1:32); "those who hate to be rebuked are stupid" (Prov. 12:1)—and instead, "lay aside immaturity and live, and walk in the way of insight" (Prov. 9:6).[130] Along with appeals from wise teachers and prophetic calls to repentance, several penitential psalms invite sinners to seek the mercy and forgiveness of Yahweh: "I said, 'I will confess my transgressions to the LORD,' and you forgave the guilt of my sin" (Ps. 32:5; see also Pss. 6:1–2; 51:1–12).

We have seen how the Gospels' kingdom proclamation demands readiness by means of repentance (e.g., Matt. 3:2, 7–10; Luke 3:10–14), but only Jesus' sermons and lessons directly address the problem of sin. Far from declaring hopeless judgment, Jesus invites his hearers to adopt a more serious attitude toward God's standards and to embrace an inward obedience to the covenant —"You have heard that it was said . . . But I say to you . . ." (e.g., Matt. 5:21–22) —which culminates in the highest ideal: "Be perfect, therefore, as your heavenly Father is perfect" (Matt. 5:48).[131] There are lessons and parables about avoiding sin and offering forgiveness for the sake of brothers or sisters (Matt. 18; Luke 17:1–4), but the Gospels also record Jesus' own resistence to temptation (Matt. 4:1–11; Mark 1:12–13; Luke 4:1–13), grounded in his use of the Scriptures and echoing Israel's own trials in the wilderness but succeeding where they fell short (Deut. 6:13, 16; 8:3).[132] Although much of his behavior is exemplary, his devotion to the will of God—"not what I want, but what you want" (Mark 14:36)—and determination to complete his mission (Luke 9:51) are also part of his obedience on behalf of sinners.

Paul's letters do not mince words about the extensive and intensive character of human sin (Rom. 1:18–2:24).[133] He believes in the need for humankind's salvation, their deliverance from the "slavery" of sin, the wages of which is death (Rom. 1:16–17; 6:12–23; 10:10–13). Sometimes Paul lists "works of the flesh" that must be avoided, but his tone is not primarily negative; rather, he calls believers to live freely in Christ, guided by and manifesting the fruit of the Spirit (Gal. 5:1, 13, 19–26). Paul commands the Corinthian community to deal harshly with a wayward member (1 Cor. 5:1–5) and then to show love and forgiveness (2 Cor. 2:5–11). Other New Testament writings emphasize an exchange of old ways for new ones (Col. 3:5–17; Eph. 4:25–32), the ideals of holy living (1 Thess. 3:13; 1 Pet. 1:15–16) and loving one another (1 John 4:7–12), or warnings about apostasy (Heb. 6:4–6; 10:26–31). In some places an apocalyptic tone hints of the power of sin becoming especially focused in the "last days" through a "desolating sacrilege" (Matt. 24:15; see Dan. 12:11), "the lawless one" (2 Thess. 2:3), "antichrists" (1 John 2:18–25), or "the beast" who utters blasphemy (Rev. 13).[134] Behind these figures, various New Testament writers assume the existence of "demons" and "unclean spirits" whom Jesus is able to "cast out" (e.g., Mark 1:21–27, 32–34) as well as "powers and principalities" that would seek to destroy God's work (Eph. 6:12–13).[135]

Summary

In spite of creation and covenant obligations that call humankind into relationship with God, disobedience permeates the biblical story. Indeed, the biblical story presupposes the existence of sin within the human community, whether considered individually or corporately, since all of the covenants, along with the promised regularity of creation (Gen. 8:22), are narrated against the backdrop of brokenness and imperfection. Knowing this, God graciously offers ways through which people may seek him in worship, find meaning in the midst of sin and suffering, and reckon with the tension between God's promised presence and the human perception of his absence at certain moments of life. Drawing on the insights of theological methods of human experience and existence, we now turn to activities and areas through which humans relate to God.

Through Worship and Life

A category as broad as "worship and life" indicates not only the need to embrace a wide variety of themes but also that our survey will only touch upon a few of the significant ones. The following word-pairs move through different aspects of place, religious experience, intellectual reflection, and the challenge of the "elusive presence" of God.

Temple and Church

Old Testament theology does not conceive of relationship with God as occurring in some otherworldly, spiritual sphere but as taking place in the midst of our physical existence.[136] In other words, a life lived with God is necessarily grounded in and integrated with dimensions of space and time, leading perhaps to the early image of "walking with God" (Enoch in Gen. 5:24; Noah in Gen. 6:9). The ancestors built altars, as Abraham did in the land where the Lord appeared to him, giving his relationship with Yahweh a sense of place (Gen. 12: 5–8; see 22:1; 28:16–18). Much of the book of Exodus concerns itself with the building and using of the tabernacle (Exod. 25–31; 35–40),[137] and Deuteronomy refers to "the place that the LORD your God will choose out of all your tribes as his habitation to put his name there" (Deut. 12:5–7; see 14:23).[138] Prior to the building of a temple, there was the Israelite shrine at Shiloh (1 Sam. 1:3), and the ark would be taken into battle to represent Yahweh's presence (1 Sam. 4:3–4), but the ark fell into enemy hands and manifested Yahweh's power over the Philistine god Dagon (1 Sam. 5:1–5).[139] Ultimately, David's dream of building a temple in Jerusalem (2 Sam. 7; 1 Chron. 22–29) was fulfilled by his son Solomon in a project that emphasized the beauty and expense of the temple (1 Kgs. 5–8).[140] Long after the temple was built, however, people of Israel and Judah continued to hold sacred various "high places" that vied with Jerusalem for religious significance (1 Kgs. 12:25–33; 2 Kgs. 18:4; 23:8, 15–20; Hos. 10:8; Amos 5:4–5).[141] Although the prophets sharply critiqued the formal worship of Israel and Judah and the false theology of the temple's inviolability (Jer. 7:1–20; 26:1–19), its destruction caused great agony for the faithful (Lam. 2:6–7). And although its rebuilding was long delayed, the temple was supposed to be the first thing to be rebuilt after the return from exile (Ezra 3:1–7; 5:1–2; Hag. 1:1–15). While Solomon's prayer affirmed that no earthly place can contain the presence of the Lord (1 Kgs. 8:27), the temple nevertheless maintained a special place in Israel's official worship (see numerous psalms, esp. Pss. 84 and 122), and it was central to Ezekiel's vision of God's future, glorious presence with people (Ezek 40–44).

The New Testament documents were written in the decades before and after the destruction of Jerusalem and the temple in 70 CE, but the Gospel of Luke clearly portrays Jesus and his family as honoring the temple and its institutional worship (Luke 2:22–24, 41–51). It is Jesus' earliest sense of call to be in his "Father's house" (Luke 2:49), and the Gospel ends, as it began, with faithful people worshiping in the temple (Luke 1:8–23; 24:53; see also Acts 2:46; 3:1).[142] According to John's Gospel, Jesus carried on a significant ministry in the temple precincts (John 2:13–22; 7:14–8:59), and all four Gospels agree that Jesus zealously defended its sanctity (Matt. 21:12–17; Mark 11:15–19; Luke 19:45–46; John 2:14–16). There is, however, also the awareness that the temple was not to remain forever, with Jesus' predicting its destruction (Matt. 24:2) and implying that his own body was a "temple" that would be rebuilt after its destruction (John 2:19–22). Jesus also describes a coming time when people "will worship the Father neither on this mountain nor in Jerusalem . . . [but] true worshipers will worship the Father in spirit and truth" (John 4:21–23). This decentering of the temple as the sole location for true worship seems compatible with the early Christian concept of the body of believers as "God's temple" (1 Cor. 3:17), though Paul himself continued to regard the temple as an appropriate location for religious observance (Acts 21:26).[143] Even so, the New Testament concept of "church" seems to gain its primary reference from the people themselves, rooted in the Old Testament concept of "assembly."[144] In this way, while groups of believers as the church necessarily met in specific places—"the church in their house" (Rom. 16:5)—the worldwide mission of the gospel reflects a universalizing theme that ultimately supplants one or a few select locations as the only places God meets with people. Indeed, John's vision of heavenly worship, one that seems to provide a pattern for the temple (Rev. 4:1–6), begins to shift the attention from temple as building to the preeminence of God's presence in the New Jerusalem: "I saw no temple in the city, for its temple is the Lord God the Almighty and the Lamb" (Rev. 21:22).[145]

Ceremony and Sacrifice

Related in many ways to the topic of temple and church, the ceremonial and sacrificial aspects of religion point to a sense of order, remembrance, corporate experience, and especially the need to deal with guilt. The story of Cain and Abel presupposes the logic and reasonableness of bringing offerings and sacrifices to Yahweh (Gen. 4:3–5),[146] as do the stories of Noah (Gen 8:20–21) and Abraham (Gen 15:9; 22:13).[147] And the essential sign of the Abrahamic covenant was the rite of circumcision (Gen. 17:9–14), establishing a ceremony of initiation into the covenant people and, therefore, into relationship with Yahweh. The exodus narrative integrates the first celebration of the Passover and feast of unleavened bread into the last of the "plagues" on Egypt, namely, the death of the firstborn (Exod. 11–13). Levitical laws of offering and sacrifice occur near the center of the Torah and recount a detailed system for responding to different experiences in the life of Israelites, with special emphasis placed on the "everlasting" observance of a day of atonement (Lev. 16).[148] The exilic era produced another concept, one in which the righteous servant would be "wounded for our transgressions, crushed for our iniquities" (Isa.

53:5). Here the people sense that this servant's sacrifice—"like a lamb that is led to the slaughter" (Isa. 53:7)—is one in which "the LORD has laid on him the iniquity of us all" (Isa. 53:6).[149]

While the practice of sacrifice was the predominant *functional* religious expression—the tabernacle and temple existed for that purpose—those places represented something greater, namely, the relationship with God with which the sacrifices were concerned. Thus, the practices of prayer, song, and worship were also vital to the religion of the Old Testament, as the psalms of praise so eloquently testify: enthronement psalms (e.g., Pss. 95–99), entrance liturgies (e.g., Ps. 24), and numerous general hymns (e.g., Pss. 29, 100, 145).[150] The reading of the law of Moses was also part of Israel's worship, and this too was to bring the people joy, as Nehemiah said, for "the joy of the LORD is your strength" (Neh. 8:10). Nevertheless, the prophets warned the people about vain or false worship in both preexilic (Hos. 4:12–13) and postexilic times (Isa. 58:3–5), often connecting those practices with injustice toward the poor. No sharper critique can be found than that of Amos: "I hate, I despise your festivals, and I take no delight in your solemn assemblies" (Amos 5:21). Thus, here too, various witnesses attest to Yahweh's ultimate desire being a relationship of dependence and obedience to God: "Surely, to obey is better than sacrifice" (1 Sam. 15:22), and "the sacrifice acceptable to God is a broken spirit; a broken and contrite heart, O God, you will not despise" (Ps. 51:17).

As with the theme of temple, the New Testament's views on religious ceremony and sacrifice were no doubt affected by the fall of Jerusalem and the cessation of the temple cultus. Given the lack of absolute certainty regarding the date and setting of the Gospels and many of the Letters, it is difficult to know the distinct situations they were addressing. Hence, in the Gospels and Acts we have Jesus, his disciples, and Paul all participating in various ceremonial activities, from the Passover (e.g., Matt. 26:17–19; John 2:13) to temple prayers (Acts 3:1) and other observances (Acts 20:16; 21:23–26). Even so, there is also a theme of freedom regarding certain traditional rites such as fasting, which Jesus does not require of his disciples during his ministry but sees as natural for those in mourning (Mark 2:18–20). And while Jesus does not call for an end to the sacrificial system, Matthew and Mark record the tearing of the curtain in the temple at the moment of Jesus' death (Matt. 27:51; Mark 15:38), opening up a more direct way of relating to God. And in John's Gospel, John the Baptist speaks of Jesus as "the Lamb of God" (John 1:29, 36), comparing him to the Passover sacrificial animal, whose blood is poured out in death (John 19:34; see 1 John 5:8) and whose body is offered as spiritual nourishment: "For my flesh is true food and my blood is true drink" (John 6:55).[151] Paul tells the Romans that they must "present [their] bodies as a living sacrifice" (Rom. 12:1), and the Letter to the Hebrews is the most explicit in contrasting Jesus' sacrificial death with those sacrifices offered under the old covenant (Heb. 10:11–14).

The New Testament also explores new expressions of rites of initiation and remembrance. Not only do the Gospels witness to Jesus' own baptism (Matt. 3:13–17; Mark 1:9–11; Luke 3:21–22; implied in John 1:32–34), but Jesus explicitly includes baptism as part of the disciple-making mission of his followers (Matt. 28:19), which the book of Acts testifies that they practiced (e.g., Acts 2:38, 41). John's Gospel presents baptism as part of the new birth and entry into God's kingdom (John 3:5), while Paul focuses on how baptism unites recipients into Christ's death (Rom. 6:3). The Letter to the Colossians even interprets baptism in terms of "spiritual circumcision" (Col. 2:10–11; see Phil. 3:3).[152] The Gospels also recount Jesus' special interpretation of the Passover as a symbolic act that unites the guest with him in a new covenant through his body and blood (e.g., Mark 14:22–24), something Jesus asks the disciples to do "in remembrance" of him (Luke 22:19). The book of Acts records instances of the sharing of meals and breaking bread (e.g., Acts 2:46), though it is difficult to trace first-century developments that would distinguish a sacramental meal from a meal strictly for nourishment and fellowship (see Paul's classic treatment of these matters in 1 Cor. 11:17–34).

Praise and Prayer

In Old Testament theology, praise and prayer are Israel's way of speaking to (and about) God in order to express both the joy of that relationship and the sense of complete dependence on God.[153] Numerous individuals in the long course of Israel's story pray for themselves or others, and for all kinds of needs: Abraham (Gen. 20:17), Jacob (Gen. 32:9–12), Moses (Exod. 32:11–14), Hannah (1 Sam. 1:10–18; 2:1–10), Solomon (1 Kgs. 8:22–54), Nehemiah (Neh. 1:4–11), and Daniel (Dan. 6:10). Corporate praise is enjoined in the earliest Hebrew poetry, as Israel celebrated God's mighty act of salvation through the Red Sea (Exod. 15), and it is arranged for by the Chronicler at the far end of Israel's history through several chapters of temple appointments (1 Chron. 22–26).[154] Of course, no biblical theology of prayer and praise would be complete without mentioning the role of the psalms in Israel's worship. The Psalter's theology of prayer and praise, writes Patrick Miller, "confronts the reader with a point of view about God and humankind and the purpose and work of God in and through Israel as well as in relation to the larger community of humankind." Miller adds that not only is the meaning of trusting God's ways explored; its reflections on God's character and creative activity present something of a "doctrine of God."[155]

In the New Testament, prayer and praise are so woven into the fabric of the writings that to remove them would be to unravel the whole tapestry. Consonant with its emphasis on the temple, Luke's Gospel opens by weaving prayers and songs into its introductory narrative: Elizabeth and Mary (1:42–45, 46–55), Zechariah (1:67–79), angels (2:13–14), Simeon (2:29–32), and Anna (2:38). Likewise, the last two verses of Luke's Gospel depict the disciples worshiping joyfully and blessing God in the temple (Luke 24:52–54). Jesus' own practice of and teachings about prayer indicate that he thought of it as a natural and integral part of one's life with God. He prayed before dawn (Mark 1:35) and in the evening (Matt. 14:23), before choosing his disciples (Luke 6:12) and facing his death (Mark 14:32–39). He taught the simplicity, patience, and humility of prayer that was focused on essential needs (Matt. 6:9–13; Luke 11:2–13) and meant for God alone, not offered for attention (Matt. 6:5–8) or self-gratification (Luke 18:9–14). Jesus' "high priestly prayer" (John 17) both revealed the depth of his concern for his disciples and expressed a high theology of union with God. The early Christian community in Jerusalem incorporated prayer into its decision making (Acts 1:24), daily worship (Acts 3:1), and leadership activities (Acts 6:4), and their whole life together was characterized by "praising God" (Acts 2:47). Paul's letters offer excellent examples of his practice and theology of prayer, as he revels in the life, glory, and purposes of God (e.g., Rom. 1:8–12; 1 Cor. 1:4–9; 2 Cor. 1:3–7; Phil. 1:3–11). Prayer and praise are, for Paul, two hands that reach out for God in faith and hope as one ceaselessly prays (1 Thess. 5:17) and always rejoices (Phil. 4:4), drawn into God's presence by the very Spirit who "intercedes with sighs too deep for words" (Rom. 8:26). The pattern for Christian worship, then, is summarized in this way: "Be filled with the Spirit, as you sing psalms and hymns and spiritual songs among yourselves, singing and making melody to the Lord in your hearts, giving thanks to God the Father at all times and for everything in the name of our Lord Jesus Christ" (Eph. 5:18–20). Finally, some of the most profound theological reflection occurs in the prayers and hymns embedded in the New Testament documents, speaking of themes as diverse as the sovereignty of God (Acts 4:24–31), the wisdom of God (Rom. 11:34–35), the humble incarnation and glorious exaltation of Christ (Phil. 2:6–11; see 1 Tim. 3:16), the mysterious purposes of God (Eph. 1:3–14), and the mediatorial work of Jesus (1 Tim. 2:5–6).

Wisdom and Experience

Modern biblical theology has wrestled with how to integrate the Wisdom literature into a comprehensive presentation of the Bible's message. Historical and narrative approaches may emphasize the material in the Torah and Former Prophets but struggle to include the insights about human experience of life within creation and society that grow out of the Wisdom books. A canonical theology such as Rendtorff's considers these books as having their own legitimate focus, in which "*people speak* to and of God," and where "convictions, experiences and insights from Israel's 'everyday life' are represented or . . . reflected upon critically and queried."[156] At the same time, Rendtorff rightly sees several themes that connect the Wisdom literature to both Torah and Prophets, such as creation and instruction. Although wisdom is mentioned far less frequently in earlier Old Testament writings, the book of Exodus alludes to the practical wisdom, or "skill" and "understanding," that God gave to those who constructed the tabernacle (e.g., Exod. 28:3), and the term of course appears prominently in the Solomonic narratives of 1 Kings 3–11.[157] These latter texts correspond to the regular attribution to Solomon for wisdom sayings in Proverbs 1:1, 10:1, and 25:1 (see also the apocryphal Wisdom of Solomon). The presence of three primary wisdom books (Proverbs, Ecclesiastes, and Job), each with its own perspective, shows the need felt by the postexilic community to canonize both traditional and nontraditional forms of wisdom.[158]

What, then, is the theological outlook of these books when they are considered together?[159] Underlying the book of Proverbs is the belief that God's goodness and providence can be trusted: "The fear of the LORD is the beginning of knowledge" (Prov. 1:7), or "Trust in the LORD with all your heart, and do not rely on your own insight. In all your ways acknowledge him, and he will make straight your paths" (Prov. 3:5–6; see 3:9, 11–12, etc.). There is the confidence that "the blessing of the LORD makes rich" (Prov 10:22), which echoes the general tenor of the book, namely, that people's actions will lead them either to goodness, prosperity, and blessing, or to evil, poverty, and curse. God can be trusted to save the righteous (Prov. 18:10; 19:23) and maintain order and justice in the world (Prov. 29:25–26; 30:5). Presenting a far less optimistic appraisal of life is the book of Ecclesiastes, which recognizes wisdom's superiority over folly but does not see any difference in terms of ultimate destiny:

> Then I saw that wisdom excels folly as light excels darkness.
>
> The wise have eyes in their head,
> but fools walk in darkness.
>
> Yet I perceived that the same fate befalls all of them. Then I said to myself, "What happens to the fool will happen to me also; why then have I been so very wise?" And I said to myself that this also is vanity. (Eccl. 2:13–15)

The book is not completely pessimistic, however, since it recognizes God as the one who "has given [work] to everyone to be busy with" (3:10) and sees some order of the times and seasons of human life: "a time for every matter under heaven" (3:1–8). Thus, the author often returns to the best that one can hope for under the circumstances of a finite existence: "to eat and drink and find enjoyment in all the toil with which one toils under the sun the few days of the life God gives us; for this is our lot" (5:18; see 2:24; 3:13; 8:15; 9:7).

Traditional, proverbial wisdom is augmented in still another way by the insights of the book of Job, which depicts the struggle of the innocent sufferer to find God at work in the midst of his pain and anguish. While much of the dialogue between Job and his friends (chaps. 3–31) takes up the theme of God's just and righteous dealings with sinful human beings, Job's own argument is that suffering does not necessarily mean that sinfulness stands behind it as a cause. At the same time, God's speeches (chaps. 38–41) also place Job's correct theology—"My servant Job has [spoken of me what is right]" (42:7)—under the larger umbrella of human limitations, the basic inability to understand fully everything that God has done in creation and is doing in our lives (42:1–6). Some of the "wisdom psalms" tie in with the debate between Job and his friends over the fate of the wicked, insofar as they suggest that the success and happiness of the wicked is temporary (Pss. 37, 73).[160]

The New Testament does not set apart specific books devoted predominantly to teaching wisdom, but the same tension between traditional and nontraditional outlooks exists in the New Testament. One finds a reaffirmation of proverbial wisdom in how people should live obediently before God and the world, but the questions raised by Ecclesiastes and Job about life's purpose and fairness are sharply focused in the life, death, and teachings of Jesus. Luke's Gospel narrates that Jesus himself "increased in wisdom" as he grew up (Luke 2:52), and Paul's high Christology describes him as the very "wisdom of God" (1 Cor. 1:24). The author of the Letter to the Colossians prayed that his readers would "be filled with the knowledge of God's will in all spiritual wisdom and understanding" (Col. 1:9), and James encouraged those "lacking in wisdom [to] ask God, who gives to all generously and ungrudgingly" (Jas. 1:5). Jesus' Sermon on the Mount calls on disciples to "do to others as you would have them do to you" (Matt. 7:12), but his own life reveals that there is a cost to following God, a way of the cross (Luke 9:22–24) that relativizes any facile formulas about rewards and punishments. Replicating the sense of abandonment experienced in the righteous sufferings of Job and the psalmist (Job 6:4, 10; Ps. 22:1), Jesus' death on the cross may be the only answer that can be given to the world's senseless pain (Matt. 27:46; Mark 15:34). The paradox of Jesus' innocent suffering leads us to consider one more theme within the human relationship with God.

Presence and Absence

Among Yahweh's promises in the ancestral covenant was the assurance of presence with Abraham's descendants. To Isaac, Yahweh declares, "Reside in this land as an alien, and I will be with you, and will bless you" (Gen. 26:3). The same promise is reaffirmed for Jacob's journeys: "Know that I am with you and will keep you wherever you go, and will bring you back to this land; for I will not leave you until I have done what I have promised you" (Gen. 28:15). Other key figures in the Old Testament receive similar comfort for their tasks, whether known to the narrator—"The LORD was with Joseph" (Gen. 39:2, 3, 21)—or revealed to human beings like Moses (Exod. 3:12). The promise to be Israel's God is vividly portrayed during the exodus and wilderness era in the symbols of Yahweh's presence, the fire and cloud (Exod. 13:21–22; Num. 14:14), the latter of which becomes associated especially with the tent of meeting (Exod. 33:9, 10; Num. 12:5; Deut. 31:15) and the temple in Jerusalem (1 Kgs. 8:10–11). When people are tempted to be overcome with fear, Yahweh makes a solemn promise of presence: "I am/will be with you." Appearing in a variety of contexts—to new leaders and prophets (Josh. 3:7; Jer. 1:8), returning exiles (Isa. 41:10; 43:5), or those rebuilding the temple (Hag. 1:13; 2:4)—these words are the quintessential expression of God's presence in the Old Testament.[161]

The promise of God's presence is not always enjoyed to the same degree, for individuals and whole generations ask where God is in the midst of suffering and loss. The Old Testament does not probe the mystery of evil and its effects on a philosophical level. For example, Genesis offers no explanation for the behavior of the serpent in the garden but rather traces human toil, death, and troubled relationships to the choices made by the man and the woman (Gen. 3:16–19).[162] The predominant expression of this sense of absence and of the loss of relationship with God comes in psalms of lament, offered by individuals—"How long, O LORD? Will you forget me forever? How long will you hide your face from me?" (Ps. 13:1)—or on behalf of the whole community: "Yet you have rejected us and abased us, and have not gone out with our armies" (Ps. 44:9). And yet, while it is true that "laments" outnumber various types of "praise" psalms, the lament forms themselves often contain expressions of trust and praise, such that feelings of complete and utter despair occur infrequently (see Ps. 88).[163] The challenge of dealing with adversity, suffering, or a sense of divine displeasure is handled in different ways: Jeremiah actively wrestles with God's will (e.g., Jer. 12:1–4; 15:15–18; 20:7–18), Habakkuk tries to be patient and confident (Hab. 3:16–19), Ecclesiastes assigns all to "vanity" and the mystery that God stands behind both prosperity and adversity (Eccl. 1:1, 14; 6:10), and Lamentations prays for restoration even as it contemplates the possibility that Yahweh has "utterly rejected" Israel and is "angry . . . beyond measure" (Lam. 5:21–22).

The Gospels and Letters of the New Testament offer promises of God's presence that are comparable to those in the Old Testament. Jesus' parting words to the disciples are, "And remember, I am with you always, to the end of the age" (Matt. 28:20), and the Letter to the Hebrews reaffirms an earlier assurance given to Moses and Joshua: "I will never leave you or forsake you" (Heb. 13:5; see Deut. 31:6; Josh. 1:5). In several cases, Jesus draws on the Old Testament message about God's presence, regularly telling his followers and others, "Do not be afraid" (e.g., Matt. 14:27; 28:10; Mark 5:36; Acts 18:9–10). But with these promises comes an equally firm revelation that disciples will experience rejection and abandonment from a world that also rejected their master: "If they persecuted me, they will persecute you" (John 15:20). Jesus must drink of the cup of suffering (Matt. 26:39, 42), and his disciples will also share in it (Matt. 20:22–23). Nevertheless, embedded—sometimes deeply—in the narrative of the early Christian witness to suffering is the steady hope that God remains true to his promise. Jesus can still call the one who forsakes him on the cross "my God" (Matt. 27:46), the certainty of tribulation is balanced by Jesus' conquering of the world (John 16:33), and even as persecution falls upon the church at Stephen's death, the gospel spreads through the scattering of disciples (Acts 8:2–8).

The rest of the New Testament documents all assume that God remains present in spite of the hardships believers must face to enter the kingdom of God (Acts 14:22). Paul feels the support of others' prayers during an imprisonment (Phil. 1:7), and he connects the sufferings the Thessalonians experience both to his own and to Christ's (1 Thess. 2:14–15). The Letter to the Hebrews understands such trials to have a disciplinary effect to strengthen believers, again based on the pattern of Jesus' own enduring of hostility (Heb. 12:1–11; see 13:12–13). Perhaps the most extensive teaching on this subject occurs in the Petrine letters, which remind their readers that the "fiery ordeal that is taking place" is not a cause for surprise (1 Pet. 4:12). Rather, all of their trials should be occasions for the strengthening of faith (1 Pet. 1:6–7), experiencing God's approval (1 Pet. 2:19–21), and looking forward to an inheritance of blessing (1 Pet. 3:9). And of course, the book of Revelation portrays the larger drama of the church's experience of the world's rejection and wrath. But here, as elsewhere in both testaments, the complexity and inscrutability of God's ways in permitting suffering is consistent with "the more knowing story that is in the rest of scripture."[164]

Summary

The preceding discussion has summarized the various means of relating to God—those areas of life by which human beings express their relationship through devotion, reflection, worship, and sometimes cries of destitution and grief. All of these ways occur against the backdrop of creation and covenant which themselves are part of the story told with gratitude for the past, faith in the present, and hope for the future. But none of these themes is about isolated individuals; we live in communities that overlap with each other. How we ought to live in the world and relate to other human beings within the logically prior relationship with God is the question to which we turn for the last major part of our study.

LIVING IN RELATIONSHIP
WITH OTHER HUMAN BEINGS

A biblical theology of human relationships could be studied along several lines. My approach here emphasizes one way to unfold the scope of ideas within the second great commandment—"You shall love your neighbor as yourself" (Matt. 22:39; Lev. 19:18)—and those explicit and implicit concepts in the "second table" of the Ten Commandments. The many contextual issues raised in previous chapters increased our sensitivity to these horizontal dimensions of human existence and our awareness of the diversity of concerns in Scripture itself. In what follows I will unfold this diversity from the more general themes of the national and international contexts within which biblical writers reflected on humankind to more specific areas of community life, both the principles upon which human beings are to relate as well as the structures they use to order their life together.

Nation and Nations: The Larger Context
of Human Relationships

The Bible is a collection of writings with Jewish roots, reflecting Jewish culture, but these works also contain universal interests from the opening chapters of Genesis. It is true, of course, that even when these universal aspects come to the forefront, the particular perspective is never far away. Having said that, however, it is possible to address various interrelationships within concentric circles, moving from tribe and nation to the life of all nations in a global community.[165]

People and Tribes: Unity and Strife

There is surely a sense in which the primeval story has a more universal scope than the ancestral accounts that follow it, but even within Genesis 1–11 much of the text remains focused on the activities of particular families: a man and woman in the garden (chaps. 2–3), two brothers (chap. 4); Noah's family (chaps. 6–9). Thus, by the time readers learn of the call of Abraham and Sarah in Genesis 12, they are acquainted with some of the ways these family units experience tension and strife. As the tribes of Israel looked back upon their roots, they would have known that their ancestors struggled in their relationships with each other: Abraham and Lot's choosing pasturage (Gen. 13:8–13), Jacob and Esau's conflict over the birthright (Gen. 27), Rachel and Leah's rivalry within Jacob's household (Gen. 29:31–30:24), and Jacob's twelve sons finding their own place amidst family jealousies (Gen. 37–45; see the blessings spoken by Jacob on his sons in Gen. 49, and by Moses on the tribes in Deut. 33). The Former Prophets continue this theme, with decisions over tribal boundaries (Josh. 13–19), the horrors of internecine warfare (Judg. 19–21), a tenuous unity under the early kings (1 Sam. 10:27; 2 Sam 2:8–11), and ultimately division of the tribes into separate kingdoms: "What share do we have in David? We have no inheritance in the son of Jesse. To your tents, O Israel! Look now to your own house, O David" (1 Kgs. 12:16). Nevertheless, behind the historical facts of disunity and division lay the ideal that the tribes, together, were meant to be one people and nation before Yahweh (Exod. 19:6), with each tribe concerned for the well-being of others (Judg. 4:14–18).[166] Hezekiah invited the remnant of the northern tribes to come to a great Passover celebration in Jerusalem, though many scorned him (2 Chron. 30:10–12), and Jeremiah's oracle of a new covenant, delivered long after the fall of the northern kingdom, specifies that Yahweh will make this covenant "with the house of Israel and the house of Judah" (Jer. 31:31). The tribes are to retain their distinctive qualities, and they are connected with the land their ancestors inherited. But they also know that their blessing lies in the unity they share as descendants of Abraham and Sarah (Isa. 51:2).

The unity of the tribes is not a central issue in the New Testament, but even there one gets hints of deeper tensions among the Jews inhabiting different parts of Palestine in the first century CE.[167] The Gospels may assume a certain level of discord between Galilee and other regions, especially Judah, and even within Galilee prejudices surface: "Can anything good come out of Nazareth?" (John 1:46).[168] Parallels to this theme occur when New Testament authors raise the question of unity among "brothers and sisters" in the body of Christ regardless of ethnic and racial differences. But one *theological* way in which this theme of tribal unity works in Paul's letter to the Romans is the notion that "all Israel will be saved" (Rom. 11:26). Although Paul is not reflecting on tribal unity in any political sense, he has made it clear that his heart breaks for the current situation of his "own people, [his] kindred according to the flesh," with respect to the gospel (Rom. 9:1–3). Of course, Paul's argument has as much, if not more, to do with a distinction between ethnic Jews and Abraham's "true descendants" (Rom. 9:6–7), but he also longs for an end to the "hardening [that] has come upon *part* of Israel" so that "*all* Israel will be saved" (Rom. 11:25–26).[169]

Israel and the Nations: Tensions and Promise

If the Old Testament tells the story of how the tribes struggled to get along with each other, there is significantly more animosity between the nation of Israel (united or divided) and other nations or peoples near and far away. In spite of many cross-cultural continuities, the writings themselves witness to a deep-seated theological suspicion of "the nations." To be sure, the primeval story affirms the connections between the families of the earth, relating all the nations in Genesis 10 to "the families of Noah's sons . . . spread abroad on the earth after the flood" (Gen. 10:32). Narratives like the one that singles out Canaan for special judgment (Gen. 9:20–27) or the division of languages at the tower of Babel (11:1–9) reminded Israel that they were part of the one human family, but the primary focus of the Old Testament is nevertheless on the line of Shem (11:10–26), and from him, Abraham and his descendants (11:27–32). With Abraham, however, there is the promise that "in [him] all the families of the earth shall be blessed" (12:3; 28:14; "nations," 26:4), and this from the very beginning of the ancestral history that focuses on his family. For better or for worse, Israel cannot escape its connection to the peoples who derive from their larger family line: Ammon and Moab, descendants of Lot (19:30–38); Ishmaelites, from Abraham's son through Hagar (16); and Edom, descended from Esau (36). Indeed, a profound promise is extended to Ishmael, that God will "bless him and make him fruitful and exceedingly numerous; he shall be the father of twelve princes, and [God] will make him a great nation" (17:20). The divine intention of blessing for the nations through the ancestral line is perhaps best seen in Genesis when Joseph is providentially raised up to provide food for "all the world" that was affected by famine (41:57).

But the generations of slavery in Egypt and the events leading up to the exodus marked Israel as unique among the nations, chosen by Yahweh from among all peoples (Exod. 19:5; see Amos 3:2), and it is set in an antagonistic relationship with others. Their experiences in the wilderness (Exod. 17:8–16; Num. 22–25; 31), their entrance into Canaan (Josh. 1–11), the time of the judges, and the threat of the Philistines all point to the basic stance of Deuteronomy: "When the LORD your God gives them over to you and you defeat them, then you must utterly destroy them. Make no covenant with them and show them no mercy" (Deut. 7:2). In spite of brief moments where outsiders were accepted or esteemed (Rahab in Josh. 6:25; the queen of Sheba in 1 Kgs. 10:1–13; and Ruth), other nations were "enemies" of God's anointed king and chosen people (Pss. 2, 46, 48), used by God to punish Israel (2 Kgs. 17; 25; Hab. 1:6–11) but also destined to be judged themselves (e.g., Isa. 13–28; Jer. 45–52; Ezek. 25–35).[170] And while Ezra and Nehemiah accept imperial power and privilege to aid them in their cause, they disallow intermarriage between the remnant in Judah and the surrounding people (Ezra 9–10; Neh. 10, 13). In the final analysis, the tension remains within the Old Testament witness because the primarily negative tone toward other peoples and nations never completely drowns out the positive, hopeful notes sounded in places where the nations receive forgiveness (e.g., Jonah), are invited to praise Yah-

weh (Pss. 67, 96, 99, 148), or share with Israel in God's eschatological blessings (Mic. 4:1–4; Zech. 14:16).[171]

As it did with the issue of tribal relationships, the New Testament exhibits
far less concern than the Old Testament over Israel's national or political existence. Having said that, there is of course no question about the Roman occupation of Palestine forming the backdrop for events in the Gospels and Acts.
Jesus foresees armies surrounding Jerusalem and weeps over its impending
destruction (Luke 19:41–44). As for his ministry, Jesus tells the disciples to
avoid going to Gentile or Samaritan regions, instead giving priority "to the
lost sheep of the house of Israel" (Matt. 10:5–6). Even so, Jesus himself heals
a Roman centurion's servant (Matt. 8:5–13), praising the centurion for his
matchless faith (Matt. 8:10), and he commissions the apostles to "make disciples of all nations" (Matt. 28). His teachings and encounters also affirm Samaritans as witnesses and examples of compassion and gratitude (John 4:39; Luke
10:30–37; 17:11–19). But there are also moments when Jesus seems less than
compassionate himself toward a Gentile, as in the difficult story of the Syro-
Phoenician woman (Mark 7:24–30), whose daughter he nevertheless heals.
The book of Acts traces the expansion of the early Christian community
throughout Judea and Samaria and beyond to the larger Greco-Roman world.
In his ministry, Paul also begins working among Jewish synagogues in most
communities (Acts 13:5, 14; 14:1), but even after arguing for the full inclusion
of Gentiles in the body of Christ (Acts 15:12), Paul never denies or disparages
his Jewish heritage (Acts 22:3; 26:4–5; Gal. 1:14), even though he denounces
the pride he took in it (Phil. 3:5–11).[172]

Humankind and the World: A Global Community

The Old Testament also acknowledges Israel's identity with the human race in
the world. The universal tone of Genesis 1–11, punctuated by the genealogy
of Adam (Gen. 5) and the "table of nations" (Gen. 10), communicates Israel's
understanding of its ties to the antiquity and unity of the human race.[173] The
opening of Chronicles reaffirms these connections, its first word being
"Adam" (1 Chron. 1:1). Of course, Old Testament writers rarely offered abstract
reflections on their common humanity outside the context of covenant, but
certain psalms and passages in the Wisdom literature ponder the basic existential situation shared by all people. The psalmist asks, "What are human
beings that you are mindful of them, mortals that you care for them? Yet you
have made them a little lower than God, and crowned them with glory and
honor" (Ps. 8:4–5). The immediately following verses tighten the reference
to Genesis 1's teaching of creation in God's image by referring to the theme
of "dominion" over all animal life (Ps. 8:6–8; Gen. 1:26–27). The author of
Ecclesiastes was not encouraged by the human predicament, seeing it rather

as a cause for a realistic faith in the face of the inevitable effects of time's passing (Eccl. 11:9–12:8). But in some psalms, reflection on human limitation and
death leads to prayer for and praise of the compassion of God: "For he knows
how we were made; he remembers that we are dust" (Ps. 103:14, 15–16; see
Ps. 90:3, 13). Part of the rhetorical force of the book of Jonah is Yahweh's
expectation that the prophet will feel some of Yahweh's concern for the
Ninevites as human beings who do not know the right way and are therefore
objects of divine and human compassion (Jonah 4:11). Finally, Israel was called
to live within the prophetic hope of a world in which all people would benefit
from the establishment of Yahweh's kingship in Zion (Isa. 2:1–4).

New Testament authors assume the distinctiveness of God's work among
Israel and the dawn of the kingdom among the Jews of the first century CE,
but they also reflect on what is common to our humanity. In Matthew's Gospel,
Jesus appeals to God's knowledge of basic human needs (food, water, clothing)
in order to lift his hearers out of their anxiety about possessions (Matt. 6:32).
Luke's genealogy of Jesus traces his descent to "Adam, son of God" (Luke
3:38), and John's prologue asserts that the eternal Word is "the true light which
enlightens everyone" (John 1:9). Jesus envisions a kingdom of God that draws
people "from east and west, from north and south" (Luke 13:29). Luke carries
this image further in the international flavor of the crowd at Pentecost, listing
no fewer than fifteen nations and language groups (Acts 2:8–11). It is true that
this is an audience primarily of "devout Jews from every nation" (Acts 2:5), but
many of these are proselytes, and it is clearly Luke's concern to see divine
power and prophetic fulfillment in the Spirit's outpouring "upon all flesh"
(Acts 2:17; see Joel 2:28). The diversification of language at Babel is not
reversed, but rather a new unity is provided through the one message of "God's
deeds of power" delivered in many languages (Acts 2:11).[174] Thus, the narrative proceeds with stories about the conversion of an Ethiopian official (Acts
8:26–40) and Cornelius, a Roman centurion (Acts 10). Paul goes to great
lengths in his analysis of sin to show that there is no fundamental difference
between human beings when one considers that "all, both Jews and Greeks,
are under the power of sin" (Rom. 3:9). All people have died in Adam (Rom.
5:12–14), and "just as we have borne the image of the man of dust, we will also
bear the image of the man of heaven" (1 Cor. 15:49). John's vision of worship
around the throne of God specifies the fact that the blood of the lamb has "ran-
somed for God saints from every tribe and language and people and nation"
(Rev. 5:9; see 14:6). In sum, the New Testament carries forward the universal
hope that was rooted in the Old Testament calling of the people of God. There
is, therefore, a certain particularity to the universal plan of God's redemption
in Jesus Christ, such that "the vision of the unity of humankind is *grounded in
the vision of the oneness of God.*"[175]

Need and Justice: The Basic Principles of Human Relationships

Citizens of Israel and members of the early church may have been able to offer some justification for wrestling with the challenge of being part of a global community of God's people, perhaps owing to the great emphasis on particularity and distinctiveness, but there could be no similar explanation offered for mistreatment of those nearest to them. The Deuteronomic and Holiness Codes of the Old Testament and the teachings of Jesus and his apostles in the New understood the fundamental principle of human relationships in terms of love for one's neighbor. Although the explicit command to "love your neighbor as yourself" is wedged in the midst of more mundane regulations for holiness (Lev. 19:18), the second half of the Ten Commandments focuses completely on just and loving relationships with others, a connection Paul makes when he says that these commandments "are summed up in this word, 'Love your neighbor as yourself.' Love does no wrong to a neighbor; therefore, love is the fulfilling of the law" (Rom. 13:9–10).[176] In like manner, Jesus identified love of neighbor as a great commandment, second only to wholehearted love for God, which together supported "all the law and the prophets" (Matt. 22:39–40; Mark 12:29–31; Luke 10:27–28; see John 13:34–35). In what follows I isolate three themes of human relationship that call for a loving response to sin, to need, and to injustice.

Judging and Forgiving: Dealing with Human Sin

The book of Genesis shares stories of vengefulness and lack of forgiveness (e.g., Cain and Lamech in Gen. 4:8; 23–24), but there are also accounts of a reconciliation that overcomes jealousy and hatred (e.g., Esau and Jacob in Gen. 27:41; 33:4–11; Joseph and his brothers in 37:8, 11; 45:15; 50:18–21). While granting that Yahweh is "the Judge of all the earth" (18:25), the Torah's instructions for determining matters of guilt and innocence required an ordered system of justice, with persons set apart to make judgments (Exod. 18:21–23). Principles of fairness and proportionality, such as the *lex talionis* or law of retribution—"eye for eye, tooth for tooth . . ."—undergirded the law so as to limit the human propensity for revenge (Exod. 21:24–25; Lev. 24:20; Deut. 19:21). Judges were commanded, "You shall not be partial to the poor or defer to the great: with justice you shall judge your neighbor" (Lev. 19:15; Deut. 1:16–17), but the prophet Isaiah recognized that the poor, orphans, and widows were the more frequent victims of injustice (Isa. 1:23). It is true that many psalms of almost every genre contain some language about enemies, and a few psalms stand out for their vehemence and retribution (e.g., Ps. 137). While in no way condoning or encouraging these attitudes, a theology of the

Psalms also recognizes the harsh reality of Israel's situation among other nations bent on its destruction. Even the most intense curses and judgments are placed in God's knowledge and justice: "Remember, O LORD, against the Edomites" (Ps. 137:7). As Jonah heard of God's compassion for even the greatest of Israel's enemies—grounded in the classic statement of God's forgiveness (Exod. 34:6–7)—so also Israel was regularly reminded of the divine pattern of calling and using outsiders, sinners, and those of lowest standing to advance the work of the kingdom and the line of the Davidic king (e.g., Tamar in Gen. 38:26–30; Rahab in Josh. 2:1–21; Ruth 4:17).

The theme of forgiveness is one of the hallmarks of New Testament theology. In both his teachings and example, Jesus made forgiveness an essential feature of the life to which he was calling people. His Sermon on the Mount took several key Old Testament texts or rabbinic traditions and emphasized their deeper rationale: Not to kill means not even being angry with or insulting to others (Matt. 5:21–22); instead of hating enemies, people should love and pray for them (Matt. 5:43–44); instead of the law of retribution one should not resist evildoers (Matt. 5:38–39). Judging others has no place in a disciple's life, since everyone has a "log" in their eye that makes them liable to judgment (Matt. 7:1–5; Luke 6:37; see 1 Cor. 4:5); instead, one should be prepared to forgive "another member of the church . . . seventy-seven times" (Matt. 18:21–22). In the face of efforts to avoid the claim of neighbor-love, Jesus told the parable in which a Samaritan, not a priest or Levite, "was a neighbor to the man who fell into the hands of robbers" (Luke 10:36). Paul's letters also warn his readers not to "pass judgment on servants of another [i.e., God]" (Rom. 14:4) but instead to be guided by the principle of love (1 Cor. 13). In extreme cases where one person's sins called for his removal from the fellowship in Corinth, Paul later stated that the punishment was enough: "Now instead you should forgive and console him, so that he may not be overwhelmed by excessive sorrow. So I urge you to reaffirm your love for him" (2 Cor. 2:7–8; see Jude 22–23). The ultimate rationale for a Christian's love and forgiving spirit flows both from God's act of forgiveness and from God's loving nature: "Be kind to one another, tenderhearted, forgiving one another, as God in Christ has forgiven you" (Eph. 4:32); "Beloved, let us love one another, because love is from God . . . [and] God is love" (1 John 4:7–8; see 2 John 5–6).

Caring and Healing: Dealing with Human Need

A biblical theology of human relationships not only addresses judgmental attitudes toward human moral failings; it also considers those needs that come upon people through no fault of their own, that is, simply from the frailty common to our human situation. In particular, both testaments advocate human compassion and concern toward victims of illness, natural disasters, or war. As the Israelites traveled through the wilderness and faced the prospect of little food or water, God miraculously provided for their needs through the agency of Moses. In a later time, when drought served as an expression of Yahweh's judgment on Ahab and his successors, Elijah and Elisha performed miracles to meet the needs of the faithful poor such as the woman of Shunem (2 Kgs. 4:8–37) or various companies of prophets (2 Kgs. 2:19–22; 4:38–44), sometimes extending the blessing to non-Israelites such as the widow of Zarephath (1 Kgs. 17:8–24) and Gehazi (2 Kgs. 5:1–27; see Luke 4:24–27). One might ask whether there is a lack of compassion in laws that isolate victims of skin diseases (Lev. 13:45–46), prohibit eunuchs from worship (Deut. 23:1), or require a certain number of days of "purification" after childbirth (Lev. 12). These regulations obviously long preceded the insights of modern medicine, and many of them are tied in with the elaborate ceremonial system that distinguished between what was "clean" or "unclean," "holy" or "common."[177] But rather than rationalizing their purpose, a biblical-theological exploration points both to the Levitical emphasis on God's holiness as a pattern for human relationships (Lev. 11:44–45) and to the ways in which other biblical texts critique the purity laws.[178] Paul House explains how this ceremonial legislation is "one more means by which Israel and Yahweh cement their relationship."[179] Other Old Testament writings, however, expose the hypocrisy of adhering to detailed rituals while also committing serious moral offenses (Ps. 50:7–21) and exhort their readers to manifest the true nature of worship by achieving justice for the poor (Isa. 58:6–9). Moreover, in places one hears the eschatological message that welcomes the day when ceremonial regulations will have outlived their usefulness: "And the foreigners who join themselves to the LORD, to minister to him, to love the name of the LORD, and to be his servants . . .—these I will bring to my holy mountain, and make them joyful in my house of prayer" (Isa. 56:6–7; cf. Deut. 23:3–6). Thus, a clear tension exists when considering the breadth of the Old Testament on this question, but it seems as if the strictures that protect Israel's distinctiveness gradually come to be interpreted in light of "the weightier matters of the law: justice and mercy and faith" (Matt. 23:23).

In the New Testament, Jesus' healing miracles stand out as one of the most important characteristics of his ministry. The four Gospels together narrate many specific healings and exorcisms while summarizing Jesus' work as follows: "And he cured many who were sick with various diseases, and cast out many demons" (Mark 1:34; see Matt. 4:24; Luke 4:40; 6:18–19). He feeds crowds of thousands (Matt. 14:13–21; 15:32–39), motivated in each instance by his compassion for them in their need (Matt. 14:14; 15:32). When he looks upon the crowds, he sees them as "harassed and helpless, like sheep without a shepherd" (Matt. 9:36), a condition that moves him to send out the disciples for a similar ministry of help and healing (Matt. 10:8; Luke 9:1). As Jesus foresees the final judgment, he states that the principle whereupon the nations shall be judged is whether they gave food to the hungry and drink to the thirsty, welcomed strangers, and visited the sick and imprisoned: "Truly I tell you, just as you did it to one of the least of these who are members of my family, you did it to me" (Matt. 25:40). The book of Acts picks up where the Gospels finish, with the apostles healing the sick, casting out evil spirits, or raising the dead (Acts 3:1–10; 8:7; 9:36–42; 19:12; 20:7–12). Paul exhorts the Corinthians to comfort and console one another in times of suffering, thereby sharing the consolation of God himself (2 Cor. 1:3–7). In other places, the New Testament commands believers to "bear one another's burdens" (Gal. 6:2), "show hospitality to strangers" (Heb. 13:2), "remember those who are in prison" (Heb. 13:3), and to pray for and anoint the sick (Jas. 5:14–15).

Poverty and Riches: Dealing with Problems of Social Justice

As God expresses covenant loyalty toward human beings, so also should human relationships be characterized by the expression of *hesed*, as Ruth shows loyalty toward Naomi (Ruth 1:8), or as Rahab says to the Israelite spies, "Now then, since I have dealt kindly with you, swear to me by the LORD that you in turn will deal kindly with my family" (Josh. 2:12).[180] Perhaps nowhere in the Old Testament is this commitment to the well-being of others as eloquently stated as in the theme of social justice. Israel's scriptures wrestle with how to live in a world marked by the extremes of poverty and wealth, and by the realities of slavery, injustice, and prejudice toward outsiders. We do not have a great deal of historical evidence for how well the daily realities in ancient Israel matched the ideals given in the law. For instance, although the Book of the Covenant did not abolish slavery, some of its first stipulations call for fair treatment of slaves (Exod. 21:2–11, 20–27). In other places, Moses and Joshua make provision for the refuge of persons accused of murder, to keep "the avenger of blood" from killing the accused "when a death sentence was not deserved" (Deut. 19:6; see Josh. 20). The law takes a particular interest in the poor, prohibiting creditors from exacting interest on their loans (Exod. 22:25), ensuring that no one would "pervert the justice due to your poor in their lawsuits" (Exod. 23:6), and requiring the remission of all debts every seven years (Deut. 15:1). Resident aliens did not receive all of the same advantages, but they were not to be oppressed (Exod. 23:9).

Along with these standards for justice, the Old Testament contains enough reference to the plight of the poor to suggest that Israelite society fell short of its high ideals. In the premonarchical era, Hannah's prayer implies that the poor needed God's help (1 Sam. 2:7–8), and in spite of the picture painted by the narrator of Kings—"Judah and Israel were as numerous as the sand by the

sea; they ate and drank and were happy" (1 Kgs. 4:20)—Solomon's administrative structure and many building projects "made [their] yoke heavy" and
contributed to the division of the kingdoms (1 Kgs. 12:4). The prophets offer
the strongest and harshest critique of Israelite and Judean society, charging the
rich with exploitation of the poor. In the northern kingdom, Amos mocked the
rich for lying on their couches to have their fill of food and wine (Amos 6:4–7;
see 2:6–8) while "they trample on the poor and take from them levies of grain"
(5:11; see 8:6). Instead, they should "let justice roll down like waters, and righteousness like an everflowing stream" (5:24). Isaiah expressed similar conster-
nation over Jerusalem's attraction to festivals and rituals when the people
needed to "learn to do good; seek justice, rescue the oppressed, defend the
orphan, plead for the widow" (Isa. 1:17; see 3:14). Jeremiah delivered this oracle directly to the king: "Execute justice in the morning, and deliver from the
hand of the oppressor anyone who has been robbed. . . . And do no wrong or
violence to the alien, the orphan, and the widow, or shed innocent blood in
this place" (Jer. 21:12; 22:3).[181] For its part, proverbial wisdom tended to blame
poverty on laziness (Prov. 10:4), but it could also declare the happiness of
"those who are kind to the poor" (14:21) and warn against encroaching "on
the fields of orphans" (23:10; see 15:25). The desired balance is to receive "neither poverty nor riches" in order to avoid denying God out of plenty or pro-
faning God from intense need (30:8). Job defended his righteousness partly
because he had "delivered the poor who cried, and the orphan who had no
helper . . . and [he] caused the widow's heart to sing for joy" (Job 29:12–13; see
31:16–23). The lament psalms often base their plea to God on the basis of the
poverty and need of the psalmist (Ps. 86:1; see 12:5), while in other places worshipers are directly challenged: "Give justice to the weak and the orphan;
maintain the right of the lowly and the destitute. Rescue the weak and the
needy; deliver them from the hand of the wicked" (Ps. 82:3–4).

The New Testament does not have a sustained critique of societal injustice
along the lines of the Old Testament prophets, but there can be no question
about its sharing the same essential perspective on poverty and riches. Jesus'
teachings about wealth are replete with warnings not to be preoccupied with
possessions: by teaching that one "cannot serve God and wealth" (Matt. 6:24)
and that the rich have great difficulty entering the kingdom of heaven (Mark
10:25); in parables about the rich fool (Luke 12:16–21) or the rich man and
Lazarus (Luke 16:19–31); and in the Sermon on the Mount's admonitions
about worry (Matt. 6:25–34) and blessings for the poor and hungry (Luke
6:20–21). Different emphases surface in the way three Gospels remember
Jesus' telling his disciples, "You always have the poor with you, but you will
not always have me" (Matt. 26:11; John 12:8); Mark's Gospel inserts the
encouragement, "and you can show kindness to them whenever you wish"

(Mark 14:7). The book of Acts does not condemn wealth or teach a complete end to ownership of private property, but it does affirm that the Jerusalem community was noted for extravagant altruism to meet needs even as it exposes the danger of greed and acclamation for "generosity" in the story of Ananias and Sapphira (Acts 4:32–37; 5:1–11).

Paul's theology of possessions and other justice issues is difficult to characterize. On the one hand he extolled the virtues of sacrificial giving patterned on Jesus' freely chosen "poverty" in the incarnation (2 Cor. 8:9). Paul thus encouraged the Corinthians to "be wronged" rather than to take other Christians to the secular courts (1 Cor. 6:7–8). Again, citing the incarnation and the crucifixion as the theological ground, he exhorted the Philippians to exhibit a humility that regards "others as better than yourselves" (Phil. 2:3–11), and he wanted them to know he had learned "to be content" with whatever he had (Phil. 4:11). On the other hand, Acts portrays a Paul who certainly defended his rights as a Roman citizen when he was the victim of injustice (Acts 16:35–39). Accepting Roman justice and its power of the sword (Rom. 13:1–7), Paul did not explicitly condemn the institution of slavery, though he urged Philemon to accept Onesimus "no longer as a slave but more than a slave, a beloved brother" (Phlm. 16).[182]

Other New Testament writings are known for their warnings about excessive wealth. The Pastoral Letters admonish "those who in the present age are rich . . . not to be haughty, or to set their hopes on the uncertainty of riches, but rather on God who richly provides us with everything for our enjoyment. They are to do good, to be rich in good works, generous, and ready to share" (1 Tim. 6:17–18). Indeed, "the love of money is a root of all kinds of evil" (1 Tim 6:10). Likewise, Hebrews cautions its readers, "Keep your lives free from the love of money, and be content with what you have" (Heb. 13:5). The Letter of James is even more harsh in its critique of mistreatment of the poor (Jas. 2:6, 15; 5:1). The commandment to love one's neighbor means showing no partiality in matters of wealth (Jas. 2:8–9), and "religion that is pure and undefiled before God the Father, is this: to care for orphans and widows in their distress, and to keep oneself unstained by the world" (Jas. 1:27).

Summary

A biblical theology of need and justice reveals no contradiction between the importance of speaking and doing in relationships, so long as words and actions evidence a basic integrity and outlook of compassion. We have seen that human needs are addressed on different levels, using the varied gifts of individuals in any given community of faith. While the Wisdom literature and the sayings of Jesus may seem to have a more individual claim, the Mosaic legislation and Paul's letters to churches address believers in community, with the implicit assumption that no individual can carry out all of the implications of neighbor-love on one's own. Thus, the community of faith must be a fellowship that nurtures individuals in their life in the world and in callings to serve others, which leads us into the final major thematic area.

Community and Calling: The Structures for Human Relationships

There are far too many aspects of human community to treat in an overview such as this, but I have highlighted five themes designating basic structures within which human beings relate to one another. The topics range from sexuality and family to leadership and community. Individuals in community, locally and globally, will experience these contexts as opportunities for and challenges to being just and caring toward their neighbor.

Male and Female: Bearing the Image of God

Feminist interpretation has helped biblical theologians appreciate the importance of listening to the various levels of voice and witness in Scripture. The Old Testament stories, poetry, wisdom, and legislation were passed down in oral and written form within the context of a patriarchal society. Thus, as one seeks to discern biblical-theological themes related to human existence as male and female, one must remain sensitive to the variety of approaches suggested by feminist theologians, approaches that may be more or less suspicious of the message being communicated in a given text. The creation account in Genesis 1 teaches that men and women are both the image of God in the world, and are therefore both responsible for living out the divine call to have dominion and to populate the earth (Gen. 1:26–28). Genesis 2, which focuses more on the life of humans in the created world, places the man and woman in relation to each other. While Yahweh's larger concern is that a human being not exist in complete solitude from all other life (2:18), the account proceeds by explaining how Yahweh made man and woman with the potential for mutuality and intimacy (2:21–25), a state that was disrupted and confused as a result of the disobedience in the garden.[183] Far from living in mutual trust and shared responsibility for the earth, the relationship of the man and woman takes on the character of struggle. They need each other for survival and for procreation, but there is now the potential for the man to "rule over" the woman (3:16).[184] The tension set forth in Genesis 1–3 between the potential for mutuality on the one hand and subordination on the other hand seems to play itself out in the rest of the Old Testament. The stories and legislation in the Torah and Former Prophets do not advocate or encourage mistreatment of women, but neither do they go out of their way to challenge the societal norms. For his part, Abraham makes matters worse by placing Sarah in danger on more than one occasion (12:10–20; 20:1–18), yet one time Yahweh tells him to listen to the voice of his wife (21:12). The rivalry between Rachel and Leah points to the dysfunctional nature of that polygamous family situation (29:31–30:24), but the narrator does not level any strong indictment against such practices. The Mosaic laws proscribed male-female relationships that were outside of the expectations for the Israelite community (e.g., Lev. 18:6–23); they also communicated differences in the relative value of male and female through rules that, for example, required different times for a woman's ceremonial uncleanness after the birth of a son or daughter (Lev. 12:2–5), though the offerings she made were the same in either case (Lev. 12:6–8). Several "texts of terror" reveal the horrible treatment to which some women were subjected (e.g., Judg. 19:22–30), while other stories show how women were subject to the decisions and actions of men (e.g., Bathsheba in 2 Sam. 11). Even so, there are stories of women's courage, wisdom, and compassion (e.g., Ruth, Abigail, Esther) in the midst of situations controlled by men. One final example of the tension in the Old Testament is the ambivalence in the Wisdom literature. The Song of Songs celebrates the passion of two lovers (Song 1:2; 5:1; 8:6–7), but the book of Proverbs, which praises Woman Wisdom (Prov. 8–9) and the "capable wife" (Prov. 31:10–31) also goes to great lengths to warn young men of the "loose woman" (Prov. 5:3–14; 7:4–27).[185] Overall, then, the Old Testament expresses high ideals for the potential of mutual blessing in male-female relationships, but the patriarchal assumptions that underlie most of the canonical writings cannot be avoided.

The New Testament writings reflect first-century Judaism's patriarchal understanding of the roles of men and women in society, but one also begins to hear a few more notes of equality than in the Old Testament. Although the situation described in the Gospels may not conclusively point to the egalitarian community Schüssler Fiorenza envisions, in various ways it does establish the dignity of women among Jesus' followers and those who received his healing and heard his teaching. Luke especially contains several stories about women not found in the other Gospels (e.g., Mary's faith and obedience, Luke 1:26–38, 46–55; 2:19), and John highlights Mary's role as one who petitions Jesus for help and stands faithfully in the fellowship of women at the cross (John 2:1–12; 19:25–27). Other individual acts of sacrifice and compassion are singled out by Jesus for commemoration (Matt. 26:13; Mark 12:42–44), and all four Gospels agree that the first witnesses to the resurrection were women.[186] Like the Gospels, the book of Acts does not describe specific women within the circle of leadership among the disciples, but they continue to have an active role in the ministry (Acts 1:14; 2:1–4; 16:14–15; 18:2, 26). In certain circumstances, Paul recognizes women who have served in important ways, such as Phoebe and Junia in Rome (Rom. 16:1, 7), and he states the fundamental principle that "there is no longer male and female; for all of you are one in Christ" (Gal. 3:28). However, he also directs the church at Corinth to observe certain cultural customs in worship (1 Cor. 11:2–16) and to limit the teaching role of women (1 Cor. 14:34–36). The Pastoral Letters also designate men for leadership positions and place women in submission to their teaching (1 Tim. 2:11–15; 3:1–13; Titus 1:5–9).

Marriage and Family: Learning to Be the Household of God

Much of the above discussion carries over to this circle of relationships, but biblical insights into marriage and family involve a greater range of dynamics than the focus on human beings as male and female. It is not possible to completely separate insights about husbands and wives from those about parents and children or brothers and sisters, but within the framework of Israelite society, the Old Testament narratives and laws highlighted certain standards and expectations. The overriding impression one gets is of the connectedness within families (including the extended family), both through dictates or principles and through the stories that tell of problems. The notion of marriage is rooted in Genesis 2, not only in the man's exclamation that the woman is "bone of my bones and flesh of my flesh" but also in the narrator's observation, "Therefore a man leaves his father and his mother and clings to his wife, and they become one flesh" (Gen. 2:23–24). Many stories and legal texts concern themselves with securing a spouse within the circle of the Israelite people. Abraham and Isaac are insistent that their sons not marry a Canaanite but one of their own kindred (Gen. 24:3; 28:1). Moreover, the laws of levirate marriage seek to ensure the continuation of one's family line (Deut. 25:5–10), "to perpetuate [a] brother's name in Israel" (v. 7) and to "build up [a] brother's house" (v. 9). The sanctity of marriage is affirmed by the Ten Commandments (Exod. 20:14) and other regulations that prohibit adulterous relationships (Deut. 22:22); even the giving of a "certificate of divorce" indicates that marriage was not to be undertaken lightly (Deut. 24:1; see Mal. 2:14–16).[187]

Relationships between parents and children as well as those between siblings emphasized the connections that unite them within the bond of family. Parents are enjoined to teach their children the law of God and the meaning of their sacred traditions (Deut. 6:7, 20–25; see Josh. 24:15) but also to instruct them in the traditional wisdom. Much of Proverbs 1–9 is set as parental teaching: "Hear, my child, your father's instruction, and do not reject your mother's teaching" (Prov. 1:8). The seriousness of these matters, at least in the Deuteronomic traditions, is borne out by the harshest of punishments for a "stubborn and rebellious son" (Deut. 21:18–21). One of the ironies of Israel's history, however, is that otherwise godly parents were not always successful in raising children who shared their convictions: Eli (1 Sam. 2:12), Samuel (1 Sam. 8:3), and Hezekiah (2 Kgs. 21:1–9). Moreover, the Old Testament narratives tend to highlight the *lack* of connections among brothers and sisters. The first siblings are torn apart by anger, as Cain murders his brother Abel (Gen. 4:1–16). The strife between Jacob and Esau (Gen. 27), between Joseph and his brothers (Gen. 37), and among David's children (2 Sam. 12–24) all reveal in their own ways the jealousies and resentments that lead to disastrous consequences.

The teachings of the New Testament also hold marriage and family relationships in high esteem—"Let marriage be held in honor by all, and let the marriage bed be kept undefiled" (Heb. 13:4)—but we also see a subtle shift away from making the biological family itself the supreme expression of human relationships. Jesus' teachings on marriage and divorce reaffirm the Old Testament standards, if also heightening their application to inward thoughts and intentions (Matt. 5:27–30; 19:3–12), and Paul sought to clarify expectations for marriage, interjecting his interpretation of God's will with his own opinion (1 Cor. 7:1–16, 25–40). And while supporting traditional, patriarchal roles, the "household codes" did set family relationships within the larger rubric of mutual subjection among all Christians (e.g., Eph. 5:21).[188] It is within the Gospels, however, that a new understanding of "family" begins to emerge: Jesus calls those who do "the will of my Father in heaven . . . my brother and sister and mother" (Matt. 12:50); the child Jesus obeys his parents but calls the temple his "Father's house" (Luke 2:49, 51); and in John's Gospel, Jesus' encounters with Mary in Cana and at the cross show that while he still honors his mother, he also creates new community (John 2:4–8; 19:25–27). As parents bring their little children to Jesus, he identifies their focus on himself—"Let [them] come to me"—as making them possessors of "the kingdom of heaven" (Matt. 19:13–15). In the Pastoral Letters, Timothy unquestionably benefited from the faith of his mother and grandmother (2 Tim. 1:5), but Paul also calls him "my beloved child" (2 Tim. 1:2), indicating the way faith creates its own family relationships. Baptism unites believers with Christ and thus with one another in the church in a sevenfold unity: "There is one body and one Spirit, just as you were called to the one hope of your calling, one Lord, one faith, one baptism, one God and Father of all, who is above all and through all and in all" (Eph. 4:4–6).

Ethnicity and Race: Moving from Exclusion to Inclusion

In addition to relating in terms of sex, gender, and family, human beings also relate to each other in light of racial and ethnic categories.[189] I have already addressed the larger concept of relationships between different nations and how the Old Testament books affirm the unity of humankind and an ideal of global peace under Yahweh's reign in Zion. I now refer to how the biblical texts express suspicion of the "other" in a national or political sense and how they also encourage Israel to maintain its racial and ethnic purity while not entirely closing the door to relationships with other peoples, even if this latter openness was a minority voice. From the ancestral concern to marry within one's own kindred to the laws that forbade intermarriage, Israelites were officially committed to avoiding intimate connection with the indigenous peoples of Canaan. As the narrator of Kings censured Solomon, "[He] loved many foreign women . . . : Moabite, Ammonite, Edomite, Sidonian, and Hittite women, from the nations concerning which the LORD had said to the Israelites, 'You shall not enter into marriage with them, neither shall they with you; for they will surely incline your heart to follow their gods'" (1 Kgs. 11:1–2). The rationale here and in other places (Exod. 34:16; Deut. 7:3–4; 1 Kgs. 16:31–33; 2 Kgs. 17:7–8; Neh. 13:23–27) is always the avoidance of the religious customs of these nations, not so much racial prejudice for its own sake.[190] Moses himself married a Cushite woman (Num. 12:1), but the context does not precisely identify her ethnicity and origin, nor is it clear that Miriam and Aaron's objection to the marriage was based solely on those grounds (see Num. 12:2). The writings of the postexilic period bring the issue of ethnicity to the fore with the policies of Ezra and Nehemiah, who "separated from Israel all those of foreign descent" (Neh. 13:3). On the other hand, the book of Ruth does not even mention the prohibitions against marrying Moabites, and Ruth's role in the line of the Davidic kings places an exclamation mark on the book's rhetoric of inclusion (Ruth 4:18–22). The postexilic prophet declares: "Do not let the foreigner joined to the LORD say, 'The LORD will surely separate me from his people' . . . The foreigners who join themselves to the LORD . . . I will bring to my holy mountain and make them joyful in my house of prayer; . . . for my house shall be called a house of prayer for all peoples" (Isa. 56:3, 6–8).

We have seen how Jesus' ministry was focused first upon "the house of Israel" but that he also interacted with and praised the faith of Samaritans and foreigners. Matthew's genealogy makes special note of Jesus' non-Jewish ancestors, such as Rahab and Ruth (Matt. 1:5). All of the Synoptic Gospels record the name and origin of the man who carried the cross—Simon of Cyrene (Matt. 27:32; Mark 15:21; Luke 23:26)—showing the importance of this tradition as a profound symbol: Disciples of all lands share in the sufferings of Christ and are called to carry their own cross daily (Luke 9:23). The book of Acts describes a variety of efforts to embrace all peoples in the kingdom of God: the speaking of languages on Pentecost (Acts 2:4–11); the resolution to conflicts between "Hellenists" and "Hebrews" over food distribution (6:1–6); Philip's ministry in Samaria and to the Ethiopian official (8:5–13, 26–40); Peter's realization "that God shows no partiality" (10:34); the Council of Jerusalem's decision to welcome Gentile believers without requiring circumcision, because God "has made no distinction between them and us" (15:9); and Paul's eventual travels to predominantly Gentile regions. The main theological dynamic is the distinction between Jews and Gentiles, to which Paul laid down the fundamental principle: "There is no longer Jew or Greek" (Gal. 3:28). The Letter to the Ephesians eloquently speaks of the way God "has made both groups [Jews and Gentiles] into one and has broken down the dividing wall, that is, the hostility between us" (Eph. 2:14). The unity is so profound that the letter calls it "one new humanity," "one body," and one "household of God" (Eph. 2:15, 16, 19; see 3:6).

Leadership and Service: Sharing Responsibility in Humility

Within the larger set of basic categories of relationship comes each person's sense of vocation, a calling that informs one's understanding of one's place in God's world. The human race, of course, shares the calling given in Genesis 1–2 to fill the earth and care for it, a mandate that reflects the divine vocation of creation and redemption. But there is also a great deal in both testaments that speaks of the distinct callings that humans bring to their relationships, such that even Cain's line could witness the blessings of work and culture (Gen. 4:20–22). The Old Testament's primary history can be organized around Israel's leaders (Moses, Joshua, major judges, Samuel, and the kings), but even during their tenure some tasks required shared leadership, such as dispensing justice (Exod. 18:13–26) or using special abilities to build the tabernacle (Exod. 35:10, 25, 30–35; 36:1–8).

The Old Testament pays the greatest attention to leadership and service in the religious and political spheres of human relationships, especially in terms of the potential success or failure of priests, prophets, and kings. *Priests*, assisted by the Levites, were charged with supervising the entire ceremonial and cultic system of sacrifices and offerings, the teaching of the law, and temple worship (Exod. 28–30; Lev. 8–9; 16; 22; Num. 3–4; 1 Chron. 23–26). So crucial was this ministerial presence among the people that Moses and Joshua arranged for forty-eight Levitical cities distributed throughout Israel (Num. 35:1–8; Josh. 21), and the tribes supported the Levites through the system of tithing (see Lev. 27:30–33; Num. 18:24; Deut. 12:6; 14:27–29).[191] The Torah and Former Prophets do not offer much description of the regular practice of priestly ministry, but we do hear of failures to execute their duties properly: Nadab and Abihu (Lev. 10:1–3), and the sons of Eli (1 Sam. 2:12–17, 22–25).[192] The Latter Prophets add to this impression with numerous indictments of the priests (Isa. 24:2; 28:7; Jer. 2:8, 26; 13:13–14; Ezek. 22:26; Hos. 5:1; 6:9).

The political leadership of *kings* arose out of the inadequacy of the judges to bring Israel safety from external threats and internal unity and justice.[193] Joshua succeeded Moses as a strong, central leader (Deut. 31:7–8; Josh. 1:2–9), but no such person arose in the period of the judges (Judg. 21:25), even though Samuel himself served faithfully as a priest, prophet, and judge (1 Sam. 3:1; 3:19–20; 7:15). The book of Deuteronomy sets the standards and scope of kingly author-ity (Deut. 17:14–20), foreshadowing the eventual failings of monarchs in both the northern and southern kingdoms (see 1 Sam. 8:10–18).[194] Even with the human failings of the kings, the prophets and psalms envisioned a renewed, Davidic dynasty that would fulfill the blessings of the covenant Yahweh made with David (Isa. 9:6–7; 11:1–10; Jer. 23:5–6; Ezek. 34:23–24; Zech. 9:9–10; Pss. 72; 110). It is here that one might use "messianic" language, insofar as the majority of Old Testament uses of the word "messiah" refer to the earthly king as God's "anointed one" (e.g., 1 Sam. 12:3, 5; Pss. 2:2; 18:50; 20:6).[195]

Finally, God raised up *prophets* as messengers of the divine will, to call Israel to repentance, declare judgment for disobedience, and offer hope for restora-tion after judgment. The prophets were also bound to the expectations of the Deuteronomic law (Deut. 13:1–5; 18:14–22), and they served in a variety of capacities, from offering direct support for a monarch (such as Nathan for David), to the latter prophets who declared judgment and hope for society as a whole. In between these types were "peripheral prophets" such as Elijah and Elisha, who might assist or denounce kings as well as work among the poor-est members of society.[196] False prophets were a perpetual danger for Israel (Isa. 9:15; Jer. 23:9–14; Ezek. 14:9–11), but there were also those who were truly called of God yet disobeyed his commands (1 Kgs. 13; Jonah).

A New Testament theology of leadership and service can be depicted as two concentric circles. The inner circle considers Jesus as the culmination of vari-ous Old Testament expressions of leadership,[197] and the outer circle develops the connections between Jesus the servant-leader and the ministry of his body, the church. Much of the energy in the Gospel accounts derives from the ques-tion over whether Jesus is the Messiah: "So the Jews gathered around him and said to him, 'How long will you keep us in suspense? If you are the Messiah, tell us plainly'" (John 10:24; see Matt. 26:63; Mark 14:61; Luke 22:67). Given the first-century Palestinian context, that question lines up with the Old Tes-tament usage of "messiah": a royal or quasi-political figure who could free Israel from Roman occupation and bring in the kingdom. For his part, Jesus avoids referring to himself as the Messiah and prefers instead the title "Son of Man" (e.g., Matt. 26:64; see Dan. 7:13–14), which itself had far-reaching implications for his identity within first-century Judaism.[198] In addition to messianic lan-guage, the New Testament speaks of Christ in terms of the classic offices of priest (Heb. 4:15; 5:5; 7:15–17; 9:11), prophet (Luke 24:19; Acts 3:22–23), and king (John 18:33–37; 19:19–21; Rev. 19:16).[199] But far from being a ruler in the earthly model, exercising power with brute force or lording his position over others, Jesus set the example of a humble servant (Mark 10:45; John 13:14–15) and a good shepherd who lays down his life for his flock (John 10:11).

These christological reflections connect with human leadership and service precisely on this point: that leadership among God's people is marked by humble service (Mark 9:35), shared with others through a diversity of gifts (1 Cor. 12:4–11). Jesus shared his ministry with the disciples almost from the beginning, calling them in Galilee (Mark 1:17–18) and sending them out to minister in his name (Mark 6:7–13), later involving many others in ministry (Luke 10:1–12, 17–20). Not only did Jesus commission the church to make disciples in all the world (Matt. 28:19–20; Acts 1:8), but he endowed the church with gifts by virtue of his ascension (Eph. 4:7–12). But like the example Jesus gave, Paul taught that the body of Christ should have no personality cults (1 Cor. 1:12–13) but rather only imitate leaders as they imitate Christ (1 Cor. 11:1; see also 1 Cor. 4:16; Phil. 3:17; 1 Thess. 1:6; 2:14; 2 Thess. 3:7, 9; Eph. 5:1). This is not to say that the concept of "office" was discontinued in the early church; to the contrary, it was asserted both in Jerusalem by the apostles and in other churches through the guidance of the apostles (Acts 1:24–26; 6:2–6; 20:17; 1 Tim. 3:1–13; Titus 1:5–9; 1 Pet. 5:1–5). Even so, such officers were to "clothe [themselves] with humility" (1 Pet. 5:5), and they were but one expression of the diverse ministries that existed among the body of Christ (Rom. 12:4–8; 1 Cor. 12:12–31). Finally, much like the Old Testament prophets, the New Testament writings contain a number of sharp critiques of leaders, both those within first-century Judaism (Matt. 23) as well as all kinds of false teachers among Christians (1 Tim. 4:1–3; 6:3–5; Titus 1:10–16; 2 Pet. 2:1–13; Jude 3–23; 1 John 4:1–6; 2 John 7–11; but compare 3 John 7–9).

Individuality and Community: Living Together in Unity and Peace

The larger drama of the challenge that Israelite tribes faced as they became a nation contained within it smaller stages on which threats to unity and peace were played out. What type of role was there for individuals in a community defined primarily by its corporate calling to be a "kingdom" and "nation" (Exod. 19:6)? One way of getting at the biblical theology of community is to recognize that while God's covenants with creation and Israel considered people in global or national terms, the Old Testament still expresses a strong theme of individual responsibility. For example, when Yahweh first declares his will at Sinai for the people delivered from slavery, the Ten Commandments address Israel in the singular, with commands for each person to obey: "I am the LORD *your* God, who brought *you* out of the land of Egypt, out of the house of slavery; *you* shall have no other gods before me" (Exod. 20:2–3).[200] Moreover, in the midst of the national history recounted in the Torah and Former Prophets, there are numerous stories where one or a few members of the community acted for good or ill, thus affecting the course of the people as a whole: the courage of Shiphrah and Puah, the Hebrew midwives (Exod. 1:15–22); the faith of Joshua and Caleb (Num. 14:6–10); the rebelliousness of Korah, Dathan, and Abiram (Num. 16); Phineas's zeal that stayed Yahweh's wrath (Num. 25:6–13); the selfish greed of Aachan (Josh. 7); David's desire to defend Yahweh's honor (1 Sam. 17:26); and Obadiah's hiding of Yahweh's prophets (1 Kgs. 18:3–4). Although some of these individuals eventually played a major role in Israel's history (e.g., Joshua, David), it would be wrong to think of them as especially noteworthy when they responded to the situations described in those passages. Even the manner in which Israel organized its populace ("thousands, hundreds, fifties, and tens," Exod 18:21) gave each member of the community a sense of connectedness to the whole while also ensuring their sense of belonging to an intimate fellowship. The organization of families, clans, and tribes did not "keep people in their place" but rather enabled individuals to experience covenant responsibilities and blessings for themselves as they also considered the needs of others, indeed, loving their neighbors as themselves (Lev. 19:18; see Ps. 133:1).

Israel's life in community was to be characterized by peace, the shalom that was not merely the absence of warfare and strife (e.g., Deut. 20:10–11; 1 Kgs. 4:24) but also a holistic sense of well-being, characterized by the community's freedom from fear (Ps. 4:8), rejection of evil (Ps. 34:12–14), comfort and healing (Isa. 57:18–19), and rest in death (Gen. 15:15).[201] Israel's shalom was very much tied to the righteousness and justice of the king (Ps. 72:3, 7) and could therefore be focused on "the peace of Jerusalem" (Ps. 122:6–8). The prophets, of course, had to resist a false sense of security, wherein leaders who abused the people with injustice were "saying, 'Peace, peace,' when there is no peace" (Jer. 6:14; 8:11). There was a price to pay for such disregard for others, when individuals "turned to [their] own way": The suffering servant bore "the punishment that made us whole" (Isa. 53:5, 6).[202] Ultimately, Israel could anticipate the eschatological reign of the "Prince of Peace," bringing "endless peace" by his just and righteous rule forever (Isa. 9:6–7).

We have seen how the New Testament's teachings about leadership emphasize the humble service offered by each part of the body of Christ. This sharing of spiritual gifts stands as a visible manifestation of the underlying unity of that body, a unity that works through acts of forgiveness, compassion, and justice. As in the Old Testament passages above, New Testament authors do not understand individuality to be swallowed up in the community but rather to find full expression there, making each member an essential part: "living stones . . . built into a spiritual house" (1 Pet. 2:5; see 1 Cor. 3:17). The book of Acts, for example, moves seamlessly from a concern for the whole church to descriptions of individual faith or disobedience. Acts 2 offers a general summary of the church's growth and generosity (vv. 43–47) but turns immediately to the ministry of Peter and John to a lame man in the temple (Acts 3:1–10). A similar summary at the end of Acts 4 mentions the gift of Barnabas only to contrast his action with that of Ananias and Sapphira (4:36–37; 5:1–11). The problem of food distribution for unnamed Hebrew and Hellenist widows leads to the calling of seven named individuals (6:1–7), one of whom (Stephen) conducts a courageous preaching ministry (Acts 7). Paul tells the Corinthian believers that the health of their fellowship is compromised by their tolerance of an individual case of sin (1 Cor. 5:1–2), but he is careful not to prohibit their ministry among "the immoral of this world" (1 Cor. 5:9–13). In another place, Paul balances a consideration for other's burdens with the need for all to "carry their own loads" (Gal. 6:2, 5). In still other passages, believers are encouraged to consider the needs of others before their own (1 Cor. 10:24), but no individual should expect others to take care of him when he is capable of work (2 Thess. 3:10; see Acts 20:34). And while local congregations certainly had to work at unity among their own numbers, there were also indications that congregations themselves were united to one another in a larger fellowship with other churches (Acts 15:22–29; 1 Cor. 14:33).[203]

The New Testament's theology of peace closely matches the thematic concerns of the Old Testament. Peace literally refers to the cessation of war or hostility (Luke 19:42), but it also encompasses a life of health and wholeness (Mark 5:34; Luke 8:48). To long for peace is an essential element of hope for oneself and the kingdom of God on earth (Luke 1:79; 2:14, 29), thus strengthening the blessing Jesus pronounces on "peacemakers" in the Beatitudes (Matt. 5:9). Jesus sent his disciples out to speak "peace" to those who received his message (Matt. 10:13; Luke 10:5–6), but he also warned them that his message would divide people, bringing a sword instead of peace (Matt. 10:34; "division" in Luke 12:51). For John, peace is the gift that Jesus leaves with his disciples to equip them for their work in his absence—not a worldly peace, but a foretaste of the eschatological presence and comfort of God even in the face of persecution (John 14:27; 16:33; 20:19–20).[204] Paul's letters all begin with the characteristic greeting of "grace and peace" (Rom. 1:7; 1 Cor. 1:3; 2 Cor. 1:2; Gal. 1:3; etc.). Paul's understanding of peace, however, is also closely tied to his interpretation of God's reconciling activity: that because God has justified people, they "have peace with God" (Rom. 5:1; 8:6; see Phil. 4:7, 9). The practical outcome of reconciliation with God meant that believers were to live peacefully with each other in the church (1 Cor. 7:15; 14:33) and to acknowledge the far-reaching social implications for humankind, since God was "making peace" between Jew and Gentile through the cross of Christ (Eph. 2:14–17; see Acts 10:36).[205] Ultimately, Jesus' followers go through life knowing that "the God of peace" will be with them and ultimately achieve victory over Satan through their faith and work (Rom 15:33; 16:20).

CONCLUSION

This thematic approach to biblical theology began with the unity and oneness of Yahweh, the God of Israel, whom the church confessed to be the Father of Jesus Christ. It has now concluded with a vision of humanity's oneness in shalom, owing to the reconciling activity of that same God of peace. Throughout this chapter we have seen how the various themes reveal a rich diversity along with a certain coherence, a unity in the diversity and a diversity in the unity. Texts and topics have intertwined in a larger biblical conversation, so that the one, multifaceted story of God's work with and through Israel and the church offers insights that look backward and forward in intertextual ways. Thus, it seems fair to say that while the New Testament writers undoubtedly built upon, interpreted, and applied Old Testament themes for their own purposes and contexts, they did not do so in a supersessionistic way. Indeed, we have seen that many themes of the New Testament are virtually equivalent to those of the Old and are consistent with the milieu of first-century Judaism. To be sure, there are notes of prophetic fulfillment and some cases of identifying Christ with the fuller meaning of Old Testament stories (e.g., Matthew's quotations), but this is not the only, or even primary, way that the New Testament develops the themes of biblical theology. The main way this occurs is by a writer identifying a particular theme and then refocusing it through the lens of God's redemptive activity in Christ. Thus, the grand ideals of creation and covenant first revealed in the history and traditions of the Old Testament are reaffirmed for Jews and Gentiles, that is, for all humankind, to live in relationship with God and with one another.

6

The Prospects for Biblical Theology

This survey of biblical theology's history, issues, methods, and themes has pointed to the resiliency and vibrancy of the discipline, but it has also highlighted several continuing challenges that await the next generation of biblical theologians. I will now briefly consider some of the more serious issues and propose ways these could be approached in order for biblical theology to prosper in the future.

THE DEFINITION OF BIBLICAL THEOLOGY

Throughout the course of this book I have suggested that almost every major issue and methodological proposal in biblical theology arises from some contested aspect of the discipline's definition. The definition I proposed to get us started was: *Biblical theology seeks to identify and understand the Bible's theological message, that is, what the Bible says about God and God's relation to all creation, especially to humankind.* Now that we are near the end of this study, this otherwise workable definition could be augmented by other aspects.

First, biblical theology explores not only *what* the Bible says about God but *how* it says these things. The debate over methods in the late twentieth century gave sharp focus to the matter of witnesses, especially whether the number and diversity of witnesses still provides some essential unity within the authoritative canon. Increasing sensitivity to this diversity necessitates attention to the "how" of biblical theology: How did the historical forces that shaped the canon's theological witness influence the eventual content of that witness? To be sure, the nineteenth and twentieth centuries made indispensable contributions to the study of theological content. Although the ongoing search for the Bible's theology cannot be set aside because of its shaping and context, that search will be unsuccessful if questions about canonical shaping and diverse witnesses are overlooked.

Second, biblical theology considers not only the *what* and *how* of the Bible's theology but also the *by whom* and *for whom*, that is, the perspectives of the biblical authors and their audiences. Among the many contributions of contextual biblical theologies at the turn of the twenty-first century is their ability to raise our awareness of the rhetoric of texts, of the purposes and interests within and behind what was written and canonized as scripture. Again, this newer concern does not mean that biblical theology can stop searching for the content of the Bible's message or the means by which its message was shaped, but the discipline will not succeed in ascertaining that message without attending to matters of perspective within the biblical text.

Third, biblical theology studies not only God's relation to creation and to human beings but also the relationships between and among human beings. Chapter 5 revealed that there is simply too much thematic content about human relationships for a definition of the discipline not to account for this area. As we have seen, the horizontal dimensions of biblical theology cannot be separated from the vertical ones; love of neighbor is practiced within the claim divine love makes upon humankind. Thus, I propose a slightly revised definition in light of the above observations: *Biblical theology seeks to identify and understand the Bible's theological message and themes, as well as how the Bible witnesses to those themes and to whom and by whom it declares that message. The outcome of such investigation will lead us to hear what the Bible says about God's being, words, and actions; about God's relationship to all creation, especially humankind; and about the implications this divine-human encounter has for relationships between human beings.* This revised language does not completely remove all of the challenges of defining biblical theology, but it does create larger boundaries within which the questions asked in chapter 1 can be discussed and answered.

THE HISTORY OF BIBLICAL THEOLOGY

Chapter 2 organized the history of the discipline around seven questions related to key movements or historical developments in biblical theology. As we reflect on the legacy of past scholarship, it is important to recognize that the way forward requires us to avoid misconceptions about the discipline's history that might hinder progress on many of today's major biblical theological issues. What are these misconceptions and how can we move beyond them?

First, there is a danger of letting the general tenor of an era within the history of biblical theology become the only characteristic of that era. Thus, the late nineteenth century is often subsumed under "the history of religions," while the mid-twentieth century is labeled as the "recovery" or "rebirth" of biblical theology. All disciplines use categories to assist in organizing the vast and diverse materials of past scholarship; this activity is both unavoidable and absolutely essential for the careful assessment of the evidence within biblical theology. However, within biblical theology every era has witnessed its own complex interactions between concepts and methods. Even when historical interests or theological ones have dominated the scholarly scene, there have been communities of faith and learning that were known for the "minority" emphasis. Many of the fine surveys of biblical theology have taken pains to listen to these voices, but the discipline as a whole would benefit from reconsidering the interaction of all the voices at any given time in its history. In particular, tracing the lines of "conservative" and "critical" scholarship during the past two hundred years would reveal more of the unbroken connections from one era to the next and help us avoid the detrimental connotations of those labels in the first place.

Second, and closely related to the first tendency, there is always the temptation for scholars of every era to set themselves over against the past. While this characteristic is applied especially by postmodern scholars to the modern era, the truth is that postmodernism sets itself just as strongly over against modernism as modernism did the pre-Enlightenment era. We have seen, however, that a variety of forms of theological interpretation existed for millennia, long before the advent of the modern discipline of biblical theology, and these "premodern" scholars were often concerned with the same basic issues as their modern counterparts, namely, questions about sources, the canon, and interpretive methods. Moreover, as postmodern scholars have pointed out the genuine weaknesses within modernism, they too have relied on principles of logic, reason, and argumentation common to scholarship throughout the centuries. The way forward calls all of those interested in biblical theology to appreciate the contributions of every era. If some wish to decenter the apparent centrality of one set of methods or scholars, such decentering does not mean a complete disavowal of the insights and experiences of the former "center." Every biblical theologian will of course feel equipped to use some methods more than others, but we can all appreciate the way in which other approaches and perspectives complement and correct our own.

Having identified these two tendencies and suggested ways to lessen their deleterious effects, I am not implying a lack of progress or difference from one generation to the next. It is beyond dispute that new discoveries about the biblical world have advanced our understanding of the Bible's message, just as new methods and perspectives have shed light on forgotten or unappreciated aspects of the Bible. But such progress and advancement notwithstanding, biblical theology can only gain from seeing the differences *and* the similarities between the present challenges and past accomplishments. In other words, this modern-postmodern moment calls for the skills of both empathy and critique, exercised within diverse communities that can provide checks and balances on the level of methods, perspectives, and results. The ideal pictured in this shared effort is easier described than lived out, owing in no small measure to several issues that currently challenge the discipline of biblical theology.

THE ISSUES OF BIBLICAL THEOLOGY

Chapter 3 identified and discussed eight major issues, grouped within three areas pertaining to the scope of the discipline's sources, to basic methodological presuppositions, and to the influences that contexts and communities have on biblical theologians. I will address some of these issues in the following two sections on methods and themes. I wish to highlight here a few areas related to sources of and influences on biblical theology that will continue to impact how scholars negotiate disagreements in biblical theology in the near future.

First, the relationship of the Old and New Testaments remains a crucial issue for biblical theology, especially when "biblical" refers to the Christian Bible. We have seen that some scholars regard this relationship not just as one issue among many but as the definitive issue, and their intuition on this point seems correct.[1] Christian biblical theologians have been hesitant to develop works that comprehensively treat the theology of both testaments, Scobie's *The Ways of God* being the noteworthy exception in the past fifteen years. The instincts behind this hesitancy have been sound, given the legacy of some Christian interpretations of the Old Testament, but it also seems that the argument against reading New Testament theology back into the Old has achieved its cautionary purpose. There will certainly continue to be, and should be, works that make either the Old or New Testament their primary focus, allowing scholars to immerse themselves in the languages, cultures, content, and theological narratives of particular portions of the canon. But as their work continues, it will also provide the basis for those who wish to explore connections between the testaments.

Second, the debate over the legitimate subject matter of biblical theology seems to be reaching some consensus among scholars. The question is no longer *whether* extrabiblical linguistic and artifactual materials should be considered in the study of the Bible's message; it is a question of *how* and *why*. In chapter 3 I suggested the helpfulness of the distinction between the content of the biblical writings and the context of the biblical writers. The latter area serves as the primary subject matter of the history of religions, leaving the former as the main focus of biblical theology, but each discipline needs the expertise of the other to develop a satisfactory portrait of the Bible's theology within the Bible's world. There will, of course, be those who argue that the canon is merely a contingency of religious history and thus should not be treated with more respect than other writings from the ancient world. This is where the question of "why" arises, since many faith communities hold the canon as theologically and spiritually authoritative. One may always debate the historical evidence about the process of canonization, even as one recognizes that religious communities will practice biblical theology for guidance about faith and life, something that strictly academic communities will not—and should not—do.

A third set of issues involves contemporary contexts and perspectives, especially the inclusion of new voices and hence new insights in biblical theology, such as those arising from feminist and postcolonial scholarship. However, two factors complicate a full assessment of their contributions, namely, the diversity of positions and methods within those perspectives and the paucity of comprehensive treatments of biblical theology. As I wrote about the new opportunities afforded the discipline by these developments, I was personally challenged by the temptation to view perspectives other than my own as being "at the margins," with mine being near some imagined "center." The next generation of biblical theologians can resist such a temptation by seeking out shared language and standards by which methods and conclusions can be justly assessed. It took over a century for historical criticism to become the common mode of discourse in biblical studies. We can only hope that it will not take that long for other methods and perspectives to participate in the conversation that is biblical theology.

THE METHODS OF BIBLICAL THEOLOGY

Chapter 4 addressed the key components of the most prevalent methods used in biblical theology, but behind all of them were presuppositions about methodological issues: whether the task is descriptive as well as normative, whether historical method must be separated from theological interpretation, and whether biblical theology and systematic theology are compatible partners working toward the same goal. Generally speaking, an exclusively descriptive approach goes hand in hand with a strictly historical method and maintains a sharp distinction between biblical and systematic theology. But, as we have seen, there is a misleading impression created by this truism: that methodology always comes down to a choice between two mutually exclusive options. On the contrary, it is possible to envision biblical theology as operating with several intersecting axes, where historical, literary, theological, and contextual concerns all meet to interpret the message of the biblical text.

I arranged the methods themselves in three major areas focused on the content of biblical theology, the shape biblical theology takes, and the perspectives from which we approach the discipline. The current challenge is for scholars to draw on these methods' strengths without dismissing any method out of hand because of shortcomings in earlier expressions. Just because some "content" methods tried to press too much or too diverse material into a limited unity does not make the search for theological content illegitimate. There is room within a comprehensive biblical theology for some systematic structure that builds on the developmental aspects of biblical traditions. Moreover, sensitivity to the diverse interests in the academy or religious institutions does not necessarily leave one in a quagmire of competing rationalities. Biblical theologians will be called upon to speak from their distinct perspectives with methods that can be tested in the public sphere and to offer results that are consistent with the best available evidence. Scholars cannot ultimately set aside every impulse of their theological commitments, but they can practice biblical theology in good faith, seeking to prescind personally or corporately held beliefs while reading the text with those who hold different convictions.

THE THEMES OF BIBLICAL THEOLOGY

Chapter 5 provided a way in which different methods and interests could converge in an organized structure that was sensitive to major themes, to the impulses that shaped the Bible's message, and to some of the contemporary issues and perspectives that inform biblical theology. As I surveyed a number of themes along the vertical and horizontal planes of biblical theology, I benefited from the sustained efforts of scholars who analyzed particular biblical themes and the relationship between texts that stand in tension with one another. I also aimed to demonstrate the possibility of and the need for synthetic treatments that build on the analytic work done by others in order to propose larger, overarching studies of either testament or both.

The key thematic issue will continue to be the relationship of the Bible's different witnesses to each other within the one canon. Rolf Knierim is correct that "the canon finalized the problem" of unity and diversity, and there is even truth to his assertion about the canon "generating this problem without resolving it."[2] But while there is no complete resolution within the canon itself, it undoubtedly contains elements that offer a unifying impulse: the fact that a specific community in history saw enough coherence amidst the diversity to hold these writings together in one authoritative collection; the consistent testimony to one God, whether Yahweh in the Old Testament or the God and Father of Jesus Christ in the New; and the biblical authors' identification with the people of Israel and/or the early church.[3] Within these broad parameters, there are witnesses who express confusion over God's ways and sorrow over the faithlessness of their people. Still others simply offer different perspectives on creation, history, religious observances, or human wisdom. And so the journey continues, for "the canon itself calls for the discernment of a theological criterion for the purpose of its own proper theological understanding."[4]

The complex interaction of unity and diversity might be represented in the following analogy. The biblical canon consists of a family of writers—individuals who are related to each other by virtue of a shared history, culture, and belief system. But, like all families, these members are unique individuals who bring their own knowledge, understanding, experiences, and concerns to their task. They do not adopt the same perspective on every issue, but they nevertheless share a common calling to give voice to God's character, words, and actions, as well as to the relationship humans have with this God and with one another. Biblical theology is the exciting task of listening to their conversation, discovering their similarities and differences, understanding their deepest convictions, and making connections with them that bring to life the Bible's message for each and every generation. May biblical theology long provide the resources to sustain those who take up that task.

Notes

Chapter 1: The Challenge of Defining "Biblical Theology"

1. In this initial discussion I use the term "Bible" both for the Hebrew Bible as sacred Scripture for the Jewish community and for the Old and New Testaments in the Christian community.

2. For the time being, I am using "biblical theology" to be inclusive of the sub-disciplines of Old Testament and New Testament theology.

3. Many scholars use similar terminology to define the discipline. Charles H. H. Scobie's definition has the same basic emphases. See *The Ways of Our God: An Approach to Biblical Theology* (Grand Rapids: Wm. B. Eerdmans Publishing Co., 2003), 4–5.

4. Erhard Gerstenberger, *Theologies in the Old Testament*, trans. John Bowden (Minneapolis: Fortress Press, 2002), 1.

5. Claus Westermann, *Elements of Old Testament Theology*, trans. Douglas W. Scott (Atlanta: John Knox Press, 1982), 9.

6. See Walter Brueggemann's discussion of the problem in *Theology of the Old Testament: Testimony, Dispute, Advocacy* (Minneapolis: Fortress Press, 1997), 107–12.

7. See, for example, Brueggemann, *Theology of the Old Testament*, 1n1; Gerstenberger, *Theologies in the Old Testament*, 3. John Goldingay uses "First Testament" for most of his book, while retaining the traditional term in his title (*Old Testament Theology*, vol. 1, *Israel's Gospel* [Downers Grove, IL: InterVarsity Press, 2003], 15). Christopher Seitz presents a brief but thoughtful exploration of these issues in "Old Testament or Hebrew Bible? Some Theological Considerations," in *Word without End: The Old Testament as Abiding Theological Witness* (Grand Rapids: Wm. B. Eerdmans Publishing Co., 1998), 61–74.

8. Gerhard Ebeling, "The Meaning of 'Biblical Theology,'" in *Word and Faith*, trans. James W. Leitch (Philadelphia: Fortress Press, 1963), 93.

9. See Ben Ollenburger, ed., *So Wide a Sea: Essays on Biblical and Systematic Theology* (Elkhart, IN: Institute of Mennonite Studies, 1991); Dennis T. Olson, "The Bible and Theology: Problems, Proposals, and Prospects," *Dialog* 37 (1998): 85–91; Joel B. Green and Max Turner, eds., *Between Two Horizons: Spanning New Testament and Biblical Theology* (Grand Rapids: Wm. B. Eerdmans Publishing

Co., 2000); Patrick D. Miller, "Theology from Below: The Theological Interpretation of Scripture," in *The Way of the Lord: Essays on Old Testament Theology*
(Tübingen: Mohr Siebeck, 2004), 297–309.

10. This explanation is in many ways an oversimplification of the complexities of
modern-postmodern terminology. In these matters I have benefited from the
work of Andrew K. M. Adam in *Making Sense of New Testament Theology: "Modern" Problems and Prospects* (Macon, GA: Mercer University Press, 1995), and
What Is Postmodern Biblical Criticism? (Minneapolis: Fortress Press, 1995).

11. For a provocative discussion of this issue, see David C. Steinmetz, "The Superiority of Pre-critical Exegesis," *Theology Today* 37 (1980): 27–38.

12. Krister Stendahl, "Biblical Theology: Contemporary," in *The Interpreter's Dictionary of the Bible*, ed. George A. Buttrick (Nashville: Abingdon Press, 1962),
1:418–32. Stendahl does not use the term "normative" in this entry to describe
the hermeneutical task. On that question, see Ben C. Ollenburger, "What Krister Stendahl 'Meant'—A Normative Critique of 'Descriptive Biblical Theology,'" *Horizons in Biblical Theology* 8 (1986): 61–98; and Philip F. Esler, *New
Testament Theology: Communion and Community* (Minneapolis: Fortress Press,
2005), 29–31.

13. Stendahl, "Biblical Theology: Contemporary," 418.

14. Ibid., 419.

15. See Adam, *Making Sense of New Testament Theology*, especially chaps. 2–4.

16. Esler, *New Testament Theology*, 6–7.

17. Werner Lemke, "Theology (OT)," in *Anchor Bible Dictionary*, ed. David Noel
Freedman (New York: Doubleday, 1992), 6:455.

18. Miller, "Theology from Below," 297–301.

19. Ibid., 297–98.

20. From the side of biblical theology, Miller cites the production of theological
introductions to the Bible and the individual works in the Overtures to Biblical Theology series (ibid.). From the side of systematic theology there is the
recent *Dictionary for Theological Interpretation of the Bible*, ed. Kevin J. Vanhoozer
(Grand Rapids: Baker Academic, 2005); commentary series such as the Ancient
Christian Commentary on Scripture, edited by Thomas C. Oden (Downers
Grove, IL: InterVarsity Press, 1998–); and the forthcoming *Journal of Theological Interpretation* (published by Eisenbrauns beginning in 2007).

Chapter 2: The History of Biblical Theology

1. See, for example, William Yarchin, *History of Biblical Interpretation: A Reader*
(Peabody, MA: Hendrickson Publishers, 2004); and Stephen Fowl, ed., *The
Theological Interpretation of Scripture: Classic and Contemporary Readings* (Oxford:
Blackwell, 1997).

2. G. B. Caird and L. D. Hurst, *New Testament Theology* (Oxford: Clarendon Press,
1994), 5; emphasis mine.

3. Donald Guthrie, *New Testament Theology* (Downers Grove, IL: InterVarsity
Press, 1981), 21; emphasis mine.

4. Contemporary biblical theologians are, of course, free to limit the scope of
their sources, as Paul House does by beginning his survey with works that can
be properly called "Old Testament Theologies" (*Old Testament Theology*
[Downers Grove, IL: InterVarsity Press, 1998], 14–15), but this is quite different from claiming that there was no biblical theology at all prior to the modern era, a claim House himself avoids making.

5. For a scholarly introduction to the phenomenon of "inner-biblical exegesis" see Michael Fishbane, *Biblical Interpretation in Ancient Israel* (Oxford: Clarendon Press, 1985).

6. For two recent studies of Exod. 34:6–7, see J. Clinton McCann, "'Abounding in Steadfast Love and Faithfulness': The Old Testament as a Source for Christology," in *In Essentials Unity: Reflections on the Nature and Purpose of the Church*, ed. M. Douglas Meeks and Robert D. Mutton (Minneapolis: Kirk House Publishers, 2001), 206–11; and R. W. Moberly, "How May We Speak of God? A Reconsideration of the Nature of Biblical Theology," *Tyndale Bulletin* 53 (2002): 177–202. See also Fishbane's extensive treatment in *Biblical Interpretation*, 335–50.

7. McCann, "Abounding in Steadfast Love," 209.

8. For further discussion and other examples see James Kugel, *The Bible as It Was* (Cambridge, MA: Harvard University Press, 1997), 1–17.

9. For general treatments of this period see Jon Berquist, *Judaism in Persia's Shadow: A Social and Historical Approach* (Minneapolis: Fortress Press, 1995); Lester L. Grabbe, *Judaism from Cyrus to Hadrian*, vol. 1, *The Persian and Greek Periods* (Minneapolis: Fortress Press, 1992); and Grabbe, *Judaic Religion in the Second Temple Period: Belief and Practice from the Exile to Yavneh* (London: Routledge, 2000). For discussions of religious literature interpreting biblical texts, see Craig A. Evans, ed., *Of Scribes and Sages: Early Jewish Interpretation and Transmission of Scripture*, 2 vols. (London: T. & T. Clark, 2004); and James L. Kugel and Rowan A. Greer, *Early Biblical Interpretation*, Library of Early Christianity (Philadelphia: Westminster Press, 1986).

10. Kugel, *The Bible as It Was*, xv.

11. Kugel and Greer, *Early Biblical Interpretation*, 26.

12. Yarchin uses this fact as a means of defining a starting point for surveying the history of biblical interpretation (*History of Biblical Interpretation*, xin1).

13. Ibid., xii–xiv. For many other examples, see Kugel, *Traditions of the Bible: A Guide to the Bible as It Was at the Start of the Common Era* (Cambridge, MA: Harvard University Press, 1998).

14. For background on this matter see Jack P. Lewis, "Council of Jamnia (Jabneh)," in *The Anchor Bible Dictionary*, ed. D. N. Freedman (New York: Doubleday, 1992), 3:634–37; and Grabbe, *Judaic Religion*, 116–26. For treatment of theological issues addressed by the leader of the Jamnia community, Yohanan ben Zakkai, see Jacob Neusner, *First Century Judaism in Crisis: Yohanan ben Zakkai and the Renaissance of Torah* (Nashville: Abingdon Press, 1975), 160–75.

15. Jacob Neusner, *The Mishnah: A New Translation* (New Haven, CT: Yale University Press, 1989), xv–xvi.

16. Jacob Neusner, *The Way of Torah: An Introduction to Judaism*, 2nd ed. (Encino, CA: Dickenson Publishing Co., 1974), 6.

17. Yarchin, *History of Biblical Interpretation*, 31–32; Peter Stuhlmacher, *Historical Criticism and Theological Interpretation of Scripture: Toward a Hermeneutics of Consent*, trans. Roy A. Harrisville (Philadelphia: Fortress Press, 1977), 27.

18. John W. Rogerson, "Interpretation, History of," in *The Anchor Bible Dictionary*, ed. D. N. Freedman (New York: Doubleday, 1992), 3:426.

19. The history of canonization is complex, tracing the authoritative use of biblical books by individual early church fathers in different regions of the Mediterranean world and leading to the eventual acceptance of a set of writings by different church councils. While the regional Council of Carthage (397 CE) is

regarded as the first official listing of the current twenty-seven books of the New Testament, their Old Testament list included books that came to be regarded as apocryphal by the Protestant churches.

20. Yarchin, *History of Biblical Interpretation*, xii.
21. Typology is "a method of biblical exegesis or interpretation in which persons, events, or things of the OT are interpreted as being foreshadowings or proto-types, of persons, events, or things in the NT" (Richard N. Soulen, *Handbook of Biblical Criticism*, 2nd ed. [Atlanta: John Knox Press, 1981], 206).
22. Gerald Bray, "The Church Fathers and Biblical Theology," in *Out of Egypt: Biblical Theology and Biblical Interpretation*, ed. Craig Bartholomew et al. (Grand Rapids: Zondervan Publishing House, 2004), 26–27.
23. Origen, "On First Principles," quoted in Yarchin, *History of Biblical Interpretation*, 45.
24. Rogerson, "Interpretation, History of," 3:426.
25. Yarchin, *History of Biblical Interpretation*, 61–63. As the later classical and early medieval periods reveal, the figurative or spiritual sense eventually developed its own inner distinctions beyond the allegorical sense: one called anagogical (i.e., more mystical or spiritual meanings) and another known as moral (some-times called the tropological sense, in reference to "tropes" or major recurring themes of biblical teaching).
26. *Peshat* comes from the Hebrew meaning "plain" or "simple," whereas *derash* (and thus *midrash*) comes from the verb "to seek"; hence the deeper meanings derived from attention to the grammatical and literary features of Scripture. For a more detailed discussion of the variety and richness of Jewish exegesis in this era, see Yarchin, *History of Biblical Interpretation*, 111–67.
27. Ibid., 133.
28. Thomas Aquinas, *Summa Theologiae* (part 1, question 1, article 10), quoted in Yarchin, *History of Biblical Interpretation*, 95.
29. I am indebted to John H. Hayes and Frederick Prussner, *Old Testament Theology: Its History and Development* (Atlanta: John Knox Press, 1985), for most of the dates listed for scholars and works in this section.
30. Hans Frei, *The Eclipse of Biblical Narrative: A Study in Eighteenth and Nineteenth Century Hermeneutics* (New Haven, CT: Yale University Press, 1974), 1–3.
31. Martin Luther, "Psalm 2," trans. L. W. Spitz Jr., in *Luther's Works*, ed. Jaroslav Pelikan (St. Louis: Concordia Publishing House, 1955), 12:6.
32. John Calvin, *Commentaries on the Psalms*, trans. H. Beveridge (Grand Rapids: Baker Book House, 1984), 1:11.
33. Frei, *The Eclipse of Biblical Narrative*, 5.
34. Philip Melanchthon, "Loci Communes Theologici," in *Melanchthon and Bucer*, ed. Wilhelm Pauck, Library of Christian Classics 19 (Philadelphia: Westminster Press, 1969), 70.
35. Hayes and Prussner translate the full title of the 1671 work as *A Biblical Collection of OT and NT Texts Explicated in Relation to the Series of Standard Theological Topics* (*Old Testament Theology*, 5).
36. Ibid., 17–18.
37. Gerhard Hasel states that the first work to bear the term "biblical theology" in its title was published in 1629 (*Old Testament Theology: Basic Issues in the Current Debate*, rev. ed. [Grand Rapids: Wm. B. Eerdmans Publishing Co., 1991], 11).
38. See David H. Weir, *The Origins of the Federal Theology in Sixteenth Century Reformation Thought* (Oxford: Clarendon Press, 1990).

39. Francis Turretin, *Institutes of Elenctic Theology*, 3 vols., trans. George Giger, ed. James Dennison (Phillipsburg, NJ: P&R Publishing, 1992). Dennison relates how the Princeton theologian Charles Hodge asked Giger to translate Turretin so that Hodge's students could read those pages assigned in his theology class (xxvii).

40. Hayes and Prussner mention the influence of his Jewish heritage, "radical" scientific and political thought, the skepticism of Cartesian philosophy, and his desire for intellectual freedom in the face of dogmatism (*Old Testament Theology*, 27–28).

41. Ibid., 33.

42. Frei, *Eclipse of Biblical Narrative*, 55.

43. See William Baird's chapter, "The Attack on Revealed Religion: The English Deists" in his *History of New Testament Research*, vol. 1, *From Deism to Tübingen* (Minneapolis: Fortress Press, 1992), 31–57.

44. Hayes and Prussner, *Old Testament Theology*, 41–42.

45. John Sandys-Wunsch argues that Pietism in Germany was "not necessarily anti-intellectual" but primarily urged a more biblically sensitive treatment of doctrine ("G. T. Zachariae's Contribution to Biblical Theology," *Zeitschrift für die altestamentliche Wissenschaft* 92 [1988]: 3).

46. Philip Jacob Spener, *Pia Desideria*, trans. and ed. Theodore G. Tappert (Philadelphia: Fortress Press, 1964), 91.

47. Ibid., 95.

48. Hayes and Prussner, *Old Testament Theology*, 51.

49. Frei, *Eclipse of Biblical Narrative*, 200–201.

50. Hayes and Prussner mention things such as the end of religious wars, world exploration by European nations, the supplanting of scholastic philosophy with more individualistic methods of reason, and a growing use of historical criticism in the field of biblical studies (*Old Testament Theology*, 36–37).

51. Th. C. Vriezen, *An Outline of Old Testament Theology*, trans. S. Neuijen (Oxford: Blackwell, 1958), 13.

52. Brevard S. Childs, *Biblical Theology of the Old and New Testaments: Theological Reflection on the Christian Bible* (Minneapolis: Fortress Press, 1993), 4.

53. For a helpful overview of the ways eighteenth-century thought influenced the origins of biblical theology, see Sandys-Wunsch, "G. T. Zachariae's Contribution," 3–12.

54. Ibid., 1.

55. Its full German title is translated by Hayes and Prussner as *Biblical Theology, or an Examination of the Biblical Basis of the Principal Theological Doctrines* (*Old Testament Theology*, 60). They state that a fifth volume, edited by another scholar, appeared about ten years after Zachariae's death.

56. Sandys-Wunsch, "G. T. Zachariae's Contribution," 22.

57. Hayes and Prussner, *Old Testament Theology*, 62.

58. Ibid., 61. A division of biblical-theological topics like Zachariae's represented one of the major methodologies in the discipline.

59. Ben C. Ollenburger, *The Flowering of Old Testament Theology*, "Theological Synopsis" (Winona Lake, IN: Eisenbrauns, 1992), 489; Jon D. Levenson, "Why Jews Are Not Interested in Biblical Theology," in *The Hebrew Bible, the Old Testament, and Historical Criticism: Jews and Christians in Biblical Studies* (Louisville, KY: Westminster/John Knox Press, 1993), 35.

60. Johann P. Gabler, "An Oration on the Proper Distinction between Biblical and Dogmatic Theology and the Specific Objectives of Each," in Ollenburger et al.,

Flowering of Old Testament Theology, 492–502. This is a reprint from John Sandys-Wunsch and Laurence Eldridge, "J. P. Gabler and the Distinction between Biblical and Dogmatic Theology: Translation, Commentary, and Discussion of His Originality," *Scottish Journal of Theology* 33 (1980): 133–58.

61. Hayes and Prussner, *Old Testament Theology*, 2.
62. Sandys-Wunsch, "G. T. Zachariae's Contribution," 23.
63. Gabler, "Oration on the Proper Distinction," 495–96.
64. Robert Morgan argues that it is more accurate to speak of *three* steps, so that the collection of the ideas in the Bible is followed by a "systematizing step" prior to reaching a pure biblical theology ("Gabler's Bicentenary," *Expository Times* 98 (1986–1987): 164–65.
65. Gabler, "Oration on the Proper Distinction," 500. Hayes and Prussner (*Old Testament Theology*, 62–63) label these two stages as "True Biblical theology" and "Pure Biblical theology," based on the German words Gabler used in his oration.
66. Recent attempts are Charles H. H. Scobie, *The Ways of Our God* and C. Marvin Pate et al., *The Story of Israel: A Biblical Theology* (Downers Grove, IL: InterVarsity Press, 2004). There are, of course, scholarly works that have explored the connection of biblical theology to related fields (e.g., Graeme Goldsworthy, *Preaching the Whole Bible as Christian Scripture: The Application of Biblical Theology to Expository Preaching* [Grand Rapids: Wm. B. Eerdmans Publishing Co., 2000]). Other works may trace a particular theme in one part of the canon (e.g., Daniel Smith-Christopher, *A Biblical Theology of Exile* [Minneapolis: Augsburg Fortress, 2002]).
67. Baird, *History of New Testament Research*, 1:187–88.
68. This development of ideas was traced according to these basic periods: earliest Hebrew society, the Mosaic era, the time of the prophets, Jewish interaction with foreign cultures, and the time of Christ (Hayes and Prussner, *Old Testament Theology*, 69).
69. Bauer, quoted in Baird, *History of New Testament Research*, 1:189. Baird identifies the focus of the four volumes as follows: the Christology of the Synoptic Gospels, the theology and anthropology of the Synoptics as well as the religious ideas of John, the book of Revelation and the letters of Peter, and the writings of Paul.
70. Ben C. Ollenburger states that Bauer's thinking on this point anticipated much of later scholarship ("From Timeless Ideas to the Essence of Religion," in *Flowering of Old Testament Theology*, 5–6).
71. Hayes and Prussner suggest that "the rationalistic emphasis on the inferiority of the Old Testament" represented a predisposition to disparage it from an "anti-Hebraic bias" (*Old Testament Theology*, 70). Gerhard Hasel states that the "higher evaluation" of the New Testament had been recently expressed in a biblical theology by Christoph von Ammon in 1792 (*Old Testament Theology*, 15).
72. The lengthy title of Kaiser's work defined biblical theology, in part, as "Judaism and Christianity according to the grammatical-historical method." The three volumes appeared between 1813 and 1821 (Hayes and Prussner, *Old Testament Theology*, 91–92). Von Cölln's *Biblical Theology* appeared posthumously in 1836 (ibid., 94).
73. Baird, *History of New Testament Research*, 1:228.
74. Hasel mentions M. Lossius and D. Cramer, whose works included such terminology in their titles (*New Testament Theology: Basic Issues in the Current Debate* [Grand Rapids: Wm. B. Eerdmans Publishing Co., 1993], 32–33).

75. Ibid., 33; Hayes and Prussner, *Old Testament Theology*, 105–7.

76. Hayes and Prussner, *Old Testament Theology*, 82–84.

77. J. C. K. von Hofmann, *Interpreting the Bible*, trans. Christian Preus (Minneapolis: Augsburg, 1959), 180.

78. Childs, *Biblical Theology of the Old and New Testaments*, 7.

79. Gerhard Hasel sees this domination by philosophical movements as the first of three stages in nineteenth-century biblical theology, the others being conservative reaction to higher criticism and the ultimate victory of the history of religions school (*Old Testament Theology*, 18).

80. Friedrich Schleiermacher, *On Religion: Speeches to Its Cultured Despisers*, trans. John Oman (New York: Harper & Row, 1958), 93.

81. Friedrich Schleiermacher, *The Christian Faith*, trans. W. R. Matthews et al., ed. H. R. MacKintosh and J. S. Stewart (New York: Harper & Row, 1963), 1:131–41.

82. Baird, *History of New Testament Research*, 1:212.

83. Ibid., 1:218.

84. Schleiermacher, *Christian Faith*, 2:608–11.

85. Hayes and Prussner, *Old Testament Theology*, 77.

86. Frei, *Eclipse of Biblical Narrative*, 318–24.

87. Georg Wilhelm Friedrich Hegel, *The Philosophy of History*, trans. J. Sibree (New York: Dover Publications, 1956), 9.

88. Ibid., 63.

89. Various forms of Hegelianism existed in the nineteenth century and became represented in the political climate of Europe. Leftist, moderate, and conservative expressions all appeared, and scholars sometimes moved among these options through the course of their careers (Baird, *History of New Testament Research*, 1:245n1).

90. Hayes and Prussner, *Old Testament Theology*, 100–103; Hasel, *Old Testament Theology*, 19.

91. Hayes and Prussner, *Old Testament Theology*, 103–5.

92. Quoted in Marcus Borg, "Profiles in Scholarly Courage: Early Days of New Testament Criticism," *Bible Review* 10 (October 1994): 44.

93. David F. Strauss, *The Life of Jesus Critically Examined*, trans. George Eliot (Ramsey, NJ: Sigler Press, 1994), 750.

94. Ibid., 755.

95. Ibid., 757–84.

96. Ibid., 780.

97. Frei speaks of Strauss's theology in the 1830s "as vaguely pantheistic as only a young Hegelian's could be at that time" (*Eclipse of Biblical Narrative*, 234). By the mid-1840s Strauss had abandoned the Hegelian model (246).

98. For a study of the relationship of their work, see Robert Morgan, "Ferdinand Christian Baur," in *Nineteenth Century Religious Thought in the West*, ed. Ninian Smart (New York: Cambridge University Press, 1985), 261–89.

99. Baird, *History of New Testament Research*, 1:259.

100. F. C. Baur, "Introduction to Lectures on the History of Christian Dogma," in *Ferdinand Christian Baur on the Writing of Church History*, trans. and ed. Peter C. Hodgson (New York: Oxford University Press, 1968), 275.

101. Baird, *History of New Testament Research*, 1:260.

102. On the relationship of Baur's historical method and Hegelian framework, see Robert Morgan, "F. C. Baur's Lectures on New Testament Theology," *Expository Times* 88 (1977): 202–6.

103. Hasel, *New Testament Theology*, 31.
104. Hayes and Prussner discuss "supernaturalists" who "did not advance the discussion appreciably, but their presence is witness to the fact that, slowly but surely, the old monopoly of the Rationalists was coming to an end" (*Old Testament Theology*, 105). Baird devotes a chapter to "moderate and mediating criticism," especially among Roman Catholic and British theologians (*History of New Testament Research*, 1:330–61).
105. Von Hofmann, *Interpreting the Bible*, 14.
106. E. W. Hengstenberg, *Christology of the Old Testament*, trans. Theod. Meyer and James Martin (Grand Rapids: Kregel Publications, 1956), 4:345.
107. Frei calls Hengstenberg's "the most notable puristic stand against all biblical criticism" (*Eclipse of Biblical Narrative*, 163).
108. Hayes and Prussner, *Old Testament Theology*, 22–23; Hasel, *Old Testament Theology*, 22n79; Frei, *Eclipse of Biblical Narrative*, 181, 182.
109. Hasel, *Old Testament Theology*, 21. Hayes and Prussner remark, "For fullness of discussion, attention to detail, and consistency of viewpoint Oehler's work stands second to none" (*Old Testament Theology*, 114).
110. G. F. Oehler, *Theology of the Old Testament*, trans. George E. Day (Minneapolis: Klock & Klock Publishers, 1978), 5. Oehler thought that in some writings von Hofmann tended to set the revelation in events over against revelation in word (37).
111. Ibid., 9.
112. Hasel, *Old Testament Theology*, 21. Hayes and Prussner correctly point out the lack of proportion in Oehler's book, with roughly two-thirds assigned to the Mosaic theology and less than one-tenth of the book discussing wisdom (*Old Testament Theology*, 118).
113. Hayes and Prussner, *Old Testament Theology*, 69. They add that with Vatke and others this approach began to come to fruition (129).
114. Ibid., 74–90.
115. Julius Wellhausen, *Prolegomena to the History of Ancient Israel*, trans. J. Black and A. Menzies (New York: Meridien Books, 1957), 295.
116. For a discussion of this threefold movement, see Patrick Miller, "Wellhausen and the History of Israel's Religion," *Semeia* 25 (1982): 63.
117. Ibid., 65.
118. Wellhausen, *Prolegomena*, 319–20.
119. Hermann Gunkel, *The Stories of Genesis*, trans. John J. Scullion (Vallejo, CA: BIBAL, 1994), quoted in Yarchin, *History of Biblical Interpretation*, 244.
120. Hayes and Prussner, *Old Testament Theology*, 133. But see the treatment of the final question in this chapter, as well as the next chapter for the issue of how the two disciplines may overlap. See James Barr, *The Concept of Biblical Theology: An Old Testament Perspective* (Minneapolis: Fortress Press, 1999), 136.
121. Hermann Gunkel, "The 'Historical Movement' in the Study of Religion," *Expository Times* 33 (1927): 533, 534.
122. Hasel, *New Testament Theology*, 46.
123. Robert Morgan calls Wrede "a Baur shorn of his Hegelian fleece" (introduction to *The Nature of New Testament Theology*, ed. and trans. Robert Morgan, Studies in Biblical Theology 25 [Naperville, IL: Alec R. Allenson, 1974], 14). See also Hans Rollmann, "From Baur to Wrede: The Quest for a Historical Method," *Studies in Religion* 17 (1988): 443–54.

124. William Wrede, "The Task and Methods of 'New Testament Theology,'" in Morgan, *Nature of New Testament Theology*, 100.

125. Ibid., 71.

126. Ibid., 116. In the German title of his work, Wrede included the term *sogenann-ten* or "so-called," which Morgan's translation reflects by placing the words "New Testament Theology" in quotation marks.

127. Hasel, *New Testament Theology*, 50–52.

128. Adolf Schlatter, "The Theology of the New Testament and Dogmatics," in Morgan, *Nature of New Testament Theology*, 117–66.

129. On the question of Schlatter's place in turn-of-the-century biblical studies, see Hasel, *New Testament Theology*, 39n169; and Peter Stuhlmacher, "Adolf Schlat-ter's Interpretation of Scripture," *New Testament Studies* 24 (1978): 433–46.

130. Schlatter, "Theology of the New Testament and Dogmatics," 124, 120.

131. See, for instance, Adolf Schlatter, *The Church in the New Testament Period*, trans. Paul P. Levertoff (London: SPCK, 1961).

132. Schlatter, "Theology of the New Testament and Dogmatics," 128.

133. The terms are those of Hendrikus Boers in *What Is New Testament Theology?* (Philadelphia: Fortress Press, 1979), 67–75.

134. Schlatter, "Theology of the New Testament and Dogmatics," 148.

135. See, for example, Ben C. Ollenburger, "From Timeless Ideas to the Essence of Religion," 15; Hayes and Prussner, *Old Testament Theology*, 126; Hasel, *Old Tes-tament Theology*, 24.

136. See Patrick D. Miller, "Israelite Religion," in *The Hebrew Bible and Its Modern Interpreters*, ed. Douglas A. Knight and Gene M. Tucker (Philadelphia: Fortress Press, 1985), 201–37.

137. Ollenburger, et al., *Flowering of Old Testament Theology*; Hasel, *Old Testament Theology*, 26; Hayes and Prussner, *Old Testament Theology*, 143; Reventlow, "Theology, (Biblical), History of," in *The Anchor Bible Dictionary*, ed. David Noel Freedman (New York: Doubleday, 1992), 6:487.

138. Hermann Gunkel, "What Remains of the Old Testament?" in *What Remains of the Old Testament and Other Essays*, trans. A. K. Dallas (New York: Macmillan, 1928), 53. The German edition of Gunkel's essay appeared in 1914.

139. Hayes and Prussner, *Old Testament Theology*, 143. Baird mentions how World War I, with its accompanying anti-German sentiment in England and Amer-ica, renewed "old animosities toward German criticism" (*History of New Testa-ment Research*, vol. 2, *From Jonathan Edwards to Rudolf Bultmann* [Minneapolis: Fortress Press, 2003], 178).

140. This forms a large part of Karl Barth's argument in his preface to the second edition of his famous commentary on Romans. Prefaces to all six editions of his commentary are recorded in *The Epistle to the Romans*, trans. Edwyn C. Hoskyns (London: Oxford University Press, 1933), 2–15.

141. Hayes and Prussner discuss several reasons behind the negative attitudes toward the Old Testament, Judaism, and even religion in general (*Old Testa-ment Theology*, 149–51).

142. Gunkel, "What Remains of the Old Testament?" 19.

143. Rudolf Kittel, *The Religion of the People of Israel*, trans. R. C. Micklem (New York: Macmillan, 1925), 223.

144. Ollenburger, "From Timeless Ideas to the Essence of Religion," 15–16. Ollen-burger points out that it was not so much that the history of religions school

changed the definition of Old Testament theology into a purely historical discipline, but rather that it reflected changes that had been present in the decades immediately after Gabler (17).

145. Otto Eissfeldt, "The History of Israelite-Jewish Religion and Old Testament Theology," in Ollenburger et al., *Flowering of the Old Testament*, 24, 25.

146. Walter Eichrodt, "Does Old Testament Theology Still Have Independent Significance within Old Testament Scholarship?" in Ollenburger et al., *Flowering of the Old Testament*, 32–36.

147. Ibid., 36–37.

148. Barth, *Epistle to the Romans*, 35.

149. Ibid., 7.

150. Karl Barth, "The Strange New World within the Bible," in *The Word of God and the Word of Man*, trans. Douglas Horton (New York: Harper & Row, 1957), 28–50. This essay originally was a lecture delivered to a church in 1916.

151. For example, Barth saw the need for "careful investigation and consideration" into the "differences between then and now, there and here," but ultimately "such investigation can only be to demonstrate that these differences are, in fact, purely trivial." Barth felt as if some of his critics did not balance those types of statements with his efforts to be "bound to the actual words of the text, and did not in any way propose to engage myself in free theologizing" (*Epistle to the Romans*, 1, ix).

152. Adolf Jülicher, "A Modern Interpreter of Paul," trans. Keith R. Crim, in *The Beginnings of Dialectic Theology*, vol. 1, ed. James M. Robinson (Richmond: John Knox Press, 1963), 73, 81, 78.

153. Quoted in C. E. B. Cranfield, *The Epistle to the Romans* (Edinburgh: T. & T. Clark, 1975), 1:41.

154. Adolf Schlatter, "Karl Barth's Epistle to the Romans," trans. Keith R. Crim, in Robinson, *Beginnings of Dialectic Theology*, 1:121–25. In the preface to the third edition of his commentary, Barth was surprised by Schlatter's "friendly rejection" of it, seeing that they shared a similar concern for the place of theology in the church (*Epistle to the Romans*, 16).

155. Walter Eichrodt, *Theology of the Old Testament*, 2 vols., trans. J. A. Baker (Philadelphia: Westminster Press, 1961, 1967). Eichrodt states that he is indebted to Otto Procksch for this structure (1:33n1). Hayes and Prussner emphasize the significance of the year 1933 for the publication of volume 1 in Germany, coinciding with the rise to power of the National Socialist party, which of course attacked both the Jews and their scriptures (*Old Testament Theology*, 179).

156. Eichrodt, *Theology of the Old Testament*, 1:36.

157. Ibid., 1:27. He also proposed this method in his essay, "Does Old Testament Theology Still Have Independent Significance?" 33.

158. Eichrodt, *Theology of the Old Testament*, 1:32.

159. Hayes and Prussner, *Old Testament Theology*, 183.

160. Eichrodt, *Theology of the Old Testament*, 1:25–26.

161. Werner Lemke, "Theology (OT)," in *The Anchor Bible Dictionary*, ed. David Noel Freedman (New York: Doubleday, 1992), 6:452.

162. For a brief discussion of several of these, see Hayes and Prussner, *Old Testament Theology*, 184–201.

163. For a comparison of Eichrodt and von Rad, see D. G. Spriggs, *Two Old Testament Theologies* (Naperville, IL: Alec R. Allenson, 1974).

164. Gerhard von Rad, *Old Testament Theology*, vol. 1, trans. D. M. G. Stalker (New York: Harper & Row, 1962), 105, 115, 121.

165. Other important summaries appear in Josh. 24:2–13; Pss. 78, 105, 136; and Neh. 9:6–31.

166. See von Rad's important essay written in 1938: "The Form-Critical Problem of the Hexateuch," in *The Problem of the Hexateuch and Other Essays*, trans. E. W. Trueman Dicken (Edinburgh: Oliver & Boyd, 1966), 1–78.

167. Walter Brueggemann, "A Convergence in Recent Old Testament Theologies," in *Old Testament Theology: Essays on Structure, Theme, and Text*, ed. Patrick D. Miller (Minneapolis: Fortress Press, 1992), 95. This essay was originally published in 1980.

168. See, for example, the testimony of Robert Morgan: "The series of lesser [New Testament Theologies] which have appeared since Bultmann's classic have done as little to advance the discipline methodologically as Bultmann's immediate predecessors and contemporaries" ("New Testament Theology," in *Biblical Theology: Problems and Perspectives*, ed. Steven J. Kraftchick et al. (Nashville: Abingdon Press, 1995), 121.

169. Rudolf Bultmann, *Theology of the New Testament*, 2 vols. (New York: Charles Scribner's Sons, 1951, 1955), 2:244. Morgan nuances their similarity: "Bultmann avoided Baur's need for too much history, but settled for too little" ("New Testament Theology," 120). By "too little," Morgan is saying that Bultmann's definition of history in terms of "human existence" is too narrow for the meaning most people give the word.

170. Rudolf Bultmann, "New Testament and Mythology: The Problem of Demythologizing the New Testament Proclamation," in *New Testament and Mythology and Other Basic Writings*, ed. Schubert M. Ogden (Philadelphia: Fortress Press, 1984), 23.

171. Ibid., 1–15.

172. Rudolf Bultmann, "Karl Barth's Epistle to the Romans," trans. Keith R. Crim, in *The Beginnings of Dialectic Theology*, vol. 1, ed. James M. Robinson (Richmond: John Knox Press, 1963), 100–120.

173. Bultmann, *Theology of the New Testament*, 2:237.

174. Ibid., 1:3.

175. On this view, at least for Bultmann's treatment of Paul, see Boers, *What Is New Testament Theology?* 75–84. Boers states that the treatment of John is far less systematic than that of Paul (80). See also Dan O. Via, *What Is New Testament Theology?* Guides to Biblical Scholarship Series (Minneapolis: Fortress Press, 2002), 2–3.

176. On some of these matters, see James F. Kay, *Christus Praesens: A Reconsideration of Rudolf Bultmann's Christology* (Grand Rapids: Wm. B. Eerdmans Publishing Co., 1994). Via remarks that "we forget at our peril" some of Bultmann's themes and that other interpreters "take his contribution to be of such a magnitude that we can still build on it and/or should be in dialogue with it" (*What Is New Testament Theology?* 4).

177. This impression forms one of Jon Levenson's arguments for why Jews traditionally have avoided doing biblical theology. See his "Why Jews Are Not Interested in Biblical Theology," in *The Hebrew Bible, the Old Testament, and Historical Criticism: Jews and Christians in Biblical Studies* (Louisville, KY: Westminster/John Knox Press, 1993), 45–46.

178. Baird, *History of New Testament Research*, 1:17; Stuhlmacher, *Historical Criticism and Theological Interpretation of Scripture*, 56.

179. Baird, *History of New Testament Research*, 1:157, 330.

180. The infallibility of the pontiff when speaking *ex cathedra* for the church is defined in chapter 4 of the "Dogmatic Constitution *Pastor Aeternus* on the Church of Christ," in *The Christian Faith in the Doctrinal Documents of the Catholic Church*, ed. J. Neuner and J. Dupuis (New York: Alba House, 1982), 234.

181. Baird, *History of New Testament Research*, 2:163.

182. Hasel, *New Testament Theology*, 63.

183. Pius XII, *Divino Afflante Spiritu*, excerpted in *Christian Faith in the Doctrinal Documents*, 83.

184. Hasel does discuss some New Testament theologies that generally followed a doctrinal approach to the Bible (*New Testament Theology*, 61–62). Barr says the same for Old Testament theologies (*Concept of Biblical Theology*, 28).

185. L. Praamsma, *The Church in the Twentieth Century*, vol. 7, *Elect from Every Nation* (St. Catherines, Ont.: Paideia Press, 1981), 183.

186. Stuhlmacher, *Historical Criticism and Theological Interpretation of Scripture*, 57–58.

187. From the Dogmatic Constitution *Dei Verbum* (1965), in *Christian Faith in the Doctrinal Documents*, 90.

188. Hasel, *New Testament Theology*, 63.

189. John L. McKenzie, *A Theology of the Old Testament* (Garden City, NY: Doubleday, 1974), 23.

190. For a study of post–Vatican II developments, see Francis Martin, "Some Directions in Catholic Biblical Theology," in *Out of Egypt: Biblical Theology and Biblical Interpretation*, ed. Craig Bartholomew et al. (Grand Rapids: Zondervan Publishing House, 2004), 65–87.

191. See James D. Smart, *The Past, Present, and Future of Biblical Theology* (Philadelphia: Westminster Press, 1979). Smart takes exception on both accounts, arguing that a "movement" needs "some form of an organization to forward its interests," but that was not true of "the few" who worked on biblical theology in the 1940s (23). Moreover, he contends that the "crisis" was not in biblical theology but in the "hermeneutical anarchy of the historical critics" (22, quoting Friedrich Mildenberger).

192. Brevard S. Childs, *Biblical Theology in Crisis* (Philadelphia: Westminster Press, 1970), 11–21. Hayes and Prussner provide some parts of the larger international context of the renewal in biblical theology (*Old Testament Theology*, 210–13).

193. See Childs, *Biblical Theology in Crisis*, chap. 2.

194. G. Ernest Wright, *God Who Acts: Biblical Theology as Recital* (London: SCM Press, 1952), 13, 59.

195. See Childs, *Biblical Theology in Crisis*, especially chaps. 3–4. Many scholars point to the work of Langdon Gilkey as undermining the movement's understanding of history.

196. See James Barr, *The Semantics of Biblical Language* (Oxford: Oxford University Press, 1961).

197. Steven J. Kraftchick, "Facing Janus: Reviewing the Biblical Theology Movement," in *Biblical Theology: Problems and Perspectives*, ed. Steven J. Kraftchick, Charles D. Meyers, and Ben C. Ollenburger (Nashville: Abingdon Press, 1995), 56, 57.

198. James Barr, "Biblical Theology," in *The Interpreter's Dictionary of the Bible*, Supplementary Volume, ed. Keith Crim (Nashville: Abingdon Press, 1976), 104.

199. See James Dunn, *Unity and Diversity in the New Testament: An Inquiry into the Character of the Earliest Christianity* (Philadelphia: Westminster Press, 1977); and John Goldingay, *Theological Diversity and the Authority of the Old Testament* (Grand Rapids: Wm. B. Eerdmans Publishing Co., 1987). See also the chapters related to the "center" of Old or New Testament theology in Hasel, *Old Testament Theology*, 139–71; and Hasel, *New Testament Theology*, 140–70.

200. This phrase is from Peter Balla, *Challenges to New Testament Theology: An Attempt to Justify the Enterprise* (Peabody, MA: Hendrickson Publishers, 1997), 183.

201. There were, of course, other guiding principles, as in Donald Guthrie's *New Testament Theology* (Downers Grove, IL: InterVarsity Press, 1981), which followed a doctrinal outline and studied the way different New Testament books or authors expressed those doctrines.

202. Childs, *Biblical Theology in Crisis*, 99, 102.

203. An independent but concurrent development to Childs's work was James A. Sanders's emphasis on the origin and function of canon within the community, a task he called "canonical criticism." See his *Torah and Canon* (Philadelphia: Fortress Press, 1972).

204. Commentaries for example: *The Book of Exodus: A Critical, Theological Commentary*, Old Testament Library (Philadelphia: Westminster Press, 1974). Introductions: *Introduction to the Old Testament as Scripture* (Philadelphia: Fortress Press, 1979); *The New Testament as Canon: An Introduction* (Philadelphia: Fortress Press, 1985). Works on biblical theology: *Old Testament Theology in a Canonical Context* (Philadelphia: Fortress Press, 1986); *Biblical Theology of the Old and New Testaments* (Minneapolis: Fortress Press, 1993).

205. Paul R. House, *Old Testament Theology* (Downers Grove, IL: InterVarsity Press, 1998); Rolf Rendtorff, *The Canonical Hebrew Bible: A Theology of the Old Testament*, trans. David E. Orton (Leiden: Deo Publishing, 2005); Frank Thielman, *Theology of the New Testament: A Canonical and Synthetic Approach* (Grand Rapids: Zondervan Publishing House, 2005); Scobie, *Ways of Our God*.

206. Dunn, *Unity and Diversity in the New Testament*, 376.

207. Balla, *Challenges to New Testament Theology*, 199.

208. Brueggemann, "Convergence in Recent Old Testament Theologies," 95–96, 101–2. See also Westermann, *Elements of Old Testament Theology*; Paul D. Hanson, *Dynamic Transcendence: The Correlation of Confessional Heritage and Contemporary Experience in a Biblical Model of Divine Activity* (Philadelphia: Fortress Press, 1978); Samuel Terrien, *The Elusive Presence: Toward a New Biblical Theology* (San Francisco: Harper & Row, 1978).

209. See Brueggemann's pair of articles: "A Shape for Old Testament Theology, I: Structure Legitimation" and "A Shape for Old Testament Theology, II: Embrace of Pain," in Miller, *Old Testament Theology*, 1–21 and 22–44. Both were originally published in *Catholic Biblical Quarterly* 47 (1985): 28–46, 395–415.

210. Walter Brueggemann, *Theology of the Old Testament: Testimony, Dispute, Advocacy* (Minneapolis: Fortress Press, 1997), 119.

211. Brueggemann, "Convergence in Recent Old Testament Theologies," 96.

212. Erhard Gerstenberger, *Theologies in the Old Testament*, trans. John Bowden (Minneapolis: Fortress Press, 2002), 273.

213. Balla suggests that the position of diversity over unity may be "the dominant view of scholarship of our day" (*Challenges to New Testament Theology*, 148).

214. Ernst Käsemann, "The Problem of a New Testament Theology," *New Testament Studies* 19 (1973): 242. Käsemann also thought the Pauline doctrine of justification could serve as something of "a canon within the canon" (Hasel, *New Testament Theology*, 160–61).

215. Heikki Räisänen, *Beyond New Testament Theology: A Story and a Programme* (London: SCM Press, 1990), 137.

216. Hasel lists with Käsemann, Günther Bornkamm, Herbert Braun, James M. Robinson, Ernst Fuchs, and Gerhard Ebeling (*New Testament Theology*, 87).

217. See Ernst Käsemann, "The Problem of the Historical Jesus," in *Essays on New Testament Themes*, trans. W. J. Montague (Naperville, IL: Alec R. Allenson, 1964), 31. See also his "Blind Alleys in the 'Jesus of History' Controversy," in *New Testament Questions of Today*, trans. W. J. Montague (Philadelphia: Fortress Press, 1969), 23–65.

218. James M. Robinson, *A New Quest of the Historical Jesus* (1959; repr., Philadelphia: Fortress Press, 1983). Compare the critique by Van A. Harvey and Schubert Ogden, "How New Is the 'New Quest of the Historical Jesus'?" in *The Historical Jesus and the Kerygmatic Christ*, ed. Carl Braaten and Roy Harrisville (New York: Abingdon Press, 1964), 197–242.

219. See, for example, Joachim Jeremias, *New Testament Theology: The Proclamation of Jesus*, trans. J. Bowden (New York: Charles Scribner's Sons, 1971).

220. One of the numerous surveys of the participants in the "third quest" is Ben Witherington, *The Jesus Quest: The Third Quest for the Jew of Nazareth*, 2nd ed. (Downers Grove, IL: InterVarsity Press, 1997).

221. Hasel, *New Testament Theology*, 58–59. See James M. Robinson and John B. Cobb Jr., eds., *The New Hermeneutic*, New Frontiers in Theology 2 (New York: Harper & Row, 1964).

222. Norman Perrin, "The Significance of Knowledge of the Historical Jesus and His Teaching," in *Rediscovering the Teaching of Jesus* (New York: Harper & Row, 1967), 207–48.

223. Peter Stuhlmacher, *Historical Criticism and Theological Interpretation of Scripture*, 83–91. Stuhlmacher describes this ethos in terms of an openness to transcendence, methodological verifiability, and effective-historical consciousness.

224. Hans Conzelmann, *An Outline of the Theology of the New Testament*, trans. John Bowden (New York: Harper & Row, 1969), xvii–xviii, 98.

225. Notice especially the subtitle of Kümmel's work: *The Theology of the New Testament: According to Its Major Witnesses: Jesus—Paul—John*.

226. See J. Louis Martyn, *History and Theology in the Fourth Gospel*, 2nd ed. (Nashville: Abingdon Press, 1979); Joel B. Green, *The Theology of the Gospel of Luke* (Cambridge: Cambridge University Press, 1995).

227. For a general overview see Leo G. Perdue, *Reconstructing Old Testament Theology: After the Collapse of History*, Overtures to Biblical Theology (Minneapolis: Fortress Press, 2005), chap. 7. See also two collections of essays edited by A. K. M. Adam: *Handbook of Postmodern Biblical Interpretation* (St. Louis: Chalice Press, 2000); *Postmodern Interpretations of the Bible: A Reader* (St. Louis: Chalice Press, 2001).

228. Andrew K. M. Adam, *Making Sense of New Testament Theology: "Modern" Problems and Prospects* (Macon, GA: Mercer University Press, 1995), 169–81, 210.

229. Many scholars point to Brueggemann's *Theology of the Old Testament* as being written from a postmodern perspective. Brueggemann is not averse to such descriptions of his work, but neither does he reject all critical approaches out

of hand. Instead, his primary concern is allowing for a diversity of views to be expressed so that the many voices of the Bible can be heard ("*Theology of the Old Testament*: A Prompt Retrospect," in *God in the Fray: A Tribute to Walter Brueggemann*, ed. Tod Linafelt and Timothy K. Beale (Minneapolis: Fortress Press, 1998), 307.

230. James Muilenburg, "Form Criticism and Beyond," *Journal of Biblical Literature* 88 (1969): 8. For a fuller development of the method, see Phyllis Trible, *Rhetorical Criticism: Context, Method, and the Book of Jonah*, Guides to Biblical Scholarship (Minneapolis: Fortress Press, 1994).

231. See chap. 4. For a survey, see George Stroup, *The Promise of Narrative Theology: Recovering the Gospel in the Church* (Eugene, OR: Wipf & Stock, 1997).

232. John J. Collins, *The Bible after Babel: Historical Criticism in a Postmodern Age* (Grand Rapids: Wm. B. Eerdmans Publishing Co., 2005), 12. Collins calls rejection of objectivity "the most widely shared assumption of postmodernists."

233. John J. Collins, *Encounters with Biblical Theology* (Minneapolis: Fortress Press, 2005), 18, 22.

234. See the response by Gerhard F. Hasel, "Recent Models of Biblical Theology: Three Major Perspectives," *Andrews University Studies* 33 (Spring–Summer 1995): 55–61.

235. Leo G. Perdue, *The Collapse of History: Reconstructing Old Testament Theology*, Overtures to Biblical Theology (Minneapolis: Fortress Press, 1994), 70.

236. Collins, *Encounters with Biblical Theology*, 21–22; Perdue, *Collapse of History*, 71.

237. See Norman K. Gottwald, "Sociological Method in the Study of Ancient Israel," in *The Bible and Liberation*, ed. Norman K. Gottwald (Maryknoll, NY: Orbis Books, 1986), 26–37; Gottwald, *The Tribes of Yahweh* (Maryknoll, NY: Orbis Books, 1979); and Gottwald, *The Hebrew Bible: A Socio-Literary Introduction* (Philadelphia: Fortress Press, 1985).

238. Philip F. Esler, *New Testament Theology: Communion and Community* (Minneapolis: Fortress Press, 2005), 36.

239. Leo G. Perdue, *Reconstructing Old Testament Theology: After the Collapse of History*, 25. Perdue's second chapter provides an excellent survey to the whole problem in Old Testament studies.

240. Hayes and Prussner, *Old Testament Theology*, 267. So, too, Collins, *Encounters with Biblical Theology*, 26; and Barr, *Concept of Biblical Theology*, 136.

241. Rainer Albertz, *A History of Israelite Religion in the Old Testament Period*, trans. John Bowden (Louisville, KY: Westminster John Knox Press, 1994), 1:16. Perdue lists Werner Schmidt, A. H. J. Gunneweg, and Erhard Gerstenberger as other representatives of this approach (*Reconstructing Old Testament Theology*, 60–69).

242. Mark S. Smith, *The Early History of God: Yahweh and the Other Deities in Ancient Israel*, 2nd ed. (Grand Rapids: Wm. B. Eerdmans Publishing Co., 2002), 9.

243. Ibid., 7–8, 9. See also Mark S. Smith, *The Origins of Biblical Monotheism: Israel's Polytheistic Background and the Ugaritic Texts* (Oxford: Oxford University Press, 2001).

244. For a brief summary of the archaeological and historical issues, see Collins, *Bible after Babel*, 105–20.

245. Bultmann, *Theology of the New Testament*, 2:250–51.

246. Dan Via mentions Heikki Räisänen, Burton Mack, Walter Schmithals, and Georg Strecker as emphasizing the historical, whereas Oscar Cullmann,

G. B. Caird, and Peter Balla are scholars who pursue history "in support of theological claims" (*What Is New Testament Theology?* 31–48).

247. Elisabeth Schüssler Fiorenza, *Bread Not Stone: The Challenge of Feminist Biblical Interpretation* (Boston: Beacon Press, 1995), 87–88.

248. See Bart D. Ehrman, *Lost Christianities: The Battles for Scripture and the Faiths We Never Knew* (Oxford: Oxford University Press, 2003). The debate is by no means new, having been forcefully presented in 1934 by Walter Bauer. See his *Orthodoxy and Heresy in Earliest Christianity*, 2nd ed., trans. Paul J. Achtemeier et al., ed. Robert A. Kraft and Gerhard Kroedel (Philadelphia: Fortress Press, 1971).

249. Collins, *Bible after Babel*, 9.

250. I think here of Hasel and of Hayes and Prussner. Another way to illustrate the changing landscape of biblical scholarship is to compare the topics in Leo Perdue's two excellent volumes on Old Testament theology: *The Collapse of History: Reconstructing Old Testament Theology* (1994), and *Reconstructing Old Testament Theology: After the Collapse of History* (2005).

251. For background and survey see Perdue, *Reconstructing Old Testament Theology*, chap. 3.

252. Katharine Doob Sakenfeld, "'Feminist' Theology and Biblical Interpretation," in *Biblical Theology: Problems and Perspectives*, ed. Steven J. Kraftchick, Charles D. Meyers, and Ben C. Ollenburger (Nashville: Abingdon Press, 1995), 247–48. See also Sakenfeld, "Feminist Perspectives on Bible and Theology," *Interpretation* 42 (1988): 5–18.

253. Schüssler Fiorenza, *Bread Not Stone*, 13.

254. Numerous works could be cited here, but some of the most important are M. H. Goshen-Gottstein, "Tanakh Theology: The Religion of the Old Testament and the Place of Jewish Biblical Theology," in *Ancient Israelite Religion*, ed. Patrick D. Miller, Paul Hanson, and S. Dean McBride (Philadelphia: Fortress Press, 1987), 617–44; Jon Levenson, "Why Jews Are Not Interested in Biblical Theology," 33–61; Matitiahu Tsevat, "Theology of the Old Testament—A Jewish View," *Horizons in Biblical Theology* 8 (1986): 33–50.

255. Goshen-Gottstein, "Tanakh Theology," 627–28. Tanakh is an acronym for the three parts of the Hebrew Bible: *Torah* (= Law), *Nebi'im* (= Prophets), and *Kethuvim* (=Writings).

256. See Levenson, "Why Jews Are Not Interested in Biblical Theology."

257. See Edward W. Said, *Orientalism*, 25th anniversary ed. (New York: Vintage Books, 2003).

258. R. S. Sugirtharajah, *The Bible and the Third World: Precolonial, Colonial, and Postcolonial Encounters* (Cambridge: Cambridge University Press, 2001), 7.

259. Perdue, *Reconstructing Old Testament Theology*, 297n25.

260. R. S. Sugirtharajah, *Asian Biblical Hermeneutics and Postcolonialism: Contesting the Interpretations* (Maryknoll, NY: Orbis Books, 1998), 11.

261. Brueggemann, *Theology of the Old Testament*, 102.

262. Bultmann, *Theology of the New Testament*, 2:250–51.

263. Miller, "Theology from Below: The Theological Interpretation of Scripture," in *The Way of the Lord: Essays on Old Testament Theology* (Tübingen: Mohr Siebeck, 2004), 299–300.

264. See Michael Welker, *God the Spirit*, trans. John F. Hoffmeyer (Minneapolis: Fortress Press, 1994).

265. See Francis Watson, *Text, Church, and World: Biblical Interpretation in Theological Perspective* (Grand Rapids: Wm. B. Eerdmans Publishing Co., 1994); and

Watson, *Text and Truth* (Grand Rapids: Wm. B. Eerdmans Publishing Co., 1997).

266. Ollenburger, "From Timeless Ideas to the Essence of Religion," 4.

Chapter 3: The Issues Raised in Biblical Theology

1. As was my practice in chapter 2, I am here considering the issues as part of biblical theology as a whole. Where distinctions must be made for differences in Old and New Testament theology, I will do so.

2. For general overview and bibliography see D. L. Baker, *Two Testaments, One Bible: A Study of Some Modern Solutions to the Theological Problem of the Relationship between the Testaments* (Downers Grove, IL: InterVarsity Press, 1976); and the appropriate chapters in Hasel, *Old Testament Theology*, 172–93; Reventlow, *Problems of Biblical Theology*, 10–144; and James Barr, *The Concept of Biblical Theology: An Old Testament Perspective* (Minneapolis: Fortress Press, 1999), 172–88, 253–65. There are also the collections of essays in James Efird, ed., *The Use of the Old Testament in the New and Other Essays* (Durham, NC: Duke University Press, 1972); and Craig A. Evans, ed., *From Prophecy to Testament: The Function of the Old Testament in the New* (Peabody, MA: Hendrickson Publishers, 2004).

3. Craig Bartholomew, "Biblical Theology and Biblical Interpretation: Introduction," in Bartholomew et al., *Out of Egypt*, 11.

4. Brevard Childs, *Biblical Theology of the Old and New Testaments*, 78.

5. These terms come from the three major sections of *Biblical Theology of the Old and New Testaments*.

6. See below for discussion of Jewish biblical theology, which, of course, would also argue for the independence of the Hebrew Bible from New Testament theological interpretation.

7. Wilhelm Vischer, *The Witness of the Old Testament to Christ*, trans. A. B. Crabtree (London: Lutterworth Press, 1949), 7–8.

8. Ibid., 7.

9. See, for example, Baker, *Two Testaments, One Bible*.

10. Hasel, *Old Testament Theology*, 177–78.

11. Bernhard Anderson, *Contours of Old Testament Theology* (Minneapolis: Fortress Press, 1999), 9–15. In his conclusion, Anderson emphasizes both the continuities and discontinuities between the testaments (330–31).

12. John Goldingay, *Old Testament Theology*, vol. 1, *Israel's Gospel* (Downers Grove, IL: InterVarsity Press, 2003), 20.

13. Ibid., 20–21. Goldingay goes on to provide a more complete and nuanced explanation for ways in which both testaments can be understood in light of each other. See also Paul R. House, *Old Testament Theology* (Downers Grove, IL: InterVarsity Press, 1998), which concludes with a chapter on the character of God that seeks "to build bridges to New Testament and biblical theology," thus showing "that the God of the Old Testament is the God of the New Testament as well" (539–40).

14. See, for example, Donald Guthrie, *New Testament Theology* (Downers Grove, IL: InterVarsity Press, 1981), 60–62.

15. Philip F. Esler, *New Testament Theology*, 194–96. See also George Eldon Ladd, *A Theology of the New Testament* (Grand Rapids: Wm. B. Eerdmans Publishing Co., 1974), for an example of exploring the Old Testament literature for each topic he studies.

16. Rudolf Bultmann, "Prophecy and Fulfillment," trans. James C. G. Greig, in *Essays on Old Testament Hermeneutics*, ed. Claus Westermann (Richmond: John Knox Press, 1963), 72–75.

17. Walter Eichrodt speaks of a "two-way relationship between the Old and New Testaments," with a "historical movement" from Old to New and "a current of life" from New to Old (*Theology of the Old Testament*, 1:26).

18. A classic example of this may be found in J. Barton Payne's massive work, *Encyclopedia of Biblical Prophecy: The Complete Guide to Scriptural Predictions and Their Fulfillment* (Grand Rapids: Baker Book House, 1991).

19. See Hengstenberg, *Christology of the Old Testament*, esp. 4:332–42.

20. See, for example, Walther Zimmerli, "Promise and Fulfillment," trans. James Wharton, in Westermann, *Essays on Old Testament Hermeneutics*, 89–122.

21. Ibid., 111–12, 113.

22. Ibid., 113–20.

23. Vischer, *Witness of the Old Testament to Christ*, 27, 13.

24. See Francis Watson, *Text and Truth: Redefining Biblical Theology* (Grand Rapids: Wm. B. Eerdmans Publishing Co., 1997).

25. Even Vischer did not argue that his method "directly finds Jesus" in the Old Testament, but rather that such exegesis would "affirm that the thoughts expressed and the stories narrated in the Old Testament, as they are transmitted in the Bible, point towards the crucifixion of Jesus" (*Witness of the Old Testament to Christ*, 28).

26. Thus, for example, F. F. Bruce's inductive, exegetical approach highlights several themes in *New Testament Development of Old Testament Themes* (Grand Rapids: Wm. B. Eerdmans Publishing Co., 1968).

27. Vos, *Biblical Theology*, 5.

28. See Walter Kaiser, *Toward an Old Testament Theology* (Grand Rapids: Zondervan Publishing House, 1978). See also the proposal for "promise and fulfillment," above.

29. See John Bright, *The Kingdom of God: The Biblical Concept and Its Meaning for the Church* (Nashville: Abingdon Press, 1953). From the perspective of the Gospels, Herman Ridderbos also identified the kingdom of God as a central motif. See *The Coming of the Kingdom*, trans. H. DeJongste (Philadelphia: Presbyterian & Reformed Publishing Co., 1962).

30. Von Rad, *Old Testament Theology*, 2:329. Baker provides a helpful analysis, critique of von Rad on these matters (*Two Testaments, One Bible*, 271–306).

31. Hasel identifies the primary contributors as Oscar Cullmann, Leonard Goppelt, and George Eldon Ladd (*New Testament Theology*, 111–32).

32. Childs, *Biblical Theology of the Old and New Testaments*, 77; see also pp. 16–18 for other concerns with the method. See also Barr's discussion of Hartmut Gese's particular formation of this position (*Concept of Biblical Theology*, 362–77).

33. See Walter Eichrodt, "Is Typological Exegesis an Appropriate Method?" trans. James Barr, in Westermann, *Essays on Old Testament Hermeneutics*, 224–45; and Gerhard von Rad, "Typological Interpretation of the Old Testament," trans. John Bright, in Westermann, *Essays on Old Testament Hermeneutics*, 17–39.

34. Eichrodt, "Is Typological Exegesis Appropriate?" 244. His *Theology of the Old Testament* (1:501–11) also develops the notion of "prediction and fulfillment" as a link between the testaments.

35. Von Rad, "Typological Interpretation," 27, 35–39.
36. H. W. Wolff, "The Hermeneutics of the Old Testament," trans. Keith Crim, in Westermann, *Essays on Old Testament Hermeneutics*, 180, 182. Wolff discusses several ways in which the testaments contribute to typological interpretation, especially by the New Testament's explicit examples and the concept of eschatological intention from the perspective of the Old Testament.
37. For an overview, D. A. Carson and H. G. M. Williamson, *It Is Written: Scripture Citing Scripture: Essays in Honour of Barnabas Lindars* (Cambridge: Cambridge University Press, 1988).
38. I am drawing here on the work of Richard B. Hays. See, for example, *Echoes of Scripture in the Letters of Paul* (New Haven, CT: Yale University Press, 1989).
39. Per Jarle Bekken, "Paul's Use of Deut 30,12–14 in Jewish Context: Some Observations," in *The New Testament and Hellenistic Judaism*, ed. Peder Borgen and Søren Giversen (Peabody, MA: Hendrickson Publishers, 1997), 183–203; James Kugel, "Stephen's Speech (Acts 7) in Its Exegetical Context," in Evans, *From Prophecy to Testament*, 206; D. Moody Smith, "The Use of the Old Testament in the New," in Efird, *Use of the Old Testament in the New and Other Essays*, 63.
40. Sanders, *Torah and Canon*, xvii.
41. James A. Sanders, "From Prophecy to Testament: An Epilogue," in Evans, *From Prophecy to Testament*, 256–57.
42. Childs, *Biblical Theology of the Old and New Testaments*, 73–79; see also 85–90, 717–27. See Mary C. Callaway, "Canonical Criticism," in *To Each Its Own Meaning: An Introduction to Biblical Criticisms and Their Application*, rev. and exp. ed., ed. Steven L. McKenzie and Stephen R. Haynes (Louisville, KY: Westminster John Knox Press, 1999), 145–47.
43. Childs, *Biblical Theology of the Old and New Testaments*, 77.
44. For a significant discussion and full bibliography up to the early 1980s, see "Excursus: Israel and the Church," in Reventlow, *Problems of Biblical Theology*, 64–132.
45. I am referring to the fact that Judaism does not regard midrashic literature in the same way that Christianity does the New Testament writings. While historically these two sources may be described as writings grounded in first-century Judaism's interaction with the Hebrew Bible, they are quite different in their authority and function with Judaism and Christianity today.
46. N. T. Wright, *Christian Origins and the Question of God*, vol. 1, *The New Testament and the People of God* (Minneapolis: Fortress Press, 1992), 469, 476.
47. Anderson, *Contours of Old Testament Theology*, 12–15.
48. Hasel, *Old Testament Theology*, 183–84, 191–93.
49. Brueggemann, *Theology of the Old Testament*, 731–33.
50. Eichrodt, *Theology of the Old Testament*, 25; Walter Zimmerli, *Old Testament Theology in Outline*, trans. David E. Green (Atlanta: John Knox Press, 1978), 13; Bultmann, *Theology of the New Testament*, 2:237; Kümmel, *Theology of the New Testament*, 17.
51. Eichrodt, *Theology of the Old Testament*, 25.
52. See, for example, Patrick D. Miller, *They Cried unto the Lord: The Form and Theology of Biblical Prayer* (Minneapolis: Fortress Press, 1994), 5–31.
53. Childs, in pointing out that the New Testament writers shared the same canon with Pharasaic Judaism, writes that "the New Testament does not *cite as scripture*

any book of the Apocrypha or Pseudepigrapha," adding that "the reference to Enoch in Jude 14–15 is not an exception" (*Biblical Theology of the Old and New Testaments*, 62).

54. For the Belgic Confession, see *Ecumenical Creeds and Reformed Confessions* (Grand Rapids: CRC Publications, 1988), 80–81; for the Westminster Confession, see *The Book of Confessions* (Louisville, KY: Office of the General Assembly, 1994), 125–26.

55. Barr, *Concept of Biblical Theology*, 578, 580.

56. Goldingay, *Old Testament Theology*, 1:16.

57. Gabler, "Oration on the Proper Distinction," 493, 497, 498.

58. According to Wrede, even "the conservative wing" of the academic community considered "the old doctrine of inspiration . . . to be untenable" ("Task and Methods," 69).

59. Hermann Gunkel, "The 'Historical Movement' in the Study of Religion," *Expository Times* 33 (1927): 534, 535.

60. Wrede, "Task and Methods," 71.

61. Schlatter, "Theology of the New Testament and Dogmatics," 148, 122.

62. Hartmut Gese, "Tradition and Biblical Theology," trans. R. Philip O'Hara and Douglas A. Knight, in *Tradition and Theology in the Old Testament*, ed. Douglas A. Knight (Philadelphia: Fortress Press, 1977), 317–24.

63. G. Ernest Wright, *The Old Testament against Its Environment*, SBT 2 (London: SCM Press, 1950); Floyd V. Filson, *The New Testament against Its Environment: The Gospel of Christ the Risen Lord*, SBT 3 (London: SCM Press, 1950).

64. Schlatter, "Theology of the New Testament and Dogmatics," 121, 124.

65. See Balla, *Challenges to New Testament Theology*, 88–90.

66. Via, *What Is New Testament Theology?* 25.

67. Gerstenberger, *Theologies of the Old Testament*, 16, 15.

68. Brueggemann, *Theology of the Old Testament*, 117.

69. House, *Old Testament Theology*, 54.

70. Walter Kaiser (*Toward an Old Testament Theology*, 15) appeals to Jesus' testimony that the Scriptures speak about himself. John Goldingay also accepts the limits of the canon for theological interpretation, without using Kaiser's appeal to Jesus (*Old Testament Theology*, 16).

71. Francis Watson, *Paul and the Hermeneutics of Faith* (London: T. & T. Clark International, 2004), 2, ix.

72. N. T. Wright, *New Testament and the People of God*, 469.

73. Leonard Goppelt, *Theology of the New Testament*, vol. 1, trans. John E. Alsup, ed. Jürgen Roloff (Grand Rapids: Wm. B. Eerdmans Publishing Co., 1981), 19.

74. For a basic introduction to this issue, see the surveys by Hasel (*Old Testament Theology*, 139–71; *New Testament Theology*, 140–70) and Reventlow (*Problems of Old Testament Theology*, 125–33), and the monographs by Goldingay (*Theological Diversity and the Authority of the Old Testament*) and James Dunn (*Unity and Diversity in the New Testament*).

75. In Gabler's words, the effort is "to distinguish among each of the periods of the Old and New Testaments, each of the authors, and each of the manners of speaking" ("Oration on the Proper Distinction," 497). See also Hayes and Prussner, *Old Testament Theology*, 70–71.

76. See the classic work by A. T. Robertson, *A Harmony of the Gospels for Students of the Life of Christ: Based on the Broadus Harmony in the Revised Version* (New

York: Harper & Row, 1922); also Kurt Aland, ed., *Synopsis of the Four Gospels*, 3rd ed. (New York: United Bible Societies, 1979).

77. See Joseph Plevnik, "The Center of Pauline Theology," *Catholic Biblical Quarterly* 51 (1989): 461–78.

78. Gese, "Tradition and Biblical Theology," 307. See also Gerhard Ebeling's remark that a biblical theologian should "give an inclusive account of his understanding of the Old and New Testament, i.e. above all of the theological problems that come of enquiring into the inner unity of the manifold testimony of the Old and New Testament" ("Meaning of 'Biblical Theology,'" 95–96).

79. The word *Mitte* has a range of meanings analogous to those for the English term "center," some of which are locative in nature and others conceptual, such as "focus of attention." See W. Scholze-Stubenrecht and J. B. Sykes, eds., *The Oxford-Duden German Dictionary* (Oxford: Clarendon Press, 1994), 515. Walter Kaiser indicates that other German terms besides *Mitte*, as well as several English words, have been suggested for this basic concept: "middle-point," "central concept," "focal point," essential root idea," and "underlying idea" (*Toward an Old Testament Theology*, 21).

80. Kaiser, *Toward an Old Testament Theology*, 20–21.

81. Hasel, *Old Testament Theology*, 139–57.

82. Hasel, *New Testament Theology*, 144–64.

83. Vos, *Biblical Theology*, 23.

84. Bright, *Kingdom of God*, 10.

85. Von Rad, *Old Testament Theology*, 1:115.

86. Barr, *Concept of Biblical Theology*, 37.

87. Elmer A. Martens, *God's Design: A Focus on Old Testament Theology* (Grand Rapids: Baker Book House, 1981), 12, 20.

88. Gese, "Tradition and Biblical Theology," 322. In this regard, Hasel speaks of von Rad's own program of God's acts in history as a type of "secret center" (*Old Testament Theology*, 146), a conclusion Barr also shares (*Concept of Biblical Theology*, 339).

89. Quoted in Hasel, *New Testament Theology*, 61.

90. Frank Matera, "New Testament Theology: History, Method, and Identity," *Catholic Biblical Quarterly* 67 (2005): 21. Matera denies "that the whole story is present in every writing or block of material," but instead affirms "that the NT writings witness in diverse ways to an overarching narrative of revelation, redemption, life in community, new moral life, and eschatological hope, all of which are rooted in the story of Israel, Jesus, and the church" (21).

91. See the discussion in chapter 2 on "new developments."

92. Ronald E. Clements, *Old Testament Theology: A Fresh Approach* (Atlanta: John Knox Press, 1978), 16–19, 152–54.

93. Balla, *Challenges to New Testament Theology*, 209.

94. Caird and Hurst, *New Testament Theology*, 18–19, 24. In a similar vein, Frank Matera writes that New Testament theology "should seek to provide a theological interpretation of the NT that integrates and relates the diverse theologies of the NT into a unified whole without harmonizing them, as elusive as this task may be" ("New Testament Theology," 16).

95. Käsemann, "Problem of a New Testament Theology," 242.

96. See the discussion of these and other examples in Balla, *Challenges to New Testament Theology*, 178–83.

97. One thinks here of the Reformation principle of "Scripture interprets Scripture." For example, the Westminster Confession of Faith states, "When there is a question about the true and full sense of any scripture (which is not manifold but one), it may be searched and known by other places that speak more clearly" (1:9). See John Webster, "Biblical Theology and the Clarity of Scripture," in Bartholomew, *Out of Egypt*, 352–84.

98. Thielman, *Theology of the New Testament*, 38, 41.

99. Gerstenberger, *Theologies of the Old Testament*, 1.

100. Brueggemann, *Theology of the Old Testament*, 710. In this regard one might mention the perspective of Jon Levenson, who points out the differences between Jewish interpretation and Christian biblical theology. Judaism understands the biblical text "as a *problem* with many facets" and has "a far higher tolerance for theological polydoxy (within limits) and far less motivation to flatten the polyphony of the sources into a monotony" ("Why Jews Are Not Interested in Biblical Theology," 56).

101. Dunn, *Unity and Diversity in the New Testament*, 374, 376.

102. Dunn describes several important functions, such as "affirm the diversity of Christianity" and "mark out the limits of acceptable diversity" (ibid., 376–86).

103. Hasel, *Old Testament Theology*, 168–71.

104. Scobie, *Ways of Our God*, 93.

105. Barr, *Concept of Biblical Theology*, 340–41.

106. Hasel, *Old Testament Theology*, 34.

107. On John's use of the "I am" formula and its connections to Deutero-Isaiah, see "Appendix IV: *EGŌ EIMI*—'I AM,'" in Raymond E. Brown, *The Gospel according to John I–XII*, Anchor Bible (Garden City, NY: Doubleday, 1966), 533–38.

108. Gabler, "Oration on the Proper Distinction," 495–96.

109. Hasel uses the three-name rubric at least seven times as the Gabler-Wrede-Stendahl dichotomy, in *Old Testament Theology*, 28, 34, 36, 46, 83, 102, 109. Interestingly, this rubric is not employed at all in his companion volume on the New Testament, but he does speak of the "descriptive approach to NT theology advocated by K. Stendahl who follows the tradition of Gabler-Bauer-Wrede" (*New Testament Theology*, 79–80).

110. Adam, *Making Sense of New Testament Theology*, 50, 212. For an alternative view of the impact and prominence of Stendahl's model, see Barr, *Concept of Biblical Theology*, chap. 12.

111. House, *Old Testament Theology*, 52. Paul Hanson has spoken of a moral responsibility of biblical studies to the church. See his "The Responsibility of Biblical Theology to Communities of Faith," *Theology Today* 37 (1980): 39–50.

112. Robert Morgan, "Can the Critical Study of Scripture Provide a Doctrinal Norm?" *Journal of Religion* 76 (1996): 207, 215.

113. See also Peter Balla (*Challenges to New Testament Theology*, 210–20) who, while maintaining the position that biblical theology is a historical, descriptive enterprise, presents a balanced discussion of the ways that scholars recognize the limitations of this approach.

114. Schlatter, "Theology of the New Testament and Dogmatics," 122. On Schlatter as a historical biblical theologian, see Boers, *What Is New Testament Theology?* 67–75.

115. For example, Bultmann cautions, "Therefore, the theological thoughts of the New Testament can be normative only insofar as they lead the believer to develop out of his faith an understanding of God, the world, and man in his own concrete situation" (*Theology of the New Testament*, 2:238).

116. Vos, *Biblical Theology*, 10, 11.
117. Via, *What Is New Testament Theology?* 39–48.
118. Caird, *New Testament Theology*, 1. It should be noted that the descriptive approach has never been a fault line for so-called conservative and liberal theologians. George Eldon Ladd, whose New Testament theology has been used by evangelical colleges and seminaries, states, "Biblical Theology is that discipline which sets forth the message of the books of the Bible in their historical setting. Biblical Theology is primarily a descriptive discipline" (*Theology of the New Testament*, 25).
119. Caird, *New Testament Theology*, 22.
120. Balla, *Challenges to New Testament Theology*, 34.
121. Childs, *Biblical Theology of the Old and New Testament*, 8, 9. Ebeling writes, "'Biblical theology' as a historical discipline is, like any historical work, not independent of the author's standpoint in history and therefore not of the conception either which the author has of the Christian faith" ("Meaning of 'Biblical Theology,'" 90).
122. Goldingay, *Old Testament Theology*, 18. In the same paragraph, he also states, "I am interested in [Old Testament theology] because I have found that the Old Testament has a capacity to speak with illumination and power to the lives of communities and individuals. . . . I want to see it let loose in the world of theology, in the church and in the world."
123. Esler, *New Testament Theology*, 1. He adds, "While I agree that Christianity should be outward-looking and actively involved with the world, where there are upsurges of great good as well as of great evil, I cannot see a problem in occasionally recalling that the relationship Christians have with the New Testament is necessarily different from that of non-Christians" (2).
124. Brueggemann, "*Theology of the Old Testament*: A Prompt Retrospect," in *God in the Fray: A Tribute to Walter Brueggemann*, ed. Tod Linafelt and Timothy K. Beal (Minneapolis: Fortress Press, 2005), 318. See also his *Theology of the Old Testament*, 731.
125. Brueggemann, *Theology of the Old Testament*, 87, 740–42. Erhard Gerstenberger offers other examples of how biblical theology addresses our contemporary context in the appendix entitled, "God in Our Time" (*Theologies in the Old Testament*, 307–21).
126. Räisänen, *Beyond New Testament Theology*, 137, 120–21, 141.
127. Gordon D. Fee and Douglas Stuart, *How to Read the Bible for All Its Worth*, 2nd ed. (Grand Rapids: Zondervan Publishing House, 1993), 26. Fee and Stuart try to allow for some cases where a prophetic text, for instance, might "have an additional (or fuller or deeper) meaning, beyond its original intent," but the main task of their book is to help students identify the original authorial intentions of biblical writings (26). They don't see their work as laying down "rules" but offering "guidelines" (27).
128. Ben C. Ollenburger, "What Krister Stendahl 'Meant'—A Normative Critique of 'Descriptive Biblical Theology,'" *Horizons in Biblical Theology* 8 (1986): 90, 89.
129. Adam, *Making Sense of New Testament Theology*, 132.
130. Brueggemann, *Theology of the Old Testament*, 731.
131. Ollenburger, "What Krister Stendahl 'Meant,'" 64, 65.
132. Caird, *New Testament Theology*, 1.
133. The classic discussion of "essential elements" in the historical method is in a 1898 work by Ernst Troeltsch, "Historical and Dogmatic Method in Theology,"

in *Religion in History*, trans. James Luther Adams and Walter F. Bense (Minneapolis: Fortress Press, 1991), 11–32. In the following discussion, I am using the word "history" as a general concept for the presuppositions and methods that are employed in "historical-critical" research of the Bible, which includes not only source-, form-, and tradition-critical study of the biblical text but also work with inscriptional, iconographical, archaeological, and sociohistorical materials. There are, to be sure, other expressions of historical study that predate higher criticism or reject some of its presuppositions and methods, but critical study best fits the understanding employed by the majority of scholars whose views we will encounter on this issue. R. Kendall Soulen speaks of four senses: (1) "past events as they truly happened," (2) "the tide of public events and circumstances that shape a given epoch," (3) "the academic or scholarly discipline that historians pursue," and (4) "the kind of books and articles that historians produce." See his "The Believer and the Historian: Theological Interpretation and Historical Investigation," *Interpretation* 57 (2003): 175.

134. Boers, *What Is New Testament Theology?* 85.
135. Thielman, *Theology of the New Testament*, 30.
136. Boers, *What Is New Testament Theology?* 86.
137. Perdue, *Collapse of History*, 25.
138. Barr, *Concept of Biblical Theology*, 189–205.
139. Alan Richardson, *An Introduction to the Theology of the New Testament* (New York: Harper & Row, 1958), 13. See the review article of Richardson's approach by Leander E. Keck, "Problems of New Testament Theology: A Critique of Alan Richardson's *An Introduction to New Testament Theology*," *Novum Testamentum* 7 (1964): 217–41.
140. Childs, *Old Testament Theology in a Canonical Context*, 16, 15.
141. Barr, *Concept of Biblical Theology*, 207.
142. Peter Stuhlmacher, *Historical Criticism and Theological Interpretation of Scripture: Toward a Hermeneutics of Consent*, trans. Roy A. Harrisville (Philadelphia: Fortress Press, 1977), 85–87.
143. See Richard Hays, "Salvation by Trust? Reading the Bible Faithfully," *Christian Century* 114 (1997): 218–23. John Goldingay has also argued that theological insight is far more likely to result from our interpretation if we subject our framework of thought to the Bible's rather than the other way around (*Old Testament Theology*, 19).
144. Gregory Dawes, *The Historical Jesus Quest: Landmarks in the Search for the Historical Jesus* (Louisville, KY: Westminster John Knox Press, 1999), 270. The reference is to Barth's *Church Dogmatics*, I/2, *The Doctrine of Word*.
145. Caird, *New Testament Theology*, 2. For a recent assessment of the practical implications of Barth's approach, see Mark R. Lindsey, "History, Holocaust, and Revelation: Beyond the Barthian Limits," *Theology Today* 61 (2005): 455–70.
146. Barth, *Epistle to the Romans*, 1.
147. Childs, "On Reclaiming the Bible for Christian Theology," in *Reclaiming the Bible for the Church*, ed. Carl E. Braaten and Robert W. Jenson (Grand Rapids: Wm. B. Eerdmans Publishing Co., 1995), 8, 14–15. For a critique of the similarities and differences between Barth and Childs, see Barr, *Concept of Biblical Theology*, 405–12.
148. For a balanced response to charges about the inadequacies of the historical-critical method, see J. J. M. Roberts, "Historical-Critical Method, Theology, and Contemporary Exegesis," in *Biblical Theology: Problems and Perspectives*, ed.

Steven J. Kraftchick, Charles D. Meyers, and Ben C. Ollenburger (Nashville: Abingdon Press, 1995), 131–41.

149. Brueggemann, *Theology of the Old Testament*, 726–29; see also p. 118, esp. notes 3 and 4. For a characteristic critique of Brueggemann's viewpoint on this matter, see Christopher Seitz, "Scripture Becomes Religion(s): The Theological Crisis of Serious Biblical Interpretation in the Twentieth Century," in *Renewing Biblical Interpretation*, ed. Craig Bartholomew, Colin Greene, and Karl Möhler (Grand Rapids: Zondervan Publishing House, 2000), 55.

150. Albertz, *History of Israelite Religion in the Old Testament Period*, 16–17. See another list of differences between the two disciplines in Perdue, *Reconstructing Old Testament Theology*, 47–48.

151. Perdue, *Reconstructing Old Testament Theology*, 44–45.

152. See, e.g., Patrick D. Miller, *The Religion of Ancient Israel* (Louisville, KY: Westminster John Knox Press, 2000). Miller's approach is more systematic, topical, and thematic (xviii–xx). See also his essay "Israelite Religion."

153. Collins, "Biblical Theology and the History of Israelite Religion," in *Encounters with Biblical Theology*, 26, 27. Others who agree that some "overlap" exists between biblical theology and the history of religions are Roland Murphy, though he expresses reservations about how to elaborate the relationship ("Questions concerning Biblical Theology," *Biblical Theology Bulletin* 30 [2000]: 85–86), and James Barr, who nevertheless sees "differences of scope and interest which justify the recognition of the two as separate but overlapping disciplines" (*Concept of Biblical Theology*, 139).

154. Barr certainly disagrees with Collins's precise formulation as going "too far," but his criticism has as much to do with how Collins reads the state of the discipline (*Concept of Biblical Theology*, 83).

155. Over against this approach, Conzelmann declared that "the 'historical Jesus' is not a theme of New Testament theology. . . . The basic problem of New Testament theology is not, how the proclaimer, Jesus of Nazareth, became the proclaimed Messiah, Son of God, Lord? It is rather, why did faith maintain the identity of the Exalted One with Jesus of Nazareth after the resurrection appearances?" (*An Outline of the Theology of the New Testament*, trans. John Bowden [New York: Harper & Row, 1969], xvii–xviii). See Caird's discussion of four errors that led to a dichotomy of positions, namely, either that Jesus himself was the sole originator of the Gospel traditions or that the Gospel writers themselves were responsible for articulating their theology (*New Testament Theology*, 345–51).

156. Witherington, *Jesus Quest*, 14.

157. Via, *What Is New Testament Theology?* chap. 4.

158. Balla, *Challenges to New Testament Theology*, 45.

159. Ibid., 16, 46.

160. But note Via's critique that Balla, in actual practice, does seem to have a normative quality to his conclusions (*What Is New Testament Theology?* 43–45). An example of relating thoroughgoing historical analysis to Old Testament theology is Dan Block, *The God of the Nations: Studies in Ancient Near Eastern National Theology*, ETS Monograph Series 2 (Jackson, MS: ETS, 1988).

161. *The New Testament and the People of God* (Minneapolis: Fortress Press, 1992); *Jesus and the Victory of God* (Minneapolis: Fortress Press, 1996); and *The Resurrection of the Son of God* (Minneapolis: Fortress Press, 2003). The project envisions five volumes in all.

162. Wright, *New Testament and the People of God*, 24–25, 26–27, 471.

163. Barr states that language is, for him, the more important concept, or "the base for modern critical scholarship" (*Concept of Biblical Theology*, 80).

164. Ulrich Mauser, "Historical Criticism: Liberator or Foe of Biblical Theology?" in *The Promise and Practice of Biblical Theology*, ed. John Reumann (Minneapolis: Fortress Press, 1991), 110. Mauser goes on to summarize the great gains made by historical criticism as well as its limitations, that its methods do not on their own "lead to the truth of history of which biblical texts speak" (ibid.). Its role can be most productive as "a servant of biblical theology" (ibid., 111).

165. Joel B. Green, "Modernity, History, and the Theological Interpretation of the Bible," *Scottish Journal of Theology* 54 (2001): 321.

166. Vos, *Biblical Theology*, 16.

167. Trevor Hart, "Systematic—In What Sense?" in Bartholomew et al., *Out of Egypt*, 348.

168. For a brief survey of the historical aspects of this question, see Robert Morgan, "The Bible and Christian Theology," in *The Cambridge Companion to Biblical Interpretation*, ed. John Barton (Cambridge: Cambridge University Press, 1998), 114–28.

169. Gabler, "Oration on the Proper Distinction," 497.

170. Hasel, *Old Testament Theology*, 195–96.

171. Olson, "Bible and Theology," 85–86. See below for Olson's assessment of these objections.

172. Räisänen, *Beyond New Testament Theology*, 137–38.

173. The specific language is from Walter Wink and George Lindbeck, cited in J. J. M. Roberts, "Historical-Critical Method, Theology, and Contemporary Exegesis," 131–32.

174. Ibid., 132–33.

175. Stephen Fowl, *Engaging Scripture: A Model for Theological Interpretation* (Malden, MA: Blackwell, 1998), 13. Fowl acknowledges that not all biblical theologians adopt the "dominant tradition."

176. Ibid., 19; see also chap. 2, in which he discusses the problem of determinacy.

177. Luke Timothy Johnson, "Imagining the World Scripture Imagines," *Modern Theology* 14 (1998): 165. In like manner, Stephen Fowl has written that "the discipline of biblical theology, in its most common form, is systematically unable to generate serious theological interpretation of scripture" (*Engaging Scripture*, 1).

178. Johnson, "Imagining the World Scripture Imagines," 169, 170, 171.

179. Ebeling, "Meaning of 'Biblical Theology,'" 96.

180. Olson, "Bible and Theology," 90.

181. One possible way to envision this redefinition of "system" is to follow Carol Newsom's suggestion that scholars of the Bible and theology employ a "dialogic" notion of truth, based on the work of Russian philosopher and literary critic Mikhail Bakhtin (d. 1975). Critical biblical scholarship denied that the Bible was "monologic," that it spoke in terms of a unified system that can be grasped by a single consciousness. But dialogic truth affirms that even as we recognize the polyphonic voices in a work of literature, there is still the possibility of identifying the ideas that emerge through the dialogue of viewpoints. See Newsom, "Bakhtin, the Bible, and Dialogic Truth," *Journal of Religion* 76 (1996): 290–306.

182. Olson, "Bible and Theology," 90. Childs states that both sides need "a recovery of the church's exegetical tradition," especially pre-Enlightenment thinkers

such as the church fathers, medieval scholastics, and Reformation teachers ("On Reclaiming the Bible for Christian Theology," 16–17).

183. Scobie, *Ways of God*, 46, 77.

184. Elmer Martens, "Moving from Scripture to Doctrine," *Bulletin for Biblical Research* 15 (2005): 86, 88. The chart is reproduced from Martens's article with permission of the author.

185. Ibid., 88.

186. Dennis Olson, "Biblical Theology as Provisional Monologization: A Dialogue with Childs, Brueggemann, and Bakhtin," *Biblical Interpretation* 6 (1998): 178–79. On the challenges of ecumenical dialogue and conversations within faith communities, such as the Roman Catholic Church, see Paul M. Van Buren, "Historical Thinking and Dogmatics," *Journal of Ecumenical Studies* 17 (1980): 94–99; and Roland E. Murphy, "When Is Theology 'Biblical'?—Some Reflections," *Biblical Theology Bulletin* 33 (2003): 21–27.

187. A. K. M. Adam, *What Is Postmodern Biblical Criticism?* (Minneapolis: Fortress Press, 1995), 1.

188. Hans Bertens, *The Idea of the Postmodern: A History* (London: Routledge, 1995), 20. Via calls attention to the fact that "the terms *postmodernism* and *postmodernity* are sometimes distinguished and sometimes used interchangeably." He states that the latter is more "a style of thought that is suspicious of classical notions of truth, reason, and objectivity." The former "may refer to a style of culture that is depthless and playful and that blurs distinctions" (*What Is New Testament Theology?* 97).

189. Bertens, *Idea of the Postmodern*, 11.

190. Adam, *What Is Postmodern Biblical Criticism?* 1.

191. Collins, *Bible after Babel*, 12. Leo Perdue discusses the same critique as "essentially an epistemological one, in that [modernism's] meaning, sources, claimed objectivity, and assumed veracity—derived from historicism, in particular, positivism, and its locus in the Enlightenment—are challenged and negated" (*Reconstructing Old Testament Theology*, 240).

192. Perdue, *Reconstructing Old Testament Theology*, 240. Burke O. Long writes that postmodernists "turned their attention away from objects-out-there toward the plurality of socially grounded processes through which human beings construct their truths about the world" ("Ambitions of Dissent: Biblical Theology in a Postmodern Future," *Journal of Religion* 76 [1996]: 278).

193. Adam, *What Is Postmodernism Biblical Criticism?* 5–16.

194. Via, *What Is New Testament Theology?* 120.

195. Perdue, *Reconstructing Old Testament Theology*, 274–76; Collins, *Bible after Babel*, 25.

196. Barry Harvey, "Anti-postmodernism," in *Handbook of Postmodern Biblical Interpretation*, ed. Andrew K. M. Adam (St. Louis: Chalice Press, 2000), 3.

197. David W. Odell-Scott, "Deconstruction," in Adam, *Handbook of Postmodern Biblical Interpretation*, 56.

198. See Yvonne Sherwood, "Derrida," in Adam, *Handbook of Postmodern Biblical Interpretation*, 72–75.

199. Jacques Derrida, "Des Tours de Babel," in *A Derrida Reader: Between the Blinds*, ed. Peggy Kamuf (New York: Columbia University Press, 1991), 244.

200. Adam, *What Is Postmodern Biblical Criticism?* 31.

201. Collins, *Bible after Babel*, 14. Collins also mentions ideological criticism aimed at moral claims in the Bible (24–25).

202. Ibid., 16. This concern is not unique to scholars who align themselves with the classic stance of higher criticism. Evangelical scholars as well resist implications of postmodernism. D. A. Carson states, "Hermeneutically sophisticated biblical theologians will happily concede that exhaustive knowledge of the meaning of a text is impossible, but they will nevertheless insist that true knowledge of the meaning of a text is not impossible." See Carson, "Current Issues in Biblical Theology: A New Testament Perspective," *Bulletin for Biblical Research* 5 (1995): 34. A thoughtful and balanced discussion is by Terry Eagleton, *The Illusions of Postmodernism* (Oxford: Blackwell, 1996).

203. Perdue, *Reconstructing Old Testament Theology*, 276.

204. Edgar V. McKnight, *The Bible and the Reader: An Introduction to Literary Criticism*, quoted in Yarchin, *History of Biblical Interpretation*, 378, 381.

205. Perdue, *Collapse of History*, 264.

206. Arthur W. Walker-Jones, "The Role of Imagination in Biblical Theology," *Horizons in Biblical Theology* 11 (1989): 91.

207. Perdue, *Collapse of History*, 264.

208. See Walter Brueggemann, *The Prophetic Imagination*, 2nd ed. (Minneapolis: Fortress Press, 2001).

209. Johnson, "Imagining the World Scripture Imagines," 171.

210. Stephen B. Chapman, "Imaginative Readings of Scripture and Theological Interpretation," in Bartholomew et al., *Out of Egypt*, 422, 437.

211. For a discussion of this Rankean understanding of history and its relation to New Testament studies, see Schüssler Fiorenza, *Bread Not Stone*, 94–98.

212. See Paul Lakeland, "The Habit of Empathy: Postmodernity and the Future of the Church-Related College," in *Professing in the Postmodern Academy: Faculty and the Future of Church-Related Colleges*, ed. Stephen R. Haynes (Waco, TX: Baylor University Press, 2002), 36–39.

213. Ibid., 40.

214. Perdue, *Reconstructing Old Testament Theology*, 278.

215. See Philip D. Kenneson, "Truth," in Adam, *Handbook of Postmodern Biblical Interpretation*, 2000), 268–75.

216. Hays, "Salvation by Trust? Reading the Bible Faithfully," 221. But compare the approach of Christopher Seitz, who wants to emphasize that even a hermeneutics of trust "must encounter the specific claims of election and estrangement, for Jew and Gentile respectively, and their reconfiguration in Christ" ("And without God in the World," in *Word Without End*, 42).

217. Hays, "Salvation by Trust?" 221. Hays clarifies: "Reading receptively and trustingly does not mean accepting everything in the text at face value, as Paul's own critical sifting of the Torah demonstrates. Cases may arise in which we must acknowledge internal tensions within scripture that require us to choose guidance from one biblical witness and to reject another. . . . At the same time we should be suspicious of the institutions that govern and shape interpretation. This means not only ecclesiastical but also academic institutions" (221–22).

218. Moberly, "How May We Speak of God?" 198.

219. For discussions of the authority of Scripture in the church, see Charles M. Wood, "Scripture, Authenticity, and Truth," *Journal of Religion* 76 (1996): 189–205. On the topic of keeping revelation as a category, see Werner G. Jeanrond, "The Significance of Revelation for Biblical Theology," *Biblical Interpretation* 6 (1998): 243–57.

220. Gregory Dawes, "A Degree of Objectivity: Christian Faith and the Limits of History," *Stimulus* 6 (1998): 36. As John Meier puts it, "There is no neutral Switzerland of the mind in the world of Jesus research." See Meier, *A Marginal Jew: Rethinking the Historical Jesus* (New York: Doubleday, 1991), 5.

221. Meier, *Marginal Jew*, 2, 4–5, 6.

222. Brueggemann, "Biblical Theology Appropriately Postmodern," in *The Book That Breathes New Life: Scriptural Authority and Biblical Theology*, ed. Patrick D. Miller (Minneapolis: Fortress Press, 2005), 131, 133.

223. Brueggemann, "*Theology of the Old Testament*: A Prompt Retrospect," 307.

224. Collins, *Bible after Babel*, 161.

225. Schüssler Fiorenza, *Bread Not Stone*, 13.

226. Schüssler Fiorenza states, "If liberation theologians make the 'option for the oppressed' the key to their theological endeavors, then they must articulate that 'the oppressed' are women" (*Bread Not Stone*, 44).

227. Mary Ann Tolbert, "Defining the Problem: The Bible and Feminist Hermeneutics" *Semeia* 28 (1983): 119.

228. Sakenfeld, "Feminist Perspectives on Bible and Theology," 6–7, 7–8.

229. Ibid., 9–11; Tolbert, "Defining the Problem," 121–26.

230. Perdue, *Reconstructing Old Testament Theology*, 104.

231. Watson, *Text, Church, and World*, 156.

232. See Carol Meyers, *Discovering Eve: Ancient Israelite Women in Context* (New York: Oxford University Press, 1988); Elisabeth Schüssler Fiorenza, *In Memory of Her: A Feminist Theological Reconstruction of Christian Origins*, 2nd ed. (New York: Crossroad, 1994).

233. This stance is reminiscent of Schüssler Fiorenza's women-church "as a feminist movement of self-identified women and women-identified men" (*Bread Not Stone*, 7).

234. Phyllis Trible, *God and the Rhetoric of Sexuality* (Philadelphia: Fortress Press, 1978); Trible, *Texts of Terror: Literary-Feminist Readings of Biblical Narratives* (Philadelphia: Fortress Press, 1984).

235. Sakenfeld, "'Feminist' Theology and Biblical Interpretation," 249. She goes on to offer a strong caution against any generalization, something a text like my own is bound to make in its desire to summarize the data.

236. Renita J. Weems, *Battered Love: Marriage, Sex, and Violence in the Hebrew Prophets* (Minneapolis: Fortress Press, 1995), 9.

237. Phyllis Trible, "Five Loaves and Two Fishes: Feminist Hermeneutics and Biblical Theology," in *The Promise and Practice of Biblical Theology*, ed. John Reumann (Minneapolis: Fortress Press, 1991), 62–64.

238. Brueggemann, *Theology of the Old Testament*, 99.

239. Perdue, *Reconstructing Old Testament Theology*, 175.

240. Tolbert, "Defining the Problem," 118.

241. Perdue speaks of this problem in light of Gadamer's understanding of "distanciation" (*Reconstructing Old Testament Theology*, 181–82). Francis Watson sees "a danger that a critique of patriarchal ideology will overlook the possibility of a *self*-critique within the text or its broader context" (*Text, Church, and World*, 178).

242. Sakenfeld, "'Feminist' Theology and Biblical Interpretation," 255–59.

243. Childs, *Biblical Theology of the Old and New Testaments*, 376–78. See also Roland Mushat Frye, "Language for God and Feminist Language: A Literary and Rhetorical Analysis," *Interpretation* 43 (1989): 45–57.

244. Brueggemann alludes to "the dismissive tendency of Brevard Childs concerning a feminist hermeneutic" (*Theology of the Old Testament*, 98n101). See also Barr, *Concept of Biblical Theology*, 410–11.

245. Marvin A. Sweeney, "Reconceiving the Paradigms of Old Testament Theology in the Post-*Shoah* Period," *Biblical Interpretation* 6 (1998): 146.

246. Ibid., 147.

247. Eichrodt, *Theology of the Old Testament*, 1:26; von Rad, *Old Testament Theology*, 2:321.

248. Werner Lemke, "Is Old Testament Theology an Essentially Christian Discipline?" *Horizons in Biblical Theology* 11 (1989): 59, 62.

249. See Johannes Beutler, "The Jewish People and Their Scriptures in the Christian Bible," *Theology Digest* 50 (2003): 104; and Anna Brawley, "Grafted In: Why Christians Are Thinking about a Jewish Biblical Theology," *Biblical Theology Bulletin* 30 (2000): 127.

250. Matitiahu Tsevat,"Theology of the Old Testament—A Jewish View," *Horizons in Biblical Theology* 8 (1986): 44, 40–41. But see Bernhard Anderson's critique of Tsevat's view of objectivity in "Response to Matitiahu Tsevat: 'Theology of the Old Testament—A Jewish View,'" *Horizons in Biblical Theology* 8 (1986): 51–59.

251. Levenson, "Why Jews Are Not Interested in Biblical Theology," 51. Of course, Lemke also recognizes these obstacles but does not see them as insurmountable.

252. Jon Levenson, "Jews and Christians in Biblical Studies," in *The Hebrew Bible, the Old Testament, and Historical Criticism: Jews and Christians in Biblical Studies* (Louisville, KY: Westminster/John Knox Press, 1993), 104. Looking back from a perspective of twenty years since the essay was published, Perdue considers Levenson's argument as "outdated" and "sharply polemical" (*Reconstructing Old Testament Theology*, 236).

253. Childs, *Old Testament Theology in a Canonical Context*, 7, 8. See also the later comment on Jewish biblical theology in Childs, *Biblical Theology of the Old and New Testaments*, 25–26.

254. On this point see Olson, "Biblical Theology as Provisional Monologization," 167–69. For a different view of Childs's handling of the issue, see Barr, *Concept of Biblical Theology*, 674n42.

255. Sweeney, "Reconceiving the Paradigms of Old Testament Theology," 150.

256. Brueggemann, *Theology of the Old Testament*, 95.

257. Ibid.

258. Perdue, *Reconstructing Old Testament Theology*, 238.

259. Seitz, "Old Testament or Hebrew Bible," 71–73. See also Nuria Calduch-Benages, "*The Theology of the Old Testament* by Marco Nobile: A Contribution to Jewish-Christian Relations," in Bartholomew et al., *Out of Egypt*, 88–101. I am admittedly speaking of a Protestant shaping of the Old Testament canon. On the differences between normative canons in Roman Catholicism and Judaism, see Beutler, "Jewish People and Their Scriptures," 104.

260. Goshen-Gottstein, "Tanakh Theology: The Religion of the Old Testament and the Place of Jewish Biblical Theology," 633–634, 628.

261. Dunn, "The Problem of 'Biblical Theology,'" in Bartholomew et al., *Out of Egypt*, 183.

262. Sugirtharajah, *Bible and the Third World*, 246–247.

263. Ibid., 266.

264. Gerstenberger, *Theologies of the Old Testament*, 10.

265. Sugirtharajah carefully distinguishes between three major "streams of post-coloniality": "The first carries the notion of invasion and control; the second places enormous investment in recovering the cultural soul; and the third stresses mutual interdependence and transformation" (*Bible and the Third World*, 248).

266. Sakenfeld, "Feminist Perspectives on Bible and Theology," 5.

267. Gustavo Gutierrez, *A Theology of Liberation: History, Politics, and Salvation*, trans. and ed. Caridad Inda and John Eagleson (Maryknoll, NY: Orbis Books, 1973), 6–7, 11, 15.

268. Sugirtharajah, *Bible and the Third World*, 250–258, 261. See also Wonil Kim, "Minjung Theology's Biblical Hermeneutics: An Examination of Minjung Theology's Appropriation of the Exodus Account," in *God's Word for Our World*, ed. J. Harold Ellens et al. (London: T. & T. Clark International, 2004), 2:159–76.

269. See George V. Pixley, *On Exodus: A Liberation Perspective* (Maryknoll, NY: Orbis Books, 1987).

270. Jon Levenson, "Exodus and Liberation," in *Hebrew Bible, the Old Testament, and Historical Criticism*, 132, 133, 137–38, 144.

271. Collins, *Bible after Babel*, 58, 68.

272. Brueggemann, *Theology of the Old Testament*, 101.

273. Sugirtharajah, *Bible and the Third World*, 251, 252, 259. Sugirtharajah formulates these questions based on the work of Gloria Anzaldúa, who comments on the task of postcoloniality in general.

274. Stephen Fowl, "Texts Don't Have Ideologies," *Biblical Interpretation* 3 (1995): 17, 31, 29.

275. Leander Keck, "The Premodern Bible in the Postmodern World," *Interpretation* 50 (1996): 136.

276. Christopher J. H. Wright, "Mission as a Matrix for Hermeneutics and Biblical Theology," in Bartholomew, *Out of Egypt*, 120.

Chapter 4: The Methods Used in Biblical Theology

1. John Reumann identifies several traditional methods (New Testament use of Old Testament, allegory, typology, etc.), some of which we examined in chapters 2 and 3. See his "Introduction: Whither Biblical Theology?" in *The Promise and Practice of Biblical Theology*, ed. John Reumann (Minneapolis: Fortress Press, 1991), 12–19.

2. Ibid., 3.

3. See Hasel, *Old Testament Theology*, 38–114; *New Testament Theology*, 72–132. Reumann helpfully draws connections between some of the Old and New Testament methods, such as topical (OT) and thematic (NT), diachronic (OT) with salvation history (NT), and so on ("Introduction," 3).

4. In his 1999 work, James Barr classifies five basic types of Old Testament theologies, though he acknowledges there are "numerous other forms": (1) collection of ideas or doctrines (Köhler), (2) synthetic, comprehensive (Eichrodt), (3) explicit Christian approach (Vriezen), (4) development of traditions (von Rad), (5) canonical (Childs) (Barr, *Concept of Biblical Theology*, 27). For New Testament theologies, G. B. Caird lists five approaches: (1) dogmatic, (2) chronological, (3) kerygmatic, (4) author by author, (5) conference table approach (*New Testament Theology*, 5–26). See also Via, *What Is New Testament Theology?* 7–23.

5. Reumann, "Introduction," 4.

6. Barr, *Concept of Biblical Theology*, 27.
7. Collins, "Is a Critical Biblical Theology Possible?" 18.
8. Gabler, "Oration on the Proper Distinction," 493.
9. Bauer's section on Christology was an appendix to the other two parts focusing on God and humankind (Hayes and Prussner, *Old Testament Theology*, 68–70; Hasel, *Old Testament Theology*, 39).
10. Hasel, *Old Testament Theology*, 49n83.
11. Eichrodt, *Theology of the Old Testament*, 1:33.
12. Vriezen, *Outline of Old Testament Theology*, 124.
13. Except for Christology, there is basically a one-to-one correspondence between the subjects covered in systematic theology and the areas discussed in his Old Testament theology.
14. Vriezen, *Outline of Old Testament Theology*, 122–23; emphasis mine.
15. Hayes and Prussner, *Old Testament Theology*, 223.
16. Richardson, *Introduction to the Theology of the New Testament*, 12, 9, 11.
17. Guthrie, *New Testament Theology*, 72–73.
18. Hasel, *New Testament Theology*, 77. But see above where Richardson's chapters do explicate four major systematic loci.
19. Anderson, *Contours of Old Testament Theology*, 3; Caird, *New Testament Theology*, 8.
20. Caird, *New Testament Theology*, 5–7.
21. Guthrie, *New Testament Theology*, 675–700. Richardson's discussion of James's understanding of "faith and works" does not refer to Luther's treatment, even in a context where it seems warranted (*Introduction to the Theology of the New Testament*, 240–41).
22. Barr, *Concept of Biblical Theology*, 40, 41.
23. Fowl, *Engaging Scripture*, 1.
24. Watson, *Text and Truth*, vii, 8, 17.
25. Ibid., 10, 11, 12, 13, 182.
26. Fowl, *Engaging Scripture*, 22, 63, 79. Another approach that considers the way community and reader are shaped by theological instruction is offered by John Webster, "Biblical Theology and the Clarity of Scripture," in *Out of Egypt: Biblical Theology and Biblical Interpretation*, ed. Craig Bartholomew et al. (Grand Rapids: Zondervan Publishing House, 2004), esp. 378–82.
27. Collins, *Bible after Babel*, 134.
28. Michael Welker, "Biblical Theology and the Authority of Scripture," trans. Arnold Neufeldt-Fast, in *Theology in the Service of the Church: Essays in Honor of Thomas W. Gillespie*, ed. Wallace M. Alston Jr. (Grand Rapids: Wm. B. Eerdmans Publishing Co., 2000), 237.
29. Welker, *God the Spirit*, xii.
30. Welker, "Biblical Theology and the Authority of Scripture," 240–41. For further background on Welker's position, see his "Sola Scriptura? The Authority of the Bible in Pluralistic Environments," trans. John Hoffmeyer, in *A God So Near: Essays on Old Testament Theology in Honor of Patrick D. Miller*, ed. Brent A. Strawn and Nancy R. Bowen (Winona Lake, IN: Eisenbrauns, 2003), 375–91.
31. Eichrodt, "Does Old Testament Theology Still Have Independent Significance," 33; Kaiser, *Toward an Old Testament Theology*, 33.
32. Eichrodt, *Theology of the Old Testament*, 1:27.
33. Kaiser, *Toward an Old Testament Theology*, 20–21.
34. Eichrodt, *Theology of the Old Testament*, 1:27.
35. Ibid., 1:32, 33, 30, 28.

36. Ibid., 1:25, 26, 33. In his extensive discussion of the development of the "covenant" concept, Eichrodt acknowledges that the Hebrew concept of *berīt* contains different, even divergent facets. One is more particular, focusing on the relationship Yahweh had with Israel through the legal and cultic system, while the other is more universal, enveloping redemption and the "consummation of all things" (66).
37. Hayes and Prussner are representative of such assessment: "For thoroughness of treatment, for range and amount of material discussed, and for persistence in trying to give Old Testament thought some form of systematic coherence, Eichrodt's monumental study knows no superior" (*Old Testament Theology*, 183).
38. For example, connections are made to the themes of "the image of God" and "immortality." Of course, many Old Testament theologians would regard this failure in a positive light, since too many connections might mean the importing of New Testament thought, or in the case of Barr's critique, views from particular denominational or theological traditions, such as a Calvinist influence (*Concept of Biblical Theology*, 259).
39. Hayes and Prussner, *Old Testament Theology*, 182; Hasel, *Old Testament Theology*, 50–51.
40. Clements, *Old Testament Theology*, 24; see also pp. 26–52.
41. Kaiser, *Toward an Old Testament Theology*, 11, 12.
42. These constitute the bulk of the book (chaps. 5–15), but the summary of the structure is on pp. 43–49.
43. For a discussion of Bultmann's theological anthropology, see the treatment of "existence" later in this chapter.
44. See Jeremias, *New Testament Theology*.
45. Joachim Jeremias, *The Central Message of the New Testament* (New York: Charles Scribner's Sons, 1965). He notes that it was especially the message of God's gracious act of justification of sinners that "was the centre of Jesus' preaching" (69). Another "new quest" theologian, Ernst Käsemann, held a similar position (though on different grounds from Jeremias) by suggesting that the various "Christologies" of the New Testament point to "the justification of the godless [as] the center of all Christian proclamation and therefore also of Scripture" (quoted in Hasel, *New Testament Theology*, 161).
46. Anderson, *Contours of Old Testament Theology*, 39; emphasis mine.
47. Ibid., 39, 40. This compares in several respects to Walther Zimmerli's focus on faith in Yahweh as what provides continuity in Israel's theology (*Old Testament Theology in Outline*, 14).
48. Clements, *Old Testament Theology*, 104, 110, 149.
49. Ronald Youngblood, *The Heart of the Old Testament* (Grand Rapids: Baker Book House, 1971), 3.
50. Kümmel, *Theology of the New Testament*, 17, 329, 330, 332.
51. Dunn, *Unity and Diversity in the New Testament*, 5, 6.
52. Ibid., 226–27, 369.
53. Scobie, *Ways of Our God*, 93–94.
54. His overview of these areas is on pp. 94–99.
55. Ibid., 99.
56. One thinks here of Hasel's identification of "God/Yahweh [as] the dynamic, unifying center of the OT" (*Old Testament Theology*, 168) or of his suggestion that "Jesus Christ is the dynamic, unifying center of the NT" (*New Testament Theology*, 164). In a later publication he defines "the center of both testaments

as the triune God who revealed Himself in the OT in multiple ways and who has manifested Himself in the NT in the incarnation of Jesus Christ the God-man" ("Proposals for a Canonical Biblical Theology," *Andrews University Seminary Studies* 34 [1996]: 32).

57. Frei, *Eclipse of Biblical Narrative*, 16. For further critique and analysis, see Watson, *Text, Church, and World*, chaps. 1, 7, and 8; and Fowl, *Engaging Scripture*, 23–24.

58. George Lindbeck, "The Bible as Realistic Narrative," *Journal of Ecumenical Studies* 17 (1980): 84.

59. Darrell Jodock, "Story and Scripture," *Word and World* 1 (1981): 132. Jodock discusses ten key aspects to reading the Bible as story.

60. Stroup, *Promise of Narrative Theology*, 145–46.

61. Barr, *Concept of Biblical Theology*, 353; see the full discussion in 347–54. He adds "that story, as manifested in the Bible, is often theologically vague, obscure, ambiguous or non-committal" (356).

62. Ibid., 356, 355. In general, John Collins welcomes the emphasis on the genre of "story" for his critical biblical theology ("Is a Critical Biblical Theology Possible?" 18–23).

63. See, for example, Scobie, *Ways of Our God*, 36–37.

64. Collins, "Is a Critical Biblical Theology Possible?" 21. Collins does acknowledge that the critical historian can never rule out "real novelty in history" but argues that our confidence in any given proposition be proportionate to the evidence for it (19). John Goldingay writes similarly: "The fact that these narratives give prominence to *God's* involvement in events does not imperil their right to be designated history . . . [and] in this understanding of history authors are not bound to confine themselves to events that can be understood within the terms of regular cause and effect" (*Old Testament Theology*, 861).

65. Craig G. Bartholomew and Michael W. Goheen, "Story and Biblical Theology," in Bartholomew et al., *Out of Egypt*, 162. Perdue also rehearses some of these in *Collapse of History*, 259–262.

66. Bartholomew and Goheen, "Story and Biblical Theology," 168.

67. Goldingay, *Old Testament Theology*, 1:28. The subject matter of volumes 2 and 3 are, respectively, the Prophets and the Writings.

68. Ibid., 30, 696. Goldingay also follows the ten chapters on Old Testament story with one more, entitled "God Sent: The Coming of Jesus" (789–858).

69. In this regard his approach is similar to the Old Testament theologies of Paul House, who works with descriptive statements of God who exists and acts in specific ways, and of Walter Brueggemann, who recounts biblical testimony through "verbal sentences."

70. Matera, "New Testament Theology," 17, 19.

71. Wright, *New Testament and the People of God*, 144. On this page Wright summarizes a long discussion of the "tools for the task" (29–144), which he brings to biblical theology.

72. Ibid., 45. Wright follows the literary and narrative theory of A. J. Griemas (69–73), which he illustrates using the parable of the tenants (74–77). All of his literary and historical analysis is accomplished against the backdrop of his theory of knowledge, what he calls "critical realism" (see pp. 32–46).

73. Ibid., 79.

74. Pate et al., *Story of Israel*, 23.

75. Four chapters cover the Old Testament (Pentateuch, Deuteronomistic History, Psalms and Wisdom literature, and Prophets), one the Second Temple litera-

ture, and six the New Testament (Synoptic Gospels, John, Acts, Paul, General Epistles and Hebrews, and Revelation).

76. Pate et al., *Story of Israel*, 25, 27.
77. See Rolf Knierim, "The Task of Old Testament Theology," *Horizons in Biblical Theology* 6 (1984): 25–31.
78. Von Hofmann, *Interpreting the Bible*, 236.
79. For background on these and other influences, see Hayes and Prussner, *Old Testament Theology*, 82–84. Recall the Rankean understanding of history as accessible events.
80. Von Hofmann, *Interpreting the Bible*, 27. Frei calls this "the distinctive positioning of the reader or interpreter . . . [and] the Bible's unitary meaning is not accessible except by the special self-positioning of the reader as a person toward the text and what it 'witnesses to'" (*Eclipse of Biblical Narrative*, 180–81).
81. Ibid., 136.
82. Ibid., 181.
83. Ibid., 210.
84. Martin Hengel, "'Salvation History': The Truth of Scripture and Modern Theology," in *Reading Texts, Seeking Wisdom*, ed. David F. Ford and Graham Stanton (Grand Rapids: Wm. B. Eerdmans Publishing Co., 2003), 229, 235–38. Hasel regards Cullmann as "the foremost representative of the salvation history approach to the NT in this [twentieth] century" (*New Testament Theology*, 111).
85. Oscar Cullmann, *Christ and Time: The Primitive Christian Conception of Time and History*, rev. ed., trans. Floyd V. Filson (Philadelphia: Westminster Press, 1964), 27. The first German edition was published in 1945.
86. Ibid., 18, 32, 51–55. By "Christ event," Cullmann is speaking particularly of "the death and resurrection of Jesus Christ" (33). In an addendum to the "introductory chapter to the third edition," Cullmann responds to James Barr's criticism about the former's dependence on a lexicography too much concerned with individual words taken out of context (14–16).
87. Oscar Cullmann, *Salvation in History*, trans. Sidney G. Sowers (New York: Harper & Row, 1967), 152, 166; emphasis mine.
88. Ibid., 172, 326.
89. Ibid., 186–291.
90. Ibid., 53–54. However, Hasel takes issue with Cullmann's understanding of von Rad (*New Testament Theology*, 115–17), and Räisänen contends that Cullmann "fuses" von Rad's Old Testament sense of tradition-history and the different "view of the New Testament writers concerning 'God's plan'" (*Beyond New Testament Theology*, 52).
91. So Hengel, "Salvation History," 238–44. George Eldon Ladd's *A Theology of the New Testament* is outlined around the major blocks of material (Synoptic Gospels, John, primitive church, Paul, general letters and Revelation), but his approach draws heavily on salvation history themes, particularly in the way he discusses the kingdom of God in terms of a "this age/the age to come" tension (68–69). Leonard Goppelt also adopted a salvation history perspective for his *Theology of the New Testament* (1:276–81). Finally, for a theologian's treatment of the question, see Wolfhart Pannenberg, "Redemptive Event and History," trans. Shirley Guthrie, in Westermann, *Essays on Old Testament Hermeneutics*, 314–335.
92. Von Rad, *Old Testament Theology*, 1:105–6, 121–22.
93. Von Rad, "Form-Critical Problem of the Hexateuch," 54.

94. Von Rad, *Old Testament Theology*, 2:325.
95. Ibid., 1:106; 2:106, 1:106; emphasis mine. See Hasel, *New Testament Theology*, 115; and Perdue, *Collapse of History*, 52.
96. Perdue mentions several of these in his review (*Collapse of History*, 63–68). On history as center, see Hasel, *Old Testament Theology*, 146–47.
97. Gese, "Tradition and Biblical Theology," 307–8, 322.
98. For a discussion of these differences, see Hasel, *Old Testament Theology*, 81; and Barr, *Concept of Biblical Theology*, 377.
99. Balla, *Challenges to New Testament Theology*, 15–16. See Stuhlmacher, *Biblische Theologie des Neuen Testaments*, vol. 1 (Göttingen: Vandenhoeck & Ruprecht, 1992).
100. Balla, *Challenges to New Testament Theology*, 248. A related methodology is that of Hans Hübner, who undertakes New Testament theology on the basis of how the Old Testament writings were received and interpreted in the New. See his *Biblische Theologie des Neuen Testaments* (Göttingen: Vandenhoeck & Ruprecht, 1990) 1:66–67.
101. Barr writes, "Perhaps the New Testament sees itself not as the completion of a long development of tradition coming right up to its own time, but as the fulfillment of an *ancient* scripture" (*Concept of Biblical Theology*, 366).
102. Räisänen, *Beyond New Testament Theology*, 81.
103. Dunn, "Problem of 'Biblical Theology,'" 176.
104. See chapter 2 and the bibliography for a list of these. Before his introductions and theologies, Childs was reflecting on doing biblical theology within the tension of its two sources, the academy and church. See his "Some Reflections on the Search for a Biblical Theology," *Horizons in Biblical Theology* 4 (1982): 1–12.
105. Childs, *Biblical Theology of the Old and New Testaments*, 83, 85, 92, 93.
106. Ibid., 78, 104–5.
107. The topic of "exile and restoration" is taken up, which of course depends on information from books such as Ezra and Nehemiah, part of the Writings. Only about thirteen pages discuss the entire latter prophet tradition as opposed to, say, over fifty pages for the Torah. Also, the traditions in the Writings are treated in this order: apocalyptic, wisdom, and Psalms.
108. Childs, *Biblical Theology of the Old and New Testaments*, 217; see also 76–77, 211.
109. The remaining eight chapters cover "covenant, election, people of God," "Christ the Lord," "reconciliation with God," "law and gospel," "humanity: old and new," "biblical faith," "God's kingdom and rule," and "the shape of the obedient life: ethics."
110. House, *Old Testament Theology*, 56.
111. Ibid., 47, 46-47. Note that House is here specifically commenting on Childs's *Old Testament Theology in a Canonical Context*; however, he makes clear that these criticisms also apply to *Biblical Theology of the Old and New Testaments* (50).
112. Ibid., 56.
113. Rendtorff, *Canonical Hebrew Bible*, 1. The ultimate rationale for a canonical focus "is grounded largely in the fact that the texts in this form became the foundation of faith, doctrine, and life of the two biblical communities, the Jewish and Christian, remaining so right through to the beginning of the modern period" (2).
114. Ibid., 3.
115. Like Sanders (*Torah and Canon*, 52, 120–21), Rendtorff understands Torah to be the theological core of the Hebrew Bible (*Canonical Hebrew Bible*, 5–6, 11).

His section on the Former Prophets is organized as much around the events of the narrative rather than a highlighting of the individual books, as he does in the Latter Prophets (as opposed to House's explicit discussion of the books themselves).

116. Rendtorff, *Canonical Hebrew Bible*, 3. Rendtorff acknowledges that this systematizing is more about "our own access to the topics," not necessarily finding "their justification in the Old Testament material itself" (3). Still, he contends that "there is scarcely a theme that does not appear in some way in several or all parts of the canon" (8).

117. Ibid., 6.

118. Thielman seeks to balance the concerns and warnings of both Wrede and Schlatter (Thielman, *Theology of the New Testament*, 9).

119. Ibid., 56. After treating the Gospels individually, Thielman has a chapter entitled "Four Diverse Witnesses to the One Gospel of Jesus Christ."

120. For a sympathetic treatment of Childs's approach and concerns, see the review by Christopher Seitz in *Word without End*, 102–9.

121. Even in his 1974 commentary on Exodus, Childs declared that "the term 'precritical' is both naive and arrogant" (*Book of Exodus*, x). In defense of Childs's sensitivity to diverse voices, see Olson, "Biblical Theology as Provisional Monologization," 168–69.

122. John Collins presses this point in "Is a Critical Biblical Theology Possible?" 15.

123. Childs, *Biblical Theology of the Old and New Testaments*, 325–47. Childs's response to the criticism is to distinguish the tradition of sources from the final form of the text so that one can study the diachronic dimensions as part of the process of understanding the canonical form (104).

124. This is how Rendtorff states the objection as he attempts to respond to it (*Canonical Hebrew Bible*, 719).

125. Ibid.

126. Perdue, *Collapse of History*, 191. For a different approach to the question, see Nicholas Wolterstorff, "The Unity behind the Canon," in *One Scripture or Many? Canon from Biblical, Theological, and Philosophical Perspectives*, ed. Christine Helmer and Christof Landmesser (Oxford: Oxford University Press, 2004), 217–32.

127. For Collins, the method does not help advance scholarly dialogue ("Is a Critical Biblical Theology Possible?" 16); for Goldingay, the Old Testament "antedates Jesus and never mentions him" (*Old Testament Theology*, 26). For an assessment of christological as opposed to Trinitarian approaches, see Brent A. Strawn, "And These Three Are One: A Trinitarian Critique of Christological Approaches to the Old Testament," *Perspectives in Religious Studies* 31 (2004): 191–210.

128. Watson, *Text, Church, and World*, 44–45.

129. Collins, *Bible after Babel*, 141–42; Perdue, *Collapse of History*, 193.

130. Knierim, "Task of Old Testament Theology," 27.

131. Hasel, *Old Testament Theology*, 86–94; see chapter 2, as well as Brueggemann, "Convergence in Recent Old Testament Theologies."

132. Brueggemann, "Shape for Old Testament Theology, I: Structure Legitimation," 1–2. On the matter of oversimplification of categories, Brueggemann takes great pains to acknowledge the need for nuance in comparing these different approaches to the bipolar character of their biblical theology ("Convergence in Recent Old Testament Theologies," 102).

133. Westermann, *Elements of Old Testament Theology*, 31–32. Brueggemann chooses to highlight the "deliverance/blessing" polarity in Westermann's work ("Convergence in Recent Old Testament Theologies," 101).

134. Terrien, *Elusive Presence*, 3. Again, Brueggemann is attracted to an "ethical/aesthetic" polarity in Terrien.

135. Ibid., 476. The absence is not cause for despair, for Terrien states, "In biblical faith, presence eludes but does not delude" (ibid.).

136. Paul Hanson, *The Diversity of Scripture: A Theological Interpretation*, Overtures to Biblical Theology (Philadelphia: Fortress Press, 1982), 63–64. These concepts develop the thesis laid out in *Dynamic Transcendence* (1978).

137. Brueggemann, "Shape for Old Testament Theology, I: Structure Legitimation," and "Shape for Old Testament Theology, II: Embrace of Pain."

138. Perdue discusses Brueggemann in a chapter on postmodernism but prefers to associate his work in the category of "imagination" (*Reconstructing Old Testament Theology*, 251). Collins has used both terms ("Is a Critical Biblical Theology Possible?" 5–6; *Bible after Babel*, 143–47).

139. Brueggemann, "*Theology of the Old Testament*: A Prompt Retrospect," 307.

140. Even in those foundational essays, Brueggemann employed the term "countertheme" to describe the embrace of pain ("Shape for Old Testament Theology, II: Embrace of Pain," 42).

141. Brueggemann, *Theology of the Old Testament*, 118, and notes 3 and 4 on that page.

142. Ibid., 121. In other words, the testimony constitutes reality for the court, and theologically speaking, "the testimony becomes revelation" (ibid.).

143. Ibid., 122, 125, 129, 174.

144. By "larger canon," I mean that Brueggemann suggests that the New Testament witness to the crucifixion is a way that the early church claimed that "God's own life embraces the abandonment of broken covenant" (ibid., 311).

145. Ibid., 313. On the issue of exile, see Brueggemann's essay, "A Shattered Transcendence? Exile and Restoration," in *Biblical Theology: Problems and Perspectives*, ed. Steven J. Kraftchick, Charles D. Meyers, and Ben C. Ollenburger (Nashville: Abingdon Press, 1995), 169–82.

146. In addition to the issues of historical method and Jewish-Christian relations, Brueggemann directs most of his attention to various facets of the problem of justice (*Theology of the Old Testament*, 735–42).

147. Gerstenberger, *Theologies of the Old Testament*, 12: He goes so far as to claim that "in their canonical theology they are in fact following a fundamentalist path" (ibid., 13).

148. Ibid., 15–16, 19. His "sketch of the social history of Israel" (chap. 3) briefly describes what is in view here.

149. Ibid., 280–81.

150. Caird, *New Testament Theology*, 22.

151. Ibid., 18, 20, 26.

152. L. D. Hurst, foreword to Caird, *New Testament Theology*, x. Hurst states that Caird did not make "perfect harmony or agreement as the criterion of an apostolic conference. Dialogue was its essential characteristic" (ibid.).

153. Ibid., 419.

154. Though he refers to Brueggemann's use of rhetoric as "the outstanding characteristic of this work," Barr is especially critical of the nonhistorical way in which Brueggemann uses it (*Concept of Biblical Theology*, 544–46, 557–59).

155. Collins, "Is a Critical Biblical Theology Possible?" 5.

156. Collins, *Bible after Babel*, 145. The references are to Brueggemann, *Theology of the Old Testament*, 712, 718. See also Goldingay, *Old Testament Theology*, 22.

157. Collins, *Bible after Babel*, 145.

158. Brueggemann, *Theology of the Old Testament*, 713.

159. Barr, *Concept of Biblical Theology*, 559.

160. Brueggemann, *Theology of the Old Testament*, 121.

161. Bultmann, *Theology of the New Testament*, 1:3.

162. For a general introduction to many aspects of Bultmann's method, see John Painter, *Theology as Hermeneutics: Rudolf Bultmann's Interpretation of the History of Jesus* (Sheffield: Almond Press, 1987), esp. 119–62.

163. Bultmann, "Is Exegesis without Presuppositions Possible?" in *New Testament and Mythology and Other Basic Writings*, ed. Schubert M. Ogden (Philadelphia: Fortress Press, 1984), 145. The Latin *tabula rasa* basically means a "clean slate," implying a mind that is completely unaffected by any previous experiences or innate knowledge.

164. Ibid., 149.

165. Bultmann, "New Testament and Mythology," 23, 27.

166. Bultmann, "Is Exegesis without Presuppositions Possible?" 148.

167. Bultmann, *Jesus Christ and Mythology* (New York: Charles Scribner's Sons, 1958), 16–17, 18, 32.

168. Bultmann, *Theology of the New Testament*, 1:3.

169. Ibid., 1:324; 2:251.

170. Hasel, *New Testament Theology*, 87–88, 89.

171. Räisänen, *Beyond New Testament Theology*, 62.

172. Herbert Braun, "The Problem of a New Testament Theology," quoted in Hasel, *New Testament Theology*, 146.

173. Perrin, "Significance of Knowledge of the Historical Jesus," 240, 234–35, 238.

174. Conzelmann, *Outline of the Theology of the New Testament*, xv.

175. Ibid., 207–8.

176. Via, *What Is New Testament Theology?* 59.

177. In both cases, their respective philosophical categories influenced the treatment and structure of biblical theology. They both wrestled with the question of mythology, though they proposed different methods of handling the biblical language. Where the two differed is on what might be called a "pure biblical theology," seeing that Bultmann was strongly influenced by Barthian neo-orthodoxy and the goal of apprehending the theological subject matter of the Bible.

178. Morgan, "New Testament Theology," 119. See below for how Morgan balances this praise with critique.

179. Via, *What Is New Testament Theology?* 60.

180. Ibid., 62.

181. Morgan, "New Testament Theology," 120.

182. Rolf Knierim, "Revisiting Aspects of Bultmann's Legacy," in *God's Word for Our World*, ed. J. Harold Ellens et al. (London: T. & T. Clark International, 2004), 2:184–85; Morgan, "New Testament Theology," 120.

183. Morgan, "New Testament Theology," 120.

184. Dieter Georgi, "Rudolf Bultmann's *Theology of the New Testament* Revisited," in *Bultmann, Retrospect and Prospect: The Centenary Symposium at Wellesley*, ed. Edward C. Hobbs (Philadelphia: Fortress Press, 1985), 81.

185. Räisänen, *Beyond New Testament Theology*, 38. As an example, Räisänen says Bultmann ignores the way "Paul wrestles with the salvation-historical problem of Israel" in Romans 9–11 (ibid., 41). While Bultmann does refer to those chapters in his *Theology*, it is true that they focus on anthropological rather than historical matters.
186. Watson, *Text and Truth*, 153–69.
187. Georgi, "Rudolf Bultmann's *Theology of the New Testament* Revisited," 80.
188. Via, *What Is New Testament Theology?* 69–70. To cite Hasel, "The existentialist approach can only deal with such sections of the NT as are amenable to existentialist interpretation" (*New Testament Theology*, 101).
189. Morgan, "New Testament Theology," 124.
190. Here I think of A. K. M. Adam's proposal for what Bultmann's *Theology of the New Testament* might look like if read in a "non-modern key" (*Making Sense of New Testament Theology*, 195–210).
191. See Via, *What Is New Testament Theology?* 83–93.
192. Long, "Ambitions of Dissent," 280.
193. Over the past twenty-five years a number of works have introduced this field: Robert Alter, *The Art of Biblical Narrative* (New York: Basic Books, 1981); Edgar V. McKnight, *The Bible and the Reader: An Introduction to Literary Criticism* (Philadelphia: Fortress Press, 1985); David Gunn and Danna Nolan Fewell, *Narrative in the Hebrew Bible* (New York: Oxford University Press, 1993); Phyllis Trible, *Rhetorical Criticism: Context, Method, and the Book of Jonah*. See especially Trible's list of such works on p. 80n120.
194. Brueggemann, *Theology of the Old Testament*, 53–60, 64–71.
195. Alter, *Art of Biblical Narrative*, 12–13.
196. Trible, *Rhetorical Criticism*, 92, 94, 95, 99, 102–4.
197. Trible, "Five Loaves and Two Fishes," 59, 62–63.
198. Wright, *New Testament and the People of God*, chap. 3.
199. Morgan, "New Testament Theology," 123, 124.
200. Perdue, *Collapse of History*, 226, 304. On the matter of narrative readings being compatible with an affirmation of "extra-textual reality," see Fowl, *Engaging Scripture*, 24.
201. John R. Donahue, "The Literary Turn and New Testament Theology: Detour or New Direction?" *Journal of Religion* 76 (1996): 272–73. For Donahue, literary approaches need to be wedded to developments in "new historicism," which brings together "an array of reading practices that investigate a series of issues that emerge when critics seek to chart the ways texts, in dialectical fashion, both represent a society's behavior patterns and perpetuate, shape, or alter that culture's dominant codes" (266).
202. Francis Watson, "Literary Approaches to the Gospels: A Theological Assessment," *Theology* 99 (1996): 127–32.
203. Meyers, *Discovering Eve*, 43.
204. Ibid., chap. 5, "The Genesis Paradigms for Female Roles, Part II: Genesis 3:16." For a different understanding, see Phyllis A. Bird, "Sexual Differentiation and Divine Image in the Genesis Creation Texts," in *Image of God and Gender Models in Judeo-Christian Tradition*, ed. K. E. Børresen (Oslo: Solum Forlag, 1991), 11–31. Bird argues that the verse contains "an explicit statement of the woman's subordination to man—not, however, as representing the order of creation but rather as a sign of its sinful perversion" (21).
205. Ibid., 118, 169. With respect to a balanced understanding of men and women in religious activities, see Phyllis Bird, "The Place of Women in the Israelite

Cultus," in *Ancient Israelite Religion*, ed. Patrick D. Miller, Paul Hanson, and S. Dean McBride (Philadelphia: Fortress Press, 1987), 397–419.

206. Schüssler Fiorenza, *In Memory of Her*, xiv, xliv, 29. For more detail on feminist hermeneutics, see Schüssler Fiorenza, *But She Said: Feminist Practices of Biblical Interpretation* (Boston: Beacon Press, 1992).

207. Schüssler Fiorenza, *In Memory of Her*, xxiii, xxiv.

208. Ibid., 235, 343.

209. Bird, "Place of Women in the Israelite Cultus," 398–399.

210. Collins, *Bible after Babel*, 81, 93n102.

211. Schüssler Fiorenza, *In Memory of Her*, 132–140; Watson, *Text, Church, and World*, 206–7.

212. Perdue, *Reconstructing Old Testament Theology*, 271n37.

213. Weems, *Battered Love*, 6. She writes, "Metaphors remind us what is imaginable"(ibid., 115).

214. Ibid., 5, 3. Weems believes that "the prophets' success or failure as orators depended in the end on their ability to convince their audiences that viable connections could be drawn between the norms governing the sexual behavior of women and God's demands on Israel" (ibid., 3).

215. Ibid., 34, 35–67.

216. Sugirtharajah, *Bible and the Third World*, 255.

217. Ibid., 256.

218. Sugirtharajah, *Asian Biblical Hermeneutics and Postcolonialism*, 11.

219. Wonil Kim, "Minjung Theology's Biblical Hermeneutics: An Examination of Minjung Theology's Appropriation of the Exodus Account," in Ellens et al., *God's Word for Our World*, 2:162, 169. Kim quotes minjung theologian Gi Deuk Song, who admits that "the adjective 'Korean' should mean not so much a theology 'of' Korea as a theology 'for' Korean Minjung" (168).

220. Ibid., 175, 176.

221. For a discussion of the way such charges are leveled in biblical scholarship, see Perdue, *Reconstructing Old Testament Theology*, 271–74.

222. Jacqueline Lapsley, "'Am I Able to Say Just Anything?' Learning Faithful Exegesis from Balaam," *Interpretation* 60 (2006): 23–24, 26, 28.

223. Esler, *New Testament Theology*, 2, 4, 1, 8. In chapter 2, Esler surveys the effects of Gabler's distinctions, particularly what he considers to be the unfortunate stress on the dogmatic destination of the fruits of biblical theology. Thus, the date of Gabler's Altdorf address "was actually a black day for Christianity" (19).

224. Ibid., 35–37. The emphasis on contemporary context and the communion of the saints does not lead Esler to downplay historical method; to the contrary, "the results of such historical investigation are, *in and of themselves*, the bearers of theological truth" (36).

225. Esler develops these at length in chapters 2 and 5, with the intervening chapters devoted to an argument for our ability to know something about history and about an ancient author's intention.

226. Esler, *New Testament Theology*, 229, 265, 267–271.

227. Ibid., 87. Esler is informed by Carol Newsom, "Bakhtin, the Bible, and Dialogic Truth," which we encountered in the discussion of biblical and systematic theology in chapter 3.

228. Michael V. Fox, "Bible Scholarship and Faith Based Study: My View," *SBL Forum* 4.2 (February/March 2006). Accessed at http://www.sbl-site.org/Article .aspx?ArticleId=490.

229. Long, "Ambitions of Dissent," 283, 284. For Long, the only way forward is for "objectivists" (who appeal to "unassailable grounds") and "constructivists" (who doubt the metaphysical "other") to "share space" with each other. He hopes that because of "the strategic force of dissent, neither will assume imperialistic privilege in the compensatory arena of pluriform knowledge-making" (285).

Chapter 5: The Themes Developed through Biblical Theology

1. There is, of course, always the matter of prejudicing the material. Unlike describing the issues raised or the methods proposed by biblical theologians, my focus now turns to the biblical text itself and requires important decisions about what can and should be mentioned about biblical themes in a chapter-length presentation of this sort. To be sure, treating the history, issues, and methods of biblical theology required prior decisions about the order and emphasis given to the material, so it is not as if this chapter is the only one in which I interject my perspective. Nevertheless, in organizing the biblical themes themselves, I am making decisions about both the Bible and the scholars who have interpreted its theology.
2. Brueggemann uses this phrase for Old Testament theology (*Theology of the Old Testament*, 117).
3. House, *Old Testament Theology*, 85.
4. I here refer to Brueggemann's insight about the "characteristic shape" of the witness in active, verbal sentences (*Theology of the Old Testament*, 122–26). In like manner, we saw that Goldingay's chapter headings all focus on God as acting ("God began," "God started over," etc.) and Rendtorff views the Hebrew canon as broadly teaching that God acts (Torah), God speaks (Prophets), and people speak to God (Writings) (*Canonical Hebrew Bible*, 6).
5. Many English versions of the Bible, including the NRSV followed here, use "Lord" to translate the divine name "Yahweh." As suggested in Exodus 3:14–15, this name derives from the Hebrew verb "to be" (*hayah*). For a discussion of the historical-grammatical background of the name, see Frank Moore Cross, *Canaanite Myth and Hebrew Epic: Essays in the History of the Religion of Israel* (Cambridge, MA: Harvard University Press, 1973), 60–75.
6. See Smith, *Origins of Biblical Monotheism*; and Smith, *Early History of God*.
7. Miller, *Religion of Ancient Israel*, 1.
8. Ibid., 23–29.
9. Gerstenberger, *Theologies in the Old Testament*, 273.
10. The word *shema* is a Hebrew imperative form of the verb "to hear." There is disagreement over the best translation of the second part of the verse, with the NRSV itself identifying three other ways of translating it. For a careful discussion of the grammar, see Moshe Greenfeld, *Deuteronomy 1–11*, Anchor Bible (New York: Doubleday, 1991), 330–31, 337–38. He opts for "YHWH our God is one YHWH," arguing that "the connotation of 'one' here is not solely unity but also aloneness" (337).
11. Miller, *Religion of Ancient Israel*, 79.
12. On the importance of continuing to interpret the Decalogue within Israel's covenantal context, see S. Dean McBride, "The Essence of Orthodoxy: Deuteronomy 5:6–10 and Exodus 20:2–6," *Interpretation* 60 (2006): 133–50.
13. For a systematic-theological analysis, see Colin E. Gunton, *The Promise of Trinitarian Theology*, 2nd ed. (Edinburgh: T. & T. Clark, 1997).

14. "Father" is not found in 3 John; "Son" (in reference to Jesus) does not occur in nine letters, mostly the Pastorals and General Letters; "Spirit" (in reference to God's spirit) is absent from 2 Timothy, Philemon, and four General Letters.

15. On the challenging issue of whether the term "monotheism" should be used in biblical theology to describe the views of either testament, see Richard Bauckham, "Biblical Theology and the Problems of Monotheism," in Bartholomew et al., *Out of Egypt*, 187–232. Bauckham also addresses the New Testament's use of the Shema (218–29).

16. Ibid., 228–29.

17. On the challenge this confession made for early Christians, see Patrick Miller, *The God You Have: Politics and the First Commandment* (Minneapolis: Fortress Press, 2004); and Joel Marcus, "Idolatry in the New Testament," *Interpretation* 60 (2006): 152–64.

18. Ulrich Mauser, "God in Human Form," *Ex Auditu* 16 (2000): 81.

19. Ulrich Mauser, "One God and Trinitarian Language in the Letters of Paul," an unpublished paper presented to the graduate colloquium at Princeton Seminary, April 21, 1998.

20. I already noted the prospects and pitfalls of christological readings of the Old Testament (see Strawn, "And These Three Are One"). Other scholars have approached the two testaments with a Trinitarian perspective, unfolding the biblical story in terms of a "promising father," a "prodigious son," and a "powerful and prophetic spirit." For this, see Ben Witherington and Laura M. Ice, *The Shadow of the Almighty: Father, Son, and Spirit in Biblical Perspective* (Grand Rapids: Wm. B. Eerdmans Publishing Co., 2002).

21. See Tremper Longman, *Making Sense of the Old Testament: Three Crucial Questions* (Grand Rapids: Baker Books, 1998).

22. In this context, however, God's personal and exclusive knowledge of Israel is the reason why he immediately adds, "therefore I will punish you for all your iniquities" (Amos 3:2b).

23. Later in 1 Corinthians, Paul anticipates a greater manifestation of this: "Then I will know fully, even as I have been fully known" (13:12).

24. For a more complete study of the theme, see Geoffrey Grogan, "A Biblical Theology of the Love of God," in *Nothing Greater, Nothing Better: Theological Essays on the Love of God*, ed. Kevin J. Vanhoozer (Grand Rapids: Wm. B. Eerdmans Publishing Co., 2001), 47–66.

25. See Katharine Doob Sakenfeld, *The Meaning of Hesed in the Hebrew Bible: A New Inquiry*, HSM 17 (Missoula, MT: Scholars Press, 1978). The common Hebrew verb "to love" (*'ahab*) is also used to express God's love for people (e.g., Solomon, in 2 Sam. 12:24). In the same context, another root (*dwd*) is employed for the prophetically revealed name of Solomon, that is "Jedidiah," meaning "loved of Yahweh" (2 Sam. 12:25).

26. The terms for "compassion" in these verses are from the roots *naham* and *raham*, respectively. In Jeremiah 8:18–9:22, the intensity of God's compassion is described by the act of crying. On the debate over this passage, see Kathleen M. O'Connor, "The Tears of God and the Divine Character in Jeremiah 2–9," in *God in the Fray: A Tribute to Walter Brueggemann*, ed. Tod Linafelt and Timothy K. Beal (Minneapolis: Fortress Press, 1998), 172–85.

27. L. Juliana M. Claassens, *The God Who Provides: Biblical Images of Divine Nourishment* (Nashville: Abingdon Press, 2006). The above texts are among the

major ones that Claassens studies. She also considers the problem of famine, "when God does not feed" (chap. 3).

28. Ibid., 107–11.

29. Grogan, "Biblical Theology of the Love of God," 49. Grogan is here drawing on a study by D. H. Palmer which shows that in the Synoptic Gospels Jesus does not use the Greek verbs *agapao* and *phileo* to speak of God's love toward humans.

30. Claassens argues that "the occurrences of the God who feeds form part of the memory embedded in the Eucharist" (*God Who Provides*, 105).

31. Grogan, "Biblical Theology of the Love of God," 57.

32. Grogan argues that this verse does not mean that love "exhaustively define[s] God" (ibid., 66).

33. This verse is not present in all Greek manuscript traditions. There is strong evidence for its exclusion in the Alexandrian texts, but there are also good arguments for its inclusion as an authentic saying. The matter remains inconclusive. See I. Howard Marshall, *Commentary on Luke*, New International Greek Testament Commentary (Grand Rapids: Wm. B. Eerdmans Publishing Co., 1978), 867–68.

34. Anderson, *Contours of Old Testament Theology*, 40. For a more complete discussion see chap. 5, "The Experience of the Holy."

35. Vriezen, *Outline of Old Testament Theology*, 149.

36. For a thorough analysis of the linguistic data on the various Hebrew words based in the root *ṣadaq*, see David J. Reimer, "צדק" in *New International Dictionary of Old Testament Theology and Exegesis*, ed. Willem A. VanGemeren (Grand Rapids: Zondervan Publishing House, 1997), 3:744–69.

37. Guthrie, *New Testament Theology*, 99. A marked contrast, however, is in the significant increase over the Old Testament in references to the *Holy* Spirit, occurring in the Gospels and Pauline letters but especially in Luke-Acts.

38. For a recent study of the theme of God's holiness, see Thomas B. Dozeman, "The Holiness of God in Contemporary Jewish and Christian Biblical Theology," in Ellens et al., *God's Word for Our World*, 2:24–36.

39. Guthrie, *New Testament Theology*, 99.

40. Brueggemann, *Theology of the Old Testament*, 229–66.

41. Guthrie, *New Testament Theology*, 108–15.

42. One could add still other aspects of the creative word, such as its goodness ("God saw that it was good") and that it "blesses" (vv. 22, 28), but these are cases where the narrator is describing God's word or response rather than quoting it.

43. On Johannine Christology, see Paul N. Anderson, *The Christology of the Fourth Gospel: Its Unity and Disunity in the Light of John 6* (Valley Forge, PA: Trinity Press International, 1997). On a christological interpretation of Old Testament themes of creation and image of God, see Watson, *Text and Truth*, 225–75 and 277–304.

44. Claus Westermann's classic study lays out the basic categories of promise in *The Promises to the Fathers: Studies on the Patriarchal Narratives*, trans. David E. Green (Philadelphia: Fortress Press, 1980).

45. Ibid., 162. See also Walter Kaiser's theology based on the "promise/blessing" motif in *Toward an Old Testament Theology*.

46. Paul also occasionally uses allegory to connect the church's experience to the Old Testament (e.g., Gal. 3:21–29).

47. Bernhard Anderson, "Standing on God's Promises: Covenant and Continuity in Biblical Theology," in Kraftchick et al., *Biblical Theology*, 145–54.

48. James Hanson, "The Endangered and Reaffirmed Promises of God: A Fruitful Framework for Biblical Theology," *Biblical Theology Bulletin* 30 (2000): 90–101.

49. In Gen. 15:1, "the word of the Lord came to Abraham in a vision," using a cognate form of the root *hazah*, a term generally found later in the Hebrew Bible. In Gen. 18:1, God "appeared" to Abraham, apparently through the agency of angelic beings in human form.

50. The Masoretic Text has the singular prophet in v. 15, though the passage goes on to imply a plurality of prophets, something assumed in Deut. 13:1–5.

51. For a study of the relationship of "narrative action" and "verbal content" in prophetic narratives, see Simon J. De Vries, "The Interface between Prophecy as Narrative and Prophecy as Proclamation," in Ellens et al., *God's Word for Our World*, 1:211–46.

52. On the connection between the book of Deuteronomy and the use of law in the so-called Deuteronomistic History, see Ronald E. Clements, "The Former Prophets and Deuteronomy—A Re-examination," in Ellens et al., *God's Word for Our World*, 1:83–95.

53. On the role of preexilic and postexilic editors in shaping the Torah, see Sanders, *Torah and Canon*, 31–53.

54. Patrick Miller calls attention to the continuing role in Christian community of the Decalogue—in spite of serious difficulties and challenges—as "the *starting point* and *ground*" for the way Scripture deals with a full range of ethical issues. See his "The Sufficiency and Insufficiency of the Commandments," in *Way of the Lord*, 31–36.

55. Frank Thielman, *Paul and the Law: A Contextual Approach* (Downers Grove, IL: InterVarsity Press, 1994), 243. On the larger question of Paul's understanding of Scripture, see J. Ross Wagner, *Heralds of the Good News: Isaiah and Paul in Concert in the Letter to the Romans* (Leiden: E. J. Brill, 2003).

56. Wright, *God Who Acts*, 38.

57. There is in biblical theology the question of the *extent* of this goodness *in time* (i.e., how it relates to the events that befall humankind in Gen. 3 and the re-creative activity of the flood in Gen. 6–9) and *in being* (i.e., whether there is complete perfection of all aspects of creation). For an assessment of these questions, see Levenson, *Creation and the Persistence of Evil*; and James Barr, "Was Everything That God Created Really Good? A Question in the First Verse of the Bible," in Linafelt and Beal, *God in the Fray*, 55–65.

58. While *bara'* ("to create") is never used of humans as the subject, Gen. 1 also uses the verb *'aśāh* ("to make") of divine activity (vv. 1, 16, 25, 31), and that verb does denote a kind of activity of which humans are capable. That God "rested from all the work that he had done in creation" (2:3) suggests that humans will now commence their activities of making and doing.

59. Terence E. Fretheim, *God and the World in the Old Testament: A Relational Theology of Creation* (Nashville: Abingdon Press, 2005), 233, 244.

60. Patrick D. Miller, "Creation and Covenant," in Kraftchick et al., *Biblical Theology*, 165.

61. With respect to Israel's history I refer especially to the events of the exodus and wilderness, but prophetic texts of restoration also use imagery (such as the flowing of wine in Amos 9:13) that can be picked up in the Gospel accounts. Scholars have also studied the way Jesus' miracles connect the Gospels' theology with other Old Testament narratives. See Craig A. Evans, "Luke's Use of

the Elijah/Elisha Narratives and the Ethic of Election," *Journal of Biblical Literature* 106 (1987): 75–83.

62. This story is picked up in the postexilic period with respect to relations between Judah and Edom (Mal. 1:2–5).

63. N. T. Wright, *Paul, In Fresh Perspective* (Minneapolis: Fortress Press, 2005), 127–28.

64. The events of the book of Ruth also work out for the benefit of Ruth and Naomi, as well as the preparation for the line of David (Ruth 4:17–22). On the role Gen. 50:20 plays in the conclusion of Genesis, see Patrick D. Miller, "The End of the Beginning: Genesis 50," in *The Ending of Mark and the Ends of God: Essays in Memory of Donald Harrisville Juel*, ed. Beverly Roberts Gaventa and Patrick D. Miller (Louisville, KY: Westminster John Knox Press, 2005), 122–24.

65. On the problem of hardening Pharaoh's heart, see G. K. Beale, "An Exegetical and Theological Consideration of the Hardening of Pharaoh's Heart in Exodus 4–14 and Romans 9," *Trinity Journal* 5 (1984): 129–54.

66. Of course, in the decree as found on the famous Cyrus Cylinder, Cyrus credits the Babylonian deity Marduk for his success. The biblical perspective is to see Yahweh behind earthly events regardless of what non-Israelites might think. Both Ezra and Nehemiah continually thank God for their success, even though they relied on Persian authority to achieve their goals (Ezra 6:1–12; Neh. 2:7–8; see also Esth. 8:8).

67. The Semitic idiom "kingdom of heaven," found exclusively in Matthew (thirty-four times), uses "heaven" as a "substitute for the divine name" (Ladd, *Theology of the New Testament*, 64).

68. See Bright, *Kingdom of God*; and Ridderbos, *Coming of the Kingdom*.

69. Ladd, *Theology of the New Testament*, 63.

70. These are the emphases of the seven kingdom parables in Matt. 13.

71. Miller, *Way of the Lord*, 224–25. See also Walter Brueggemann, *The Message of the Psalms: A Theological Commentary* (Minneapolis: Augsburg, 1984), 74–77.

72. See, for example, David M. Gunn, "Colonialism and the Vagaries of Scripture: Te Kooti in Canaan," in Linafelt and Beal, *God in the Fray*, 127–42.

73. For example, after working through the questions raised by Yahweh's hardening of Pharaoh's heart and the killing of the Egyptian firstborn, Brian McCarthy settles for an open view of the character of Yahweh who "can grow and mature." See his "The Characterization of YHWH, the God of Israel, in Exodus 1–15," in Ellens et al., *God's Word for Our World*, 1:6–20.

74. Brueggemann, "A Shattered Transcendence? Exile and Restoration," in Kraftchick et al., *Biblical Theology*, 169–82.

75. Terence Fretheim, "Some Reflections on Brueggemann's God," in Linafelt and Beal, *God in the Fray*, 31.

76. Regardless of whether von Rad's reconstruction of the Old Testament's literary and tradition history is correct, at some point the creation narratives were joined with Israel's story as a people. In other words, creation now stands as the preamble to Israel's own remembrance of the past, as some creation psalms testify by linking Yahweh's rule of the cosmos with his rule over history (e.g., Pss. 65:5–13; 148:13–14).

77. See Frank Moore Cross and David Noel Freedman, *Studies in Ancient Yahwistic Poetry* (Missoula, MT: Scholars Press, 1975).

78. The precise editorial history of these books remains contested. Martin Noth's classic model of an exilic historian who edited the history of Israel and Judah

was carefully emended by Frank Moore Cross and Richard Nelson in their studies of a double redaction of the history, which accounted for editorial activity during Josiah's reign (c. 620 BCE). I am also persuaded that an even earlier, Hezekian redaction is likely. On all of this see Baruch Halpern and David S. Vanderhooft, "The Editions of Kings in the 7th–6th Centuries B.C.E.," *Hebrew Union College Annual* 62 (1991): 179–244.

79. Goldingay, *Old Testament Theology*, 33.
80. Martin Hengel calls this perspective of a "history of the word of God" a type of "salvation history." He writes, "For me as a Christian theologian *this history receives its unity and its foundation from its center and its goal, the person of Jesus Christ*" ("'Salvation History,'" 240).
81. Richard Hays, "The Conversion of the Imagination: Scripture and Eschatology in 1 Corinthians," *New Testament Studies* 45 (1999): 395.
82. See Moberly, "אמן" in *New International Dictionary of Old Testament Theology and Exegesis*, 1:427–33. Moberly reminds us that there are other Hebrew roots that communicate a life of "trust" (*bth*) and "fear of God." He adds that, unlike the New Testament, terms for "faith" do not "hold a position of similar importance in the OT. The difference, however, is perhaps more one of terminology than of basic outlook" (427).
83. Childs, *Old Testament Theology in a Canonical Context*, 220.
84. Westermann, *Elements of Old Testament Theology*, 71.
85. J. J. M. Roberts, *Nahum, Habakkuk, and Zephaniah*, Old Testament Library (Louisville, KY: Westminster/John Knox Press, 1991), 112. Roberts points out that the apostle Paul applies this verse to his message about justification, a meaning not directly tied to the original context but one that "may be more profound. . . . In the context of Habakkuk's oracle, however, the verb 'will live' refers to life in the interim before the time fixed for the fulfillment of the vision" (111–12).
86. I am drawing on the list of poetic genres in W. H. Bellinger, *Psalms: Reading and Studying the Book of Praises* (Peabody, MA: Hendrickson Publishers, 1990), 23.
87. There are many important thinkers associated with this perspective, notably E. P. Sanders, James Dunn, and N. T. Wright. For a summary of the debate, see Thielman, *Paul and the Law*, 14–47, and more recently Wright, *Paul, In Fresh Perspective*.
88. As Wright argues, "*God's covenant faithfulness is revealed, through the faithfulness of the Messiah, for the benefit of all who believe, Jew and Gentile alike.* That is the point of [Romans] 3.21–26. This is my primary reason for understanding *pistis Christou*, in other passages as well, as referring in shorthand form to the Messiah's faithfulness to God's plan rather than to human belief or trust in the Messiah, though of course that remains important as well; the two are closely correlated" (Wright, *Paul, In Fresh Perspective*, 119–20).
89. See Thielman, *Paul and the Law*, 24.
90. This is also Wright's point about Paul's thesis in Romans, that it redefines, "around the Messiah, what it means to be the people of God" (*Paul, In Fresh Perspective*, 119). Thus, he adds, "*Justification, for Paul, is a subset of election*, that is, it belongs as part of his doctrine of the people of God" (121).
91. Balancing von Rad's optimistic interpretation of 2 Kgs. 25 with Noth's pessimistic view is Walter Brueggemann, "The Kerygma of the Deuteronomistic Historian," *Interpretation* 22 (1968): 387–402.

92. In addition to Amos, the "day of the LORD" theme occurs frequently in the Book of the Twelve: Joel 2:31; Obad. 15; Zeph. 1:7, 14; Mal. 4:1–6. On its use in these contexts, see Rolf Rendtorff, "Alas for the Day! The 'Day of the LORD' in the Book of the Twelve," in Linafelt and Beal, *God in the Fray*, 186–97.

93. Many other images are used to depict the peaceful and fruitful world of the restoration (Isa. 4:2–6; 9:2–7; 11:1–9; Jer. 23:5–8; Hos. 2:19–23). To these texts may be added the more developed apocalyptic passages that envisage final and cosmic restoration as well as judgment (Isa. 65:17–25; Zech. 12:1–14; Dan. 12:1–13).

94. The references are Matt. 12:21; Luke 6:34; 23:8; 24:21; John 5:45.

95. For a fuller discussion, see James H. Charlesworth, "Ancient Apocalyptic Thought and the New Testament," in Kraftchick et al., *Biblical Theology*, 222–32.

96. Paul does not answer the questions we might ask about the precise nature and setting of Jesus' anticipated return. Given the enormous interest in matters of the "end times," it should be stated that neither Paul nor the Gospel writers seem overly concerned about the timing and sequence of future events, except to challenge believers to watchfulness (the Synoptics) and to reassure believers that they need not fear for loved ones who have already died (1 Thess. 4:13–18).

97. Hays, "Conversion of the Imagination," 394.

98. Herman Ridderbos, *Paul: An Outline of His Theology*, trans. John R. De Witt (Grand Rapids: Wm. B. Eerdmans Publishing Co., 1975), 44, 90.

99. Other references occur, such as those to the Lord's "manifestation" (1 Tim. 6:14; Titus 2:13) or simply "the day" (2 Pet. 1:19; 2:4–9).

100. Goldingay, *Old Testament Theology*, 33.

101. A good example of this ongoing work may be found in Patrick Miller's suggestion that the Apostles' Creed would be strengthened with the addition of a brief statement in the first article, to read as follows: "I believe in God the Father Almighty, Creator of heaven and earth, *who delivered Israel from Egyptian bondage*." See his "Rethinking the First Article of the Creed," *Theology Today* 61 (2005): 499–508.

102. See Donald H. Juel, "A Disquieting Silence: The Matter of the Ending," in Gaventa and Miller, *Ending of Mark and the Ends of God*, 1–13.

103. Ellen Charry, "Following an Unfollowable God," in Gaventa and Miller, *Ending of Mark and the Ends of God*, 156–57.

104. On the many facets of Christian hope, see the classic treatment by Jürgen Moltmann, *Theology of Hope: On the Ground and the Implications of a Christian Eschatology*, trans. James W. Leitch (New York: Harper & Row, 1967).

105. Patrick D. Miller, "Creation and Covenant," in Kraftchick et al., *Biblical Theology*, 168. See this same essay for a discussion on various views of creation and convenant.

106. Fretheim understands both terms positively in their Gen. 1 context. To have "dominion" (*rādāh*) suggests "caregiving, even nurturing, not exploitation," and "subdue" (*kābaš*) here means "ordering of the not yet ordered" (*God and the World in the Old Testament*, 51–52). On the whole matter of God's ongoing responsibility, creativity, and sustenance, vis-à-vis humankind's work, see ibid., 3–9.

107. Ibid., 50.

108. Ibid., 43–44.

109. Fretheim shows how the Hebrew terms used here (*'abad*, which carries the sense of "serve," and *šamar*, "to keep, observe") imply a deep sense of care and concern for the well-being of creation (ibid., 53–54).

110. Fretheim exegetes Jer. 12 and its other creation imagery (ibid., 174–81).
111. Ibid., 219.
112. Collins, *Encounters with Biblical Theology*, 103; Fretheim, *God and the World in the Old Testament*, 273.
113. On the use of this imagery here and in 1 Cor. 3:16–17, see Gordon D. Fee, *The First Epistle to the Corinthians*, New International Commentary on the New Testament (Grand Rapids: Wm. B. Eerdmans Publishing Co., 1987), 145–50, 263–66.
114. In addition to the classic study of the theme in Eichrodt, see the historical study by Delbert Hillers, *Covenant: The History of a Biblical Idea* (Baltimore: Johns Hopkins University Press, 1969); for a canonical and theological perspective, see Rolf Rendtorff, *The Covenant Formula: An Exegetical and Theological Investigation*, trans. Margaret Kohl (Edinburgh: T. & T. Clark, 1998).
115. Anderson, *Contours of Old Testament Theology*, 239.
116. Miller, *God You Have*, 63.
117. Anderson, *Contours of Old Testament Theology*, 245–46.
118. See Barr, *Concept of Biblical Theology*, 30. He cites Brevard Childs in support of this claim (644n7).
119. Some ancient versions of Matthew and Mark include the term "new" as a modifier for "covenant," probably seeking consistency with the Lukan tradition.
120. Childs, *Biblical Theology of the Old and New Testaments*, 438.
121. Childs points out that in Hebrews the contrast between old and new covenants also works with "the double meaning of *diathēkē* as both covenant and testament to illustrate his point that Christ died to ensure the validity of the promised eternal inheritance" (ibid., 439).
122. For a study of the historical and literary dynamics of these images in the Hebrew Bible, see Jon Levenson, *Sinai and Zion: An Entry into the Jewish Bible* (Minneapolis: Winston Press, 1985).
123. Childs, *Biblical Theology of the Old and New Testaments*, 439.
124. See Anderson, "Standing on God's Promises."
125. Johannine language is similar: "By this we know that we abide in him and he in us, because he has given us his Spirit" (1 John 4:13).
126. Ridderbos, *Paul*, 59.
127. Mark E. Biddle, *Missing the Mark: Sin and Its Consequences in Biblical Theology* (Nashville: Abingdon Press, 2005), 44.
128. Lesser characters, too, stand out as illustrative of various human failings, such as Aachan's greed at Jericho (Josh. 7). At the same time, different authors may choose to focus only on someone's positive achievements, as in the Chronicler's treatment of Solomon (2 Chron. 1–9).
129. Biddle, *Missing the Mark*, 121.
130. Several of these types of terms are discussed by Biddle in ibid., 151–52n22.
131. Biddle notes that the Greek term rendered "perfect" can have a range of meanings. Given the context of the Sermon of the Mount, he believes the verse teaches that Jesus is "calling for 'wholeness' in the sense of integrity, consistency of being and doing, of identity and action" (*Missing the Mark*, 161n31).
132. For a fuller treatment of the entire theme, see Ulrich Mauser, *Christ in the Wilderness: The Wilderness Theme in the Second Gospel and Its Basis in the Biblical Tradition*, Studies in Biblical Theology 39 (London: SCM Press, 1963).
133. On Pauline teaching about sin, see Ridderbos, *Paul*, 91–158.

134. On different theories about these figures, see Anthony A. Hoekema, *The Bible and the Future* (Grand Rapids: Wm. B. Eerdmans Publishing Co., 1979), 154–63.

135. For a summary of views on spiritual powers, see Walter Wink, *Naming the Powers: The Language of Power in the New Testament* (Philadelphia: Fortress Press, 1983), and the successive volumes in the "Powers" series.

136. According to Jon Levenson, "God's localization and his ubiquity, are not *generally* perceived in the Hebrew Bible as standing in tension. On the contrary, the Temple is the epitome of the world, a concentrated form of its essence, a miniature of the cosmos" (*Sinai and Zion*, 138).

137. The repetition of material in Exod. 35–40 (from chaps. 25–31) becomes understandable when we consider the final form of the book of Exodus as placing the "golden calf" incident between them. Hence, the author affirms that God remains faithful to his promises and blessings even after Israel has sinned. See Gören Larsson, *Bound for Freedom: The Book of Exodus in Jewish and Christian Traditions* (Peabody, MA: Hendrickson Publishers, 1999), 264–67.

138. For a study of this concept, see Sandra Lynn Richter, *Deuteronomistic History and the Name Theology* (Berlin: Walter de Gruyter, 2002).

139. See Walter Brueggemann, *Ichabod toward Home: The Journey of God's Glory* (Grand Rapids: Wm B. Eerdmans Publishing Co., 2002).

140. The location is associated both with Abraham's offering on the mountains of Moriah, mentioned only twice in the Bible (Gen. 22:2; 2 Chron. 3:2) and David's offering at the "threshing floor of Araunah the Jebusite" (2 Sam. 24:16–25; 2 Chron. 3:1).

141. See Miller, *Religion of Ancient Israel*, 52–54, 76–77.

142. But note that Acts refers to the growing body of believers in Jerusalem as the "church," at least from Acts 5:11 onward. Some Greek manuscripts have the term in Acts 2:47.

143. Except for three references in Matthew (16:18; 18:17 twice), the Gospels do not use the term "church" to describe Jesus' followers. This fact may suggest not only that first-century Christians continued to think of Jerusalem and its temple as a central worship place but also that their Gospels did not endeavor to bolster the church's standing by placing the term "church" regularly in Jesus' sayings.

144. The Greek *ekklesia* was used in the Septuagint to translate the Hebrew term *qahal*, the assembly or congregation of the people.

145. G. K. Beale argues that "the OT tabernacle and Temple were symbolically designed to point to the cosmic eschatalogical reality that God's tabernacling presence, formerly limited to the holy of holies, was to be extended throughout the whole earth" (*The Temple and the Church's Mission: A Biblical Theology of the Dwelling Place of God*, New Studies in Biblical Theology 17, ed. D. A. Carson [Downers Grove, IL: InterVarsity Press, 2004], 25).

146. Although Gen. 4 does not make explicit connection to the events of chap. 3 as giving rise to a situation that requires sacrifice, the numerous literary echoes between chaps. 3 and 4 suggest that the biblical author was demonstrating a parallel between the circumstances of the parents and those of the sons.

147. The term for the "ram" that Abraham offered in these passages is elsewhere found clustered mainly in Torah texts related to sacrifices (e.g., Exod. 29:15–34; Lev. 5:14–19; 8:18–29).

148. On the system of sacrifice and offering in Israel, see Miller, *Religion of Ancient Israel*, 106–30.

149. For a discussion of the major views associated with the servant's identity, see John L. McKenzie, *Second Isaiah*, Anchor Bible (Garden City, NY: Doubleday, 1968), xxxviii–lv.

150. Bellinger, *Psalms*, 23.

151. In other places, John's account portrays Jesus' ministry as a new way of relating to God, such as when he transforms the water into wine, water that John specifically notes came from jars used "for the Jewish rites of purification" (John 2:6).

152. Classic studies on baptism that present quite different views are Oscar Cullmann, *Baptism in the New Testament*, trans. J. K. S. Reid, Studies in Biblical Theology 1 (London: SCM Press, 1950); and George R. Beasley-Murray, *Baptism in the New Testament* (Grand Rapids: Wm. B. Eerdmans Publishing Co., 1973).

153. For an in-depth study of this area, see Miller, *They Cried unto the Lord*.

154. As with the other areas we have considered, people also misconstrued the meaning and use of prayer and praise, as indicated by stories of idolatry (Exod. 32–33), efforts to purchase divine influence (Num. 22–24), and the prophetic critiques of empty, formal worship.

155. Miller, *Way of the Lord*, 217, 221–25.

156. Rendtorff, *Canonical Hebrew Bible*, 6, 8.

157. In approximately seven places in Exod. 28–36, the NRSV translates the basic Hebrew term for wisdom (*hokmah*) as "skill" or "understanding."

158. John Collins, who sees an important role for "wisdom literature as a resource for the ongoing enterprise of natural theology," nevertheless cautions, "Wisdom cannot in any sense supersede the historical and prophetic materials that constitute the great bulk of the OT. If the 'Biblical Theology Movement' erred by neglecting wisdom, no purpose is served by inverting that error" (*Encounters with Biblical Theology*, 103).

159. There is, of course, an important aspect of Wisdom literature that speaks to relationships among human beings; this will be addressed below in the section on justice, poverty, and riches.

160. Bellinger lists the following as wisdom psalms: 1, 32, 37, 49, 73, 112, 119, 127, 128, 133 (*Psalms*, 23).

161. For a more complete analysis of the contents of oracles of salvation, particularly in the context of prayer, see Miller, *They Cried to the Lord*, 135–77.

162. Ambiguity over the role of supernatural influence in temptations to sin rises to the surface when comparing the different explanations the Deuteronomist and Chronicler give for David's decision to take a census of Israel: Yahweh "incited David" (2 Sam. 24:1); the Satan (literally, "the accuser") "incited David" (1 Chron. 21:1). Readers of Job learn that Satan's (literally, "the accuser's") activity is behind Job's suffering (Job 1:11–12; 2:5–7), but each time Yahweh grants permission for this within strict limits. Yahweh even tells Satan, "You incited me against him, to destroy him for no reason" (2:3).

163. Likewise, Brueggemann's terminology of "psalms of disorientation" (*Message of the Psalms*, 51–121) or countertestimony (*Theology of the Old Testament*, 317–403) always assume some sense of "orientation" and "core testimony." He also adds that while all testimony is "subject to cross-examination," there will never be "a cross-examination to which the consensus testimony does not make a vigorous response" (*Theology of the Old Testament*, 318).

164. Patrick D. Miller, "Prayer and Divine Action," in Linafelt and Beal, *God in the Fray*, 228.

165. Since I will discuss biblical-theological themes of "family" in another section, I will not study this present topic from the perspective of smaller groups such as the "house of the father" or clans. On the religious and theological dimensions, see Miller, *Religion of Ancient Israel*, 62–76; and Gerstenberger, *Theologies in the Old Testament*, 25–91.

166. Even when the tribes turn on each other, as happens with Benjamin at the conclusion of the book of Judges, there is the sense that something better is expected. After the carnage, the author narrates, "The people had compassion on Benjamin because the LORD had made a breach in the tribes of Israel" (Judg. 21:15).

167. Only one of Jesus' sayings makes explicit reference to the tribes. He informs the disciples that "when the Son of Man is seated on the throne of his glory, you who have followed me will also sit on twelve thrones, judging the twelve tribes of Israel" (Matt. 19:28; Luke 22:30).

168. The scholarly debate on the state of first-century Judaism in Palestine is quite complex. For an accessible introduction to the issues and proposals, see John Dominic Crossan and Jonathan L. Reed, *Excavating Jesus: Beneath the Stones, Behind the Texts* (San Francisco: HarperSanFrancisco, 2002).

169. On taking "all Israel" in v. 26 to include the "part of Israel" in v. 25, see Thomas W. Gillespie, "Prophetic Surprise in Romans 9–11," in Gaventa and Miller, *Ending of Mark and the Ends of God*, 99–102.

170. Other specific prophetic critiques are against Egypt and Edom (Joel 3:19–21), Edom (Obadiah), Nineveh (Nah. 1:1), and Philistia, Moab, Ammon, and Ethiopia (Zeph. 2).

171. See Miller, "Creation and Covenant," 168.

172. This issue also touches on matters of ethnicity and race. See the section below on that theme.

173. For a discussion of literary and historical issues behind biblical genealogies in their ancient context, see Robert R. Wilson, *Genealogy and History in the Biblical World* (New Haven, CT: Yale University Press, 1977).

174. Recalling the argument that the "diversity" interpretation of the Babel episode was exploited for the purposes of apartheid, it may be said that the early chapters of Acts witness to the unity of the body of believers (Acts 2:43–47; 4:32–37) in spite of the struggles they faced to embrace that unity (e.g., Acts 6:1).

175. Stephen C. Barton, "The Unity of Humankind as a Theme in Biblical Theology," in Bartholomew et al., *Out of Egypt*, 254.

176. There is no difference between the verb in these commands; it is *'ahab* (Hebrew) and *agapaō* (Greek) for both the "love" of God and of neighbor.

177. Brevard Childs summarizes the main interpretative approaches to these laws in *Old Testament Theology in a Canonical Context*, 84–86.

178. Ibid., 86–90.

179. House, *Old Testament Theology*, 136–37.

180. Rahab uses the verb *'asah*, "to do, to make," so that the action she is describing is the doing of *hesed*, that is, the showing of covenant loyalty and steadfast love to others.

181. Most of the canonical prophets contain similar oracles of judgment (e.g., Mic. 2:1–2; Hab. 1:2–4; Zeph. 1:12–13). In Malachi's case, he also condemns the postexilic community for its failure to tithe, thus depriving the priests and Levites of their basic needs and, in essence, "robbing God" (Mal. 3:8–10). And Micah

eloquently teaches that Yahweh has plainly shown people "to do justice, and to love kindness, and to walk humbly with [their] God" (Mic. 6:8).

182. On recent interpretation of this issue, see J. Albert Harrill, *Slaves in the New Testament: Literary, Social, and Moral Dimensions* (Minneapolis: Fortress Press, 2006).

183. One does not have to interpret this narrative exactly as Trible does—namely, that the ancient Israelites believed there was originally an androgynous "earth creature" undifferentiated by sex—in order to agree with her that Gen. 2 on its own does not intend to communicate any subordination of the woman to the man (Trible, *God and the Rhetoric of Sexuality*, 97–105). The NRSV rendering of v. 18 ("a helper as his partner") seems to express the sense of the original Hebrew phrase *'ezer kenegdô*.

184. Here, too, while it seems best to interpret the "judgments" of Gen. 3 as setting forth the consequences of disobedience—consequences that are not meant to become a positive norm for sexual relationships or gender roles—I tend to agree with Susan Lanser that Trible's interpretation of the message of Gen. 3 is too optimistic. If the text made a clear statement of equal responsibility for the sin, it is difficult to "explain why male dominance should be the particular consequence of a transgression for which both man and woman are equally . . . responsible" (Collins, quoting Susan Lanser, in *Bible after Babel*, 94).

185. Even in Prov. 31:1, King Lemuel warns his son, "Do not give your strength to women," a saying that seems strangely ironic in view of the subsequent praise of the "strong woman" (v. 11, Hebrew, *'ešet hayil*). For an introduction to this issue in the book of Proverbs, see Kathleen M. O'Connor, *The Wisdom Literature* (Collegeville, MN: Liturgical Press, 1988), 59–85.

186. Many more stories call attention to women's compassion and faith: the Syro-Phoenician woman (Matt. 15:28), Mary and Martha (Luke 10:42; John 11:24), the woman healed of hemorrhaging (Mark 5:27–34), and the Samaritan woman at the well (John 4:29).

187. Renita Weems's conclusions in her study of the negative connotations of the marriage metaphor in the prophetic literature are consistent with the way Torah regulations generally (though not always) take a patriarchal perspective, considering these matters from a husband's point of view (Num. 5:11–31; Deut. 21:10–17; 22:13–21; 24:4).

188. These "codes" all place wives in a subordinate role within the marriage (Eph. 5:22–24; Col. 3:18; 1 Pet. 3:1–6), but they also place extraordinary expectations on husbands that were not necessarily in keeping with first-century Jewish or Gentile customs (Eph. 5:25–33; Col. 3:19; 1 Pet. 3:7).

189. I am using the terms "race" and "ethnicity" somewhat interchangeably. The biblical documents do not use terms such as "nation," "people," or "foreigner" with the same specificity that modern languages give them. Moreover, the academic discipline of anthropology today would generally deny any biological category called "race," arguing instead that race is a cultural construct. See, for example, the 1997 "Official Statement on 'Race'" of the American Anthropological Association, which says "Biophysical diversity has no inherent social meaning except what we confer upon it" (quoted in Aaron Podolefsky and Peter J. Brown, eds., *Applying Cultural Anthropology: An Introductory Reader*, 6th ed. [Boston: McGraw-Hill, 2003], 123–24).

190. Charles Scobie correctly states that "the OT basically views all races and cultures as equal in God's sight" (*Ways of God*, 819). This was my point above in the section on "global community," that Israel understood its essential unity with the rest of humankind. But the word "basically" in Scobie's quotation should probably be emphasized in light of tensions over intermarriage. To say, as Scobie does, that "the OT shows no trace of discrimination on the basis of race or color" (819) seems to be true only in a larger biblical-theological sense. Israel's actual practice was prejudicial, but it provides no warrant for racial prejudice today.

191. It is difficult to know what connections the story of Abraham's tithing to Melchizedek, a "priest of God Most High," has with the later ordinances of tithing (Gen. 14:18–20). This enigmatic character is mentioned only one other time, in Ps. 110:4.

192. There are also "positive" impressions, from the point of view of the biblical narrators, such as the story of Phineas's zeal (Num. 25:7–13).

193. In spite of the negative view that biblical theologians often have of the monarchy, the prophetic vision of a worldwide, peaceful messianic kingdom cannot be viable if the idea of kingship is inherently evil. On this view, see J. J. M. Roberts, "In Defense of the Monarchy: The Contributions of Israelite Kingship to Biblical Theology," in Miller et al., *Ancient Israelite Religion*, 377–96.

194. In spite of the generally sad condition of kingship in Judah—only eight of its twenty monarchs "did what was right in the sight of the LORD, as [their] father David had done" (e.g., 1 Kgs. 15:11)—there was a marked difference in Judah's stability compared to Israel. The former had one dynasty with twenty monarchs for about 340 years, providing an average reign of seventeen years, about seven years longer than those of the northern kingdom.

195. About thirty of the thirty-seven occurrences of the word *mašîah* in the Old Testament refer to the human king, with most of these instances clustered in 1–2 Samuel (for Saul or David) and the Psalms.

196. See David L. Petersen, *The Roles of Israel's Prophets*, Journal for the Study of the Old Testament: Supplement Series 17 (Sheffield: JSOT Press, 1981).

197. See Mauser, "God in Human Form," 81–82.

198. On this question, see John Collins, "The Son of Man in First Century Judaism," *New Testament Studies* 38 (1992): 448–66. According to Collins, while "Daniel 7 remains the source of Jewish expectation of an apocalyptic Son of Man" (449), writings such as the *Similitudes of Enoch* and *4 Ezra* contributed to first-century understanding of the Daniel passage (464–66).

199. These terms also form part of the classic systematic-theological approach to the person and work of Christ in medieval Catholicism and the Reformers. See John Calvin, *Institutes of the Christian Religion* 2.15.1; trans. Ford Lewis Battles, ed. John T. McNeill (Philadelphia: Westminster Press, 1960).

200. The singular force of the commands continues throughout the Decalogue. Of course, the verbal commands are grammatically in the masculine gender.

201. For an overview of the Old Testament's theology of shalom, see Scobie, *Ways of God*, 881–87.

202. In Isa. 53:5 the NRSV renders the word *shalom* as "whole"; in Ps. 72:3 the NRSV translates it as "prosperity."

203. We could supplement this theme with Philip Esler's emphasis on a communion of saints through the ages (*New Testament Theology*, chaps. 8–10).

204. Bultmann, *New Testament Theology*, 2:83.

205. Donald Guthrie writes, "When it is a question of reconciliation between God and man, so essential is the part of Christ in it that he is here called 'our peace' (Eph 2:14)" (*New Testament Theology*, 491).

Chapter 6: The Prospects for Biblical Theology

1. See Bernd Janowski, "The One God of the Two Testaments," trans. Christine Helmer, *Theology Today* 57 (2000): 297–324.
2. Knierim, "Task of Old Testament Theology," 27.
3. Again, see Janowski, "One God of the Two Testaments."
4. Knierim, "Task of Old Testament Theology," 27.

Bibliography

Adam, Andrew K. M., ed. *Handbook of Postmodern Biblical Interpretation*. St. Louis: Chalice Press, 2000.

———. *Making Sense of New Testament Theology: "Modern" Problems and Prospects*. Macon, GA: Mercer University Press, 1995.

———, ed. *Postmodern Interpretations of the Bible: A Reader*. St. Louis: Chalice Press, 2001.

———. *What Is Postmodern Biblical Criticism?* Minneapolis: Fortress Press, 1995.

Aland, Kurt. *Synopsis of the Four Gospels*. 3rd ed. New York: United Bible Societies, 1979.

Albertz, Rainer. *A History of Israelite Religion in the Old Testament Period*. 2 vols. Translated by John Bowden. Louisville, KY: Westminster John Knox Press, 1994.

Alexander, Desmond, and Brian Rosner. *New Dictionary of Biblical Theology*. Downers Grove, IL: InterVarsity Press, 2000.

Alter, Robert. *The Art of Biblical Narrative*. New York: Basic Books, 1981.

American Anthropological Association. "Official Statement on 'Race.'" In *Applying Cultural Anthropology: An Introductory Reader*, 6th ed., edited by Aaron Podolefsky and Peter J. Brown, 123–24. Boston: McGraw-Hill, 2003.

Anderson, Bernhard. *Contours of Old Testament Theology*. Minneapolis: Fortress Press, 1999.

———. "Response to Matitiahu Tsevat: 'Theology of the Old Testament—A Jewish View.'" *Horizons in Biblical Theology* 8 (1986): 51–59.

———. "Standing on God's Promises: Covenant and Continuity in Biblical Theology." In *Biblical Theology: Problems and Perspectives*, edited by Steven J. Kraftchick, Charles D. Meyers, and Ben C. Ollenburger, 145–54. Nashville: Abingdon Press, 1995.

Anderson, Paul N. *The Christology of the Fourth Gospel: Its Unity and Disunity in the Light of John 6*. Valley Forge, PA: Trinity Press International, 1997.

Baird, William. *History of New Testament Research*. Vol. 1, *From Deism to Tübingen*. Minneapolis: Fortress Press, 1992.

———. *History of New Testament Research*. Vol. 2, *From Jonathan Edwards to Rudolf Bultmann*. Minneapolis: Fortress Press, 2003.

Baker, D. L. *Two Testaments, One Bible: A Study of Some Modern Solutions to the Theological Problem of the Relationship between the Testaments*. Downers Grove, IL: InterVarsity Press, 1976.

Balla, Peter. *Challenges to New Testament Theology: An Attempt to Justify the Enterprise.* Peabody, MA: Hendrickson Publishers, 1997.

Barr, James. "Biblical Theology." In *The Interpreter's Dictionary of the Bible*, Supplementary Volume, edited by Keith Crim, 104–11. Nashville: Abingdon Press, 1976.

———. *The Concept of Biblical Theology: An Old Testament Perspective.* Minneapolis: Fortress Press, 1999.

———. *The Semantics of Biblical Language.* Oxford: Oxford University Press, 1961.

Barth, Karl. *The Epistle to the Romans.* 6th ed. Translated by Edwyn C. Hoskyns. London: Oxford University Press, 1933.

———. *The Word of God and the Word of Man.* Translated by Douglas Horton. New York: Harper & Row, 1957.

Bartholomew, Craig. "Biblical Theology and Biblical Interpretation: Introduction." In *Out of Egypt: Biblical Theology and Biblical Interpretation*, edited by Craig Bartholomew et al., 1–19. Grand Rapids: Zondervan Publishing House, 2004.

Bartholomew, Craig G., and Michael W. Goheen. "Story and Biblical Theology." In *Out of Egypt: Biblical Theology and Biblical Interpretation*, edited by Craig Bartholomew et al., 144–71. Grand Rapids: Zondervan Publishing House, 2004.

Barton, Stephen C. "The Unity of Humankind as a Theme in Biblical Theology." In *Out of Egypt: Biblical Theology and Biblical Interpretation*, edited by Craig Bartholomew et al., 233–58. Grand Rapids: Zondervan Publishing House, 2004.

Bauckham, Richard. "Biblical Theology and the Problems of Monotheism." In *Out of Egypt: Biblical Theology and Biblical Interpretation*, edited by Craig Bartholomew et al., 187–232. Grand Rapids: Zondervan Publishing House, 2004.

Bauer, Walter. *Orthodoxy and Heresy in Earliest Christianity.* 2nd ed. Translated by Paul J. Achtemeier et al. Edited by Robert A. Kraft and Gerhard Kroedel. Philadelphia: Fortress Press, 1971.

Baur, Ferdinand Christian. "Introduction to Lectures on the History of Christian Dogma." In *Ferdinand Christian Baur on the Writing of Church History*, translated and edited by Peter C. Hodgson, 259–366. New York: Oxford University Press, 1968.

Beale, G. K. "An Exegetical and Theological Consideration of the Hardening of Pharaoh's Heart in Exodus 4–14 and Romans 9." *Trinity Journal* 5 (1984): 129–54.

———. *The Temple and the Church's Mission: A Biblical Theology of the Dwelling Place of God.* New Studies in Biblical Theology 17. Edited by D. A. Carson. Downers Grove, IL: InterVarsity Press, 2004.

Beasley-Murray, George R. *Baptism in the New Testament.* Grand Rapids: Wm. B. Eerdmans Publishing Co., 1973.

Beckwith, Roger T. "Toward a Theology of the Biblical Text." In *Doing Theology for the People of God*, edited by Donald Lewis and Alister McGrath, 43–50. Downers Grove, IL: InterVarsity Press, 1996.

Bekken, Per Jarle. "Paul's Use of Deut 30,12–14 in Jewish Context: Some Observations." In *The New Testament and Hellenistic Judaism*, edited by Peder Borgen and Søren Giversen, 183–203. Peabody, MA: Hendrickson Publishers, 1997.

Bellinger, W. H. *Psalms: Reading and Studying the Book of Praises.* Peabody, MA: Hendrickson Publishers, 1990.

Berquist, Jon. *Judaism in Persia's Shadow: A Social and Historical Approach.* Minneapolis: Fortress Press, 1995.

Bertens, Hans. *The Idea of the Postmodern: A History.* London: Routledge, 1995.

Beutler, Johannes. "The Jewish People and Their Scriptures in the Christian Bible." *Theology Digest* 50 (2003): 103–9.

Biddle, Mark E. *Missing the Mark: Sin and Its Consequences in Biblical Theology.* Nashville: Abingdon Press, 2005.

Bird Phyllis A. "The Place of Women in the Israelite Cultus." In *Ancient Israelite Religion*, edited by Patrick D. Miller, Paul Hanson, and S. Dean McBride, 397–419. Philadelphia: Fortress Press, 1987.

———. "Sexual Differentiation and Divine Image in the Genesis Creation Texts." In *Image of God and Gender Models in Judeo-Christian Tradition*, edited by K. E. Børresen, 11–31. Oslo: Solum Forlag, 1991.

Block, Dan. *The God of the Nations: Studies in Ancient Near Eastern National Theology.* ETS Monograph Series 2. Jackson, MS: ETS, 1988.

Boers, Hendrikus. *What Is New Testament Theology?* Philadelphia: Fortress Press, 1979.

Brawley, Anna. "Grafted In: Why Christians Are Thinking about a Jewish Biblical Theology." *Biblical Theology Bulletin* 30 (2000): 120–28.

Bray, Gerald. "The Church Fathers and Biblical Theology." In *Out of Egypt: Biblical Theology and Biblical Interpretation*, edited by Craig Bartholomew et al., 23–40. Grand Rapids: Zondervan Publishing House, 2004.

Bright, John. *The Kingdom of God: The Biblical Concept and Its Meaning for the Church.* Nashville: Abingdon Press, 1953.

Brown, Raymond E. *The Gospel according to John I–XII.* Anchor Bible. Garden City, NY: Doubleday, 1966.

Bruce, F. F. *New Testament Development of Old Testament Themes.* Grand Rapids: Wm. B. Eerdmans Publishing Co., 1968.

Brueggemann, Walter. "Biblical Theology Appropriately Postmodern." In *The Book That Breathes New Life: Scriptural Authority and Biblical Theology*, edited by Patrick D. Miller, 131–40. Minneapolis: Fortress Press, 2005.

———. "A Convergence in Recent Old Testament Theologies." In *Old Testament Theology: Essays on Structure, Theme, and Text*, edited by Patrick D. Miller, 95–110. Minneapolis: Fortress Press, 1992.

———. "A First Retrospect on the Consultation." In *Renewing Biblical Interpretation*, edited by Craig Bartholomew, Colin Greene, and Karl Möller, 342–47. Grand Rapids: Zondervan Publishing House, 2000.

———. "Futures in Old Testament Theology." In *Old Testament Theology: Essays on Structure, Theme, and Text*, edited by Patrick D. Miller, 111–17. Minneapolis: Fortress Press, 1992.

———. *Ichabod Toward Home: The Journey of God's Glory.* Grand Rapids: Wm B. Eerdmans Publishing Co., 2002.

———. "The Kerygma of the Deuteronomistic Historian." *Interpretation* 22 (1968): 387–402.

———. *The Message of the Psalms: A Theological Commentary.* Minneapolis: Augsburg, 1984.

———. "A Shape for Old Testament Theology, I: Structure Legitimation." In *Old Testament Theology: Essays on Structure, Theme, and Text*, edited by Patrick D. Miller, 1–21. Minneapolis: Fortress Press, 1992.

———. "A Shape for Old Testament Theology, II: Embrace of Pain." In *Old Testament Theology: Essays on Structure, Theme, and Text*, edited by Patrick D. Miller, 22–44. Minneapolis: Fortress Press, 1992.

———. "A Shattered Transcendence? Exile and Restoration." In *Biblical Theology: Problems and Perspectives*, edited by Steven J. Kraftchick, Charles D. Meyers, and Ben C. Ollenburger, 169–82. Nashville: Abingdon Press, 1995.

————. "*Theology of the Old Testament*: A Prompt Retrospect." In *God in the Fray: A Tribute to Walter Brueggemann*, edited by Tod Linafelt and Timothy K. Beal, 307–20. Minneapolis: Fortress Press, 1998.

————. *Theology of the Old Testament: Testimony, Dispute, Advocacy*. Minneapolis: Fortress Press, 1997.

Bultmann, Rudolf. "Is Exegesis without Presuppositions Possible?" In *New Testament and Mythology and Other Basic Writings*, edited by Schubert M. Ogden, 145–53. Philadelphia: Fortress Press, 1984.

————. *Jesus Christ and Mythology*. New York: Charles Scribner's Sons, 1958.

————. "Karl Barth's Epistle to the Romans." Translated by Keith R. Crim. In *The Beginnings of Dialectic Theology*, vol. 1, edited by James M. Robinson, 100–120. Richmond: John Knox Press, 1963.

————. "New Testament and Mythology: The Problem of Demythologizing the New Testament Proclamation." In *New Testament and Mythology and Other Basic Writings*, edited by Schubert M. Ogden, 1–43. Philadelphia: Fortress Press, 1984.

————. "Prophecy and Fulfillment." Translated by James C. G. Greig. In *Essays on Old Testament Hermeneutics*, edited by Claus Westermann, 50–75. Richmond: John Knox Press, 1963.

————. *Theology of the New Testament*. 2 vols. New York: Charles Scribner's Sons, 1951, 1955.

Caird, G. B., and L. D. Hurst. *New Testament Theology*. Oxford: Clarendon Press, 1994.

Calduch-Benages, Nuria. "*The Theology of the Old Testament* by Marco Nobile: A Contribution to Jewish-Christian Relations." In *Out of Egypt: Biblical Theology and Biblical Interpretation*, edited by Craig Bartholomew et al., 88–101. Grand Rapids: Zondervan Publishing House, 2004.

Callaway, Mary C. "Canonical Criticism." In *To Each Its Own Meaning: An Introduction to Biblical Criticisms and Their Application*, rev. and exp. ed., edited by Steven L. McKenzie and Stephen R. Haynes, 142–55. Louisville, KY: Westminster John Knox Press, 1999.

Calvin, John. *Commentaries on the Psalms*. Vol. 1. Translated by H. Beveridge. Grand Rapids: Baker Book House, 1984.

————. *Institutes of the Christian Religion*. Translated by Ford Lewis Battles. Edited by John T. McNeill. Philadelphia: Westminster Press, 1960.

Carson, D. A. "Current Issues in Biblical Theology: A New Testament Perspective." *Bulletin for Biblical Research* 5 (1995): 17–41.

Carson, D. A., and H. G. M. Williamson. *It Is Written: Scripture Citing Scripture: Essays in Honour of Barnabas Lindars*. Cambridge: Cambridge University Press, 1988.

Chapman, Stephen B. "Imaginative Readings of Scripture and Theological Interpretation." In *Out of Egypt: Biblical Theology and Biblical Interpretation*, edited by Craig Bartholomew et al., 409–47. Grand Rapids: Zondervan Publishing House, 2004.

Charlesworth, James H. "Ancient Apocalyptic Thought and the New Testament." In *Biblical Theology: Problems and Perspectives*, edited by Steven J. Kraftchick, Charles D. Meyers, and Ben C. Ollenburger, 222–32. Nashville: Abingdon Press, 1995.

Charry, Ellen. "Following an Unfollowable God." In *The Ending of Mark and the Ends of God: Essays in Memory of Donald Harrisville Juel*, edited by Beverly Roberts Gaventa and Patrick D. Miller, 155–63. Louisville, KY: Westminster John Knox Press, 2005.

Childs, Brevard S. *Biblical Theology in Crisis*. Philadelphia: Westminster Press, 1970.

————. *Biblical Theology of the Old and New Testaments: Theological Reflection on the Christian Bible*. Minneapolis: Fortress Press, 1993.

———. *Old Testament Theology in a Canonical Context*. Philadelphia: Fortress Press, 1986.

———. "On Reclaiming the Bible for Christian Theology." In *Reclaiming the Bible for the Church*, edited by Carl E. Braaten and Robert W. Jenson, 1–17. Grand Rapids: Wm. B. Eerdmans Publishing Co., 1995.

———. "Some Reflections on the Search for a Biblical Theology." *Horizons in Biblical Theology* 4 (1982): 1–12.

Claassens, L. Juliana M. *The God Who Provides: Biblical Images of Divine Nourishment*. Nashville: Abingdon Press, 2006.

Clements, Ronald E. "The Former Prophets and Deuteronomy—A Re-examination." In *God's Word for Our World*, vol. 1, edited by J. Harold Ellens et al., 83–95. London: T. & T. Clark International, 2004.

———. *Old Testament Theology: A Fresh Approach*. Atlanta: John Knox Press, 1978.

Collins, John J. *The Bible after Babel: Historical Criticism in a Postmodern Age*. Grand Rapids: Wm. B. Eerdmans Publishing Co., 2005.

———. *Encounters with Biblical Theology*. Minneapolis: Fortress Press, 2005.

———. "The Son of Man in First Century Judaism." *New Testament Studies* 38 (1992): 448–66.

Conzelmann, Hans. *An Outline of the Theology of the New Testament*. Translated by John Bowden. New York: Harper & Row, 1969.

Cross, Frank Moore. *Canaanite Myth and Hebrew Epic: Essays in the History of the Religion of Israel*. Cambridge, MA: Harvard University Press, 1973.

Cross, Frank Moore, and David Noel Freedman. *Studies in Ancient Yahwistic Poetry*. Missoula, MT: Scholars Press, 1975.

Crossan, John Dominic, and Jonathan L. Reed. *Excavating Jesus: Beneath the Stones, Behind the Texts*. San Francisco: HarperSanFrancisco, 2002.

Cullmann, Oscar. *Baptism in the New Testament*. Translated by J. K. S. Reid. Studies in Biblical Theology 1. London: SCM Press, 1950.

———. *Christ and Time: The Primitive Christian Conception of Time and History*. Rev. ed. Translated by Floyd V. Filson. Philadelphia: Westminster Press, 1964.

———. *Salvation in History*. Translated by Sidney G. Sowers. New York: Harper & Row, 1967.

Dahl, Nils A. *Jesus the Christ: The Historical Origins of Christological Doctrine*. Edited by Donald H. Juel. Minneapolis: Fortress Press, 1991.

Dawes, Gregory. "A Degree of Objectivity: Christian Faith and the Limits of History." *Stimulus* 6 (1998): 32–37.

———, ed. *The Historical Jesus Quest: Landmarks in the Search for the Historical Jesus*. Louisville, KY: Westminster John Knox Press, 1999.

De Vries, Simon J. "The Interface between Prophecy as Narrative and Prophecy as Proclamation." In *God's Word for Our World*, vol. 1, edited by J. Harold Ellens et al., 211–46. London: T. & T. Clark International, 2004.

Dodd, C. H. *The Old Testament in the New*. Philadelphia: Fortress Press, 1963.

Donahue, John R. "The Literary Turn and New Testament Theology: Detour or New Direction?" *Journal of Religion* 76 (1996): 250–75.

Dozeman, Thomas B. "The Holiness of God in Contemporary Jewish and Christian Biblical Theology." In *God's Word for Our World*, vol. 2, edited by J. Harold Ellens et al., 24–36. London: T. & T. Clark International, 2004.

Dunn, James D. G. "The Problem of 'Biblical Theology.'" In *Out of Egypt: Biblical Theology and Biblical Interpretation*, edited by Craig Bartholomew et al., 172–83. Grand Rapids: Zondervan Publishing House, 2004.

————. *The Theology of Paul the Apostle*. Grand Rapids: Wm. B. Eerdmans Publishing Co., 1998.

————. *Unity and Diversity in the New Testament: An Inquiry into the Character of the Earliest Christianity*. Philadelphia: Westminster Press, 1977.

Eagleton, Terry. *The Illusions of Postmodernism*. Oxford: Blackwell Publishers, 1996.

Ebeling, Gerhard. "The Meaning of 'Biblical Theology.'" In *Word and Faith*, translated by James W. Leitch, 79–97. Philadelphia: Fortress Press, 1963.

Efird, James, ed. *The Use of the Old Testament in the New and Other Essays*. Durham, NC: Duke University Press, 1972.

Ehrman, Bart D. *Lost Christianities: The Battles for Scripture and the Faiths We Never Knew*. Oxford: Oxford University Press, 2003.

Eichrodt, Walter. "Does Old Testament Theology Still Have Independent Significance within Old Testament Scholarship?" In *The Flowering of Old Testament Theology: A Reader in Twentieth Century Old Testament Theology, 1930–1990*, edited by Ben C. Ollenburger, Elmer A. Martens, and Gerhard F. Hasel, 30–39. Winona Lake, IN: Eisenbrauns, 1992.

————. "Is Typological Exegesis an Appropriate Method?" Translated by James Barr. In *Essays on Old Testament Hermeneutics*, edited by Claus Westermann, 224–45. Richmond: John Knox Press, 1963.

————. *Theology of the Old Testament*. 2 vols. Translated by J. A. Baker. Philadelphia: Westminster Press, 1961, 1967.

Eissfeldt, Otto. "The History of Israelite-Jewish Religion and Old Testament Theology." In *The Flowering of Old Testament Theology: A Reader in Twentieth Century Old Testament Theology, 1930–1990*, edited by Ben C. Ollenburger, Elmer A. Martens, and Gerhard F. Hasel, 20–29. Winona Lake, IN: Eisenbrauns, 1992.

Esler, Philip F. *New Testament Theology: Communion and Community*. Minneapolis: Fortress Press, 2005.

Evans, Craig A., ed. *From Prophecy to Testament: The Function of the Old Testament in the New*. Peabody, MA: Hendrickson Publishers, 2004.

————. "Luke's Use of the Elijah/Elisha Narratives and the Ethic of Election." *Journal of Biblical Literature* 106 (1987): 75–83.

————, ed. *Of Scribes and Sages: Early Jewish Interpretation and Transmission of Scripture*. 2 vols. London: T. & T. Clark International, 2004.

Fee, Gordon D. *The First Epistle to the Corinthians*. New International Commentary on the New Testament. Grand Rapids: Wm. B. Eerdmans Publishing Co., 1987.

Fee, Gordon D., and Douglas Stuart. *How to Read the Bible for All Its Worth*. 2nd ed. Grand Rapids: Zondervan Publishing House, 1993.

Felder, Cain Hope. *Stony the Road We Trod: African American Biblical Interpretation*. Minneapolis: Fortress Press, 1991.

Filson, Floyd V. *The New Testament against Its Environment: The Gospel of Christ the Risen Lord*. Studies in Biblical Theology 3. London: SCM Press, 1950.

Fishbane, Michael. *Biblical Interpretation in Ancient Israel*. Oxford: Clarendon Press, 1985.

Fowl, Stephen. *Engaging Scripture: A Model for Theological Interpretation*. Malden, MA: Blackwell, 1998.

————. "Texts Don't Have Ideologies." *Biblical Interpretation* 3 (1995): 15–34.

————, ed. *The Theological Interpretation of Scripture: Classic and Contemporary Readings*. Oxford: Blackwell, 1997.

Fox, Michael V. "Bible Scholarship and Faith Based Study: My View." *SBL Forum* 4.2, February/March 2006. http://www.sbl-site.org/Article.aspx?ArticleId=490.

Freedman, David Noel, et al., eds. *The Anchor Bible Dictionary*. 6 vols. New York: Doubleday, 1992.

Fretheim, Terence E. *God and the World in the Old Testament: A Relational Theology of Creation*. Nashville: Abingdon Press, 2005.

———. "Some Reflections on Brueggemann's God." In *God in the Fray: A Tribute to Walter Brueggemann*, edited by Tod Linafelt and Timothy K. Beal, 24–37. Minneapolis: Fortress Press, 1998.

Frye, Roland Mushat. "Language for God and Feminist Language: A Literary and Rhetorical Analysis." *Interpretation* 43 (1989): 45–57.

Gabler, Johann P. "An Oration on the Proper Distinction between Biblical and Dogmatic Theology and the Specific Objectives of Each." Translated by John Sandys-Wunsch and Laurence Eldredge. In *The Flowering of Old Testament Theology: A Reader in Twentieth Century Old Testament Theology, 1930–1990*, edited by Ben C. Ollenburger, Elmer A. Martens, and Gerhard F. Hasel, 492–502. Winona Lake, IN: Eisenbrauns, 1992.

Georgi, Dieter. "Rudolf Bultmann's *Theology of the New Testament* Revisited." In *Bultmann, Retrospect and Prospect: The Centenary Symposium at Wellesley*, edited by Edward C. Hobbs, 75–87. Philadelphia: Fortress Press, 1985.

Gerstenberger, Erhard. *Theologies in the Old Testament*. Translated by John Bowden. Minneapolis: Fortress Press, 2002.

Gese, Hartmut. "Tradition and Biblical Theology." In *Tradition and Theology in the Old Testament*, edited by D. A. Knight, 301–26. Philadelphia: Fortress Press, 1977.

Gillespie, Thomas W. "Prophetic Surprise in Romans 9–11." In *The Ending of Mark and the Ends of God: Essays in Memory of Donald Harrisville Juel*, edited by Beverly Roberts Gaventa and Patrick D. Miller, 91–105. Louisville, KY: Westminster John Knox Press, 2005.

Goldingay, John. *Old Testament Theology*. Vol. 1, *Israel's Gospel*. Downers Grove, IL: InterVarsity Press, 2003.

———. *Theological Diversity and the Authority of the Old Testament*. Grand Rapids: Wm. B. Eerdmans Publishing Co., 1987.

Goldsworthy, Graeme. *Preaching the Whole Bible as Christian Scripture: The Application of Biblical Theology to Expository Preaching*. Grand Rapids: Wm. B. Eerdmans Publishing Co., 2000.

Goppelt, Leonard. *Theology of the New Testament*. Vol. 1. Translated by John E. Alsup. Edited by Jürgen Roloff. Grand Rapids: Wm. B. Eerdmans Publishing Co., 1981.

Goshen-Gottstein, M. H. "Tanakh Theology: The Religion of the Old Testament and the Place of Jewish Biblical Theology." In *Ancient Israelite Religion*, edited by Patrick D. Miller, Paul Hanson, and S. Dean McBride, 617–44. Philadelphia: Fortress Press, 1987.

Gottwald, Norman K. *The Hebrew Bible: A Socio-Literary Introduction*. Philadelphia: Fortress Press, 1985.

———. "Sociological Method in the Study of Ancient Israel." In *The Bible and Liberation*, ed. Norman K. Gottwald, 26–37. Maryknoll, NY: Orbis Books, 1986.

———. *The Tribes of Yahweh: A Sociology of the Religion of Liberated Israel, 1250–1050 B.C.* Maryknoll, NY: Orbis Books, 1979.

Gowan, Donald E. *Theology of the Prophetical Books: The Death and Resurrection of Israel*. Louisville, KY: Westminster John Knox Press, 1998.

Grabbe, Lester L. *Judaic Religion in the Second Temple Period: Belief and Practice from the Exile to Yavneh*. London: Routledge, 2000.

———. *Judaism from Cyrus to Hadrian.* Vol. 1, *The Persian and Greek Periods.* Minneapolis: Fortress Press, 1992.

Green, Joel B. "Modernity, History, and the Theological Interpretation of the Bible." *Scottish Journal of Theology* 54 (2001): 308–29.

———. *The Theology of the Gospel of Luke.* Cambridge: Cambridge University Press, 1995.

Green, Joel B., and Max Turner, eds. *Between Two Horizons: Spanning New Testament and Biblical Theology.* Grand Rapids: Wm. B. Eerdmans Publishing Co., 2000.

Grogan, Geoffrey. "A Biblical Theology of the Love of God." In *Nothing Greater, Nothing Better: Theological Essays on the Love of God,* edited by Kevin J. Vanhoozer, 47–66. Grand Rapids: Wm. B. Eerdmans Publishing Co., 2001.

Gunkel, Hermann. "The 'Historical Movement' in the Study of Religion." *Expository Times* 33 (1927): 532–36.

———. "What Remains of the Old Testament?" In *What Remains of the Old Testament and Other Essays,* translated by A. K. Dallas, 13–56. New York: Macmillan, 1928.

Gunn, David M. "Colonialism and the Vagaries of Scripture: Te Kooti in Canaan." In *God in the Fray: A Tribute to Walter Brueggemann,* edited by Tod Linafelt and Timothy K. Beal, 127–42. Minneapolis: Fortress Press, 1998.

Gunton, Colin E. "Dogma, the Church, and the Task of Theology." *Neue Zeitschrift für Systematische und Religionsphilosophie* 40 (1998): 66–79.

———. *The Promise of Trinitarian Theology.* 2nd ed. Edinburgh: T. & T. Clark, 1997.

Guthrie, Donald. *New Testament Theology.* Downers Grove, IL: InterVarsity Press, 1981.

Gutierrez, Gustavo. *A Theology of Liberation: History, Politics, and Salvation.* Translated and edited by Caridad Inda and John Eagleson. Maryknoll, NY: Orbis Books, 1973.

Halpern, Baruch, and David S. Vanderhooft. "The Editions of Kings in the 7th–6th Centuries B.C.E." *Hebrew Union College Annual* 62 (1991): 179–244.

Hanson, James. "The Endangered and Reaffirmed Promises of God: A Fruitful Framework for Biblical Theology." *Biblical Theology Bulletin* 30 (2000): 90–101.

Hanson, Paul D. *The Diversity of Scripture: A Theological Interpretation.* Overtures to Biblical Theology. Philadelphia: Fortress Press, 1982.

———. *Dynamic Transcendence: The Correlation of Confessional Heritage and Contemporary Experience in a Biblical Model of Divine Activity.* Philadelphia: Fortress Press, 1978.

———. "The Responsibility of Biblical Theology to Communities of Faith." *Theology Today* 37 (1980): 39–50.

Harrill, J. Albert. *Slaves in the New Testament: Literary, Social, and Moral Dimensions.* Minneapolis: Fortress Press, 2006.

Hart, Trevor. "Systematic—In What Sense?" In *Out of Egypt: Biblical Theology and Biblical Interpretation,* edited by Craig Bartholomew et al., 341–51. Grand Rapids: Zondervan Publishing House, 2004.

Harvey, Barry. "Anti-postmodernism." In *Handbook of Postmodern Biblical Interpretation,* edited by Andrew K. M. Adam, 1–7. St. Louis: Chalice Press, 2000.

Harvey, Van A., and Schubert Ogden. "How New Is the 'New Quest of the Historical Jesus'?" In *The Historical Jesus and the Kerygmatic Christ,* edited by Carl Braaten and Roy Harrisville, 197–242. New York: Abingdon Press, 1964.

Hasel, Gerhard. *New Testament Theology: Basic Issues in the Current Debate.* Grand Rapids: Wm. B. Eerdmans Publishing Co., 1993.

———. *Old Testament Theology: Basic Issues in the Current Debate.* Rev. ed. Grand Rapids: Wm. B. Eerdmans Publishing Co., 1991.

————. "Proposals for a Canonical Biblical Theology." *Andrews University Seminary Studies* 34 (1996): 23–33.

————. "Recent Models of Biblical Theology: Three Major Perspectives." *Andrews University Studies* 33 (Spring–Summer 1995): 55–75.

Hayes, John H., and Frederick Prussner. *Old Testament Theology: Its History and Development.* Atlanta: John Knox Press, 1985.

Hays, Richard. "The Conversion of the Imagination: Scripture and Eschatology in 1 Corinthians." *New Testament Studies* 45 (1999): 391–412.

————. *Echoes of Scripture in the Letters of Paul.* New Haven, CT: Yale University Press, 1989.

————. "Salvation by Trust? Reading the Bible Faithfully." *Christian Century* 114 (1997): 218–23.

Hegel, Georg Wilhelm Friedrich. *The Philosophy of History.* Translated by J. Sibree. New York: Dover Publications, 1956.

Hengel, Martin. "'Salvation History': The Truth of Scripture and Modern Theology." In *Reading Texts, Seeking Wisdom,* edited by David F. Ford and Graham Stanton, 229–44. Grand Rapids: Wm. B. Eerdmans Publishing Co., 2003.

Hengstenberg, E. W. *Christology of the Old Testament.* Translated by Theod. Meyer and James Martin. Grand Rapids: Kregel Publications, 1956.

Hillers, Delbert. *Covenant: The History of a Biblical Idea.* Baltimore: Johns Hopkins University Press, 1969.

Hoekema, Anthony A. *The Bible and the Future.* Grand Rapids: Wm. B. Eerdmans Publishing Co., 1979.

Hofmann, J. C. K. von. *Interpreting the Bible.* Translated by Christian Preus. Minneapolis: Augsburg, 1959.

House, Paul R. *Old Testament Theology.* Downers Grove, IL: InterVarsity Press, 1998.

Hübner, Hans. *Biblische Theologie des Neuen Testaments.* 3 vols. Göttingen: Vandenhoeck & Ruprecht, 1990, 1993, 1995.

Janowski, Bernd. "The One God of the Two Testaments." Translated by Christine Helmer. *Theology Today* 57 (2000): 297–324.

Jeanrond, Werner G. "Criteria for New Biblical Theologies." *Journal of Religion* 76 (1996): 233–45.

————. "The Significance of Revelation for Biblical Theology." *Biblical Interpretation* 6 (1998): 243–57.

Jeremias, Joachim. *The Central Message of the New Testament.* New York: Charles Scribner's Sons, 1965.

————. *New Testament Theology: The Proclamation of Jesus.* Translated by J. Bowden. New York: Charles Scribner's Sons, 1971.

Jodock, Darrell. "Story and Scripture." *Word and World* 1 (1981): 128–39.

Johnson, Luke Timothy. "Imagining the World Scripture Imagines." *Modern Theology* 14 (1998): 165–80.

Juel, Donald H. "A Disquieting Silence: The Matter of the Ending." In *The Ending of Mark and the Ends of God: Essays in Memory of Donald Harrisville Juel,* edited by Beverly Roberts Gaventa and Patrick D. Miller, 1–13. Louisville, KY: Westminster John Knox Press, 2005.

Jülicher, Adolf. "A Modern Interpreter of Paul." Translated by Keith R. Crim. In *The Beginnings of Dialectic Theology,* vol. 1, edited by James M. Robinson, 72–81. Richmond: John Knox Press, 1963.

Kaiser, Walter. *Toward an Old Testament Theology.* Grand Rapids: Zondervan Publishing House, 1978.

Käsemann, Ernst. "Blind Alleys in the 'Jesus of History' Controversy." In *New Testament Questions of Today*, translated by W. J. Montague, 23–65. Philadelphia: Fortress Press, 1969.

———. "The Problem of a New Testament Theology." *New Testament Studies* 19 (1973): 235–45.

———. "The Problem of the Historical Jesus." In *Essays on New Testament Themes*, translated by W. J. Montague, 15–47. Naperville, IL: Alec R. Allenson, 1964.

Kay, James F. *Christus Praesens: A Reconsideration of Rudolf Bultmann's Christology*. Grand Rapids: Wm. B. Eerdmans Publishing Co., 1994.

Keck, Leander E. "The Premodern Bible in the Postmodern World." *Interpretation* 50 (1996): 130–41.

———. "Problems of New Testament Theology: A Critique of Alan Richardson's *An Introduction to New Testament Theology*." *Novum Testamentum* 7 (1964): 217–41.

Kenneson, Philip D. "Truth." In *Handbook of Postmodern Biblical Interpretation*, edited by Andrew K. M. Adam, 268–75. St. Louis: Chalice Press, 2000.

Kim, Seyoon. *The Origin of Paul's Gospel*. Grand Rapids: Wm. B. Eerdmans Publishing Co., 1982.

Kim, Wonil. "Minjung Theology's Biblical Hermeneutics: An Examination of Minjung Theology's Appropriation of the Exodus Account." In *God's Word for Our World*, vol. 2, edited by J. Harold Ellens et al., 159–76. London: T. & T. Clark International, 2004.

Kittel, Rudolf. *The Religion of the People of Israel*. Translated by R. C. Micklem. New York: Macmillan, 1925.

Knierim, Rolf. "Revisiting Aspects of Bultmann's Legacy." In *God's Word for Our World*, vol. 2, edited by J. Harold Ellens et al., 177–98. London: T. & T. Clark International, 2004.

———. "The Task of Old Testament Theology." *Horizons in Biblical Theology* 6 (1984): 25–31.

Kraftchick, Steven J. "Facing Janus: Reviewing the Biblical Theology Movement." In *Biblical Theology: Problems and Perspectives*, edited by Steven J. Kraftchick, Charles D. Meyers, and Ben C. Ollenburger, 54–77. Nashville: Abingdon Press, 1995.

Kraftchick, Steven J., Charles D. Meyers, and Ben C. Ollenburger, eds. *Biblical Theology: Problems and Perspectives*. Nashville: Abingdon Press, 1995.

Kugel, James. *The Bible as It Was*. Cambridge, MA: Harvard University Press, 1997.

———. "Stephen's Speech (Acts 7) in Its Exegetical Context." In *From Prophecy to Testament: The Function of the Old Testament in the New*, edited by Craig A. Evans, 206–18. Peabody, MA: Hendrickson Publishers, 2004.

———. *Traditions of the Bible: A Guide to the Bible as It Was at the Start of the Common Era*. Cambridge, MA: Harvard University Press, 1998.

Kugel, James L., and Rowan A. Greer. *Early Biblical Interpretation*. Library of Early Christianity. Philadelphia: Westminster Press, 1986.

Kümmel, Werner Georg. *The Theology of the New Testament: According to Its Major Witnesses: Jesus—Paul—John*. Nashville: Abingdon Press, 1973.

Ladd, George Eldon. *A Theology of the New Testament*. Grand Rapids: Wm. B. Eerdmans Publishing Co., 1974.

Lakeland, Paul. "The Habit of Empathy: Postmodernity and the Future of the Church-Related College." In *Professing in the Postmodern Academy: Faculty and the Future of Church-Related Colleges*, edited by Stephen R. Haynes, 33–48. Waco, TX: Baylor University Press, 2002.

Lapsley, Jacqueline. "'Am I Able to Say Just Anything?' Learning Faithful Exegesis from Balaam." *Interpretation* 60 (2006): 22–31.

Larsson, Gören. *Bound for Freedom: The Book of Exodus in Jewish and Christian Traditions.* Peabody, MA: Hendrickson Publishers, 1999.

Lemke, Werner. "Is Old Testament Theology an Essentially Christian Discipline?" *Horizons in Biblical Theology* 11 (1989): 59–71.

———. "Theology (OT)." In *The Anchor Bible Dictionary*, edited by David Noel Freedman, 6:448–73. New York: Doubleday, 1992.

Levenson, Jon. *Creation and the Persistence of Evil: The Jewish Drama of Divine Omnipotence.* San Francisco: Harper & Row, 1985.

———. "Exodus and Liberation." In *The Hebrew Bible, the Old Testament, and Historical Criticism: Jews and Christians in Biblical Studies*, 127–59. Louisville, KY: Westminster/John Knox Press, 1993.

———. *Sinai and Zion: An Entry into the Jewish Bible.* Minneapolis: Winston Press, 1985.

———. "Why Jews Are Not Interested in Biblical Theology." In *The Hebrew Bible, the Old Testament, and Historical Criticism: Jews and Christians in Biblical Studies*, 33–61. Louisville, KY: Westminster/John Knox Press, 1993.

Lewis, Jack P. "Council of Jamnia (Jabneh)." In *The Anchor Bible Dictionary*, edited by David Noel Freedman, 3:634–37. New York: Doubleday, 1992.

Lindbeck, George A. "The Bible as Realistic Narrative." *Journal of Ecumenical Studies* 17 (1980): 81–85.

———. *The Nature of Doctrine: Religion and Theology in a Postliberal Age.* Philadelphia: Westminster Press, 1984.

Lindsey, Mark R. "History, Holocaust, and Revelation: Beyond the Barthian Limits." *Theology Today* 61 (2005): 455–70.

Long, Burke O. "Ambitions of Dissent: Biblical Theology in a Postmodern Future." *Journal of Religion* 76 (1996): 276–89.

Longman, Tremper, III. *Making Sense of the Old Testament: Three Crucial Questions.* Grand Rapids: Baker Books, 1998.

Luther, Martin. "Psalm 2." Translated by L. W. Spitz Jr. In *Luther's Works*, vol. 12, edited by Jaroslav Pelikan, 3–93. St. Louis: Concordia Publishing House, 1955.

Marcus, Joel. "Idolatry in the New Testament." *Interpretation* 60 (2006): 152–64.

Marsden, George. *Fundamentalism and American Culture: The Shaping of Twentieth Century Evangelicalism, 1870–1925.* New York: Oxford University Press, 1980.

Marshall, I. Howard. *Commentary on Luke.* New International Greek Testament Commentary. Grand Rapids: Wm. B. Eerdmans Publishing Co., 1978.

———. "How Does One Write on the Theology of Acts?" In *Witness to the Gospel: The Theology of Acts*, edited by I. H. Marshall and David Peterson, 3–16. Grand Rapids: Wm. B. Eerdmans Publishing Co., 1998.

Martens, Elmer A. *God's Design: A Focus on Old Testament Theology.* Grand Rapids: Baker Book House, 1981.

———. "Moving from Scripture to Doctrine." *Bulletin for Biblical Research* 15 (2005): 77–103.

Martin, Francis. "Some Directions in Catholic Biblical Theology." In *Out of Egypt: Biblical Theology and Biblical Interpretation*, edited by Craig Bartholomew et al., 65–87. Grand Rapids: Zondervan Publishing House, 2004.

Martyn, J. Louis. *History and Theology in the Fourth Gospel.* 2nd ed. Nashville: Abingdon Press, 1979.

Matera, Frank J. "New Testament Theology: History, Method, and Identity." *Catholic Biblical Quarterly* 67 (2005): 1–22.

Mauser, Ulrich. *Christ in the Wilderness: The Wilderness Theme in the Second Gospel and Its Basis in the Biblical Tradition.* Studies in Biblical Theology 39. London: SCM Press, 1963.

———. "God in Human Form." *Ex Auditu* 16 (2000): 81–99.

———. "Historical Criticism: Liberator or Foe of Biblical Theology?" In *The Promise and Practice of Biblical Theology*, edited by John Reumann, 99–113. Minneapolis: Fortress Press, 1991.

———. "One God and Trinitarian Language in the Letters of Paul." Unpublished manuscript.

McBride, S. Dean. "The Essence of Orthodoxy: Deuteronomy 5:6–10 and Exodus 20:2–6." *Interpretation* 60 (2006): 133–50.

McCann, J. Clinton. "'Abounding in Steadfast Love and Faithfulness': The Old Testament as a Source for Christology." In *In Essentials Unity: Reflections on the Nature and Purpose of the Church*, edited by M. Douglas Meeks and Robert D. Mutton, 206–11. Minneapolis: Kirk House Publishers, 2001.

———. *A Theological Introduction to the Book of Psalms: The Psalms as Torah.* Nashville: Abingdon Press, 1993.

McCarthy, Brian R. "The Characterization of YHWH, the God of Israel, in Exodus 1–15." In *God's Word for Our World*, vol. 1, edited by J. Harold Ellens et al., 6–20. London: T. & T. Clark International, 2004.

McEvenue, Sean E. "The Old Testament, Scripture or Theology?" *Interpretation* 35 (1981): 228–42.

McKenzie, John L. *Second Isaiah.* Anchor Bible. Garden City, NY: Doubleday, 1968.

———. *A Theology of the Old Testament.* Garden City, NY: Doubleday, 1974.

McKnight, Edgar V. *The Bible and the Reader: An Introduction to Literary Criticism.* Philadelphia: Fortress Press, 1985.

Meier, John. *A Marginal Jew: Rethinking the Historical Jesus.* New York: Doubleday, 1991.

Melanchthon, Philip. "Loci Communes Theologici." In *Melanchthon and Bucer*, edited by Wilhelm Pauck, 1–152. Library of Christian Classics 19. Philadelphia: Westminster Press, 1969.

Meyers, Carol. *Discovering Eve: Ancient Israelite Women in Context.* New York: Oxford University Press, 1988.

Miller, Patrick D. "Creation and Covenant." In *Biblical Theology: Problems and Perspectives*, edited by Steven J. Kraftchick, Charles D. Meyers, and Ben C. Ollenburger, 155–68. Nashville: Abingdon Press, 1995.

———. "The End of the Beginning: Genesis 50." In *The Ending of Mark and the Ends of God: Essays in Memory of Donald Harrisville Juel*, edited by Beverly Roberts Gaventa and Patrick D. Miller, 115–26. Louisville, KY: Westminster John Knox Press, 2005.

———. *The God You Have: Politics and the First Commandment.* Minneapolis: Fortress Press, 2004.

———. "Israelite Religion." In *The Hebrew Bible and Its Modern Interpreters*, edited by Douglas A. Knight and Gene M. Tucker, 201–37. Philadelphia: Fortress Press, 1985.

———. "Prayer and Divine Action." In *God in the Fray: A Tribute to Walter Brueggemann*, edited by Tod Linafelt and Timothy K. Beal, 211–32. Minneapolis: Fortress Press, 1998.

———. *The Religion of Ancient Israel.* Louisville, KY: Westminster John Knox Press, 2000.

———. "Rethinking the First Article of the Creed." *Theology Today* 61 (2005): 499–508.

———. *They Cried unto the Lord: The Form and Theology of Biblical Prayer*. Minneapolis: Fortress Press, 1994.

———. *The Way of the Lord: Essays on Old Testament Theology*. Tübingen: Mohr Siebeck, 2004.

———. "Wellhausen and the History of Israel's Religion." *Semeia* 25 (1982): 61–73.

Moberly, R. W. L. "אמן" In *New International Dictionary of Old Testament Theology and Exegesis*, vol. 1, edited by Willem A. VanGemeren, 427–33. Grand Rapids: Zondervan Publishing House, 1997.

———. "How May We Speak of God? A Reconsideration of the Nature of Biblical Theology." *Tyndale Bulletin* 53 (2002): 177–202.

———. "Theology of the Old Testament." In *The Face of Old Testament Studies: A Survey of Contemporary Approaches*, edited by David W. Baker and Bill T. Arnold, 452–78. Grand Rapids: Baker Books, 1999.

Moltmann, Jürgen. *Theology of Hope: On the Ground and the Implications of a Christian Eschatology*. Translated by James W. Leitch. New York: Harper & Row, 1967.

Morgan, Robert. "The Bible and Christian Theology." In *The Cambridge Companion to Biblical Interpretation*, edited by John Barton, 114–28. Cambridge: Cambridge University Press, 1998.

———. "Can the Critical Study of Scripture Provide a Doctrinal Norm?" *Journal of Religion* 76 (1996): 206–32.

———. "F. C. Baur's Lectures on New Testament Theology." *Expository Times* 88 (1977): 202–6.

———. "Ferdinand Christian Baur." In *Nineteenth Century Religious Thought in the West*, edited by Ninian Smart, 261–89. New York: Cambridge University Press, 1985.

———. "Gabler's Bicentenary." *Expository Times* 98 (1987): 164–68.

———, ed. and trans. *The Nature of New Testament Theology*. Studies in Biblical Theology 25. Naperville, IL: Alec R. Allenson, 1974.

———. "New Testament Theology." In *Biblical Theology: Problems and Perspectives*, edited by Steven J. Kraftchick, Charles D. Meyers, and Ben C. Ollenburger, 104–30. Nashville: Abingdon Press, 1995.

Muilenburg, James. "Form Criticism and Beyond." *Journal of Biblical Literature* 88 (1969): 1–18.

Murphy, Roland E. "Questions concerning Biblical Theology." *Biblical Theology Bulletin* 30 (2000): 81–89.

———. "When Is Theology 'Biblical'?—Some Reflections." *Biblical Theology Bulletin* 33 (2003): 21–27.

Neuner, J., and J. Dupuis, eds. *The Christian Faith in the Doctrinal Documents of the Catholic Church*. New York: Alba House, 1982.

Neusner, Jacob. *First Century Judaism in Crisis: Yohanan ben Zakkai and the Renaissance of Torah*. Nashville: Abingdon Press, 1975.

———. *The Mishnah: A New Translation*. New Haven, CT: Yale University Press, 1989.

———. *The Way of Torah: An Introduction to Judaism*. 2nd ed. Encino, CA: Dickenson Publishing Co., 1974.

Newsom, Carol A. "Bakhtin, the Bible, and Dialogic Truth." *Journal of Religion* 76 (1996): 290–306.

O'Connor, Kathleen M. "The Tears of God and the Divine Character in Jeremiah 2–9." In *God in the Fray: A Tribute to Walter Brueggemann*, edited by Tod Linafelt and Timothy K. Beal, 172–85. Minneapolis: Fortress Press, 1998.

———. *The Wisdom Literature*. Collegeville, MN: Liturgical Press, 1988.

Odell-Scott, David W. "Deconstruction." In *Handbook of Postmodern Biblical Interpretation*, ed. Andrew K. M. Adam, 55–61. St. Louis: Chalice Press, 2000.

Oden, Thomas C., ed. *Ancient Christian Commentary on Scripture*. Downers Grove, IL: InterVarsity Press, 1998–.

Oehler, Gustav Friedrich. *Theology of the Old Testament*. Translated by George E. Day. Minneapolis: Klock & Klock Publishers, 1978.

Ollenburger, Ben C. "From Timeless Ideas to the Essence of Religion." In *The Flowering of Old Testament Theology: A Reader in Twentieth Century Old Testament Theology, 1930–1990*, edited by Ben C. Ollenburger, Elmer A. Martens, and Gerhard F. Hasel, 3–19. Winona Lake, IN: Eisenbrauns, 1992.

———. "What Krister Stendahl 'Meant'—A Normative Critique of 'Descriptive Biblical Theology.'" *Horizons in Biblical Theology* 8 (1986): 61–98.

Ollenburger, Ben C., Elmer A. Martens, Gerhard F. Hasel, eds. *The Flowering of Old Testament Theology: A Reader in Twentieth Century Old Testament Theology, 1930–1990*. Winona Lake, IN: Eisenbrauns, 1992.

Olson, Dennis. "The Bible and Theology: Problems, Proposals, Prospects." *Dialog* 37 (1998): 85–91.

———. "Biblical Theology as Provisional Monologization: A Dialogue with Childs, Brueggemann, and Bakhtin." *Biblical Interpretation* 6 (1998): 162–79.

Oswalt, John N. "The Book of Isaiah: A Short Course on Biblical Theology." *Calvin Theological Journal* 39 (2004): 54–71.

Painter, John. *Theology as Hermeneutics: Rudolf Bultmann's Interpretation of the History of Jesus*. Sheffield: Almond Press, 1987.

Pannenberg, Wolfhart. "Redemptive Event and History." Translated by Shirley Guthrie. In *Essays on Old Testament Hermeneutics*, edited by Claus Westermann, 314–35. Richmond: John Knox Press, 1963.

Pate, C. Marvin, et al. *The Story of Israel: A Biblical Theology*. Downers Grove, IL: InterVarsity Press, 2004.

Payne, J. Barton. *Encyclopedia of Biblical Prophecy: The Complete Guide to Scriptural Predictions and Their Fulfillment*. Grand Rapids: Baker Book House, 1991.

Perdue, Leo G. *The Collapse of History: Reconstructing Old Testament Theology*. Overtures to Biblical Theology. Minneapolis: Fortress Press, 1994.

———. *Reconstructing Old Testament Theology: After the Collapse of History*. Overtures to Biblical Theology. Minneapolis: Fortress Press, 2005.

Perrin, Norman. "The Significance of Knowledge of the Historical Jesus and His Teaching." In *Rediscovering the Teaching of Jesus*, 207–48. New York: Harper & Row, 1967.

Petersen, David L. *The Roles of Israel's Prophets*. Journal for the Study of the Old Testament: Supplement Series 17. Sheffield: JSOT Press, 1981.

Pixley, George V. *On Exodus: A Liberation Perspective*. Maryknoll, NY: Orbis Books, 1987.

Plevnik, Joseph. "The Center of Pauline Theology." *Catholic Biblical Quarterly* 51 (1989): 461–78.

Rad, Gerhard von. "The Form-Critical Problem of the Hexateuch." In *The Problem of the Hexateuch and Other Essays*, translated by E. W. Trueman Dicken, 1–78. Edinburgh: Oliver & Boyd, 1966.

———. *Old Testament Theology*. 2 vols. Translated by D. M. G. Stalker. New York: Harper & Row, 1962, 1965.

———. "Typological Interpretation of the Old Testament." Translated by John Bright. In *Essays on Old Testament Hermeneutics*, edited by Claus Westermann, 17–39. Richmond: John Knox Press, 1963.

Räisänen, Heikki. *Beyond New Testament Theology: A Story and a Programme.* London: SCM Press, 1990.

Reimer, David J. "צדק." In *New International Dictionary of Old Testament Theology and Exegesis*, vol. 3, edited by Willem A. VanGemeren, 744–69. Grand Rapids: Zondervan Publishing House, 1997.

Rendtorff, Rolf. "Alas for the Day! The 'Day of the LORD" in the Book of the Twelve." In *God in the Fray: A Tribute to Walter Brueggemann*, edited by Tod Linafelt and Timothy K. Beal, 186–97. Minneapolis: Fortress Press, 1998.

———. *Canon and Theology: Overtures to an Old Testament Theology.* Translated by Margaret Kohl. Overtures to Biblical Theology. Minneapolis: Fortress Press, 1993.

———. *The Canonical Hebrew Bible: A Theology of the Old Testament.* Translated by David E. Orton. Leiden: Deo Publishing, 2005.

———. *The Covenant Formula: An Exegetical and Theological Investigation.* Translated by Margaret Kohl. Edinburgh: T. & T. Clark, 1998.

Reumann, John. "Introduction: Whither Biblical Theology?" In *The Promise and Practice of Biblical Theology*, ed. John Reumann, 1–31. Minneapolis: Fortress Press, 1991.

Reventlow, Henning Graf. *Problems of Biblical Theology in the Twentieth Century.* Translated by John Bowden. London: SCM Press, 1986.

———. *Problems of Old Testament Theology in the Twentieth Century.* Translated by John Bowden. London: SCM Press, 1985.

———. "Theology (Biblical), History of." In *The Anchor Bible Dictionary*, edited by David Noel Freedman, 6:483–505. New York: Doubleday, 1992.

Richardson, Alan. *An Introduction to the Theology of the New Testament.* New York: Harper & Row, 1958.

Richter, Sandra Lynn. *Deuteronomistic History and the Name Theology.* Berlin: Walter de Gruyter, 2002.

Ridderbos, Herman. *The Coming of the Kingdom.* Translated by H. DeJongste. Philadelphia: Presbyterian & Reformed Publishing Co., 1962.

———. *Paul: An Outline of His Theology.* Translated by John R. De Witt. Grand Rapids: Wm. B. Eerdmans Publishing Co,, 1975.

Roberts, J. J. M. "Historical-Critical Method, Theology, and Contemporary Exegesis." In *Biblical Theology: Problems and Perspectives*, edited by Steven J. Kraftchick, Charles D. Meyers, and Ben C. Ollenburger, 131–41. Nashville: Abingdon Press, 1995.

———. "In Defense of the Monarchy: The Contributions of Israelite Kingship to Biblical Theology." In *Ancient Israelite Religion*, edited by Patrick D. Miller, Paul Hanson, and S. Dean McBride, 377–96. Philadelphia: Fortress Press, 1987.

———. *Nahum, Habakkuk, and Zephaniah.* Old Testament Library. Lousiville, KY: Westminster/John Knox Press, 1991.

Robertson, A. T. *A Harmony of the Gospels for Students of the Life of Christ: Based on the Broadus Harmony in the Revised Version.* New York: Harper & Row, 1922.

Robinson, James M. *A New Quest of the Historical Jesus.* Philadelphia: Fortress Press, 1983.

Robinson, James M., and John B. Cobb Jr., eds. *The New Hermeneutic.* New York: Harper & Row, 1964.

Rogerson, John W. "Interpretation, History of." In *The Anchor Bible Dictionary*, edited by David Noel Freedman, 3:424–33. New York: Doubleday, 1992.

Rollmann, Hans. "From Baur to Wrede: The Quest for a Historical Method." *Studies in Religion* 17 (1988): 443–54.

Said, Edward W. *Orientalism.* 25th anniversary edition. New York: Vintage Books, 2003.

Sakenfeld, Katharine Doob. "Feminist Perspectives on Bible and Theology." *Interpretation* 42 (1988): 5–18.

———. "'Feminist' Theology and Biblical Interpretation." In *Biblical Theology: Problems and Perspectives*, edited by Steven J. Kraftchick, Charles D. Meyers, and Ben C. Ollenburger, 247–59. Nashville: Abingdon Press, 1995.

———. *The Meaning of Hesed in the Hebrew Bible: A New Inquiry*. Harvard Scientific Monographs 17. Missoula, MT: Scholars Press, 1978.

Sanders, James A. *Torah and Canon*. Philadelphia: Fortress Press, 1972.

Sandys-Wunsch, John, and Laurence Eldridge. "J. P. Gabler and the Distinction between Biblical and Dogmatic Theology: Translation, Commentary, and Discussion of His Originality." *Scottish Journal of Theology* 33 (1980): 133–58.

Schlatter, Adolf. *The Church in the New Testament Period*. Translated by Paul P. Levertoff. London: SPCK, 1961.

———. "Karl Barth's Epistle to the Romans." Translated by Keith R. Crim. In *The Beginnings of Dialectic Theology*, vol. 1, edited by James M. Robinson, 120–25. Richmond: John Knox Press, 1963.

———. "The Theology of the New Testament and Dogmatics." In Robert Morgan, *The Nature of New Testament Theology*, Studies in Biblical Theology 25, 117–66. Naperville, IL: Alec R. Allenson, 1974.

Schleiermacher, Friedrich. *The Christian Faith*. 2 vols. Translated by W. R. Matthews et al. Edited by H. R. MacKintosh and J. S. Stewart. New York: Harper & Row, 1963.

———. *On Religion: Speeches to Its Cultured Despisers*. Translated by John Oman. New York: Harper & Row, 1958.

Scholze-Stubenrecht, W., and J. B. Sykes, eds. *The Oxford-Duden German Dictionary*. Oxford: Clarendon Press, 1994.

Schüssler Fiorenza, Elisabeth. *Bread Not Stone: The Challenge of Feminist Biblical Interpretation*. Boston: Beacon Press, 1995.

———. *But She Said: Feminist Practices of Biblical Interpretation*. Boston: Beacon Press, 1992.

———. *In Memory of Her: A Feminist Theological Reconstruction of Christian Origins*. 2nd ed. New York: Crossroad, 1994.

Scobie, Charles H. H. *The Ways of Our God: An Approach to Biblical Theology*. Grand Rapids: Wm. B. Eerdmans Publishing Co., 2003.

Seitz, Christopher. "Scripture Becomes Religion(s): The Theological Crisis of Serious Biblical Interpretation in the Twentieth Century." In *Renewing Biblical Interpretation*, edited by Craig Bartholomew, Colin Greene, and Karl Möller, 40–65. Grand Rapids: Zondervan Publishing House, 2000.

———. *Word without End: The Old Testament as Abiding Theological Witness*. Grand Rapids: Wm. B. Eerdmans Publishing Co., 1998.

Sherwood, Yvonne. "Derrida." In *Handbook of Postmodern Biblical Interpretation*, ed. Andrew K. M. Adam, 69–75. St. Louis: Chalice Press, 2000.

Smart, James D. *The Past, Present, and Future of Biblical Theology*. Philadelphia: Westminster Press, 1979.

Smith, D. Moody. "The Use of the Old Testament in the New." In *The Use of the Old Testament in the New and Other Essays*, edited by James Efird, 3–65. Durham, NC: Duke University Press, 1972.

Smith, Mark S. *The Early History of God: Yahweh and the Other Deities in Ancient Israel*. 2nd ed. Grand Rapids: Wm. B. Eerdmans Publishing Co., 2002.

———. *The Origins of Biblical Monotheism: Israel's Polytheistic Background and the Ugaritic Texts*. Oxford: Oxford University Press, 2001.

Soulen, R. Kendall. "The Believer and the Historian: Theological Interpretation and Historical Investigation." *Interpretation* 57 (2003): 174–86.

Soulen, Richard N. *Handbook of Biblical Criticism*. 2nd ed. Atlanta: John Knox Press, 1981.

Spener, Philip Jacob. *Pia Desideria*. Translated and edited by Theodore G. Tappert. Philadelphia: Fortress Press, 1964.

Spriggs, D. G. *Two Old Testament Theologies*. Naperville, IL: Alec R. Allenson, 1974.

Steinmetz, David C. "The Superiority of Pre-critical Exegesis." *Theology Today* 37 (1980): 27–38.

Stendahl, Krister. "Biblical Theology: Contemporary." In *The Interpreter's Dictionary of the Bible*, edited by George A. Buttrick, 1:418–32. Nashville: Abingdon Press, 1962.

Strawn, Brent A. "And These Three Are One: A Trinitarian Critique of Christological Approaches to the Old Testament." *Perspectives in Religious Studies* 31 (2004): 191–210.

Stroup, George. *The Promise of Narrative Theology: Recovering the Gospel in the Church*. Eugene, OR: Wipf & Stock, 1997.

Stuhlmacher, Peter. "Adolf Schlatter's Interpretation of Scripture." *New Testament Studies* 24 (1978): 433–46.

———. *Biblische Theologie des Neuen Testaments*. 2 vols. Göttingen: Vandenhoeck & Ruprecht, 1992, 1999.

———. *Historical Criticism and Theological Interpretation of Scripture: Toward a Hermeneutics of Consent*. Translated by Roy A. Harrisville. Philadelphia: Fortress Press, 1977.

Sugirtharajah, R. S. *Asian Biblical Hermeneutics and Postcolonialism: Contesting the Interpretations*. Maryknoll, NY: Orbis Books, 1998.

———. *The Bible and the Third World: Precolonial, Colonial, and Postcolonial Encounters*. Cambridge: Cambridge University Press, 2001.

———. *Postcolonial Reconfigurations: An Alternative Way of Reading the Bible and Doing Theology*. St. Louis: Chalice Press, 2003.

Sweeney, Marvin A. "Reconceiving the Paradigms of Old Testament Theology in the Post-*Shoah* Period." *Biblical Interpretation* 6 (1998): 142–61.

Terrien, Samuel. *The Elusive Presence: Toward a New Biblical Theology*. San Francisco: Harper & Row, 1978.

Thielman, Frank. *Paul and the Law: A Contextual Approach*. Downers Grove, IL: InterVarsity Press, 1994.

———. *Theology of the New Testament: A Canonical and Synthetic Approach*. Grand Rapids: Zondervan Publishing House, 2005.

Tolbert, Mary Ann. "Defining the Problem: The Bible and Feminist Hermeneutics." *Semeia* 28 (1983): 113–26.

Trible, Phyllis. "Five Loaves and Two Fishes: Feminist Hermeneutics and Biblical Theology." In *The Promise and Practice of Biblical Theology*, ed. John Reumann, 51–70. Minneapolis: Fortress Press, 1991.

———. *God and the Rhetoric of Sexuality*. Philadelphia: Fortress Press, 1978.

———. *Rhetorical Criticism: Context, Method, and the Book of Jonah*. Guides to Biblical Scholarship. Minneapolis: Fortress Press, 1994.

———. *Texts of Terror: Literary-Feminist Readings of Biblical Narratives*. Philadelphia: Fortress Press, 1984.

Troeltsch, Ernst. "Historical and Dogmatic Method in Theology." In *Religion in History*. Translated by James Luther Adams and Walter F. Bense, 11–32. Minneapolis: Fortress Press, 1991.

Tsevat, Matitiahu. "Theology of the Old Testament—A Jewish View." *Horizons in Biblical Theology* 8 (1986): 33–50.

Turretin, Francis. *Institutes of Elenctic Theology*. 3 vols. Translated by George Giger. Edited by James Dennison. Phillipsburg, NJ: P&R Publishing, 1992.

Van Buren, Paul M. "Historical Thinking and Dogmatics." *Journal of Ecumenical Studies* 17 (1980): 94–99.

Vanhoozer, Kevin J., ed. *Dictionary for Theological Interpretation of the Bible*. Grand Rapids: Baker Academic, 2005.

Via, Dan O. *What Is New Testament Theology?* Guides to Biblical Scholarship Series. Minneapolis: Fortress Press, 2002.

Vischer, Wilhelm. *The Witness of the Old Testament to Christ*. Translated by A. B. Crabtree. London: Lutterworth Press, 1949.

Vos, Geerhardus. *Biblical Theology: Old and New Testaments*. Grand Rapids: Wm. B. Eerdmans Publishing Co., 1948.

Vriezen, Th. C. *An Outline of Old Testament Theology*. Translated by S. Neuijen. Oxford: Blackwell, 1958.

Wagner, J. Ross. *Heralds of the Good News: Isaiah and Paul in Concert in the Letter to the Romans*. Leiden: E. J. Brill, 2003.

Walker-Jones, Arthur W. "The Role of Imagination in Biblical Theology." *Horizons in Biblical Theology* 11 (1989): 73–97.

Watson, Francis. "Literary Approaches to the Gospels: A Theological Assessment." *Theology* 99 (1996): 125–33.

———. *Paul and the Hermeneutics of Faith*. London: T. & T. Clark International, 2004.

———. *Text and Truth: Redefining Biblical Theology*. Grand Rapids: Wm. B. Eerdmans Publishing Co., 1997.

———. *Text, Church and World: Biblical Interpretation in Theological Perspective*. Grand Rapids: Wm. B. Eerdmans Publishing Co., 1994.

Webster, John. "Biblical Theology and the Clarity of Scripture." In *Out of Egypt: Biblical Theology and Biblical Interpretation*, edited by Craig Bartholomew et al., 352–84. Grand Rapids: Zondervan Publishing House, 2004.

Weems, Renita J. *Battered Love: Marriage, Sex, and Violence in the Hebrew Prophets*. Minneapolis: Fortress Press, 1995.

Weir, David H. *The Origins of the Federal Theology in Sixteenth Century Reformation Thought*. Oxford: Clarendon Press, 1990.

Welker, Michael. "Biblical Theology and the Authority of Scripture." Translated by Arnold Neufeldt-Fast. In *Theology in the Service of the Church: Essays in Honor of Thomas W. Gillespie*, edited by Wallace M. Alston Jr., 232–41. Grand Rapids: Wm. B. Eerdmans Publishing Co., 2000.

———. *God the Spirit*. Translated by John F. Hoffmeyer. Minneapolis: Fortress Press, 1994.

———. "Sola Scriptura? The Authority of the Bible in Pluralistic Environments." Translated by John Hoffmeyer. In *A God So Near: Essays on Old Testament Theology in Honor of Patrick D. Miller*, edited by Brent A. Strawn and Nancy R. Bowen, 375–91. Winona Lake, IN: Eisenbrauns, 2003.

Wellhausen, Julius. *Prolegomena to the History of Ancient Israel*. Translated by J. Black and A. Menzies. New York: Meridien Books, 1957.

Westermann, Claus. *Elements of Old Testament Theology*. Translated by Douglas W. Scott. Atlanta: John Knox Press, 1982.

———. *The Promises to the Fathers: Studies on the Patriarchal Narratives*. Translated by David E. Green. Philadelphia: Fortress Press, 1980.

Wilson, Robert R. *Genealogy and History in the Biblical World*. New Haven, CT: Yale University Press, 1977.

Witherington, Ben. *The Jesus Quest: The Third Quest for the Jew of Nazareth*. 2nd ed. Downers Grove, IL: InterVarsity Press, 1997.

Witherington, Ben, and Laura M. Ice. *The Shadow of the Almighty: Father, Son, and Spirit in Biblical Perspective*. Grand Rapids: Wm. B. Eerdmans Publishing Co., 2002.

Wolff, Hans Walter. "The Hermeneutics of the Old Testament." Translated by Keith Crim. In *Essays on Old Testament Hermeneutics*, edited by Claus Westermann, 160–99. Richmond: John Knox Press, 1963.

Wolterstorff, Nicholas. "The Unity behind the Canon." In *One Scripture or Many? Canon from Biblical, Theological, and Philosophical Perspectives*, edited by Christine Helmer and Christof Landmesser, 217–32. Oxford: Oxford University Press, 2004.

Wood, Charles M. "Scripture, Authenticity, and Truth." *Journal of Religion* 76 (1996): 189–205.

Wrede, William. "The Task and Methods of 'New Testament Theology.'" In *The Nature of New Testament Theology*, edited and translated by Robert Morgan, Studies in Biblical Theology 25, 68–116. Naperville, IL: Alec R. Allenson, 1974.

Wright, Christopher J. H. "Mission as a Matrix for Hermeneutics and Biblical Theology." In *Out of Egypt: Biblical Theology and Biblical Interpretation*, edited by Craig Bartholomew et al., 102–43. Grand Rapids: Zondervan Publishing House, 2004.

Wright, G. Ernest. *God Who Acts: Biblical Theology as Recital*. London: SCM Press, 1952.

———. *The Old Testament against Its Environment*. Studies in Biblical Theology 2. London: SCM Press, 1950.

———. *The Old Testament and Theology*. New York: Harper & Row, 1969.

Wright, N. T. *Christian Origins and the Question of God*. Vol. 1, *The New Testament and the People of God*. Minneapolis: Fortress Press, 1992.

———. *Paul, In Fresh Perspective*. Minneapolis: Fortress Press, 2005.

Yarchin, William. *History of Biblical Interpretation: A Reader*. Peabody, MA: Hendrickson Publishers, 2004.

Young, Edward J. *The Study of Old Testament Theology Today*. London: James Clarke & Co., 1958.

Youngblood, Ronald. *The Heart of the Old Testament*. Grand Rapids: Baker Book House, 1971.

Zimmerli, Walther. *Old Testament Theology in Outline*. Translated by David E. Green. Atlanta: John Knox Press, 1978.

———. "Promise and Fulfillment." Translated by James Wharton. In *Essays on Old Testament Hermeneutics*, edited by Claus Westermann, 89–122. Richmond: John Knox Press, 1963.

Index of Authors

CPSIA information can be obtained at www.ICGtesting.com
Printed in the USA
LVOW04s1609180115

423352LV00007B/98/P